Cyber Law in Kenya

Cyber Law in Kenya

Second Edition

Isaac Rutenberg

This book was originally published as a monograph in the International Encyclopaedia of Laws/Cyber Law.

Founding Editor: Roger Blanpain
General Editor: Frank Hendrickx
Volume Editor: Jos Dumortier

Wolters Kluwer

Published by:
Kluwer Law International B.V.
PO Box 316
2400 AH Alphen aan den Rijn
The Netherlands
E-mail: international-sales@wolterskluwer.com
Website: lrus.wolterskluwer.com

Sold and distributed in North, Central and South America by:
Wolters Kluwer Legal & Regulatory U.S.
7201 McKinney Circle
Frederick, MD 21704
United States of America
Email: customer.service@wolterskluwer.com

Sold and distributed in all other countries by:
Air Business Subscriptions
Rockwood House
Haywards Heath
West Sussex
RH16 3DH
United Kingdom
Email: international-customerservice@wolterskluwer.com

Printed on acid-free paper

ISBN 978-94-035-1241-9

e-Book: ISBN 978-94-035-1242-6
web-PDF: ISBN 978-94-035-1243-3

Printed in the United Kingdom.

The Author

Isaac Rutenberg is an academic and lawyer based in Nairobi, Kenya. He is currently the Director of the Centre for Intellectual Property and Information Technology Law (CIPIT) at the Strathmore Law School, Strathmore University, where he is also a senior lecturer. Isaac holds a JD (degree in law), a PhD in Chemistry, a bachelor of science in Chemistry, and a bachelor of science in Mathematics/Computer Science. He is admitted to practice law in the state of California, patent law in the United States Patent and Trademark Office, and patent/trademark law in the Kenya Industrial Property Institute. He is a member of the Chartered Institute of Arbitrators (Kenya branch) and the American Chemical Society. He previously served as a member of the Board of Directors at the Kenya Copyright Board.

This edition is based on the 1st edition authored by Michael M. Murungi.

The Author

Table of Contents

List of Abbreviations

ABL	Africa Broadcasting Ltd
AIDS	Acquired Immune Deficiency Syndrome
ARIPO	African Regional Intellectual Property Organization
ASO	Analogue Switch-Off
ASP	Application Service Provider
AUC	African Union Commission
AUCCSPDP	African Union Convention on Cyber Security and Personal Data Protection
BCAC	Broadcasting Content Advisory Council
BPO	Business Process Offshoring
BSD	Broadcasting signal distribution
CA	Communications Authority of Kenya
CAK	Competition Authority of Kenya
CBD	Central business district
CCK	Communications Commission of Kenya
CERT	Computer Emergency Response Team
CIPIT	Centre for Intellectual Property and Information Technology Law
CIPEV	Commission of Inquiry into Post-election Violence
CMA	Capital Markets Authority
CMO	Collective Management Organization
COFEK	Consumer Federation of Kenya
COMESA	Common Market for Eastern and Southern Africa
CORD	Coalition for Reform and Democracy
CSP	Content Services Provider
DAB	Digital Audio Broadcasting
DCA	Dot Connect Africa

List of Abbreviations

DMCA	Digital Millenium Copyright Act
DNS	Domain Name System
DRAKE	Domain-Name Registrar Association of Kenya
DRM	Digital Rights Management
DVB	Digital Video Broadcasting
EAC	East African Community
EAP&TC	East African Posts and Telecommunications Corporation
EASSy	Eastern Africa Submarine Cable System
EATN	East African Television Network Ltd
eKLR	Electronic Kenya Law Reports (www.kenyalaw.org)
ERS-WEC	Economic Recovery Strategy for Wealth and Employment Creation
FCC	Federal Communications Commission (USA)
FIRST	Forum for Incident Response and Security Teams
FNOs	Fixed Network Operators
FWA	Fixed Wireless Access (Networks)
GDP	Gross Domestic Product
GEA	Government Enterprise Architecture
GITS	Government Information Technology Services
GMPCS	Global Mobile Personal Communications by Satellite
GRC	Global Resource Centre
GSM	Global System for Mobile Communication
GTZ	German Technical Cooperation
NSP	Network service provider
HIV	Human Immunodeficiency Virus
ICANN	Internet Corporation for Assigned Names and Numbers
iCSIRT	Industry Computer Security and Incident Response Team
ICT	Information and Communications Technology
IFC	International Finance Corporation

IGW	International Gateway
IMF	International Monetary Fund
IMPACT	International Multilateral Partnership Against Cyber Threats
IP	Internet Protocol
IPR	Intellectual Property Rights
IPTV	Internet Protocol Television
ISP	Internet Service Provider
ITU	International Telecommunications Union
IXP	Internet Exchange Point
KAMP	Kenya Association of Music Producers
KANU	Kenya African National Union
KBC	Kenya Broadcasting Corporation
KCA	Kenya Communications Act, 1998
KDN	Kenya Data Networks
KEBS	Kenya Bureau of Standards
KECOBO	Kenya Copyright Board
KECOPAC	Kenya Consumers Protection Advisory Committee
KEMSA	Kenya Medical Supply Agency
KENET	Kenya Education Network KeNIC Kenya Network Information Centre
KES	Kenyan Shillings
KFCB	Kenya Film Classification Board
KIC Act	Kenya Information and Communications Act, 1998
KICTANet	Kenya ICT Action Network
KIMA	Kenya Internet Marketing Association
KIPI	Kenya Industrial Property Institute
KLR	Kenya Law Reports
KNBS	Kenya National Bureau of Statistics
KNEC	Kenya National Examinations Council
KPLC	Kenya Power and Lighting Company
KPTC	Kenya Posts and Telecommunications Corporation
KRA	Kenya Revenue Authority
LION2	Lower Indian Ocean Network 2 Submarine Cable
LRIC	Long Run Incremental Cost
MCK	Media Council of Kenya

List of Abbreviations

MCSK	Music Copyright Society of Kenya
MNO	Mobile Network Operator
MPAKE	Music Publishers Association of Kenya
MTC	Mobile Telecommunications Company
MVNO	Mobile Virtual Network Operator
NARC	National Rainbow Coalition
National KE-CIRT/CC	National Cybersecurity Strategy, the National Computer Incident Response Team – Coordination Centre
NCS	National Communications Secretariat
NESC	National Economic and Social Council
NFP	Network Facilities Providers
NNX	Network Numbering Exchange
NOFBI	National Fibre Optic Infrastructure
NPKI	National Public Key Infrastructure
NREN	National Research and Education Network
NRRD	Network redundancy, resilience, and diversity
OPGW	Optical Ground Wire
OSP	Online Service Provider
OTT	over-the-top
p.	page
para.	paragraph
PCK	Postal Corporation of Kenya
PoP	Point of Presence
PRiSK	Performers Rights Society of Kenya
PRS	Premium Rate Services
PRSP	Premium Rate Service Providers
PSVs	Public Service Vehicles
PTS	Post-och Telestyrelsen (Sweden)
QoS	Quality of Service
RMS	Royal Media Services Ltd
RTPMP Act	Restrictive Trade Practices, Monopolies, and Price Control Act
SADC	Southern Africa Development Community
SCN	Submarine Cable Networks
SEACOM	The South East Africa Communication
SIM	Subscriber Identification Module

SLA	Service Level Agreements
SLDs	Second-Level domains
TEAMS	East African Marine System
TESPOK	Telecommunications Service Providers Association of Kenya
TLDs	Top-Level domains
TRIPS	World Trade Organization's Agreement on Trade-Related Aspects of Intellectual Property Rights
TSPs	Telecommunications Service Providers
ULF	Unified Licensing Framework
UNCITRAL	United Nations Commission on International Trade Law
UNECA	United Nations Economic Commission for Africa
WCT	WIPO Copyright Treaty
WIPO	World Intellectual Property Organization
WPPT	WIPO Performances and Phonograms Treaty
WTO	World Trade Organization
ZACR	South Africa Central Registry

List of Abbreviations

List of Figures and Tables

List of Figures and Tables

General Introduction

Chapter 1. General Background of the Country

§1. Geography, Demographics, and Government

1. The Republic of Kenya is a country in East Africa lying along the Indian Ocean at the equator. It is neighboured by Uganda to the west, South Sudan to the north-west, Ethiopia to the north and north-east, Somalia to the east, and Tanzania to the south. Kenya has three designated cities – Nairobi, the capital, Mombasa, and Kisumu. It has a land mass measuring 580,367 km^2 (224,080 sq mi) and its economy, like those of most African and developing countries, is heavily dependent on agriculture.[1] A national census conducted in 2009 established that Kenya's population stood at 38 million people.[2] According to 2015 Kenya National Bureau of statistics (KNBS) data, the population for 2014 was projected to have grown to 43 million. (Figures 1 and 2)[3]

1. G. Mwakikagile, *Kenya: Identity of a Nation* (Pretoria, SA: New African Press, 2007).
2. Government of Kenya, Ministry of Planning and National Development and Vision 2030: *Kenya 2009 Population and Housing Census Highlights*, available at www.planning.go.ke/.
3. Kenya National Bureau of Statistics. Kenya Facts and Figures 2015 available at ww.knbs.or.ke/.

Figure 1 Map of Kenya

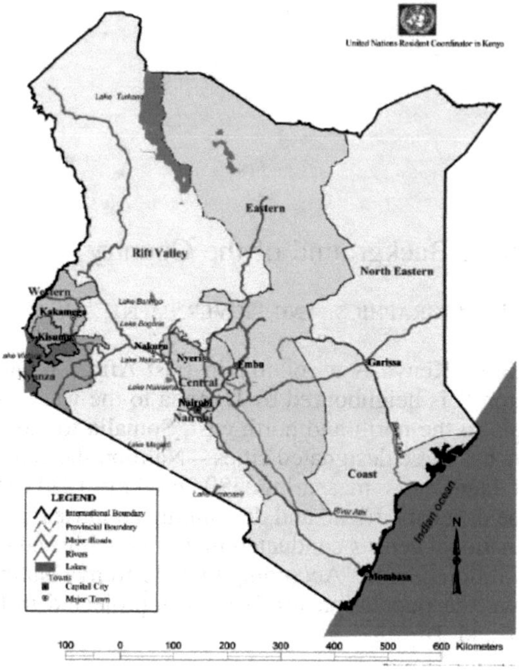

Figure 2 Kenya's National Flag and Coat of Arms

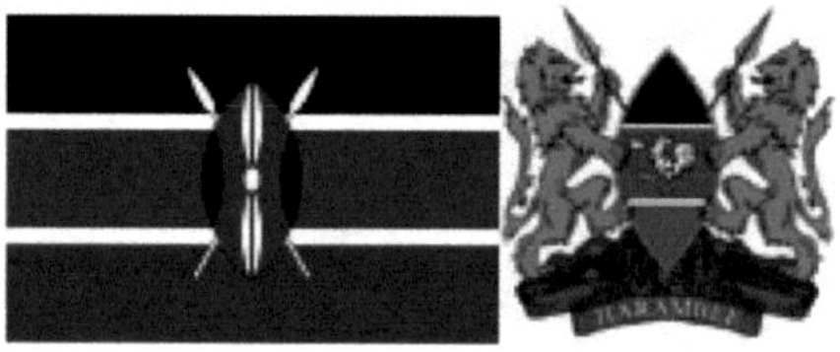

Source: Government of Kenya.

2. Kenya's Internet country code is .ke. The country is named after Mount Kenya, a significant landmark and the second among the highest mountain peaks of Africa. Before 1920, the area now known as Kenya was known as the British East Africa Protectorate.

3. The Government of Kenya is organized according to the Constitution of Kenya, 2010. Kenya is a presidential representative democratic republic, whereby the President is both the head of state and head of government. Executive power is exercised by the president, the deputy president, cabinet secretaries, attorney general, and the director of public prosecutions. Legislative power is vested in a bicameral legislature consisting of the National Assembly and the Senate. The Judiciary is independent of the executive and the legislature. Kenya's national language is Swahili. Its official languages are English and Swahili. The country is divided into forty-seven counties with county governments decentralized and with their own executive authority.[4] Since gaining independence from the British in 1963, Kenya has maintained consistent relative stability despite changes in its political system and crises in neighbouring countries. A cross-party parliamentary reform initiative in the autumn of 1997 revised some oppressive laws inherited from the colonial era that had been used to limit freedom of speech and assembly. This improved public freedoms and contributed to generally credible national elections in December 1997.

4. In December 2002, Kenyans took part in democratic and open elections, and most of which were judged free and fair by international observers. The 2002 elections marked an important turning point in Kenya's democratic evolution in that power was transferred peacefully from the Kenya African National Union (KANU), which had ruled the country since independence, to the National Rainbow Coalition (NARC), a coalition of political parties.

5. Under the presidency of Mwai Kibaki, the new ruling coalition promised to focus its efforts on generating economic growth, combating corruption, improving education, and rewriting its constitution. A few of these promises were met, including passage of a new constitution in 2010 and free, universal primary education. In 2007, the government issued a statement declaring that from 2008, secondary education would be heavily subsidized, with the government footing all tuition fees. However, the government has not been able to fully enforce this directive.

I. Elections and the Executive Branch of Government

6. In 2007–2008, the country experienced a wave of violence based on disputed elections. The violence ended with a power-sharing agreement that temporarily recreated the position of a prime minister, a position that had been abandoned at independence.

7. In 2010, the people of Kenya voted and passed a new Constitution. The Constitution of Kenya 2010 officially consolidated executive power in the presidency, and the Office of the Prime Minister was again to be abandoned after subsequent general elections in 2013. The constitution created forty-seven counties and a framework for a devolved government, with many of the government's responsibilities transferred from the central government to the county governments.

8. After relatively peaceful elections in 2012, Uhuru Kenyatta (the son of Kenya's first president) assumed the Office of the Presidency in 2013 as the first elected president under the new constitution. A major task was to ensure that Parliament implemented provisions of the new constitution according to the schedule set forth

4. Constitution of Kenya, 2010.

therein. Various new laws related to Information and Communications Technology (ICT) were legislated, including the Consumer Protection Act 2012, Kenya Information and Communications (KIC) Amendment Act 2013, the Science Technology and Innovation Act of 2013, the Access to Information Act 2016, and the Protection of Traditional Knowledge and Traditional Cultural Expressions Act 2016. Legislative activity continues with recent efforts to pass various bills related to Cybercrime, Data Protection, and Critical Infrastructure.

9. Kenya held general elections again in August 2017, and this election would prove both strikingly similar and strikingly different from the election in 2012. The race for the Office of the President was a rematch between the same two major candidates from the election in 2012. The Independent Electoral and Boundaries Commission (IEBC) declared Uhuru Kenyatta, the incumbent, the winner of the election just a few days after the voting. In a case filed at the Supreme Court of Kenya, the opposition candidate, Raila Odinga, immediately challenged the declaration of results by the IEBC. A similar challenge had been lodged in 2012, with the Supreme Court at that time ruling that Uhuru Kenyatta had been duly elected in a free and fair election.

10. In 2017, and to widespread astonishment, the Supreme Court held in a 4-2 decision that the August 2017 elections were not conducted in a manner consistent with the Constitution of Kenya 2010. The Court stated that the IEBC committed 'irregularities and illegalities' and that the election was therefore null and void. The Court ordered that the Presidential election be rerun within sixty days. This marks the first time in Africa that the courts have nullified a presidential election.

11. The election rerun, held in October 2017, was equally controversial, as the opposition leader Raila Odinga effectively boycotted the entire exercise. The resulting vote was 97% in favour of Uhuru Kenyatta, and after a failed petition to the Supreme Court, Kenyatta was sworn in for a second term as President of the Republic of Kenya.

II. Judicial Branch of Government

12. In addition to the executive and legislative branches of government, the Constitution of Kenya 2010 provides for the Judiciary as a third and independent branch. The Judiciary is mandated to deliver justice in line with the Constitution and the laws of Kenya and is expected to resolve disputes in a just manner with a view to protecting the rights and liberties of all.[5]

13. The system of courts within the Judiciary is organized into two levels.

5. *See* http://www.judiciary.go.ke/portal/page/about-the-judiciary.

A. Superior Courts

14. The superior courts are the Supreme Court, the Court of Appeal, the High Court, and such Courts as may be established by Parliament. The High Court has unlimited original jurisdiction in criminal and civil matters,[6] as well as to hear cases related to, among other things, employment and labour relations, the environment, and the use and occupation of, and title to, land.[7]

B. Subordinate Courts and Tribunals

15. The subordinate courts are the Magistrates courts, Kadhis' Courts, Courts-Martial, and any other court or local tribunal as may be established by Parliament.[8]

16. There are also tribunals which are bodies established by Parliament to exercise judicial and quasi-judicial functions. They supplement ordinary courts but lack penal jurisdiction. The High Court exercises its supervisory role over tribunals.[9] The Tribunal that deals with the information and communication sector is the Communications and Multimedia Appeals Tribunal, established by the KIC Act 1998.[10] The main purpose of the Tribunal is to arbitrate in cases where disputes arise between the parties under the Act and matters that may be referred to it by the Cabinet Secretary.[11] The jurisdiction of the Tribunal is limited to the interpretation of the KIC Act.[12] Appeals from a decision or order of the Tribunal may be made to the High Court whose decision on any such appeal is final.[13]

§2. ECONOMIC PERFORMANCE

17. The territory that is now Kenya was once part of a common market involving present-day Tanzania and Uganda. The market was founded in 1917, formalized in 1948 with the formation of the East Africa Community, and collapsed in 1977. The idea of a common market was started by the British colonial government to serve the commercial interests of the British government and those of the British settlers in the occupied territories in East Africa. The aim was to create a free and integrated market, sheltered by selective high tariff walls to simultaneously encourage Kenyan settler businessmen and the expansion of foreign manufactured exports into East Africa. This meant that either the gains from a customs union were not reaped or the distribution between partner states was not 'equitable'.

---

6. Article 165, Constitution of Kenya 2010.
7. Article 162(1), Constitution of Kenya 2010.
8. Article 169(1), Constitution of Kenya 2010.
9. *See* http://www.judiciary.go.ke/portal/page/tribunals.
10. Section 102, Kenya Information and Communications Act 1998.
11. Section 102(1), Kenya Information and Communications Act 2010.
12. Dr M.S. Raisinghani, 'Handbook of Research on Global Information Technology Management in the Digital Economy' Information Science Reference.
13. Section 102 G, Kenya Information and Communications (Amendment) Act 2013.

18. Further, after independence, these integrated activities were reconstituted, and the High Commission was replaced by the East African Common Services Organization, which many observers thought would lead to a political federation between the three territories. The new organization ran into difficulties because of the lack of joint planning and fiscal policy, separate political policies and Kenya's dominant economic position. In 1967, the East African Common Services Organization was superseded by the East African Community (EAC). Ten years later, in 1977, the EAC collapsed due to demands by Kenya to have more seats than Uganda and Tanzania in decision-making organs, amid disagreements caused by dictatorship under President Idi Amin in Uganda, socialism in Tanzania, and capitalism in Kenya. With the collapse, the three Member States lost over sixty years of cooperation and the benefits of economies of scale. Each of the former Member States had to embark, at great expense and lower efficiency, upon the establishment of services and industries that had previously been provided at the community level, including telecommunications and postal services.[14]

19. The EAC is now an intergovernmental organization comprising the five East African countries Burundi, Kenya, Rwanda, Tanzania, and Uganda. The first major step in establishing the East African Federation is the customs union in East Africa signed in March 2004, which commenced on 1 January 2005. EAC's customs union and common market protocol took effect in 2010 following ratification by all the five EAC states with the goal of creating a full political federation. In 2013, a protocol was signed outlining the Member States plans for launching a monetary union within ten years.[15]

20. Kenya is also a member of the Common Market for Eastern and Southern Africa (COMESA). COMESA is a preferential trading area with twenty Member States stretching from Libya to Swaziland. It was formed in December 1994, replacing a preferential trade area that had existed since 1981 and is one of the pillars of the African Economic Community. In 2008, COMESA agreed to an expanded free-trade zone including members of two other African trade blocs, the EAC and the Southern Africa Development Community (SADC), and launched the Tripartite Free Trade Area in 2015. This agreement sets the stage for the establishment of a single market for the twenty-six countries in the Eastern and Southern African region,[16] and it is intended to form the precursor of a continental Africa-wide free-trade area.[17]

21. Kenya has a rapidly expanding economy that is driven largely by agriculture and tourism but which has recently joined many other countries in the developing world in seeking to transform itself into a knowledge economy. Kenya also has one of the world's highest population growth rates and almost half of its population lives below the poverty line.

---

14. *See*, generally, A. Odhiambo et al., *A History of East Africa* (London: Longman Group Ltd, 1977).
15. Protocol for the Establishment of the EAC Monetary Union signed, available at www.eac.int/.
16. Mega African trade bloc paves way for continental commerce, available at www.reuters.com/.
17. TFTA (http://www.bilaterals.org/?-comesa-eac-sadc) June 2015 retrieved on 15 Sep. 2015.

22. Kenya Vision 2030 is Kenya's development blueprint covering the period 2008–2030. It aims to make Kenya a newly industrializing, 'middle-income country providing high quality life for all its citizens by the year 2030'. The vision is based on three 'pillars' namely, the economic pillar, the social pillar, and the political pillar. This vision's programme plan came after the successful implementation of the *Economic Recovery Strategy for Wealth and Employment Creation (ERS-WEC),* under which Kenya's Gross Domestic Product (GDP) steadily rose from 0.6% in 2002 to 6.1% in 2006.

23. The economic pillar aims at providing prosperity of all Kenyans through an economic development programme aimed at achieving an average GDP growth rate of 10% per annum for the next twenty-five years. The social pillar seeks to build 'a just and cohesive society with social equity in a clean and secure environment'. The political pillar aims at realizing a democratic political system founded on issue-based politics that respects the rule of law and protects the rights and freedoms of every individual in the Kenyan society.

24. For a country that is leveraging on ICT as a driver of economic growth, the challenges faced by the makers of telecommunications policy in Kenya are therefore exceptionally demanding. To meet economic needs, the country will need to continuously expand its telecommunications network, enhance service quality and features, and upgrade operational efficiency and productivity. The government of Kenya has responded to these challenges with a market-oriented economic policy, which emphasizes openness to the world economy and export-led growth, and eliminates barriers to the private sector investments in industry, including telecommunications. This market-led approach is in contrast to neighbouring countries such as Rwanda and Tanzania, which are implementing government-led transitions in the ICT sector.

25. By 2017 estimates, Kenya's total GDP, a measure of the total value of the country's production services, was about KES 7.1 trillion, or roughly USD 71 billion, with USD 1,650 per capita.[18] Until the twenty-first century, the country's performance was not in line with its potential. Compared to the first post-independence decade, Kenya performed poorly in both the 1980s and the 1990s. Negative or minimal growth was observed in the early 2000s, although this has recently improved substantially. Some key performance statistics are as follows:

- GDP growth was negative 0.2% in 2000, a modest 1.2% in 2001, and a lower 1.1% in 2002.[19] However, by 2015 and 2016, GDP growth had risen to 5.7% and 5.8%, respectively.[20] Inflation during 2015 and 2016 remained moderate at 6.6% and 6.3%, respectively.
- Income levels vary greatly from region to region.

18. Kenya Bureau of Statistics: Kenya Economic Survey (2017).
19. Kenya Bureau of Statistics: Kenya Economic Survey (2003).
20. Kenya Bureau of Statistics: Kenya Economic Survey (2017).

- Agriculture contributed 30.4% and 32.6% of GDP in 2015 and 2016, respectively, and the financial and insurance activities sector contributed 6.8% and 7.1% of GDP in 2015 and 2016. The financial and insurance sectors have seen consistent growth in their percentage of the overall economy between 2012 and 2016. In contrast, the manufacturing sector contributed 9.4% and 9.2% of GDP in 2015 and 2016, respectively and has seen a consistent decline in percentage of the overall economy between 2012 and 2016.[21] This is clear evidence of a (modest) shift towards a knowledge-based economy.

26. For more than a decade beginning around 2005, Kenya has seen dramatic growth. This period has seen a consistent, year-on-year expansion that is interrupted by occasional but brief periods of uncertainty and slower growth (particularly around the time of elections).

§3. Conclusion

27. Like many other sub-Saharan African states, Kenya has strived to establish a framework of governance and social order that creates the market conditions for rapid economic growth. Over the years, its national development policies have focused on improving the productive sectors of the economy: agriculture, manufacturing, trade, tourism and services. With the liberalization of the telecommunications and other ICT services in the country, Kenya witnessed an unprecedented growth in local and foreign investment that made both direct and indirect contributions to the economy.

21. *Ibid.*

Chapter 2. Telecommunications Infrastructure

§1. The ICT Industry

28. From 1948 to 1977, postal services in Kenya, Tanzania, and Uganda were provided by the East African Posts and Telecommunications Corporation (EAP&TC). The dissolution of the first EAC, which lasted from 1967 to 1977, made it imperative for Kenya to establish its own monopoly communications company, the Kenya Posts and Telecommunications Corporation (KPTC).

29. New government economic policies in the mid-1990s were developed and adopted, supported by the International Monetary Fund (IMF) and the World Bank. The recommendations of that process included the liberalization and separation of the postal and telecommunication operations. An IMF loan arrangement also depended on privatization of KPTC, but IMF suspended this in July 1997 over reported concerns of corruption in the government.

30. Controversy over IMF telecommunications privatization policies continued. KPTC's Board of Directors was dismissed by the government in February 1999 prior to an IMF visit to the country.

I. The Kenya Communications Act, 1998

31. With the passing of the Kenya Communications Act (KCA), 1998, which came into force on 1 July 1999, Kenya's communications industry was set for unprecedented changes. The passing of the Act was the culmination of a decade of mounting pressure from various quarters for Kenya's government to open up the industry to competition and independent regulation. The Act dissolved the KPTC and transferred its obligations to two new legal entities, namely, Telkom Kenya and the Postal Corporation of Kenya (PCK). The former was to enjoy a monopolistic head start in the provision of certain telecommunications services in the now competitive market, while the latter was the designated public postal licensee. The Communications Commission of Kenya (CCK) was established as the independent regulator for the telecommunications, radio communications, and postal service industries. The issuing of broadcasting licences remained the mandate of the Ministry of Transport and Telecommunications (now the Ministry of Information, Communications, and Technology) until 2009 when an amendment to the Act transferred that mandate to the CCK. The National Communications Secretariat (NCS) was established as an organ within the Ministry to serve as the policy advisory arm of the government on matters relating to the communications sector and finally, the Communications Appeal Tribunal (now Communications and Multimedia Appeals Tribunal), a quasi-judicial body, as the independent arbitrator of disputes in the industry. The Kenya Information Communications Amendment Act of 2013 renamed CCK to the Communications Authority of Kenya (CA),[22] set out limitations to the freedom of the media and freedom of expression, gave CA powers to make regulations for enforcement on the freedom of the media, and gave CA powers to undertake prosecution of any offence under the Act.[23]

II. Telecommunications Services

32. Table 1 shows growth and declines in the number of Telecommunications Service Providers (TSPs) by Category between 2011 and 2015. The recent uptick in Internet Service Providers (ISPs) indicates the area of the strongest growth in the industry. Various telecommunications service sectors are discussed below in Table 1.

Table 1 Number of Telecommunications Service Providers by Category

Licence Category	*2010/ 11*	*2011/ 12*	*2012/ 13*	*2013/ 14*	*2014/ 15*
Vendors and Contractors	825	656	645	643	637
Technical Personnel	252	217	214	209	251
Internet Service Providers	47	45	45	44	58
Value-Added Service Providers	39	31	30	30	30
Public Data Network Operators	8	8	10	10	12
Local Loop Operators	10	10	10	10	10
Commercial VSAT (Hub Operators)	1	1	1	1	1
Internet Backbone and Gateway Operator (IBGO)	1	–	–	–	–
Data Carrier Network Operators (DCNO)	6	2	2	2	2
Total	**1,189**	**970**	**957**	**949**	**1,001**

Source: Communications Authority of Kenya, Annual Report 2014/15.

22. For the sake of clarity and consistency, the new name and abbreviation of the Communications Authority (i.e., the CA) is used throughout this text, even when referring to the organization or its actions at a time that it was known as the CCK.
23. Kenya Information and Communications Amendment Act 2013, section 5B.

A. *Fixed-Line Telephony*

33. During the time of the KPTC and Telkom Kenya and before the introduction of mobile telephony, access to quality telephone services in Kenya was poor. Official waiting lists of customers seeking telephone service increased almost fourfold to almost 79,000 between 1977 and 1983 but had been reduced to less than 50,000 by 1986. These waiting lists only applied to areas where telephone services were available. At the time that the privatization of Telkom Kenya began in 2006, the company only provided landline services to 315,000 subscribers in a country with a population of over 35 million people.[24]

B. *Internet*

34. The Internet was introduced in Kenya in the early 1990s, largely led by Kenyans returning from overseas studies, western expatriates, international bodies and non-governmental organizations. Commercial ISPs, led by Form Net and Africa Online, entered the Internet market by the mid-1990s, primarily offering dial-up services and content services. The notable early adopters included the import/export sector, industries which had overseas operations and clients and the academic sector, with most of their users confined to Nairobi. With an increasing number of ISPs and Internet users, the need for an Internet backbone became evident, and KPTC introduced Jambonet by 1998. The key challenges in the 1990s were the limited and high cost of international Internet bandwidth, the high cost of both dial-up and domestic leased lines, the limited penetration of personal computers, limited capacity and poor quality fixed infrastructure, poor regulatory framework and the lack of appropriate information technology skills.[25]

35. The first five years of the new millennium (1999/2000–2004/2005) were dominated by Telkom Kenya as a monopoly provider of telecommunication services, with Internet bandwidth and leased line tariffs largely remaining high and unchanged.

Table 2 Internet Usage and Population Growth in Kenya

Year	*Users*	*Population*	*Penetration (%)*	*Usage Source*
2000	200,000	30,339,770	0.7	ITU
2008	3,000,000	37,953,838	7.9	ITU
2009	3,359,600	39,002,772	8.6	ITU
2010	3,995,500	41,070,934	9.7	ITU

24. International Finance Corporation: Infrastructure Advisory success stories Kenya: Telkom Kenya, available at www.ifc.org/ifccx/psa.nsf, 2009.
25. *See* www.CA.go.ke.

Year	*Users*	*Population*	*Penetration (%)*	*Usage Source*
2015	31,985,048	45,925,301	69.6	CAK

Source: Internet Live Stats (www.InternetLiveStats.com). Elaboration of data by International Telecommunication Union (ITU), World Bank, and United Nations Population Division.

36. The situation only changed after Telkom Kenya's exclusivity period came to an end in 2004 and the CA licensed new operators to compete in both Internet backbone gateway and domestic leased line services. As a result of the ensuing competition in 2005/2006, Internet tariffs began to come down while international Internet bandwidth increased. In the first decade of the twenty-first century, the challenges faced in Internet growth have been low Internet penetration, high costs of Internet services, poor or little local content to drive demand, and the focus by ISPs on Internet access rather than on quality Internet services and applications. Moreover, until 2009, the legislative and licensing framework for market operators was inadequate, as it had been quickly overtaken by rapidly changing and converging technologies.

37. According to ITU estimates in 2014, globally, there are approximately 2.9 billion people using the Internet representing 40%of the world's population. Internet user penetration in developed countries stands at 78% vis-à-vis 32% in developing countries. The European region continues to enjoy the highest Internet penetration in the world (75%), followed by Americas (66%), Arab States (41%), Asia and Pacific (32%), and Africa (19%). In Kenya, Internet usage stands at 60.8% of the population as of 2014, which is higher than the world's average of 40%. Table 2 provides population data and Internet penetration data for Kenya from the ITU and from the CA.

C. Mobile Telephony

38. Between the time the first mobile phone service provider was established in 1997 until 2014, mobile phone subscribers grew to an impressive 34.8 million. Presently, there are four licensed mobile phone service providers in Kenya, namely, Safaricom Ltd, Airtel Kenya Ltd (formerly Zain, Celtel, Kencell), Telkom Kenya Ltd (Orange) and Finserve (Equitel).

39. Safaricom was formed in 1997 as a fully owned subsidiary of Telkom Kenya, then the government-owned incumbent monopoly. In May 2000, Vodafone Group Plc of the United Kingdom (UK) acquired a 40% stake and management responsibility for the company. In December 2007, 60% of the shares held by Telkom Kenya were transferred to the Government of Kenya, which was reduced to 35% in March of 2008 after the government offered 25% of the stake for sale to the public. Safaricom's 10 billion ordinary shares are now traded on the Nairobi Stock Exchange. As at the beginning of 2015, official figures put the number of Safaricom shareholders at 8.2 million. Safaricom has established itself as the most profitable company in East Africa, posting a net profit of KES 31,871,303,000 in the financial year ending March 2015.[26]

40. The company that now operates the Airtel mobile phone brand in Kenya was first licensed in January of 2000 as Kencell Communications Ltd with 40% ownership by Sameer Group, a Kenyan investment giant, and 60% by Vivendi Telecom International. It started operations in August of that year and immediately entered into a fierce competition with Safaricom, which had captured a large portion of the mobile phone market in Kenya. In 2004, it changed its name to Celtel Kenya Ltd after Celtel International, a leading pan-African mobile communications group, bought out Vivendi. A year later, in May 2005, Mobile Telecommunications Company (MTC) bought an 85% stake in Celtel International and in 2008, dropped the Celtel brand and replaced it with Zain. In 2010, India's Bharti Airtel bought Zain African operations and changed the brand to Airtel Kenya. By 2015, estimates by CA put the number of the company's subscribers at slightly over 7 million, which constitutes about 22.6% of market share.

41. After the dissolution of the KPTC by the KCA, 1998, Telkom Kenya was established as the incumbent government-owned telecommunications monopoly. After two unsuccessful attempts to privatize the company since 2000, the Kenyan government approached the World Bank Group's International Finance Corporation (IFC) in March 2006 to act as the transaction adviser on two linked transactions: the privatization of Telkom Kenya and the negotiated sale of 9% of Safaricom to Vodafone International. Telkom Kenya was effectively on the verge of bankruptcy, and its business prospects were bleak under increased competitive pressure from the private mobile telephony players. The government's objectives were to address the restructuring of the company's deteriorating balance sheet, as well as the losses and significant overstaffing that had accumulated during its monopoly years, as well as also to benefit employees by providing adequate retrenchment compensation for redundant staff and work opportunities for remaining staff. Telkom Kenya obtained USD 81 million in financing to fund the cost of downsizing of thousands of its employees by pledging part of its 60% stake in Safaricom. The loan was to be repaid upon the completion of the privatization exercise. This allowed the company to be privatized as a competitor to Safaricom and thus increase competition in the market.[27] The unbundling of Safaricom also funded the restructuring of Telkom's balance sheet so that it could be privatized free of major government liabilities, including government debts and pension deficits. Lastly, in 2007, Telkom was awarded a mobile telephony licence that became critical to its competitiveness and attractiveness to investors during the privatization transaction. The privatization involved a bidding process for 51% of the company. A consortium led by France Telecom won the bid in late 2007 over the other two bidders: Reliance of India and Telkom South Africa. The unbundling of Telkom's stake in Safaricom would lead

26. The Business Daily, 15 May 2015.
27. International Telecommunications Union, available at www.itu.int/ituweblogs/treg/Privatisation+Of+Telkom+Kenya+Limited.aspx, 10 Jun. 2008.

to the flotation of 25% of Safaricom shares in the Nairobi Securities Exchange in June 2008. The initial public offering was five times oversubscribed, raising more than USD 800 million, which more than offset the cost of restructuring Telkom. Telkom launched its mobile telephony service under the Orange brand in August of 2008. From 2012, the shareholding structure has continued to change due to a decision by the Kenyan government to convert its shareholding into equity in order to ease Telkom Kenya's debt burden. This diluted government shareholding in the company to 40%. In January 2013, France Telecom increased its stake to 70% as a result of the Kenyan government not having provided its full portion of 2012 funding.[28] From 2014, France Telecom sought to sell its stake at Telkom Kenya and exit the Kenyan market. Several reasons were offered for the planned exit, including claims that industry regulator had not established a level playing field to help stop price wars, as well as the government's intention to withdraw control and management of the National Fibre Optic Infrastructure (NOFBI) from Telkom Kenya.[29]

42. Econet Wireless, a consortium managed by Econet Wireless International of South Africa, had a troubled entry into Kenya's mobile telephony market. After being granted a licence as early as 2003, CCK revoked the licence in the same year after the operator was drawn into litigation battles with local partners over shareholding and failed to pay the balance of the licence fees. Later, the licence was restored, and in December of 2008, the company launched its mobile telephony service under the Yu brand. In 2008, Econet Wireless sold its Kenya operation to Indian firm Essar Telecommunications. Yu Mobile managed to reach 2.7 million subscribers which was then about 8.8% market share. Nevertheless, the operator soon signalled its intention to pull out of the Kenyan market. In the final arrangement, Yu Mobile sold its infrastructure to Safaricom, while Airtel Kenya acquired Yu's 2.7 million subscribers by taking over the mobile number prefix. This allowed Yu Mobile customers to migrate to Airtel's network without having to change their identities. The deal was reported to be valued at about USD 100 million.[30]

43. Finserve Africa Ltd, which is a subsidiary of Equity Bank operating under the brand name Equitel, got a licence from CA in April 2014 to operate as a Mobile Virtual Network Operator (MVNO). An MVNO is a communications provider that offers mobile cellular services to its customers without the need for Global System for Mobile Communication (GSM) network infrastructure or a spectrum licence. MVNOs are licensed in Kenya under the Application Service Provider (ASP) licensing category and are able to provide all forms of services to end users using the communications infrastructure of a licensed mobile network operator (MNO). Subsequently, the licensed MNOs are licensed under the Network Facility Provider (NFP) Tier 1 category of licence. The licensed MNO hosts the MVNOs on the

---

28. Government loses ownership grip in Telkom Kenya, available at http://www.standardmedia.co.ke/business/article/2000074810/government-loses-ownership-grip-in-telkom-kenya, 12 Jan. 2013.
29. Orange back to drawing board as buyout bid flops, available at http://www.businessdailyafrica.com/Corporate-News/Orange-kenya-buyout-bid-flops/-/539550/2532842/-/item/0/-/11sd6ey/-/index.html, 24 Nov. 2014.
30. Safaricom, Airtel splash Sh8bn for Yu, available at http://www.businessdailyafrica.com/Corporate-News/Safaricom-and-Airtel-buy-yuMobile/-/539550/2227688/-/133nkwr/-/index.html, 2 Mar. 2014.

excess capacity on its network. MVNOs can provide cellular mobile services including customer registration, Subscriber Identification Module (SIM) cards issuance, billing, and customer care to end users without holding a spectrum licence. The MVNOs are assigned their own mobile numbering range by the regulator. The MVNOs are obliged to provide services within the set Quality of Service parameters set out by the regulator.

44. In July 2015, Finserve Africa Ltd (Equitel) launched its mobile money, voice, data, and SMS after a pilot phase of one year. Within a year of the launch, Equitel had a subscriber base of over one million customers. Equitel began offering 'thin SIM' technology, a paper-thin SIM card that is affixed onto the traditional SIM card, thereby converting a single SIM handset into a duo SIM handset. The use of this technology lowered costs for the operator, which resulted in two outcomes. First, Equitel was able to offer service at very low cost, thereby capturing low-income segment consumers that would not otherwise be able to purchase a second handset (or an actual dual-SIM handset) to use Equitel services. Second, immediately prior to the intended roll-out in 2014, Equitel and the CA were quickly sued by interested parties claiming that the thin SIM roll-out violated various regulations and failed to adequately protect consumer data.[31] The lawsuits temporarily blocked Equitel's roll-out of the technology, but by 2015 the courts removed the injunction and Equitel began offering the service.[32]

45. Other MVNOs in Kenya are Mobile Pay Ltd (running the Tangaza Pesa money service) and Zioncell Kenya Ltd, both of which are hosted on the physical infrastructure belonging to Airtel Kenya.

31. *See* http://www.businessdailyafrica.com/Corporate-News/Court-stops-rollout-of-Equity-s-thin-SIM-cards/539550-2561606-g3tpc7/index.html.
32. *See* http://www.nation.co.ke/business/Equity-gets-court-backing-to-roll-out-thin-SIM-technology/996-2733930-kccoy4/index.html.

Table 3 Mobile Network Growth Indicators

Type	*Mobile Network Growth Indicators*				
	2010/11	*2011/12*	*2012/13*	*2013/14*	*2014/15*
Capacity	47,677,000	49,977,000	55,077,000	65,077,000	62,800,000
No. of Subscribers	25,279,768	29,703,439	30,594,422	32,246,393	36,113,121
SMS	2,622,821,774	4,295,378,823	13,233,082,214	24,582,230,257	27,443,621,730

Source: Communications Authority of Kenya, Annual Report 2014/15.

Table 4 Mobile Money Transfer Growth Indicators

Operator	*June 2011*	*June 2012*	*June 2013*	*June 2014*	*June 2015*
Safaricom Limited (M-Pesa)	14,331,941	15,083,674	17,561,999	19,776,056	21,338,328
Telkom Kenya Limited (Orange Money – Iko Pesa)	117,091	140,166	166,114	185,463	192,531
Airtel Networks Kenya Limited (Airtel Money)	2,530,916	3,751,713	4,580,467	3,238,754	3,119,812
Essar Telecom Kenya Limited (Yu Cash)	415,779	530,149	2,291,473	2,147,139	0
Mobikash	–	–	–	1,263,655	1,714,170
Tangaza	–	–	–	503,556	503,556
Equitel (Finserve Ltd)	–	–	–	–	873,643
Total Number of Subscribers	17,395,727	19,505,702	24,840,404	27,114,623	27,742,040
Total Number of Agents	42,313	49,079	88,466	110,096	129,357

Source: Communications Authority of Kenya, Annual Report 2014/15.

46. The total number of 2G and 3G transceivers in Kenya doubled during the period 2010–2015, with 3G transceivers representing about 17% of the total by 2015.[33] The increase in these figures from prior years can be attributed to continued expansions of coverage area and increases in the capacity for voice and, particularly, data services. The growth in cellular services has impacted the economy positively as a larger percentage of the population now has access to voice, data, and value-added services such as mobile money transfer services. One mobile carrier, Safaricom, is currently in the process of rolling out 4G LTE service, and the CA has allocated frequency spectrum for other telecommunications companies to do the same. Tables 3 and 4 provide CA data showing the growth of mobile subscribers and usage, and the growth of mobile money services, respectively. Tables 5, 6, 7, and 8 show the decline or stagnation of fixed network users, services, and infrastructure. Table 9 shows the rapid expansion of mobile network infrastructure from various service providers.

33. Source: Kenya National Bureau of Statistics Annual Abstracts, 2016.

Table 5 Fixed Network Subscribers

Financial Year	*2009/10*	*2010/11*	*2011/12*	*2012/13*	*2013/14*	*2014/15*
Wireline Capacity	421,528	400,764	380,135	362,627	340,005	75,407
Wireline Connections	234,522	187,716	74,606	56,724	53,998	87,774
Wireless Connections (Include LLO Subscribers)	225,592	191,585	188,155	159,745	147,396	0
Total Connections (Wireline and Wireless)	460,114	379,301	262,761	216,469	201,398	87,774
Urban Wireline Connections	227,486	182,084	72,368	54,758	50,481	87,774
Rural Wireline Connections	7,036	5,632	2,238	1,694	1,520	0
International Outgoing Traffic (Minutes)	14,761,211	11,455,952	20,058,628	16,457,407	16,498,989	13,398,004
International Incoming Traffic (Minutes)	38,550,399	31,866,685	17,796,496	14,444,467	12,427,119	10,598,469
Traffic to Mobile Networks (Minutes)	31,024,688	79,616,952	104,967,748	105,287,432	105,212,956	107,889,935

Source: Communications Authority of Kenya 2014/15 annual report.

Note: Local Loop Operator (LLO).

Table 6 Additional Private Land Mobile Stations

Frequency	*Band Station Type*	*2008/09*	*2009/10*	*2010/11*	*2011/12*	*2012/13*	*2013/14*	*2015/16*
VHF	Fixed	85	61	65	74	94	112	79
	Mobile/Portable	440	376	632	697	822	565	649
	Total	**525**	**437**	**697**	**771**	**916**	**677**	**728**
HF	Fixed	14	15	1	11	3	–	4
	Mobile/Portable	16	13	13	31	7	–	5
	Total	**30**	**28**	**14**	**42**	**10**	**–**	**9**

Source: Communications Authority of Kenya.

Note: Very High Frequency (VHF) and High Frequency (HF).

Table 7 Fixed Network Traffic

Frequency Band	*No. of New Links*			*No. of Decommissioned Links*			*Cumulative No. of Fixed Links*		
	2012/13	*2013/14*	*2014/15*	*2012/13*	*2013/14*	*2014/15*	*2012/13*	*2013/14*	*2014/15*
5GHz	170	224	357				830	1,144	1,501
6GHz	–	6	0	–	–		113	66	66
7/8GHz	80	97	56	35	63	254	1,273	1,307	1,108
11GHz	–	–	1		–	0	0	4	5
13GHz	13	21	3	30	–	452	807	798	349
15GHz	198	192	193	151	356	77	2,973	2,809	2,679
18GHz	–	4	3	–	2	4	8	76	75
23GHz	44	64	54	–	24	54	533	513	513
38GHz	16	22	0	–	–	1	118	108	107
Total	**521**	**630**	**667**	**216**	**445**	**842**	**5,464***	**6,825**	**6,403**

Source: Communications Authority of Kenya 2014/15 annual report, p. 26.

*The numbers are as reported by the CA.

Table 8 Fixed Wireless Access Systems

	Number of Sites			*Number of Transceivers*		
Frequency Band	*2012/13*	*2013/14*	*2014/15*	*2012/13*	*2013/14*	*2014/15*
1.7GHz	23	23	23	276	276	276
3.3GHz	103	107	73	270	232	201
3.5GHz	511	486	412	1,958	1,915	1,692
Total	637	616	508	2,504	2,423	2,169

Source: Communications Authority of Kenya 2014/15 annual report, p. 26.

Table 9 Mobile Cellular Services

Operator	*Technology*	*2009/10*	*2010/11*	*2011/12*	*2012/13*	*2013/14*	*2014/15*
Essar Telecom Kenya Limited	2G	3,639	4,500	5,500	5,500	5,500	–
	3G	–	–	–	–	–	–
Telkom Kenya Limited	2G	3,458	4,492	6,230	6,391	6,903	7,631
	3G	–	1,254	2,269	2,375	3,056	3,192
Airtel Networks Kenya Limited	2G	6,966	8,791	13,452	14,788	15,981	16,811
	3G	–	162	973	1,096	1,686	1,892
Safaricom Limited	2G	39,048	48,026	46,702	54,215	56,247	65,552
	3G	3,568	3,623	7,811	9,304	10,639	14,216
Total No. of Transceivers	2G	53,111	65,809	71,884	80,894	84,631	89,994
	3G	3,568	5,039	11,053	12,775	15,381	19,300

Source: Communications Authority of Kenya 2014/15 annual report, p. 25.

(–) Means that the licensee had not taken up a 3G licence.

§2. FIBRE OPTICS

I. International Network

47. The telecommunications industry in Kenya has experienced a transformation brought about by numerous major initiatives to connect to the rest of the world by fibre optic cables:

- The East African Marine System (TEAMS).
- The Eastern Africa Submarine Cable System (EASSy).
- The South East Africa Communication (SEACOM).
- Lower Indian Ocean Network submarine cable (LION2).

48. Prior to 2009, East Africa had remained the only region in the world that had neither intra-African nor direct international cable network access. The region instead relied on expensive satellite communications. Data costs in the country remained among the highest in the world with costs of up to USD 7,000 per megabit of bandwidth. Kenya's hopes to become a bigger player in Business Process Off-shoring (BPO), as India has done in the recent past, were hampered by the high cost of data. Nevertheless, Kenya's nascent call centre business grew from employing 200 people in the year 2006 to 3,000 in 2009, despite relying on expensive satellite-based communications at the time.[34] The introduction of fibre optic connections has made practical what was once merely aspirational.

A. The East African Marine System

49. TEAMS was an initiative spearheaded by the government of Kenya to link the country to the rest of the world through a 5,000 km submarine fibre optic cable linking the city of Mombasa on the coast of Kenya to Fujairah in the United Arab Emirates.

50. On 11 October 2007, Alcatel-Lucent was awarded the USD 82 million contract to lay the TEAMS cable. Construction began in January 2008 on the Emirates' side. On 12 June 2009, the cable arrived in the Kenyan port city of Mombasa and was launched by the President of Kenya, Mwai Kibaki. The project is owned by Etisalat (UAE) and a consortium comprised of the government of Kenya and various investors in Kenya's telecommunications industry, including, Safaricom, Telkom Kenya, Liquid Telecom (previously Kenya Data Networks (KDN)), Wananchi Group, Jamii Telecom, Access Kenya, and BCS Group.[35] The TEAMS cable is connected to the Kenya national fibre backbone network and other major backhaul providers, thus extending the gigabit submarine capacity to the rest of the neighbouring

34. 'What Ails the BPO Sector?', *The East African Standard*, 22 Feb. 2010.
35. 'Fibre Optic Did Land, says TEAMS Secretariat', *The Daily Nation*, 1 Jul. 2009.

East African countries: Uganda, Rwanda, Burundi, Tanzania, and Ethiopia through cross-border connectivity arrangements.[36]

B. The Eastern Africa Submarine Cable System (EASSy)

51. EASSy connects countries of Eastern Africa via a high bandwidth fibre optic cable system to the rest of the world. It is considered a milestone in the development of information infrastructure in the region. EASSy runs from Mtunzini in South Africa to Port Sudan in Sudan, with landing points in nine countries, and connected to at least ten landlocked countries – who will no longer have to rely on expensive satellite systems to carry voice and data services. The project, partially funded by the World Bank, was initiated in January 2003, when a handful of companies investigated its feasibility.[37] EASSy is a high capacity cable with more than 10 terabit per second (Tbit/s), two fibre-pair configuration. It is the first to deliver direct connectivity between East Africa and Europe/North America. EASSy interconnects with multiple international submarine cable networks (SCN) for onward connectivity to Europe, the Americas, the Middle East and Asia. Commercial service started in mid-2010.[38]

C. The South East Africa Communication

52. SEACOM is a privately funded venture that built, owns, and operates a submarine fibre optic cable connecting communication carriers in South and East Africa. SEACOM sells wholesale international capacity to global networks via India and Europe. The project's business model is to provide affordable bandwidth via volume discounts and large bandwidth growth. South Africa, Madagascar, Mozambique, Tanzania, and Kenya are interconnected via a protected ring structure on the continent. A second express fibre pair connects South Africa to Kenya. According to SEACOM, these two fibre pairs have a combined design capacity of 1.28 terabits, of which 100 gigabits is currently active. The cable was commissioned for operation on 23 July 2009. Express fibre pairs are also provided from Kenya to France into a point of presence (PoP) in Marseille, with 640 gigabits capacity, and from Tanzania to India into the PoP in Mumbai with 640 gigabits capacity. SEACOM has procured fibre capacity from Marseille to London as part of the SEACOM network. The SEACOM undersea fibre optic cable system is designed to perform reliably for twenty-five years. It seeks to provide African retail carriers with equal and open access to inexpensive bandwidth, thus removing the international infrastructure bottleneck. This will help to support Eastern and Southern African economic growth.

---

36. The East African Marine System Limited, available at www.teams.co.ke/.
37. *See* www.eassy.org.
38. EASSy enters commercial service, available at http://mybroadband.co.za/news/telecoms/14278-EASSy-enters-commercial-service.html, 5 Aug. 2010.

53. On 23 July 2009, the 15,000 km (9,300 mi) subsea fibre optic cable began operations, providing the East African countries of Djibouti, South Africa, Tanzania, Kenya, Uganda, and Mozambique, with high-speed Internet connections to Europe and Asia. The cable was officially switched on in simultaneous events held across the region, including in Mombasa and Dar-es-Salaam. Investment in the SEACOM project is USD 600 million in total, with 76.25% of financing coming from African funders and the balance from Herakles Capital, a United States (US) entity. The project's ownership structure is as follows: Industrial Promotion Services with 26.56%, Remgro Ltd 25%, while Convergence Partners and Shanduka hold 12.5% each. Herakles Telecom LLC holds a 23.44% stake in the project.[39] The SEACOM fibre optic cable's enormous capacity enables high definition TV, peer-to-peer networks, and Internet Protocol Television (IPTV) while meeting the surging Internet demands in Africa.[40]

D. Lower Indian Ocean Network Submarine Cable

54. LION2, which offers a maximum capacity of 1.28 tbps, is a 2,700 km long extension of the initial Lower Indian Ocean Network (LION) that connects Madagascar to the rest of the world, providing alternate onward connectivity from Kenya to Asia and Europe. The cable is operated by Telkom Kenya, a subsidiary of France Telecom Group. The laying of LION2 cable began in late 2010, and the cable became operational in early 2012. Key shareholders for LION2 are France Telecom-Orange, Telkom Kenya, Mauritius Telecom, and Orange Madagascar as well as carrier companies Emtel Ltd and Société Réunionnaise du Radiotéléphon.[41]

II. National Fibre Network

55. Liquid Telecom (Formerly KDN) is arguably Kenya's largest private data carrier and infrastructure provider. Liquid Telecom operates a combination of microwave radio and fibre optical links, over which it provides layer two carrier services (Ethernet, Frame Relay) to corporate customers. It also houses and maintains a number of international Internet gateways, which it sells to corporate customers such as ISPs. Tables 10 and 11 show the growth of international bandwidth available to the Kenyan market from undersea and satellite infrastructure. As bandwidth has grown, the number of users has also expanded. Tables 12 and 13 provide broadband subscription data illustrating this growth.

---

39. SEACOM is privately funded and over three-quarter African owned, available at http://seacom.mu /our-company/company-structure.
40. *See* www.seacom.mu.
41. Fourth sea cable linking East Africa goes live, available at http://www.businessdailyafrica.com/ Corporate-News/Fourth-undersea-fibre-cable-linking-East-Africa-goes-live/-/539550/1385812/-/p4s 2qhz/-/index.html, 13 Apr. 2012.

56. So far, Liquid Telecom has deployed the largest fibre optic network in the region with over 5,000 km of metropolitan fibre optic cable connecting forty counties in Kenya.[42] Furthermore, Liquid Telecom in March 2015 partnered with the Nakuru County Government to take on a groundbreaking initiative that saw the design and launch of a high capacity Wi-Fi network covering a ten-kilometre radius from the central business district (CBD).[43] The project, a first of its kind in Kenya, saw Nakuru join Kigali in Rwanda and Tshwane in South Africa as one of the first major urban centres in Africa to enjoy access to free public Wi-Fi.[44]

57. The CA also licensed the Kenya Power and Lighting Company (KPLC), the licensed national electricity distributor with an established network of Optical Ground Wire (OPGW) system built on the national power grid, to roll out telecommunication infrastructure that would enable operators to buy excess capacity from the firm. CA successfully established policy guidelines on infrastructure sharing in an effort to ease the investment burden of new entrants into the market and avoid duplication of resources. Since the launch of its fibre optic business in early 2010, the Company has signed lease agreements with a number of telecommunications operators including Safaricom, Airtel, Liquid Telecom Ltd, Jamii Telecommunications, Indigo Telecommunication Ltd, and Wananchi Telecom Ltd.[45] Concerned about possible disruptions that may result from cable vandalism, Liquid Telecom entered into a similar arrangement with KPLC.[46]

---

42. allAfrica, CIO East Africa (Nairobi), Baraka Jefwa, *'Kenya: After Nakuru, Liquid Telecom Seeks to Connect Nine More Counties to WiFi'*, available at http://allafrica.com/stories/201609050883.html, accessed on 5 May 2017.
43. *Ibid. See also*: Standard Digital, Steve Mkawale, *'Nakuru Stays Wired with Free Internet'*, available at https://www.standardmedia.co.ke/article/2000166468/nakuru-stays-wired-with-free-Internet, acc essed on 5 May 2017.
44. allAfrica, CIO East Africa (Nairobi), Baraka Jefwa, '*Kenya: After Nakuru, Liquid Telecom Seeks to Connect Nine More Counties to WiFi*', available at http://allafrica.com/stories/201609050883.html, accessed on 5 May 2017.
45. Kenya Power, Kenya Power Fibre Optic Network, Telecommunications Business Unit (TBU), available at http://kplc.co.ke/content/item/35, accessed on 5 May 2017.
46. *The Daily Nation,* 20 Mar. 2010, 26.

Table 10 International Gateway Bandwidth

Financial Year	*2010/11*	*2011/12*	*2012/13*	*2013/14*	*2014/15*
Undersea Fibre Optic Cable Capacity					
1. SEACOM Capacity (Mbps)	79,626.24	308,224.00	578,400	565,440	770,000
2. TEAMS Capacity (Mbps)	102,332.16	101,990.00	101,990	119,970	820,000
3. EASSY Capacity (Mbps)	122,880.00	122,880.00	122,880	120,000	39,063
4. LION2 Capacity (Mbps)	–	40,960.00	40,960	40,000	39,220
Total Undersea Bandwidth Capacity (Mbps)	**304,838.40**	**574,054.00**	**844,230**	**846,290***	**1,668,283**
Satellite Bandwidth Capacity (Mbps)	336.10	649.80	639.52	214.4	278.00
Total Available Bandwidth Capacity (Mbps)	**305,174.50**	**574,703.80**	**844,870**	**846,504.40**	**1,668,561**

Source: Communications Authority of Kenya 2014/15 annual report.

*The numbers are as reported by the CA.

Table 11 International Leased Bandwidth

Financial Year	*2009/10*	*2010/11*	*2011/12*	*2012/13*	*2013/14*	*2014/15*
International Undersea Bandwidth (Mbps)	20,000.00	32,151.52	264,426.00	356,655	440,820.00	788,300.00
International Satellite Bandwidth (Mbps)	384.12	119.00	157.78	219.95	196.40	184.78
Total International Bandwidth (Mbps)	**20,384.12**	**32,270.52**	**264,583.78**	**356,874.95**	**441,006.43**	**788,484.78**

Source: Communications Authority of Kenya 2014/15 annual report.

Table 12 Number of Broadband Subscriptions

Financial Year	*2010/11*	*2011/12*	*2012/13*	*2013/14*	*2014/15*
Fixed Broadband (DSL, Satellite, and Fibre)	6,552	35,265	64,850	73,404	94,769
Wireless (WIMAX)	5,646	17,282	18,634	16,958	17,103
Mobile	108,928	674,255	1,315,339	2,999,794	5,215,987
Total	**121,126**	**726,802**	**1,398,823**	**3,090,156**	**5,327,859**

Source: Communications Authority of Kenya 2014/15 annual report.

Table 13 Growth of Internet Subscribers Including Broadband

Subscriptions/Users	*2010/11*	*2011/12*	*2012/13*	*2013/14*	*2014/15*
Terrestrial Mobile Data/Internet Subscriptions	4,189,720	7,655,576	12,340,005	13,930,694	19,809,709
Terrestrial Wireless Data/Internet Subscriptions	29,979	21,709	21,282	16,205	17,721
Satellite Data/Internet Subscriptions	960	519	1,278	646	635
Fixed Digital Subscriber Line (DSL Data/Internet Subscriptions	15,168	11,682	11,512	12,129	2,597
Fixed Fibre Optic Data/Internet Subscriptions	22,460	49,371	58,197	69,373	93,598
Fixed Cable Modem (Dial-Up) Data/Internet Subscriptions	–	25	25	25	25
Total Internet Subscriptions	**4,258,287**	**7,738,882**	**12,432,308***	**14,029,072**	**19,924,285**
Estimated Internet Users	**12,538,030**	**14,032,366**	**19,654,925**	**22,310,044**	**29,672,419**

Source: Communications Authority of Kenya 2014/15 annual report.

*The numbers are as reported by the CA.

Chapter 3. The ICT Market

58. The telecommunications landscape in Kenya has continued to be shaped by technological developments, a new market structure and licensing regime, and improved infrastructure. The simultaneous shift in consumer needs and expectations has compelled aggressive network roll-out and infrastructure upgrades using technologies that support high capacity services. Increased competition among the operators has also contributed to the high level of product and service innovations as a means of customer acquisition and customer retention.

59. The relationship between ICT and commercial activities is generally founded upon two types of interactions: the use of ICT devices and services in business operations and the use of ICT devices, services, or platforms in e-commerce. Business operations focuses on the day-to-day operations of a company and may include internal communications as well as business-to-business interactions, supply chain management, and vendor interactions. In general, then, e-commerce focuses on providing products and/or services to customers (whether that customer is an individual or a business) via an electronic platform. These issues are discussed in more detail in the next chapter.

60. Beyond e-commerce, the ICT market includes a variety of types of activities by users of ICT devices and platforms, such as engaging in social interactions, access to information, and access to government services. The CA regularly aggregates and publishes sector statistics that elucidate these and other activities. Data presented below are taken from the most recent quarterly report released by the CA.[47]

61. Although ICT is not synonymous with mobile technologies, the latter is easily the most relevant and accurate measure of the health and trajectory of the Kenyan ICT market. In particular, mobile penetration and subscription data have been used for many years to show growth in the industry. In the latest figures, mobile subscriptions numbered 37.8 million against a total population of 43.0 million people in Kenya. The common practice by users of maintaining more than one subscriber line means that mobile penetration cannot be directly inferred from the number of subscriptions, nevertheless it is clear that mobile penetration has reached a very high level. Furthermore, the rate at which the population is adopting mobile technology is continuing to rise: Table 14 shows that quarter-on-quarter new subscriptions are rapidly and recently increasing.

47. Communications Authority of Kenya: First Quarter Sector Statistics Report for the Financial Year 2015/2016 (July–September 2015).

Table 14 New Mobile Subscriptions and Total Internet Users

Quarter Ending	*Net Addition of Mobile Subscriptions*	*Number of Internet Users in Millions (Internet Penetration as Percentage)*
September 2014	522,435	23.2 (57.1)
December 2014	863,803	26.1 (64.3)
March 2015	1,161,826	29.2 (71.7)
June 2015	1,318,664	29.6 (69.0)
September 2015	1,752,086	31.9 (74.2)

Source: Communications Authority of Kenya.

62. As mentioned in the previous chapter, the mobile market in Kenya consists of four telecommunications providers. Safaricom Ltd is responsible for 66.3% of mobile subscriptions, followed by Airtel with 19.1%, Orange Kenya with 11.8%, and Equitel (Finserve Africa Ltd) with 2.9% of subscriptions. The vast majority, over 90%, of Safaricom's 25.1 million subscriptions are prepaid subscriptions, with less than 10% of post-paid subscriptions. The quarterly statistics showed an increasing trend for all measures of mobile usage, including the number of minutes of voice traffic per user per month, the number of outgoing SMS per user (notwithstanding the recent competition from over-the-top (OTT) services such as WhatsApp), roaming voice and roaming SMS traffic, international mobile traffic, and mobile money transfer usage.

63. Data and Internet usage also show continued upward trends. Table 14 shows that the estimated number of Internet users has increased by over 35% in just the last five quarters. The majority of Internet usage is via mobile subscriptions; a total of 21.6 million mobile data subscriptions were reported in the first quarter data.

Chapter 4. E-Commerce: Facts and Figures

64. An extensive survey of the role of ICT in Kenyan business operations was carried out during the three-month period of March–May 2016.[48] The study was sponsored by the CA and the KNBS and involved a survey of 3,530 Kenyan enterprises across all sectors and sizes. This investigation looked at the following issues: the uptake of e-commerce; online purchases and selling activities; online transactions via e-mail; benefits and limitations of online selling and buying; mobile commerce; and cloud computing. To characterize these issues, the study covered the following topics:

– Use of ICT equipment and devices.
– Internet infrastructure and use of applications.
– ICT management and security.
– Perception of enterprises on the use of ICTs.
– Comparison of data from 2016 against 2010.
– Comparative analysis of public institutions and enterprises.

Key findings of the study with regard to e-commerce are provided in Table 15.

Table 15 Survey Data for ICT Use by Kenyan Companies

Companies That:	*Companies Answering in the Affirmative (%)*
… use computers	92.1
… use Internet	90.2
… use fixed broadband	81.3
… use mobile broadband	40.5
… use Internet for communications	88.7
… use Internet for banking	35.4
… have a Local Area Network	60.4
… use cloud computing services	22.9
… have a mobile phone	85.7
… have a fixed phone line	50.5
… use facsimile	11.3
… have an IT policy in place	40
… have an e-waste management policy	37

Source: Communications Authority of Kenya: Enterprise ICT Survey 2016.

48. Communications Authority of Kenya: Enterprise ICT Survey 2016.

65. Regarding the uptake of e-commerce, the study found that, across all sectors and firm sizes, 39% of Kenyan enterprises surveyed engage in e-commerce, with larger enterprises significantly more likely to do so compared with micro and small enterprises. The highest percentage of enterprises engaged in e-commerce was found in the ICT sector (62.9%) and the electricity, gas, steam, and air conditioning supply sector (50.0%), whereas the lowest percentage was found in the mining and quarrying industry (12.5%).

66. Regarding online purchases, across all sectors and firm sizes, 32.7% of enterprises reported being engaged in online purchasing, but only 26.5% of enterprises reported being engaged in online selling. Indeed, online purchasing was more common than online selling across nearly all sectors and firm sizes. For example, no enterprises in the mining and quarrying sector (i.e., 0.0%) engaged in online selling, although 12.5% were engaged in online purchasing. Also, for example, 43.9% of large enterprises engaged in online purchasing, but only 31.8% of large enterprises engaged in online selling. For online purchases of goods, the mode of delivery reflects the lack of a nationwide physical addressing system in Kenya. Thus, 67.1% of enterprises engage in online purchases where the goods are physically delivered by the supplier, whereas 10.8% of enterprises engage in online purchases where the goods are delivered by the PCK.

67. Regarding online transactions via e-mail, across all sectors and firm sizes, 69.3% of enterprises engaged in this activity. The majority of e-mail transactions (69.3%) involved human interaction whereas a smaller percentage (39%) were via automated services.

68. Almost one-third (29.8%) of enterprises stated that they realized no benefits from transacting online. Of the remaining enterprises, the most common benefit was reduced transaction time (57.4%), followed by lower business costs (46.0%) and improved quality of customer service (37.0%). Similarly, 24.5% of enterprises identified no limitations from transacting online. Of the remaining enterprises, the most common limitation was that the enterprise's products were not well suited for sale online (32.1%), followed by an insufficient level of customer demand for purchasing online (24.4%) and a preference for maintaining their current business model (22.8%). Interestingly, security concerns were identified by 18% of enterprises as a limitation for online transacting.

69. The report further found that, across all sectors and firm sizes, 50.3% of surveyed enterprises have a website.[49] Interestingly, on average 79% of Kenyan enterprises engage with customers via social networking sites such as Facebook and

49. This may indicate substantial growth in the uptake of ICT by Kenyan industry, as well as an increase in the propensity for Kenyan consumers to make purchases online. A prior academic study in 2013 found that only 22% of SMEs surveyed had a website, and another study in 2012 found that only 4% of Kenyan consumers surveyed would consider making a purchase online. *See*: M. Joshua, N. Isaac & N. Agnes, 'The Extent of E-Commerce Adoption among Small and Medium Enterprises in Nairobi, Kenya' *JKUAT Journal* 4(9) (2013); and *see* P. Kabuba, 'E-commerce and Performance of Online Businesses in Kenya' LLM project, University of Nairobi, November 2014.

Google+, 42% of enterprises use instant messaging platforms such as WhatsApp, and 30% of enterprises engage in microblogging such as via Twitter.

70. Unsurprisingly given the high levels of mobile penetration in the region, a substantial percentage (71.1%) of enterprises reported buying or selling goods using mobile phones.

71. Finally, penetration of cloud computing services remains relatively low in Kenya. The report found that, across all sectors and firm sizes, only 22.9% of enterprises use cloud computing. Among enterprises not currently using cloud computing, only 29.2% have plans to adopt cloud services in the future. The most significant benefit brought by cloud computing was identified as increased flexibility, with 77.3% of enterprises reporting this advantage. The most common barrier to adopting cloud computing was identified as insufficient knowledge within the organization (37.1%). Only 14.9% of enterprises identified high cost as a barrier to adoption of cloud computing.

Chapter 5. E-Government Initiatives

§1. General Initiatives

72. The KIC Act does not create any general or particular obligation on the part of the government to incorporate the use of electronic records and digital signatures in the provision of public services. The intention behind the provisions on electronic transactions and digital signatures appears not to have been to create any legal obligations but to merely formally declare the legality of the use of electronic records in formal transactions. The overriding aim of the provisions was not to compel the uptake of technological aids to business transactions but to eliminate uncertainties on the legality of paperless transacting.

73. The KIC Act's provisions on e-government are therefore merely declaratory and not mandatory. It provides in section 83S(1) that:

> *where any law provides for:*
>
> (a) *the effective delivery of public goods and services, improving the quality of life for disadvantaged communities, strengthening good governance and public participation, creation of a better business environment, improving productivity and efficiency of government departments;*[50]
> (b) *the filing of any form, application or any other document with any office, authority, body or agency owned or controlled by the Government in a particular manner;*
> (c) *the issue or grant of any license, permit, sanction or approval by whatever name called in a particular manner; or*
> (d) *the receipt or payment of money in a particular manner,*
> *then ... such requirement shall be deemed to have been satisfied if such filing, issue, grant, receipt or payment, as the case may be, is effected by means of such electronic forms as may be prescribed by the Minister in consultation with the Commission.*[51]

74. According to the submissions made in the public consultative forums, the matters included in paragraph (a) of section 83S(1) were in actual fact meant to be the functions of the CA with regard to e-government. They were meant to be placed at the commencement of the section in the same fashion that section 83C provides the functions of the Commission in relation to electronic transactions. They may have been grafted onto that section through inadvertence. This becomes apparent when the paragraph is read together with the section's concluding paragraph.

50. The substantial wording of this paragraph of s. 83S of the KIC Act was adopted from a presentation made by the author on behalf of the Kenya ICT Federation (KIF) to a subcommittee of the Kenya's Parliament which was receiving public and stakeholder comments about the KIC Bill, save that in the presentation, KIF had asked Parliament to set out the matters outlined in the paragraph as the objectives of the CA with relation to e-government.
51. Section 83S.

75. Notwithstanding the lack of a legal requirement to transition government services to electronic-based systems, the Government of Kenya launched, in late 2013, the Huduma Kenya Programme. The Programme aims to transform public service delivery by providing citizens with access to various public services and information in an integrated system that includes: physical 'one-stop shop' service centres called Huduma Centres located throughout the country; a mobile platform; a web portal; a call centre; and an integrated online payment gateway. The Huduma Centres and supporting technologies provide services that include the issuance of official government documents including national identity cards and birth certificates, business support services such as the registration of business names and limited companies, and applications for access to government procurement opportunities. To date, the government has opened over thirty Huduma Centres throughout the country.

76. The Huduma Kenya Programme is one initiative of a larger effort towards modernizing the delivery of governmental services. Another initiative within the same effort is the eCitizen web portal, launched in 2014 by the Ministry of Information, Communication, and Technology. The eCitizen portal allows Kenyan citizens and residents to apply for various government services from a number of government ministries and offices. Non-Kenyans can also apply for entry visas and work permits through the portal. In another major step towards digitizing governmental services, the Kenya Revenue Authority (KRA) transitioned to a fully integrated and countrywide online tax collection system in 2014.

77. It is clear that the Government of Kenya has made many efforts at digitizing government functions and citizen services. Since the KIC Act does not mandate a transition to e-government, motivating factors for such a transition must be sought elsewhere. It appears, in fact, that governmental policy is foundational to the efforts made by the Government of Kenya to digitize services. In particular, the Kenya National ICT Master Plan, launched in 2013 and updated in 2017, provides objectives and strategies towards implementing integrated, end-to-end e-government processes in all areas of governmental activities. The central government is expected to provide common critical infrastructure such as data networking and storage, and government agencies are expected to emerge from the old concept of 'silo' delivery of services.[52] In addition to the Master Plan, e-government was mentioned in the 2006 National ICT Policy[53] and is a central tenet of the updated (although still draft) National ICT Policy.[54]

52. Section 5.1, The Kenya National ICT Master Plan, 2013/2014–2017/2018.
53. Section 2.8, National ICT Policy, January 2006.
54. Section 19, Draft National ICT Policy, 2016.

§2. Universal Service

78. The KIC Act establishes a Universal Service Fund which is to be managed and administered by CA.[55] The object and the purpose of the Fund is 'to support widespread access to, support capacity building and promote innovation in information and communications technology services'.[56] The CA is empowered by the Act to impose a universal service levy on the licensees under the Act for purposes of the Universal Service Fund.[57]

79. By CA's own analysis, the wave of investment in the ICT sector that followed the sector's liberalization has not availed communications services to all in Kenya 'as the licensed operators and service providers have tended to concentrate operations in areas where a return on investment is guaranteed'.[58] Consequently, both rural and urban areas that are perceived as commercially unviable by operators have 'remained either un-served or under-served'.[59] As the sector regulator, CA is responsible for ensuring that all in Kenya have access to affordable communications services.

80. To redress the access gaps, CA has undertaken and describes seven pilot projects in various parts of the country. The projects are: establishment of school-based ICT Centres; establishment of community telecentres as access points; development of ICT solutions for persons with disabilities; digitization of the Kenya Certificate of Secondary Education Curriculum; computerization of health centres; undertaking research and development towards Universal Access; and development of e-resource centres.[60]

§3. Conclusion

81. Like many other sub-Saharan African States, Kenya has strived to establish a framework of governance and social order that creates the market conditions for rapid economic growth. Over the years, its national development policies have focused on improving the productive sectors of the economy: agriculture, manufacturing, trade, tourism, and services. With the liberalization of the telecommunications and other ICT services in the country, Kenya witnessed an unprecedented growth in local and foreign investment that made both direct and indirect contributions to the economy.

82. The telecommunications landscape in Kenya has continued to be shaped by technological developments arising out of convergence and a new market structure and licensing regime. The subsequent shifts in consumer needs and expectations

55. Section 84J(1).
56. *Ibid.,* subs. (2).
57. *Ibid.,* subs. (3).
58. *See* www.CA.go.ke/services/universal_access/index.html, 24 Feb. 2010.
59. *Id.*
60. *See* http://ca.go.ke/index.php/projects, 30 May 2017.

have compelled aggressive network roll-out and infrastructure upgrades using technologies that support high capacity services. Increased competition among the operators has also contributed to the high level of product and service innovations as a means of customer acquisition and customer retention. This is underlined by the increase in subscriber base by the fixed network operator.

83. The number of Internet users has recently increased at a much more rapid rate compared with earlier periods. Internet usage is still not in tandem with other telecommunication services and especially lags behind the nearly ubiquitous mobile money market. CA attributed the initial slow growth of Internet usage to the infrastructure bottlenecks and the high cost of services.[61] These bottlenecks are, largely, no longer as relevant. Going forward, increases in Internet usage should roughly parallel the rate of adoption of Internet-enabled mobile phones.

61. CA Sector Statistics Report, April 2008–June 2009.

Part I. Regulation of the ICT Market

Chapter 1. Regulatory Framework of the Telecommunications Sector

§1. The Policy Framework

I. National Development Framework

84. Kenya's blueprint for national development is the Kenya Vision 2030,[62] covering the period 2008–2030. It aims to make Kenya a newly industrializing, 'middle-income country providing high quality life for all its citizens by the year 2030'.[63] The vision is based on three 'pillars' namely, the economic pillar, the social pillar, and the political pillar.

85. The pillars are anchored on key principles that form the foundation of socio-political welfare and economic growth:

- Macroeconomic stability for long-term development.
- Continuity in governance reforms.
- Enhanced equity and wealth creation opportunities for the poor.
- Infrastructure.
- Energy.
- Science, Technology, and Innovation (STI).
- Land reform.
- Human resources development.
- Security.
- Public sector reforms.

86. The economic pillar seeks to secure prosperity for Kenyans through an economic development programme aimed at achieving a GDP growth rate of 10% per year for the next twenty-five years. The social pillar seeks to build a 'just and cohesive society with social equity in a clean and secure environment'. The political

62. Developed in August 2007 by the National Economic and Social Council (NESC).
63. Kenya Vision 2030 (Abridged/Summary Edition), 1 available at www.nesc.go.ke/Meetings/FullCouncil/Speeches/SpeechesMain.htm, accessed on 20 Sep. 2009.

pillar aims at realizing a democratic political system founded on issue-based politics that respects the rule of law and protects the rights and freedoms of every individual in the Kenyan society.[64]

87. The Vision focuses on six key sectors as the engines of growth towards 2030, namely, tourism, agriculture, the wholesale and retail trade sector, manufacturing, BPO, and financial services. The Vision is to be implemented in successive five-year medium-term plans with the first plan covering the period 2008–2012 and the second medium-term plan covering the period through 2017.

II. Vision 2030 and ICT: Business Process OffSshoring

88. The Vision defines BPO as involving the provision of 'business services via the Internet to companies and organizations in the developed world, for example, Britain, USA, and Canada' and recognizes it as a 'new but promising sector to Kenya and especially to its young people'.[65] The Vision's aim for business process outsourcing is for Kenya to rapidly transform itself into one of the top three BPO destinations in Africa and to create at least 7,500 direct BPO jobs with an additional GDP contribution of USD 137 million. The plan for achieving this is to attract at least five major leading IT suppliers and at least ten large multinational corporations and global BPO players to Kenya and to identify at least five large local players as BPO champions either through stand-alone operations or joint ventures.

89. Under the flagship BPO project for the vision, the government of Kenya plans to establish one major BPO park in Nairobi that will serve as the country's focal point for BPO featuring state-of-the-art infrastructure. The government plans to offer competitive incentives for companies to locate in the park and to provide a one-stop shop for the administration of BPO ventures.

90. A number of other flagship projects under the Vision are aligned with the ICT Master Plan, which is described in detail later in this chapter.

III. The Current National ICT Policy

91. The liberalized multi-operator ICT industry in Kenya today is the culmination of a series of policy, legal, and regulatory interventions that began with the release by the government of the *Telecommunications and Postal Sector Policy Statement* in 1997. The policy outlined the government's vision of transiting the sector from a highly State-controlled market to a liberalized and competitive multi-operator environment with few or no government-owned operators. The sector

64. Kenya Vision 2030 (Abridged/Summary Edition), 2 available at www.nesc.go.ke/Meetings/FullCouncil/Speeches/SpeechesMain.htm, accessed on 20 Sep. 2009.
65. Kenya Vision 2030 (Abridged/Summary Edition), 5 available at www.nesc.go.ke/Meetings/ FullCouncil/Speeches/SpeechesMain.htm, accessed on 20 Sep. 2009.

policy paved the way for the repeal of the Kenya Posts and Telecommunications Act and the enactment of the KCA of 1998. The latter Act dissolved the KPTC, the incumbent State monopoly, and established CA as the regulator for the telecommunications, radio communications, and postal sectors; the NCS to serve as a policy advisory body; the Communications Appeals Tribunal; Telkom Kenya Ltd; and PCK.

92. Kenya's current National ICT Policy was developed by the Ministry of Information and Communications and launched in January 2006. It articulates the government's policy objectives and strategies for information technology, broadcasting, telecommunications, postal services, radio frequency spectrum and universal access. The vision of the policy is to create 'a prosperous ICT-driven Kenya' and its mission is to 'improve the livelihoods of Kenyans by ensuring the availability of accessible, efficient, reliable and affordable ICT services'.[66] The policy is based on four guiding principles: infrastructure development, human resource development, stakeholder participation, and appropriate policy and regulatory framework.[67]

93. The ICT policy acknowledges the inadequacy of Kenya's legal framework in dealing with issues of convergence, e-commerce, and e-government and proceeded from the need for a comprehensive policy, legal, and regulatory framework to:

- support ICT development, investment, and application;
- promote competition in the industry where appropriate;
- ensure affordability and access to ICT nationally;
- address issues of privacy, e-security, ICT legislation, cyber crimes, ethical and moral conduct, copyright, intellectual property rights (IPR), and piracy;
- support research and development in ICT; and
- develop an institutional framework for policy development and review.[68]

94. On this issue, however, the ICT Policy predates the 2009 amendments to the KIC Act, as well as other legislative developments throughout the 2010s. Such developments have, at least on paper, addressed many of the inadequacies raised in the policy.

95. The ICT policy aimed to achieve the following targets for the telecommunications sub-sector by 2015:

- improve the fixed-line teledensity in rural areas from 0.33 lines to 5 lines per 100 inhabitants;
- improve the fixed-line teledensity in urban areas from 1.97 lines to 20 lines per 100 inhabitants;

---

66. Ministry of Information & Communications (2006) National Information & Communications Technology (ICT) Policy, 1.
67. *Id.*
68. *Supra*, at 4.

- increase the number of mobile subscribers from 4 million to 10 million;
- expand the international Internet bandwidth from 69 Mbps to 1 Gbps;
- provide all primary schools with affordable Internet access and ensure that all secondary schools and tertiary institutions have affordable Internet access by the year 2010; and
- establish Internet access nodes at all district headquarters by 2010.

96. Many of the above goals were achieved, surpassed, or made obsolete by technological developments. For example, according to CA data as of March 2015, there were 34.8 million mobile subscribers, more than three times the target. Internet bandwidth has also far surpassed expectations: international bandwidth as of March 2015 stood at 783.5 Gbps.[69] Fixed-line teledensity is no longer a major focus due to the superiority of mobile communications.[70] Unfortunately, however, some primary and secondary schools remain without affordable and reliable Internet access.[71] Provision of Internet access to public schools is now a major focus of government and, more recently, the private sector, including start-up companies taking cues from Silicon Valley.[72]

A. *Equity Ownership in Operators in the ICT Industry*

97. The National ICT Policy provided an incentive for Kenyan-based participation and investment in the broadcasting and telecommunications sector through equity ownership of licensed operators. The incentive was also informed by the need to ensure that the broadcasting sub-sector met the needs of Kenyans. The policy, therefore, emphasized the need for effective local ownership and control of the Kenyan broadcasting system by providing that any firm licensed to provide broadcasting or telecommunications services would have at least 30% Kenyan equity ownership. For all listed companies, the equity participation would need to conform to the existing rules and regulations of the Capital Markets Authority (CMA), the statutory regulator for Kenya's financial market.[73] However, in the years that followed the implementation of the National ICT Policy, the restriction would be progressively relaxed.

---

69. Communications Authority sector statistics Q3 2014–2015.
70. In fact, fixed lines have decreased in number over the period 2005–2017.
71. In 2012, President Uhuru Kenyatta made a campaign pledge to provide a laptop for every student in his or her initial year of primary school. Various attempts have been made in President Kenyatta's first presidential term to fulfil this pledge. One major challenge initially facing implementation of the project was the lack of connections to the main electrical supply grid for many rural schools. Many programmes were implemented to address this issue, and by 2016, 95% of primary schools had been connected to the grid (as reported by the Ministry of Energy and Petroleum).
72. An example is BRCK, Inc., a Kenyan company designing Internet routers and related devices for rural areas.
73. Established under the Capital Markets Authority Act, Ch. 485A of the Laws of Kenya.

98. In 2007, the Minister for Information and Communications, Hon. Mutahi Kagwe, published a policy guideline on equity ownership in TSPs.[74] Under the guidelines, it was provided that any firm licensed to provide telecommunications services 'shall have at least 20% Kenya equity ownership' while the equity participation of listed companies would continue to be regulated by the CMA. The government also declared that it would 'support upcoming small-scale operators through proactive measures'. Later, in 2008, the incumbent Minister, Hon. Samuel Poghisio, would amend the guidelines to provide that:

> *any firm licensed to provide communication services as an operator or service provider shall be required to maintain and shall ensure that at the end of the third year from the date of the issuance of a license, or earlier as the case may be, and thereafter for the duration of the license term, that it has no less than 20% ownership and control by Kenyan persons, howsoever achieved. However, within reason and all circumstances had in due regard in any particular case, the Government may exceptionally grant a waiver to this requirement as appropriate.*[75]

99. The Minister reiterated that for all licensed listed companies, the ownership and control limitations were to conform to the Capital Markets Act and the government's plan to continue supporting small-scale licensees.

100. Indeed, Airtel Kenya was given a waiver in 2012 over the regulation requiring it to have at least 20% local ownership after it had difficulties getting a strategic local partner to acquire 15% of the company. At the time, Kenyan businessman Naushad Merali owned 5% of the company. The exemption given to Airtel was open-ended and without a timeline.[76] Furthermore, before the telecom operator Essar (Yu) exited the Kenyan market, they were also allowed to have less than 20% of local ownership after they were unable to get local investors sufficient to meet the statutory requirements.

B. Policy Objectives of the National ICT Policy

101. The National ICT Policy provides objectives and strategies for enhancing four sub-sectors of the ICT industry. For each sub-sector, Tables 16–19 below give a summary of the policy objectives outlined in Kenya's National ICT Policy, the strategies for achieving the objectives, and selected achievements and efforts within each objective.

---

74. Gazette Notice No. 7481 of 2007, 'Information and Communications Technology Sector Policy Guidelines', Vol. CIX-No. 55, 10 Aug. 2007, 2542.
75. Gazette Notice No. 10335 of 2008, 2829, 'Information and Communications Technology Sector Policy Guidelines', No. 10335 of 2008, 2829.
76. Airtel freed from 20% local ownership rule, available at www.businessdailyafrica.com/Corporate-News/Airtel-freed-from-20-per-cent-local-ownership-rule/-/539550/1632440/-/item/1/-/j0k95cz/-/index.html, 28 Nov. 2012.

102. The first sub-sector is that of broadcasting, in which the ICT Policy identifies as a major issue the lack of a rational and comprehensive framework to govern the establishment, ownership, management and control of the information, entertainment, and education services to Kenyans through broadcasting.

Table 16 Policy Objectives and Efforts in Kenya's National ICT Policy for the Broadcasting Sub-sector

Policy Objectives	*Policy Strategies*	*Achievements*
Develop a legal and regulatory framework for broadcasting; encourage growth of a competitive and efficient broadcasting industry.	New legal framework to be enacted to cover regulation, policy advisory and dispute resolution in broadcasting. CA designated as the sector regulator for broadcasting.	Kenya Information and Communications (Broadcasting) Regulations 2009 was enacted by the Ministry.[1]
Develop a licensing framework for broadcasters and the allocation of frequencies.	Mandate and obligations of Kenya Broadcasting Corporation (KBC) as the designated as public broadcaster redefined.	Kenya Information and Communications (Broadcasting) Regulations 2009 provides regulations to control licensing. The CA continues inspections and monitoring exercises to make sure the assigned spectrum is used in accordance with the licence.[2]
Ensuring the development of broadcasting services that reflect a sense of Kenyan identity, character, and cultural diversity.	CA, licences, and stakeholders to work on mechanisms for increased local content in broadcasting. Government to provide incentives for local content.	Kenya Information and Communications (Broadcasting) Regulations 2009 provides rules to regulate local content in the broadcasting regulations. Currently, broadcasters are to have minimum percentage of local content of 40%. The CA hosted an event in 2016 allowing local content creators and producers to network with broadcasters.[3]

Policy Objectives	*Policy Strategies*	*Achievements*
Promoting diversity in ownership and control of broadcasting services.	Content Advisory Council to be established to advise CA on broadcasting content standards.	Kenya Information and Communications (Broadcasting) Regulations 2009 provides rules on ownership and control of broadcasters.[4]
Promoting fair competition, innovation, and investment in broadcasting.	Professional standards: All broadcasters to act in public interest and to be guided by a code of conduct.	The Draft KIC (broadcasting) Regulations of 2016 provide for all infomercials and advertisements to conform to fair competition.[5]
Encourage the development of and respect for codes of practice in broadcasting.	Market regime: Policy to foster pluralism, fair competition, and reliance on market forces in broadcasting services. Competition to be enhanced through licensing of more radio and TV stations. Market to be segmented into normal, private and public broadcasters.	The CA developed a code of practice for the deployment of communications infrastructure in Kenya. There is, however, no enforcement mechanism for this code of practice to date.[6]
Promoting research and development.	Signal distribution: Government to license signal distribution services for maximal use of broadcasting infrastructure.	Cabinet Secretary for ICT launched the Digital Literacy Programme (DLP) in West Pokot County in November 2016. The Ministry makes regular inspections.[7]
Ensure universal access to and viability of public service broadcasting.	Digital broadcasting: Government to introduce and manage the transition to digital broadcasting.	The migration to digital broadcasting was completed in 2015 as supervised by the government.

Policy Objectives	*Policy Strategies*	*Achievements*
	Equity participation and control: Policy to encourage Kenyan participation. Broadcasting firms to have at least 30% of equity owned by Kenyans. Listed companies to conform with the regulations of the CMA.	
Cross-media ownership: Concentration of ownership of print and electronic media in a few hands to be discouraged.	Limits to media ownership to be set through regulations and competition laws.	Limitations for grant of a broadcasting licence are provided in the KIC Act.[8]

Source: Ministry of Information and Communications, National Information & Communications Technology Policy, January 2006, pp. 16 et seq.

1. Communications Authority, *Sector Regulations*, http://www.ca.go.ke/index.php/sector-regulations.

2. Communications Authority, *Sector Regulations*, http://www.ca.go.ke/index.php/sector-regulationshttp://www.ca.go.ke/index.php/frequency-spectrum.

3. Communications Authority, *"Authority Hosts Inaugural Local Content Soko"* http://ca.go.ke/index.php/what-we-do/94-news/353-authority-hosts-inaugural-local-content-soko.

4. The Kenya Communications (Broadcasting) Regulations, 2009, paragraph 10.

5. Draft KIC (broadcasting) Regulations of 2016.

6. *Codes of Practice for the Deployment of Communications Infrastructure in Kenya.*

7. *Kenya News Agency "CS Mucheru On Inspection Tour Of Digital Learning Programme in West Pokot County."* http://kenyanewsagency.go.ke/en/cs-mucheru-on-inspection-tour-of-digital-learning-programme-in-ortum-primary-school-west-pokot-county/.

8. For example, *see* section 46D of KIC Act 1998, requiring the CA to consider various factors such as diversity of views in granting a license and in prohibiting the CA from granting a license to political parties, public officers, etc.

103. The second sub-sector is telecommunications, in which there is a recognized need to harness the sector as a key contributor to social and economic growth.

Table 17 Policy Objectives and Efforts in Kenya's National ICT Policy for Telecommunications

Policy Objectives	*Policy Strategies*	*Achievements*
Create a modern and efficient national telecommunications infrastructure.	Promote competition, increased customer choice, and increased investment through sector liberalization and the licensing of new operators.	The government has made efforts to spur development of LTE services and has been doing so through the open access approach. Disputes centred on licence fees delayed the launch of LTE services by mobile network operators (MNOs). These MNOs have continued to invest in infrastructure and technology upgrades using trial licences with a number of licences being awarded since 2014.[1]
Promote research and development, innovation, and manufacturing.	Promote network and service unbundling, infrastructure sharing, and co-location.	
Promote expansion of telecommunications infrastructure and services to rural and marginalized areas.	Establish a technology-neutral licensing framework for the sub-sector.	The government launched a USD 2.89 billion National Broadband Strategy in 2013 with the objective to extend Internet access to all Kenyans. The project has so far connected 28 out of the 47 Kenyan counties with fibre connection, and development is ongoing for the remaining counties. The project is also expected to connect all ministries through a government common core network, with the objective to facilitate internal communication.[2]

Policy Objectives	*Policy Strategies*	*Achievements*
Enhance public service delivery in health and educational institutions through the use of telecommunications infrastructure.	Restructure Telkom Kenya to promote efficiency.	In 2010, the government-run National Hospital Insurance Fund (NHIF) signed a partnership with mobile operator Safaricom to allow the self-employed and informally employed to pay health insurance premiums through the M-Pesa mobile money platform. The Ministry of Health has a partnership with Merck, the international pharmaceutical company. In May 2015, Merck invested Kshs 10.2 million in the e-Health initiative.[3]
	Establish universal access mechanisms for wider access to telecommunications services.	
	Promote public–private partnerships in the development of telecommunications infrastructure and equipment.	
	Require physical infrastructure providers to make provision for future ICT installations, including: – roads, rail, pipeline, property development, power	

Policy Objectives	*Policy Strategies*	*Achievements*
	Liberalization: Government to continue with liberalization of the various market segments in the sub-sector and to put in place an appropriate regulatory framework for promoting competition.	
	Equity participation: Licensed telecommunications operator to have at least 30% of its equity owned by Kenyans. Listed companies to conform with the regulations of the CMA.	
	Market Structure: Market structure to be reviewed from time to time in order tooptimize it for attracting investment.	
	Broadband and multimedia services: Government to facilitate access to affordable Internet and other value-added services by encouraging the deployment of broadband and multimedia access technologies.	

Policy Objectives	*Policy Strategies*	*Achievements*
Security and reliability of telecommunications infrastructure.	Regulations to be developed to ensure that telecommunications infrastructure is robust, resilient, and secure.	
Enhancement of national security.	Government to create statutory obligations for telecommunications service providers to assist law enforcement in legal intercepts.	Approval at cabinet level of the Computer and Cybercrime Bill 2016 provides a legal framework to better protect the nation.[4]

1. Kenya - Mobile Infrastructure, Operators and Broadband - Statistics and Analyses. Available at:https://www.budde.com.au/Research/Kenya-Mobile-Infrastructure-Operators-and-Broadband-Statistics-and-Analyses.

2. Business Sweden, *Opportunities in the Kenyan ICT Sector.* Available at: http://www.business-sweden.se/contentassets/df353ab4798b4aa58b9131da0f3104de/factpack---ict-sector-in-kenya---2017.pdf, Page 8.

3. Oxford Business Group, *Rise of E-health Transforms Kenya's Health Sector.* Available at: https://www.oxfordbusinessgroup.com/analysis/rise-e-health-new-technology-and-expanded-ict-use-are-transfor
ming-health-sector.

4. *See* www.ifree.co.ke/2017/04/cabinet-approves-computer-cybercrime-bill-2016/, accessed on 11 May 2017.

104. The third sector identified in the Policy as an area for specific focus is the distribution of radio frequency spectrum, which is recognized as a scarce public resource. The Policy states that there is a need to maintain a balance between the public and private interest in distributing and using spectrum.

Table 18 Policy Objectives and Efforts in Kenya's National ICT Policy for the Radio Frequency Spectrum Sub-sector

Policy Objectives	*Policy Strategies*	*Achievements*
Enhanced national security and defence.	Review of the national radiofrequency spectrum policy and management.	The CA commissioned a new Radio Spectrum Monitoring and Management System (SMMS) to help regulate the frequency spectrum in March 2016. The SMMS is intended to "prevent, detect and ultimately eliminate interference in radio communications services."[1]
Enhanced emergency preparedness against disasters.	Radiofrequency spectrum sharing to be encouraged.	
Efficient national and international transportation systems.	Encourage and assess the use of non-radiofrequency spectrum based alternatives.	
Sustainable conservation of natural resources.	Apply market principles in promoting effective use of spectrum.	Following results from the World Radio Conference, the CA plans frequencies for use by the different operators every 4 years in order to use the frequency spectrum sustainably.[2]
Efficiency in the dissemination of educational information and entertainment.	CA and Kenya Bureau of Standards to develop and enforce radio communication standards.	
Efficient and affordable telecommunication services.		The CA released a Telecommunications tariff in 2014 to regulate the tariffs so that consumers are protected and get affordable services.[3]

Policy Objectives	*Policy Strategies*	*Achievements*
Research and development.		The Draft National ICT Policy 2016 is intended to implement new spectrum allocations established at the World Radiocommunications Conference in 2015
Enhanced social and economic progress.		The Draft National ICT Policy 2016 provides a framework to guide sustained ICT sector growth in the country over the next 5 years as stated by the Cabinet Secretary for the Ministry of ICT.

1. *See* http://cio.co.ke/news/main-stories/kenya-acquires-new-radio-spectrum-monitoring-system.

2. *See* http://www.ca.go.ke/index.php/frequency-spectrum, accessed on 10 May 2017.

3. *See* Telecommunications Tariff Brochure of 2014 by the Communications Authority of Kenya at http://www.ca.go.ke/index.php/tariff-information.

105. The final sector identified in the ICT Policy for specific focus is that of providing universal access to ICT resources. This area is recognized as important due to the need to enhance access to ICTs by rural, marginalized, and disadvantaged groups.

Table 19 Policy Objectives and Efforts in Kenya's National ICT Policy for the Universal Access Sub-sector

Policy Objectives	*Policy Strategies*	*Achievements*
Ensure all citizens have access to affordable ICT services.	Government to ensure the availability of free-to-air public services to all parts of the country.	Free-to-air television remains available for those with digital-enabled televisions or set-top boxes. The CA and other stakeholders developed a programming code for free-to-air broadcasting in March 2016 for implementing by the operators.[1]
Promote widespread availability and access to Internet services.	Require public service broadcasting to feature local programming reflecting the nation's cultural diversity.	

Policy Objectives	*Policy Strategies*	*Achievements*
Ensure availability of relevant education and training programmes in ICT.	Require KBC to undertake universal service broadcasting obligations.	In March 2011, the Kenyan President launched the broadcasting station granting the Kenya Institute of Education (KIE) a fully dedicated digital educational broadcast channel (Radio and Television) with outreach to all areas of the country. The government of Kenya has developed, through the Kenya Institute of Education (KIE), a comprehensive curriculum for early childhood education classes to include computer games in order to introduce and enhance computing skills in young pupils.[2]
	Ensure telecommunications services are available at affordable prices.	The government encourages competition between the four mobile operators in the country which helps consumers get services at affordable prices.[3]
	Establish community telecentres.	A central public library with publicly accessible computers is under construction in Nairobi. The CA established four community ICT access points in 2007 in various parts of the Country. These centres provide different ICT services.[4]
	Fixed and mobile telephone operators to provide free emergency calls, operator assistance, and directory enquiry services.	An emergency phone service (toll-freephone number 999) was re-established in 2013, although the services are reported to be unreliable and/or inconsistently reliable.
	Government to establish universal service fund.	The CA has received USD 1 million from telecommunications companies to start the implementation of the USF.[5]

Policy Objectives	*Policy Strategies*	*Achievements*
	Government to use Universal Service Fund to establish ICT Centre of Excellence to promote capacity building and innovation in ICT.	The CA (then CCK) in May 2007 supported the establishment of various school-based ICT centres by providing computers and Internet connectivity with the help of some telecommunication operators.[6]

1. Programming Code for free to air Radio and Television Services in Kenya, 2nd Edition – March 2016, at http://www.ca.go.ke/index.php/broadcasting,, accessed on 11 May 2017.

2. Global Economic Symposium, *Implementation- A Range of Measures by the Kenyan Government.* Available at: http://www.global-economic-symposium.org/knowledgebase/the-global-economy/reinventing-education/implementations/a-range-of-measures-by-the-kenyan-government.

3. Omae Malak, Lang'at Philip & Ndung'u Edward, *Mobile Subscription, Penetration and Coverage Trends in Kenya's Telecommunication Sector.* Available at: https://thesai.org/Downloads/IJARAI/Volume4No1/Paper_1-Mobile_Subscription_Penetration_and_Coverage_Trends.pdf.

4. The Communications Authority of Kenya, Projects, Community Telecentres, at http://www.ca.go.ke/index.php/component/content/article/96-universal-access/projects/201-community-telecentres.

5. Rebecca Wanjiku, *Kenya Starts Universal Service Fund Implementation,* 13 August 2014, ITworld, at http://www.itworld.com/article/2693785/networking-hardware/kenya-starts-universal-service-fund-implementation.html.

6. *See* http://www.ca.go.ke/index.php/projects/96-universal-access/projects/200-school-based-ict-centres, accessed on 11 May 2017.

C. National Broadband Strategy

106. A national broadband strategy was launched in 2013 with the aim to transform Kenya to a knowledge-based society driven by a high capacity nationwide broadband. The strategy focuses on providing quality broadband services to all citizens, including always-on connectivity delivering a minimum of 5 Mbps to individuals, homes, and businesses for high-speed access to voice, data, video, and applications for development. The Strategy provides for the promotion of Public and Private Partnerships so that industry stakeholders and the national and county governments work together to deploy infrastructure, invest and build awareness and capacity for the use of broadband.

107. The broadband strategy focuses on five key thematic areas that have direct impact on its implementation and success:

(1) Infrastructure, Connectivity and Devices.
(2) Content, Applications and Innovations.
(3) Capacity Building and Awareness.

(4) Policy, Legal and Regulatory Environment.
(5) Financing and Investment.

Table 20 Minimum Broadband Speeds

	2013–17	*2018–22*	*2023–27*	*2028–30*
URBAN	40 Mbps	300 Mbps	1024 Mbps	2048 Mbps
RURAL	5 Mbps	50 Mbps	100 Mbps	500 Mbps

Source: Government of Kenya, the National Broadband Strategy, 2013, p. 9.

Table 21 Broadband Penetration Targets

	Baseline	*Target by 2017*
% of penetration by households	6.3%	35%
% of penetration by schools	43.4%	100%
% of penetration by health facilities	n/a	100%

Source: Government of Kenya, The National Broadband Strategy, 2013, p. 9.

108. Several policy, legal, regulatory, and institutional reforms are suggested in the broadband strategy. They include a broadband policy, spectrum plan, universal service fund, national coordination in complementary infrastructure deployment, way leave fees, standards in ICT deployments, technical specifications on fibre deployments, infrastructure sharing, trust and security, affordability of ICT service, open access, creativity and artistic expression policy, and IPR.

109. According to the broadband strategy, the Kenyan government currently spends approximately 0.5% of the national budget on ICTs. The strategy suggests that the government spends at least 5% of its overall budget on ICTs and broadband within the first five years. Such increase in spending is necessary to achieve the various goals within the strategy, such as extending the NOFBI to 30,000 km across the country, and in improving last mile connectivity. Other suggestions in the strategy are designed to encourage private sector solutions, such as by encouraging access to Internet-ready devices (smartphones, set-top boxes, computers, etc.) by zero-rating the taxes and duties on such devices.

110. Key projects described in the strategy focus on infrastructure and connectivity, capacity building, and content and applications innovation. For example, the broadband strategy benchmarks Internet speed and accessibility targets against the

US, the European Union, Japan, and other countries from the developed and developing world.[77] Tables 20 and 21 show broadband expansion targets as provided in the strategy.

IV. National ICT Master Plan

111. Soon after releasing the National Broadband Strategy, in 2014 the Ministry of Information and Communication released the ICT Master Plan covering the period 2014–2017. The Master Plan is a descendant of the Connected Kenya Master Plan launched in February 2013 with a view to extend stakeholders participation and take into account changes in the current Government of Kenya. The vision of the Master Plan is 'Kenya as an ICT hub and a globally competitive digital economy'.

112. The master plan is aligned with the Constitution of Kenya 2010, the three pillars of Vision 2030, and new laws enacted between November 2012 and January 2013.[78] The Master Plan has six guiding principles: partnership; equity and non-discrimination; technology neutrality; environmental protection and conservation; good governance; and incentivizing.

113. The Master Plan further cites three foundations needed in order for Kenya to transition to a knowledge-based society and to position the country as a regional ICT hub. The first foundation of the Master Plan is ICT human capital and workforce development, which aims at developing quality ICT human resources as a prerequisite to the development of a viable ICT sector. Key to this is ensuring that ICT development, implementation, and exploitation are an integral and sustainable component of development. The second foundation is an integrated ICT infrastructure, which seeks to provide the integrated infrastructure backbone required to enable cost-effective delivery of ICT products and services to Kenyans. The third foundation is an integrated information infrastructure which aims at improving the quality of e-Government services and access to publicly held information.

114. For each of the foundations, the Master Plan identifies the driving forces, desired outcomes by 2017, the objectives, and the strategies for realizing the objectives. Much like Vision 2030, the Master Plan identifies a number of flagship projects for reaching the identified objectives. Table 22 provides some of this information, as well as progress made on various objectives and projects.

---

77. National Broadband Strategy Government of the Republic of Kenya, 2013. Currently the availability of broadband services is limited to urban areas and covers only 18% of the Kenyan geographic space.
78. Such laws include the Science, Technology, and Innovation Act 2013, TIVET Act 2013, and Universities Act 2012.

Table 22 ICT Master Plan Selected Flagship Projects and Expected Outcomes[1]

Project or Sub-project	*Application or Expected Outcome*	*Activities and Achievements*
Enabling legal and regulatory framework	Update National ICT Policy document	The Draft National ICT Policy 2016 is pending approval by the cabinet.[2]
Persons datahub	Citizens portal providing Huduma services	Citizen's portal providing Huduma services and driver's licence system: E-citizen portal was launched in 2014 by the Ministry of Finance[3]
Establishments data hub	Automation of business/ company registry to capture and maintain companies' records	E-citizen allows businesses to register the business name automatically online since 2015[4]
Assets datahub	Implementation of transport information management system (TIMS)	National Transportation and Safety Authority (NTSA) launched a TIMS platform in June 2016[5]
Assets data hub	Implementation of a national physical addressing system (NPAS) to provide street addressing, numbering and coding of all properties and thereby provide clear logistical support for economic activities, e.g. delivery of goods and services to persons and businesses	In October 2016, the Cabinet Secretary for the Ministry of ICT released a statement saying that the Ministry is fast tracking the process of putting into place the NAS, and that there are action and implementation plans to do this.[6]
National spatial data infrastructure (NSDI)	Set up an national spatial data infrastructure (NSDI) by mapping all land/ property parcels using GIS	March 2016 – power connections at the data centres completed, creation of Nairobi database complete. Construction of KNSDI is 85% complete. Spatial Planning Bill submitted to the AG[7]

Project or Sub-project	*Application or Expected Outcome*	*Activities and Achievements*
Affordable and quality broadband infrastructure to underserved areas		NOFBI extension phase 2 commenced in 2014[8]. Hotspots in rural towns, bus stations, and other public spaces: Safaricom launched 'VumaOnline' in 2013, a service that provides free Wi-Fi to passengers in public transport vehicles[9]. Microsoft in partnership with local companies started an initiative to bring solar-powered Wi-Fi to western Rift Valley in 2013[10]. GCCN extension: Phase one of the County Connectivity Project, whereby 28 counties were fully connected to the GCCN, was completed in 2013[11].
School network	Implementation of the school laptop project	ICT Cabinet Secretary supplied laptops to some schools in November 2016 to implement the Digital Literacy Programme.[12]
School network	Creation of a schools network and its connection to the Internet through the KENET infrastructure	There is a KENET schools connectivity initiative that connects the academic community. Schools can become members to it. It was launched in 2014.[13]
Health network	Health portal Hotspots in healthcentres	E-portal for health services was launched by the Ministry of health in April 2017[14]. The county government of Kiambu connected 41 health facilities with free Internet in March 2017[15].
Five Centres of Excellence in ICT education &training	Enactment of KOTDA bill	The bill has been submitted to the cabinet but has not yet been enacted.[16]

Project or Sub-project	*Application or Expected Outcome*	*Activities and Achievements*
Five Centres of Excellence in ICT education & training	Establish five Centres of Excellence in five universities that teach electrical engineering, computer science, and information systems to develop high-end ICT talent. This shall include new teaching laboratories, employment of at least 75% doctoral-level faculty in computer science, engineering, and information systems. In order to retain the high-end faculty, there will be a need to introduce new reward systems, attract expatriates from other countries and provide doctoral and masters level scholarships to bright students.	Oracle's Centre of Excellence was launched in September 2014 at @iLabAfrica in Strathmore University to train teachers and students. The centre was officially opened by the Cabinet Secretary of the Ministry of ICT at the time.[17]
Development of MOOCs-type ICT continuous education courses for the training of trainers and the public	Training of trainers portal Public literacy programme via e-learning	The Digital Learning Programme (DLP) was initiated by the Government of Kenya in 2013[18].
National electronic single window system	Portal on cross-bordertrade	E-portal on cross-border trade was launched in 2016 by KENTRADE[19].
National payment gateway	Legal framework on electronic payment system	The National Payment System Act of 2011 was revised in 2012 and includes electronic payment sections[20]

Project or Sub-project	*Application or Expected Outcome*	*Activities and Achievements*
National agriculture commodity	Agriculture portal Electronic tea auction Electronic animal monitoring system	Electronic animal monitoring system: as of 2015, the Kenya Dairy Board was promoting the use of the Radio Frequency Identification (RFID) bolus that facilitates electronic animal registration[21]. The Kenya Open Data Portal with a section for agriculture was launched in 2011 and redesigned in 2015[22].

Note: Konza Technopolis Development Authority (KOTDA)

1. National ICT Master Plan 2017, Annex 5.

2. *See* http://www.ict.go.ke/draft-ict-policy-set-for-dabinet-approval/, accessed on 11 May 2017.

3. *See* http://www.cio.co.ke/news/main-stories/kenya%27s-e-citizen-portal-hits-1.23-million, accessed on 11 May 2017.

4. *See* https://www.ecitizen.go.ke/ecitizen-services.html, accessed on 11 May 2017.

5. *See* http://www.hapakenya.com/2016/06/09/car-registration-ownership-tranfer-will-now-be-done-online/, accessed on 11 May 2017.

6. "Kenya to adopt National Addressing System" (*Ministry of Information, Communications and Technology* 24 October 2016) http://www.ict.go.ke/kenya-to-adopt-national-addressing-system/, accessed on 12 May 2017.

7. *See* http://www.vision2030.go.ke/495/progress-2016-march-preparation-national-spatial-plan-kenya-data-infrastructure-knsdi/.

8. *See* http://icta.go.ke/national-optic-fibre-backbone-nofbi/, accessed on 11 May 2017.

9. *See* http://www.cio.co.ke/news/main-stories/safaricom-launches-%22vumaonline%22-to-offer-free-wifi-in-matatus,, accessed on 11 May 2017.

10. *See* https://www.newscientist.com/article/mg21729045-900-microsoft-brings-solar-wi-fi-to-rural-kenya/, accessed on 11 May 2017.

11. *See* http://www.capitalfm.co.ke/business/2016/11/belgium-give-sh2-4bn-last-mile-connectivity-project/,, accessed on 11 May 2017.

12. *See* http://www.mygov.go.ke/?p=6428&http://www.ict.go.ke/.

13. *See* http://schools.kenet.or.ke/&https://www.kenet.or.ke/.

14. *See* https://www.standardmedia.co.ke/business/article/2001237859/ministry-enhances-health-services-with-new-portal,, accessed on 11 May 2017.

15. *See* http://www.ku.ac.ke/kutv/41-kiambu-hospitals-get-wi-fi-go-cashless-smart-cards/,, accessed on 11 May 2017.

16. *See* http://kenyanewsagency.go.ke/en/tag/konza-technopolis-development-authority-kotda-bill/.

17. M. Lilian "CIO East Africa" (*Oracle's Centre of Excellence to bridge IT skills gap in Kenya - CIO East Africa* 11 September 2014) http://www.cio.co.ke/news/top-stories/oracle%E2%80%99s-centre-of-excellence-to-bridge-it-skills-gap-in-kenya, accessed on 12 May 2017.

18. *See* http://icta.go.ke/digital-literacy-programme-progress-may-2016/,, accessed on 11 May 2017.

19. *See* http://www.businessdailyafrica.com/magazines/1248928-3260262-jr0p01/index.html, accessed on 11 May 2017.

20. National Payment System Act No. 39 of 2011.

21. *See* http://www.businessdailyafrica.com/magazines/New-digital-cattle-tracker-gives-farmers-peace-of-mind/1248928-2693902-yb1wu9/index.html,, accessed on 11 May 2017.

22. *See* http://ictupdate.cta.int/2017/03/02/kenya-opens-up-agricultural-data/,, accessed on 11 May 2017.

V. National Cybersecurity Strategy

115. The national cybersecurity strategy was spearheaded by the Ministry of Information, Communications, and Technology and defines Kenya's cybersecurity vision, key objectives, and ongoing commitment to support national priorities by encouraging ICT growth and aggressively protecting critical information infrastructures while continuing to promote the use of ICT to enable Kenya's economic growth.

116. The strategy seeks to provide organizations and individuals with increased confidence in online and mobile transactions, encouraging greater foreign investment, and opening a broader set of trade opportunities within the global marketplace.

117. The strategy recognizes that cyberspace plays a critical role in the global economy, national and international dimensions that include industry, commerce, intellectual property, security, technology, culture, policy, and diplomacy. The Government of Kenya considers securing its national cyberspace a national priority to continue to facilitate economic growth for the country and its citizens.

118. The strategy includes four strategic goals:

(1) Enhance the nation's cybersecurity posture in a manner that facilitates the country's growth, safety, and prosperity.
(2) Build national capability by raising cybersecurity awareness and developing Kenya's workforce to address cybersecurity needs.
(3) Foster information sharing and collaboration among relevant stakeholders to facilitate an information sharing environment focused on achieving the Strategy's goals and objectives.
(4) Provide national leadership by defining the national cybersecurity vision, goals, and objectives and coordinating cybersecurity initiatives at the national level.

119. Kenya's Cybersecurity Framework aims at enhancing the security of Kenya's cyberspace and as a result creating confidence in the use and adoption of ICTs in Kenya. This framework consists of the National Cybersecurity Strategy, the National Computer Incident Response Team – Coordination Centre (National KE-CIRT/CC), and the National Public Key Infrastructure (NPKI). The Cybersecurity Framework was launched by President Uhuru Kenyatta in June 2014.

120. The Cyber Security Strategy establishes an elaborate cybersecurity governance structure including the National Kenya Computer Incident Response Team/ Coordination Centre (KE-CIRT/CC) and a Cybersecurity Committee. The main purpose of the Cybersecurity Committee is to participate in the implementation of the National KE-CIRT/CC, facilitate coordination and collaboration in response to cybersecurity incidents, and other cybercrime management activities. CA chairs this committee.

121. The National KE-CIRT/CC, which is resident at CA, was also launched in June 2014 and is Kenya's national cybercrime management point of contact. This CIRT is described in more detail in Part VII of this manuscript.

VI. Pending Policy and Legislation

A. The Second (Draft) National ICT Policy

122. The National ICT Policy of 2006 provided a workable roadmap for development of the ICT sector, but after about five years it became clear that a review of the roadmap was needed. After multi-stakeholder consultations, the Ministry of ICT released a Draft National ICT Policy in June 2016. The draft policy is intended to complement Vision 2030 and provide key strategies for achieving Kenya's ambitious national development targets.

123. The Draft National ICT Policy 2016 is notable for two related reasons. First, the Cabinet Secretary of the Ministry of ICT under whom the policy was drafted is Joe Mucheru, formerly the Sub-Sahara Africa Lead for Google, Inc., from the Google office in Nairobi. Second, the Draft policy has a clear focus on building private sector capacity in ICT. This focus is, of course, unsurprisingly given the private sector background of the Cabinet Secretary, and it can be seen from the Broad Strategies that are prominent in the policy:

- Encourage Public–Private Partnerships (PPPs) for ICT-enabled systems.
- Promote the local-assembly ecosystem that will spur the light manufacturing industry in order to guarantee affordable communication devices.
- Institute innovation clusters that will generate a critical supply of highly skilled technical personnel required to drive the information society.
- Facilitate broadband access to all citizens and ensure Broadband connectivity of all public facilities by 2020.
- Promote investment in the ICT sector.

- Ensure availability of spectrum resources to support the development of ICT infrastructure and accessibility countrywide.
- Support human resource development and capacity building.
- Facilitate access to devices and the development of local content.
- Encourage innovation and competition in the ICT sector.
- Provide ICT training of all relevant public officials and service providers.
- Facilitate ICT-based delivery systems for healthcare, education, and infrastructure.
- Facilitate deployment of the Internet of Things (remote sensing and control of connected devices) for the public infrastructure and environmental management.
- Encourage universities to scale up education and incubation of ICT solutions, including through partnerships with the business sector.[79]

124. The Draft National ICT Policy 2016 departs from the National ICT Policy 2006 in a variety of ways, most of which stem from the evolution of the global ICT industry as well as political changes in the country. For example, the Draft Policy recognizes that the Constitution of Kenya 2010 devolved much of government to the forty-seven counties in Kenya and includes substantial focus on servicing the ICT needs of those counties.

125. The Draft Policy also covers topics that were still barely emerging or were completely unknown just a decade earlier. For example, a section recognizes big data, particularly whereby data are captured in Machine to Machine (M2M) interactions not involving any human input. The Draft Policy recognizes the importance of such data and provides the following proactive policy objectives:

- Develop policy and legislation on information privacy and data ownership.
- Standards on encryption technologies for M2M communications.
- Government data consolidation.
- National addressing policy.
- Policy around accessibility of geolocation data.

126. In addition to the above policy objectives, a number of specific strategies are provided, including strategies for encouraging the private sector:

- Develop a Big Data Strategy in consultation with stakeholders.
- Promote and accelerate the development, utilization, and sharing of big data.
- Promote the construction of a national big data platform and big data centres.
- Boost and promote big data collection, storage, processing, analysis, visualization, and other key technologies while upgrading big data technology infrastructure.
- Promote big data commercialization as well as the development of hardware and software products for big data applications.

---

79. Draft National ICT Policy June 2016, pp. 13–14.

127. Similarly, the Draft Policy also contains sections pertaining to the following emerging issues, among others: net neutrality; OTT services; Internet of Things (IoT); and E-Agriculture.

128. The June 2016 Draft version of the National ICT Policy continues to proceed through the process of adoption and is currently awaiting approval by the full Cabinet.

B. The Critical Infrastructure Protection Bill

129. A draft Critical Infrastructure Protection Bill was sponsored by the Office of the President, and in 2015 then Cabinet Secretary for the Ministry of ICT Dr Fred Matiang'i reported that the bill was soon to be tabled in parliament. At the time it was reported that Dr Matiang'i supported the bill due to 'constant destruction of some of the key infrastructures in the country by protesters.' The bill was, however, never published and the contents of the draft remain undisclosed.

§2. Administrative Framework

130. There are five important institutions in the administrative structure of Kenya's ICT industry:

(1) The Ministry of Information Communications and Technology.
(2) The NCS.
(3) CA (previously the CCK).
(4) The Communications Appeals Tribunal.
(5) The Kenya ICT Authority (ICTA).

I. The Ministry of Information Communications and Technology

131. The Ministry of Information Communications and Technology has both the managerial control and the political leadership of the ICT industry in Kenya. It is headed by a Cabinet Secretary who is nominated by the President, with the approval of the National Assembly. Under the Constitution of Kenya 2010, Cabinet Secretaries should not be members of parliament. Cabinet Secretaries are accountable individually, and collectively, to the President for the exercise of their powers and the performance of their functions. The day-to-day management of the affairs of the Ministry is vested in the Principal Secretary. Principal Secretaries are contracted employees of the government and are usually drawn from experts in the areas concerning their Ministry.

132. The Cabinet Secretary is a member of the Cabinet, which is comprised of the President, the Deputy President, the Attorney General, and other Cabinet Secretaries. The function of the Cabinet is to aid and advise the President in the government of Kenya.[80] The Cabinet Secretary is therefore answerable to both the Cabinet and the National Assembly for all matters relating to the Ministry, particularly, broadcasting, ICT, telecommunications, radio communications, and postal services.

133. Under the KIC Amendment Act 2013, the Cabinet Secretary may issue to the Authority, policy guidelines of a general nature relating to the provisions of this Act.[81] The other powers of the Cabinet Secretary under the Act include:

- the appointment of seven persons to serve as the members of the Board of Directors of CA;[82]
- by notice in the Gazette and on the official website of the Ministry, declare a vacancy in the CA Board and invite applications from qualified persons;[83]
- convene a selection panel for the purpose of selecting suitable candidates for appointment as the chairperson or member of the Board;[84]
- appoint the chairperson and the members of the CA board upon receipt of names of persons from the selection panel;[85]
- ensure that the appointees to the Board reflect the interests of all sections of society;[86]
- ensure equal opportunities for persons with disabilities and other marginalized groups;[87]
- ensure that not more than two-thirds of the members are of the same gender;[88]
- in consultation with Competition Authority of Kenya (CAK), make regulations on all matters relating to broadcasting, ICT, telecommunications, radio communications, universal access, postal services, and all matters for the better carrying out of the provisions of the Act;[89]
- designate the classes of documents and transactions to which the provisions of the Act relating to electronic transactions shall apply or not apply;[90]
- declare a computer system or a network to be protected system for the purposes of the Act;[91] and
- appoint chairperson and eight other members of the Universal Service Advisory Council.[92]

---

80. Constitution of Kenya 2010 Chapter 9, part 3.
81. Kenya Information and Communications Amendment Act 2013 s. 5C(1).
82. Information and Communications Amendment Act 2013 s. 6(1)(e).
83. *Ibid.*, s. 6B(1)(a).
84. Section 6B(1)(b).
85. Section 6B(9).
86. Section 6B(10)(a).
87. Section 6B(10)(b).
88. Section 6B(10)(c).
89. Sections 27, 83R, 84P, 84W.
90. Section 83B.
91. Section 83Q.
92. Kenya Information and Communications Amendment Act 2013 s. 39(6).

134. The functions of the Cabinet Secretary include:

- Language Policy Management.
- Information Communication Technology Policy.
- Broadcast Policy.
- Public Communications.
- Promotion of E-government.
- ICT Training and Standards Development and Administration.
- Development of National Communications Capacity and Infrastructure.
- Provision of the Public Relations Services.
- Promotion of Software Development Industry.
- Fibre Optics Infrastructure Management.
- Policy on Software Licensing Regime.
- ICT Agency.
- Provision of ICT consulting services to other Government departments.
- Provision of advisory services on the acquisition of ICT and telecommunication services and equipment to Government ministries and departments.
- Telecommunications services.
- Development of National Communications Capacity and Infrastructure.
- Dissemination of public information.[93]

135. The executive functions of the Ministry of Information, Communications, and Technology extend to cover the following institutions:

- Kenya Broadcasting Corporation (KBC).
- Kenya Institute of Mass Communication.
- PCK.
- NCS.
- Telkom Kenya.
- Multimedia University.
- Safaricom Ltd.
- Konza Technopolis Development Authority.
- Brand Kenya Board.
- Kenya Year Book Editorial.
- Kenya ICTA.

136. The Presidential Executive Order 2 of 2013 on organization of Government of Kenya listed the CA as one of the organizations in which the Ministry exercised control, but the KIC Amendment Act 2013 envisioned an Authority 'independent and free of control by government, political or commercial interests in

93. Office of the President: Presidential Executive order No. 2 of 2013 on the organization of Government of Kenya, 2013.

the exercise of its powers and in the performance of its functions'.[94] Therefore, the presidency removed CA from the list of organizations to which it has control.[95]

II. The National Communication Secretariat

137. The NCS is established under the KIC Act, 1998.[96] It is headed by a Communications Secretary. Its function is:

to advise the Government on the adoption of a communication policy which –

- *promotes the benefits of technological development to all users of postal and telecommunication facilities;*
- *fosters national safety and security, economic prosperity and the delivery of critical social services through posts and telecommunications;*
- *facilitates and contributes to the full development of competition and efficiency in the provision of services both within and outside Kenya; and*
- *fosters full and efficient use of telecommunication resources including effective use of the radio spectrum by the Government in a manner which encourages the most beneficial use thereof in the public interest.*[97]

138. The NCS is thus the policy advisory body to the Ministry. Indeed, the NCS drafted the first national ICT policy for post-liberalization Kenya, and its technical input was instrumental in the legislative reforms that were introduced by the Kenya Communications (Amendment) Act, 2008.

139. In 2013, the NCS drafted an early version of the current Draft National ICT Policy 2016. In addition, the NCS has been active in preparing draft policies and laws pertaining to a national addressing system, frequency spectrum management, data protection, and access to information.

III. The Communications Authority of Kenya

140. The former CCK was renamed to 'Communications Authority of Kenya' in 2013.[98] The CA is established under the KIC Act as a body corporate with perpetual

94. Kenya Information and Communications Amendment Act 2013 s. 5A.(1).
95. Information, Communication & Technology (ICT), available at http://www.presidency.go.ke/index.php/information-communication-technology-ict retrieved 10 Sep. 2015.
96. Part VII, s. 84.
97. Section 34(2).
98. Kenya Information and Communications Amendment Act 2013, s. 3. The CA was not able to adopt the acronym 'CAK' due to prior use of that acronym by the Competition Authority of Kenya.

succession, and its core duty is 'to license and regulate postal, information and communication services' in accordance with the provisions of the Act.[99] The Act obliges CA to have regard to the following in the course of the performance of its functions:

- any policy guidelines of a general nature relating to the provisions of the Act notified to it by the Minister and published in the Gazette;
- Kenya's obligations under any international treaty or agreement relating to the provisions of telecommunication, radio, and postal services.[100]

141. The CA is comprised of:

- a Chairperson appointed by the President;
- the Director General recruited and appointed by the Board through a competitive process for a term of four years renewable once;
- the Principal Secretary for the time being responsible for matters relating to broadcast, electronic, print, and all other types of media;
- the Principal Secretary for the time being responsible for matters relating to finance;
- the Principal Secretary for the time being responsible for matters relating to internal security;
- at least seven other persons, not being public officers, appointed by the Cabinet Secretary and of whom at least one shall have knowledge or experience and have a degree recognized in Kenya in matters relating to law, telecommunications, information and communication technology; broadcasting; postal regulation; humanities and social sciences; or any other relevant field.[101]

142. The Director General is the chief executive officer of CA responsible for the day-to-day management of its affairs and the members of the staff. He is also an ex officio member of the Board of Directors.[102] CA is funded through a budgetary provision set aside for its purposes by Parliament; money obtained from borrowing, donations, and grants; and moneys and assets payable or accruing to it whether as fines, forfeitures, licence fees, etc. under the Act.[103] CA works in coordination with the Ministry and the NCS in the preparation of rules and regulations concerning various aspects of broadcasting, ICT, telecommunications, radio communications, postal services, universal access, consumer protection, and fair competition. Save in accordance with the policy directions of the Minister as provided under the Act, CA is required by law to exercise its functions independently.[104]

143. The high stakes and the dynamics of transiting the country's ICT industry from a State-controlled to a liberalized market have, on several occasions, brought

99. Sections 3, 5.
100. Section 5(4).
101. Section 6.
102. Section 11.
103. Section 17.
104. Section 5A.

political intrigues that have seriously tested the independence of the organization and the nature of its relationship with the Ministry.

144. In March 2005, the then Minister for Information and Communications, Hon. Raphael Tuju, caused a sensation in the ICT industry when he announced that he had 'dissolved' the entire Board of Directors of CA. The decision, which the Minister reported had been taken at Cabinet level following an enquiry into allegations of misconduct and corruption, was as unprecedented as it may have been unprocedural. Under the Act, the Members of the Board other than the Chairman and the Director General (who seem to enjoy a somewhat untrammelled security of tenure) may not be removed except on the grounds of mental or physical incapacity, misconduct, bankruptcy, or conflict of interest.[105] Following the Minister's decision, various voices in the industry, particularly the Telecommunications Service Providers Association of Kenya (TESPOK) accused the Minister of interfering with the independence of CA. Some industry sources, however, agreed with the Minister's decision and welcomed the appointment of a new CA Board.[106]

145. Later in November of the same year, the Minister issued a press statement 'nullifying' the issuance of a licence for a third mobile operator to Econet Wireless Kenya Ltd. The decision was ostensibly taken after the 'government' had established, subsequent to issuing Econet with a licence in an open bidding procurement, that the operator would not be able to have the shareholding required to meet the terms of the government's policy on equity ownership of telecommunications operators. Under the KIC Act, the power to revoke a telecommunications licence was vested in CA upon due process. Though most people and indeed even some of the operators failed to see the sense in the fine distinction between the Minister and the Commission in such situations, the Minister's action in this case, though it may have been justified, may have been beyond his powers as it appeared to have been done without due process. At least to the extent that it was CA's power rather than the Minister's to order the revocation, the Minister's action amounted to a Ministerial interference with CA's independence contrary to the KIC Act. Econet subsequently filed judicial review proceedings against the Minister, CA, one of the unsuccessful bidders, and its investment partner,[107] which it subsequently abandoned after the Minister subsequently 'restored' the licence in 2007.

146. In 2013, a petition was filed challenging the constitutionality of the continued existence of the CA. The petitioner argued that the CA was not the independent body contemplated by Article 34 of the Constitution of Kenya 2010 to regulate the media and, as such, it could not superintend over the ongoing digital migration process in Kenya. In support of this contention, Hon, Muite, S.C., cited Principle 10 of the *Principles on Freedom and Broadcast* based on Article 19 of the *United Nations Declaration on Human Rights*. Principle 10 provides that all public bodies

105. First Schedule to the KIC Act: Provisions as to Conduct of Business Affairs of the Board, para. 2.
106. *See* www.afrol.com/articles/15905, accessed on 15 Nov. 2009.
107. *Republic v. Minister for Information and Communications ex parte Econet Wireless*, High Court (Nairobi) Miscellaneous Civil Application No. 1640 of 2004.

that exercise power in the areas of broadcast and/or telecommunications regulation should be independent and autonomous and that this should be guaranteed by the law. The petitioner argued that CA as then constituted was not independent of government control and therefore cannot be an independent body. The CA is therefore not entitled to issue licences or supervise the digital migration process.

147. In deciding the case, Judge D. S. Majanja held that the CA was, in fact, on constitutionally sound ground:

> *Under KICA, CA is the body mandated to regulate broadcasting and other electronic media by way of licensing. Under Section 5 of KICA, the CA is established 'to license and regulate postal, information and communication services in accordance with the provisions of this Act.'*
> *The circumstances of CA have not changed and until the transition is completed by implementation of the Kenya Information and Communications (Amendment) Bill, 2013, CA as currently established remains the body entitled under the Constitution and the law to continue to regulate the media and airwaves in accordance with the Constitution and existing law.*[108]

148. Public record bears no account of CA having complained of interference with its independence by an incumbent Minister in charge of information and communications.

149. The CA manages and guides the ICT sector through a variety of methods and instruments. Chiefly among these, the CA is responsible for advising the Cabinet Secretary on the drafting, championing, and implementing of Regulations (i.e., Subsidiary Legislation) under the KIC Act 1998. As described in detail throughout this text, there are currently no less than twenty independent Regulations covering various aspects of the ICT sector. In addition, the CA is responsible for issuing, from time to time and with the input of stakeholders, Sector Guidelines on the implementation of specific regulatory issues. There are currently eleven sector guidelines available from the CA, although most of these are over a decade old and have not been updated.[109]

IV. The Communications and Multimedia Appeals Tribunal

150. The Communications and Multimedia Appeals Tribunal is established under the KIC Amendment Act 2013[110] for the purpose of arbitrating in cases where disputes arise between parties under the Act, or for any other matters as may be referred to it by the Cabinet Secretary. The Tribunal is comprised of: a Chairperson nominated by the Judicial Service Commission, who shall be a person qualified for

---

108. *Royal Media Services Ltd & 2 others v. Attorney General & 8 others* [2013] eKLR.
109. *See* http://www.ca.go.ke/index.php/sector-guidelines, accessed 1 Jun. 2017.
110. Section 102.

appointment as a judge of the High Court of Kenya and who shall also possess experience in communication policy and law; and at least four persons possessing knowledge and experience in media, telecommunication, postal, courier systems, radio communications, information technology, or business practice and finance; and who are not in the employment of the Government, the Media Council, or the Authority.

151. The members of the Tribunal are appointed by the Cabinet Secretary from a list of names forwarded to him or her by a selection panel. The members of the Tribunal hold office for a period of three years but shall be eligible for reappointment for one further term for a period not exceeding three years. In selecting, nominating, approving, or appointing the members of the Tribunal, the selection panel and the Cabinet Secretary shall ensure that the nominees to the Tribunal reflect the interests of all sections of the society; ensure equal opportunities for persons with disabilities and other marginalized groups; and ensure that not more than two-thirds of the members shall be of the same gender.[111]The Tribunal has powers to summon and hear witnesses, receive evidence, conduct hearings, and make orders for the payment of costs.[112]

152. Any person aggrieved by a decision or order of the Tribunal may, within thirty days of such decision or order, appeal against such decision or order to the High Court.[113] Any decisions made by the Media Council or Communications Authority may be appealed at the tribunal.[114] Any person aggrieved by a decision or order of the Tribunal may, within thirty days of such decision or order, appeal against such decision or order to the High Court. The decision of the High Court on any appeal under this section shall be final.[115]

V. ICT Authority

153. The Information and Communication Technology Authority is a State Corporation under the Ministry of Information, Communications, and Technology. The corporation was established in August 2013. The ICTA is a successor to the KIC Technology Board, the Directorate of e-Government, and the Government Information Technology Services (GITS).[116]

154. The Authority has a board consisting of: a non-executive Chairman appointed by the President; the Principal Secretary responsible for matters relating to Information Communications and Technology; the Principal Secretary responsible for matters relating to the National Treasury; the Principal Secretary responsible for matters relating to Land, Housing, and Urban Development; six persons,

111. *Ibid.*
112. Section 102D, 102E.
113. Kenya Information and Communications Amendment Act 2013 s. 102G.
114. Section 102F.
115. Section 102G.
116. Kenya Gazette Supplement No. 118, 16 Aug. 2013, Legal Notice 183.

not being public officers, appointed by the Cabinet Secretary, by virtue of their specialist knowledge and distinguished service and experience of at least seven years in matters relating to information and communications technologies, e-government, e-commerce, law, finance, or human resources management; and the Chief Executive Officer.

155. The Chief Executive Officer of the Authority is appointed by the Cabinet Secretary on the recommendation of the Board after a competitive recruitment process. The Chief Executive Officer who must possess a degree shall hold office for a term of three years and is eligible for reappointment for a further one term. The Chief Executive Officer is the accounting officer with overall responsibility for the direction, organization, and administration of programmes and other affairs of the Authority.

156. The Authority is tasked with rationalizing and streamlining the management of all Government of Kenya ICT functions. Its broad mandate entails enforcing ICT standards in Government and enhancing the supervision of its electronic communication. The Authority also promotes ICT literacy, capacity, innovation, and enterprise in line with the Kenya National ICT Master Plan 2014–2017.

157. The ICTA's mandate is as follows:

- Set and enforce ICT standards and guidelines for the human resource, infrastructure, processes and system, and technology for the public office and public service.
- Deploy and manage all ICT staff in the public service.
- Facilitate and regulate the design, implementation, and use of ICTs in the public service.
- Promote ICT literacy and capacity.
- Promote e-government services.
- Facilitate optimal electronic, electronic form, electronic record, and equipment use in public service.
- Promote ICT Innovation and enterprise.
- Establish, develop, and maintain secure ICT Infrastructure and Systems.
- Supervise the design, development, and implementation of critical ICT Projects across the Public Service.
- Implement and manage the Kenya National Spatial Data Initiative.

158. The Authority is expected to promote: strategic progress in the development and use of ICTs; universal access to services through ICTs; and universal good quality broadband when carrying out its functions.

§3. The Legal Framework

159. The essential legislation for the ICT industry is the KIC Act, 1998. The Act was originally enacted in 1998 as the KCA of 1998, but it was renamed in 2009 with the coming into force of the Kenya Communications (Amendment) Act, 2008 and subsequently amended in 2013 as the KIC Amendment Act, 2013 which was the country's boldest legislative intervention in the ICT sector in over a decade. The purpose of the Act is to establish the CA and to facilitate the development of the information and communications sector (including broadcasting, multimedia, telecommunications, and postal services) and e-commerce.[117]

160. The KIC Act is complemented by a growing list of subsidiary legislations, namely:

- Kenya communications (appeals) rules, 1999.
- Kenya communications regulations, 2001.
- KIC (broadcasting) regulations, 2009.
- Kenya information and communications (dispute resolution) regulations, 2010.
- Kenya information and communications (tariff) regulations, 2010.
- Kenya information and communications (compliance monitoring, inspections, and enforcement) regulations, 2010.
- Kenya information and communications (fair competition and equality of treatment) regulations, 2010.
- Kenya information and communications (interconnection and provision of fixed links, access, and facilities) regulations, 2010.
- Kenya information and communications (consumer protection) regulations, 2010.
- Kenya information and communications (numbering) regulations, 2010.
- Kenya information and communications (postal and courier services) regulations, 2010.
- Kenya information and communications (importation, type approval, and distribution of communications equipment) regulations, 2010.
- Kenya information and communications (radio communications and frequency spectrum) regulations, 2010.
- Kenya information and communications (universal access and service) regulations, 2010.
- Kenya information and communications (licensing and quality of service) regulations, 2010.
- Kenya information and communications (electronic certification and domain name administration) regulations, 2010.
- Kenya information and communication (transitional provisions) regulations, 2012.
- Kenya information and communications (registration of subscribers of telecommunication services) regulations, 2013.
- Kenya information and communications (registration of subscribers of telecommunication services) regulations, 2014.
- Kenya information and communications (registration of SIM cards) regulations, 2015.

117. The Preamble to the Act.

I. Market Structure

161. In 2004, the Ministry of Information and Communications announced that it would bring into effect a new market definition regime for the ICT industry as a mechanism of harnessing the emerging technological opportunities as well as addressing the attendant regulatory challenges of technological convergence. Technological convergence within the ICT sub-sector had rendered the long-held technology-oriented licensing approach untenable. With the launch of the new Unified Licensing Framework (ULF), CA sought to establish a technologically neutral market and licensing regime that would allow any form of communications infrastructure to be used to provide any technically viable communications service.

162. The ULF was brought into effect by a Gazette Notice[118] published by the Minister. The notice reiterated that the Ministry's policy priority was to focus 'on establishing a market structure capable of attracting investment in the sector and allowing the creation of a versatile ICT infrastructure for leveraging national development. The market structure will be reviewed from time to time in line with changing market needs and technological trends'.[119] The notice further stated that the government was adopting a unified licensing and technology-neutral regulatory framework 'in order to enable optimum utilization of existing infrastructure for provision of diverse services'.[120]

163. The main segments of the ICT market under the new framework became:

- Network Facilities Providers (NFP) – who shall own and operate any form of communications infrastructure (based on satellite, terrestrial, mobile, or fixed).
- ASP – to provide all forms of services to end users using the network services of a facilities provider.
- Content Services Providers (CSP) – to provide content services such as television and radio broadcasts, data processing services, third-party content providers, and other information services.

164. In both the notice and communication to ICT industry stakeholders at the conclusion of the consultative process leading to the implementation of the ULF, the Ministry and CA stated that the migration to the new framework would proceed on the following understanding:

- technology neutrality and unified licensing were increasingly being adopted by policymakers and regulators and were a logical result of technological advancements as well as consumer demands and emerging business trends in the telecommunications industry;

118. Gazette Notice No. 7295 of 2008, 'Information and Communications Technology Sector Policy Guidelines', Vol. CX No. 68, 15 Aug. 2008.
119. *Ibid.*
120. *Ibid.*

- the government was committed to fostering a predictable and attractive regulatory environment capable of attracting and promoting investments in the sector. Against this background, the CA would ensure that the terms and conditions of the modified licences under the ULF would not diminish the rights of existing licences;
- to provide even more certainty in the sector, licences issued under the ULF would be on the same more favourable terms and CA would also ensure that when modifying licences, existing licensees maintain their numbering resources and assigned radio frequency spectrum for the duration for which those resources are assigned;
- consistent with the government's objective of ensuring a smooth transition to the ULF, no licensees would be charged or incur expenses relating to the horizontal migration of existing licences;
- the existing licences would be converted into the new licensing framework on the same or more favourable terms and conditions;
- the framework, in general, would apply to both existing and new licensees, and while licensees who migrate horizontally to ULF would not be required to pay additional fees, those wishing to vertically upgrade their licences would be subjected to the usual application process; and
- the implementation of the framework would not only be timely but also would take into account the existing business models in the industry while ensuring that no operator was disadvantaged.

165. Table 23 shows the market structure of the ICT industry based on CA's ULF.

Table 23 The Market Structure for the ICT Industry under CA's Unified Licence Framework

Licence Category under Unified Licence Framework	*Licence Period*	*Initial Licence Fee*	*Annual Operating Fee*	*Access Fee for Frequency Spectrum*	*Annual Spectrum Fee*
CATEGORY 1: INFRASTRUCTURE-BASED OPERATORS – NETWORK FACILITIES PROVIDERS (NFPs)					
Tier 1 NFP: National Fixed Network Operator (Telkom Kenya) and Cellular Mobile Operators	15 years	USD 205,450	0.5% of annual gross turnover	Bid/Assessed price for specific frequency spectrum reservation (National, Regional, or Local Area)	Based on bandwidth & coverage
Tier 2 NFP: Data Carrier Network Operators, Public Data Network Operators, and Regional Telecom Operators	15 years	USD 205,450	0.5% of annual gross turnover	Bid/Assessed price for specific frequency spectrum reservation (National, Regional, or Local Area)	Based on bandwidth& coverage
Tier 3 NFP: Local Loop Providers	15 years	USD 2,740	0.5% of annual gross turnover	Bid/Assessed price for specific frequency spectrum reservation (National, Regional, or Local Area)	Based on bandwidth& coverage
International Gateway Licence (Satellite and/or Terrestrial)	15 years	USD 205,450	0.5% of annual gross turnover	Not applicable	Based on bandwidth utilization
Submarine Cable Landing Licence	15 years	USD 1 million	0.5% of annual gross turnover	Not applicable	Not applicable

Licence Category under Unified Licence Framework	*Licence Period*	*Initial Licence Fee*	*Annual Operating Fee*	*Access Fee for Frequency Spectrum*	*Annual Spectrum Fee*
CATEGORY 2: NON-INFRASTRUCTURE-BASED SERVICE PROVIDERS: APPLICATIONS SERVICE PROVIDERS (ASPs)					
ASPs –Global Mobile Personal Communications by Satellite (GMPCS) Service Providers, Internet Exchange Point (IXP), Internet Service Provider, Resale Service Providers (RSP), and Other Value-Added Service (VAS) Providers	15 years	USD 1,370	USD 1,370 or 0.5 of Annual Gross Turnover whichever is higher	Not applicable	Not applicable
CATEGORY 3: CONTENT SERVICE PROVIDERS (CSPs)					
Content Service Providers (CSP): Premium Rate Service Providers –Audio-Text Service Providers; Credit Card Valuation Service Providers; and Other Web-Based Public Commercial Information Service Providers	15 years	USD 1,370	USD 1,370 or 0.5 of annual gross turnover whichever is higher	Not applicable	Not applicable
Business Process Offshoring (BPO)	Not applicable	USD 136	Not applicable	Not applicable	Not applicable

Licence Category under Unified Licence Framework	*Licence Period*	*Initial Licence Fee*	*Annual Operating Fee*	*Access Fee for Frequency Spectrum*	*Annual Spectrum Fee*
CATEGORY 4: TERMINAL EQUIPMENT VENDORS AND INSTALLATION/MAINTENANCE CONTRACTORS					
Terminal Equipment Installation/Maintenance Contractors	5 years	USD 205	USD 82	Not applicable	Not applicable
CATEGORY 5: VENDORS AND CONTRACTORs' TECHNICAL PERSONNEL AUTHORIZATIONS					
Vendors and Contractors' Technical Authorization Personnel	3 years	USD 27	USD 6.80	Not applicable	Not applicable
CATEGORY 6: PRIVATE NETWORKS: ALTERNATIVE NETWORK FACILITIES PROVIDERS (ANFP)					
Private Networks: Alternative Network Facilities Providers (ANFP)	15 years	Not applicable	Not applicable	Bid/Assessed price for specific frequency spectrum reservation (National, Regional or Local)	Based on bandwidth coverage
Private Satellite Terminal Authorization: Interactive VSAT Terminal Using Local Licensed Hub and Private VSAT Terminal Using Foreign Hub	15 years	Not applicable	Using local hub: USD 82 per VSAT. Using foreign hub: USD 2,740 per VSAT	Not applicable	Local hub: Not applicable Foreign hub: Based on spectrum usage
GMPCS Landing Rights Authorization	15 years	USD 12,500	Not applicable	Not applicable	Not applicable

II. General Provisions on Licences and Conditions

166. In the standard licences for the three tiers of operators, the following definitions are provided:

- A NFP is defined as a licensee authorized by CA to build and commercially operate Telecommunication/electronic communications Systems.
- A Content Service is defined as information of any kind normally provided at a fee and delivered over electronic communications networks and services. It includes broadcasting content, financial information services, and other information society services.
- Application Services are defined as electronic communications services which are normally provided for remuneration and consists wholly or mainly in the conveyance of signals on electronic communications networks including those used for broadcasting, but excluding services providing or exercising editorial control over content transmitted using electronic communications networks and services.

167. The following general conditions apply to all licences issued by CA, save for licences for telecommunications vendors, radio communications, and value-added or resale services:[121]

- every application for a licence should be in the form prescribed by CA and accompanied by a payment of the prescribed fee;
- CA may require the applicant to supply such additional information as it may deem necessary for the purposes of considering the application;
- at least thirty days before granting a licence, CA shall give notice to the public in the Kenya Gazette of the application and specify a time, not being less than thirty days from the date of the notice, within which written representations or objections may be made to it with respect to the application;
- in considering the application, CA will consider any such representations or objections;
- after the period provided in the Gazette Notice has expired, CA may grant the licence to the applicant 'if it is satisfied that the applicant should be licensed', subject to such conditions as it may prescribe;
- once a licence has been granted, unless it is earlier revoked, it shall continue to be in force for the duration of the period specified in it;
- where CA declines to grant or to renew a licence, it shall notify the applicant of the reasons for the refusal within thirty days of such refusal;
- an applicant who is aggrieved by the refusal may appeal to the Communications Appeal Tribunal;
- CA is to maintain a register of all licences issued by it, and the register is to be made available for inspection to any person during working hours upon the payment of any fee prescribed for that purpose.

121. *See* ss 77–83 of the KIC Act.

168. Variations to the licence may occur, such as under the following circumstances:

– CA may from time to time modify any of the conditions of the licence. However, this is to be done upon advance notice published in the Kenya Gazette stating the proposed modification, its effects, the reasons thereof and providing a period of not less than thirty days during which the licensee or any interested party may make written objections or representations with respect to the proposed modifications;
– where the proposed modification is intended to 'remedy or prevent matters which operate or are likely to operate against the public interest', CA may proceed to make the modification upon prior notice or the receiving of objections or representations. However, notice of the modification is to be given to the licensee;
– a licensee aggrieved by the decision of CA with regard to the modification of its licence may appeal to the Communications Appeal Tribunal within fifteen days of the receipt of the notice of modification; and
– the Tribunal may stay the decision of CA on the modification pending the hearing and determination of the appeal.

169. Table 24 sets out the general licensing conditions for the three broad categories of licensees under the ULF.

Table 24 Licensing Conditions for Operators under the Unified Licensing Framework

	Network Facilities Provider (Tier 1)	*Application Services Provider*	*Content Services Provider*
Subject Matter of Licence	Transmission systems, switching or routing systems, and other resources permitting conveyance of signals by wire, radio, optical, or other electromagnetic means.	Electronic communications normally provided at a fee consisting mainly in the conveyance of signals on electronic communications networks including those used for broadcasting but excluding services exercising editorial control over content transmitted using the networks or services.	Information of any kind normally provided at a fee and delivered over electronic communications networks and services. They include broadcasting content, financial information services, and other information society services.
Prohibition	Licensee to connect its systems only to: – other telecommunication system licensed by CCK;	Licensee to exercise due diligence in obtaining the authorizations of the relevant government bodies on matters	Services should be desirable to the public, and content should not include foul language,

	Network Facilities Provider (Tier 1)	*Application Services Provider*	*Content Services Provider*
Prohibition	– other systems authorized by another national regulatory authorities of the country or territory upon notice to CCK – apparatus which meets CCK's type approval and certification requirements.	relating to the provision of its services. No licence shall be provided for which a separate licence is required to be obtained by CCK. No service to be provided which is not filed with and approved by CCK.	material indicating violence, sadism, cruelty or repulsive or horrible behaviour, or anything in breach of the law; immoral acts including prostitution; material likely to mislead through inaccuracy, ambiguity, exaggeration, or omission; material that may result in any unreasonable invasion of privacy; induce an unacceptable sense of fear or anxiety; encourage or incite persons to engage in dangerous practices or to use harmful substances; induce or promote tribal and/or racial disharmony; cause grave or widespread offence; debase, degrade, or demean; and take unfair advantage of consumers.

	Network Facilities Provider (Tier 1)	*Application Services Provider*	*Content Services Provider*
			Licensee to exercise due diligence in obtaining the authorizations of the relevant government bodies on matters relating to the provision of its services. No licence shall be provided for which a separate licence is required to be obtained by CCK. No service to be provided which is not filed with and approved by CCK.
Standardization	All equipment and devices comprising the provider's system to be of an approved industrial standard and type approved by CCK.	All equipment and devices used in the provision of the licensed services to be of an approved industrial standard and typeapproved by CCK.	All equipment and devices used in the provision of the licensed services to be of an approved industrial standard and typeapproved by CCK.
Universal Access and Service Obligations	Licensee to participate in the provision of such universal services as may be specified by CCK from time to time.	Licensee to participate in the provision of such universal services as may be specified by CCK from time to time.	

	Network Facilities Provider (Tier 1)	*Application Services Provider*	*Content Services Provider*
Interconnection, Co-location, Infrastructure Sharing, and Third Parties	As far as is reasonable and practicable: Allow other licensees to interconnect, co-locate, and share infrastructure and other facilities on terms that are reasonable, just, and non-discriminatory and in accordance with regulations. Permit a requesting licensee (third party) to connect its licensed system to its systems to enable the provision of licensed services by the third party.	Enter into service level agreements with other licensees for the provision of licensed services. Ensure that its equipment does not interfere with the equipment, facilities, and operations of third parties.	Enter into service level agreements with other licensees for the provision of licensed services. Ensure that its equipment does not interfere with the equipment, facilities, and operations of third parties.
Provision of Connectivity to Third Parties	Implement interconnection procedures in accordance with regulations issued by CCK.	Implement interconnection procedures in accordance with regulations issued by CCK.	Implement interconnection procedures in accordance with regulations issued by CCK.
Quality of Service	Meet the quality of service requirements prescribed by the CCK.	Meet the quality of service requirements prescribed by CCK.	Meet the quality of service requirements prescribed by CCK.

	Network Facilities Provider (Tier 1)	*Application Services Provider*	*Content Services Provider*
Emergency and Auxiliary Services	As far as is reasonable and practicable: Make its system available and accessible for the provision of emergency services free of charge. Interconnect with the systems of the police and public emergency service providers as prescribed by CCK.	Provide such directory information services as may be directed by CCK. Services to include an access number designated by the CCK as the Public Emergency Number. Provide public emergency services free of charge to any persons who access the licensed services. In case of public emergencies or crises, provide connectivity to the relevant government agencies.	No provision.
Environment, National Security, and Public Safety	Comply with physical planning, environmental, maritime, public health, and civil aviation laws. Not to cause any health, environmental, or safety hazard or contravene any law on public safety.	Take adequate measures to safeguard life against danger, including electromagnetic emissions emanating from communications equipment.	No provision

	Network Facilities Provider (Tier 1)	*Application Services Provider*	*Content Services Provider*
Numbering and Number Portability	Adhere to the national numbering plan and requirements on number portability prescribed by CCK. Ensure that the licensed system blends with the environment. In cases of emergency, provide connectivity and such other facilities to such agency of the government as CCK may prescribe.	Utilize the numbers assigned to it by CCK. Adhere to the national numbering plan and requirements on number portability prescribed by CCK. Not to cause any health, environmental, or safety hazard or contravene any law on public safety.	Utilize the numbers assigned to it by CCK. Adhere to the national numbering plan and requirements on number portability prescribed by CCK.
Consumer Protection	Ensure accuracy of its billing system. Not exercise undue preference or discrimination against particular persons in the provision of its services.	Ensure accuracy of its billing system. As far as is reasonable and practicable: Provide the licensed services to any person	Ensure accuracy of its billing system. Ensure that the licensed service and any promotional material does not reach those for whom the service concerned is

	Network Facilities Provider (Tier 1)	*Application Services Provider*	*Content Services Provider*
	Not subsidize or cross-subsidize or give undue preference to any of its associated businesses or persons concerning the provision of its services. Pre-notification to CCK of joint venture agreements or arrangements. Meet quality of service requirements prescribed by CCK.	upon reasonable request; establish customer care and information services to subscribers featuring dedicated and free customer care lines and customer care offices/ points; and Provide or ensure the provision of maintenance services for equipment supplied to the subscriber. File with CCK its scope of services, terms of service, dispute resolution mechanisms, and all charges for the services. Meet quality of service requirements prescribed by CCK.	inappropriate. As far as is reasonable and practicable, establish customer care and information services to subscribers. File with CCK its scope of services, terms of service, dispute resolution mechanisms, and all charges for the services. Pre-notification to CCK of joint venture agreements or arrangements. Promotions transmitted via audiovisual devices such as television broadcasts to give price information in both spoken and visual means.

	Network Facilities Provider (Tier 1)	*Application Services Provider*	*Content Services Provider*
		Except for non-payment and other contractual reasons, not to interrupt or suspend the provision of a service without notification to CCK and the subscriber. Not exercise undue preference or discrimination against particular persons in the provision of its services. Not to subsidize or cross-subsidize or give undue preference to any of its associated businesses or persons concerning the provision of its services. Give advance notice to CCK on agreements or arrangements for joint ventures.	Except for non-payment and other contractual reasons, not to interrupt or suspend the provision of a service without notification to CCK and the subscriber. Not exercise undue preference or discrimination against particular persons in the provision of its services. Not subsidize or cross-subsidize or give undue preference to any of its associated businesses or persons concerning the provision of its services.

	Network Facilities Provider (Tier 1)	*Application Services Provider*	*Content Services Provider*
Privacy and Confidentiality	Ensure privacy and confidentiality of proprietary information and business secrets disclosed in the course of obtained. Except for the purpose of law enforcement, national interest, or in obedience of the law, not to use any apparatus capable of recording, silently monitoring, or intruding into a subscriber's communication traffic. Except for the purpose of law enforcement, inform in advance all parties whose traffic is to be recorded, monitored, or intruded into.	Unless otherwise required by law, to use directory information for the purposes of a directory enquiry service and not to provide it to any third party without the consent of the subject. Ensure privacy and confidentiality of proprietary information and business secrets disclosed in the course of obtained. Except for the purpose of law enforcement, national interest, or in obedience of the law, not to use any apparatus capable of recording, silently monitoring, or intruding into a subscriber's communication traffic. Except for the purpose of law enforcement, inform in advance all parties whose traffic is to be recorded, monitored, or intruded into.	Services should be desirable to the public and content should not include material that may result in any unreasonable invasion of privacy. Ensure privacy and confidentiality of proprietary information and business secrets disclosed in the course of obtained. Except for purpose of law enforcement, national interest or in obedience of the law, not to use any apparatus capable of recording, silently monitoring, or intruding into a subscriber's communication traffic. Except for the purpose of law enforcement, inform in advance all parties whose traffic is to be recorded, monitored, or intruded into.

	Network Facilities Provider (Tier 1)	*Application Services Provider*	*Content Services Provider*
Fair Competition	Not engage in activities likely to have the effect of preventing, restricting, or distorting competition.	Not engage in activities likely to have the effect of preventing, restricting, or distorting competition.	Not engage in activities likely to have the effect of preventing, restricting, or distorting competition.
Equity	Notify CCK of any change in the shareholding, ownership, or control of the operator.	Notify CCK of any change in the shareholding, ownership, or control of the operator.	Notify CCK of any change in the shareholding, ownership, or control of the operator.
Inspection and Accounting	Permit CCK to enter and inspect its premises, equipment, and facilities and provide it with all information necessary to carry out its functions. Submit to CCK information on the financial accounting mechanisms of the licensed system. At the end of every fiscal year, submit to CCK an audit balance sheet of its financial operations for the concluded year.	Permit CCK to enter and inspect its premises, equipment, and facilities and provide it with all information necessary to carry out its functions. Submit to CCK information on the financial accounting mechanisms of the licensed system. At the end of every fiscal year, submit to CCK an audit balance sheet of its financial operations for the concluded year.	Permit CCK to enter and inspect its premises, equipment, and facilities and provide it with all information necessary to carry out its functions. Submit to CCK information on the financial accounting mechanisms of the licensed system. At the end of every fiscal year, submit to CCK an audit balance sheet of its financial operations for the concluded year.

	Network Facilities Provider (Tier 1)	*Application Services Provider*	*Content Services Provider*
Force Majeure	Licensee to mitigate the impact of the occurrence of any force majeure on its system and services. CCK may, upon application, exempt operator from certain obligations in the licence on account of force majeure.	Licensee to mitigate the impact of the occurrence of any force majeure on its system and services. CCK may, upon application, exempt operator from certain obligations in the licence on account of force majeure.	
Licence Issue, Revocation, and Renewal	Initial licence fee: USD 205,450 Upfront operating fee: USD 68,500. Annual fee: 0.5% of annual gross revenue or USD 6,850 whichever is higher. Licence granted for fifteen years.	Initial licence fee: USD 1,370. Upfront operating fee: USD 1,370 Annual fee: 0.5% of annual gross revenue or USD 1,370 whichever is higher. Licence granted for fifteen years. CCK having the	Initial licence fee: USD 1,370. Upfront operating fee: USD 1,370 Annual fee: 0.5% of annual gross revenue or USD 1,370 whichever is higher. Licence granted for fifteen years. CCK having the discretion to

	Network Facilities Provider (Tier 1)	*Application Services Provider*	*Content Services Provider*
	CCKis having the discretion to renew the licence upon request for an additional ten years. Licensee may voluntarily opt to terminate the licence. CCK may revoke licence by giving six-month notice for reasons stated where licensee: – fails to commence its services nine months after licensing; – fails to pay licence fee, annual operating fees, and other applicable fees; – breaches a condition of the licence;	discretion to renew the licence upon request for an additional ten years. Licensee may voluntarily opt to terminate the licence. CCK may revoke licence by giving six-month notice for reasons stated where licensee: – fails to commence its services nine months after licensing; – fails to pay licence fee, annual operating fees, and other applicable fees; – breaches a condition of the licence; – is dissolved or enters into liquidation, bankruptcy, or an arrangement with its creditors;	renew the licence upon request for an additional ten years Licensee may voluntarily opt to terminate the licence. CCK may revoke licence by giving six months notice for reasons stated where licensee: – fails to commence its services nine months after licensing; – fails to pay licence fee, annual operating fees, and other applicable fees; – breaches a condition of the licence; – is dissolved or enters into liquidation, bankruptcy, or an arrangement with its creditors;

	Network Facilities Provider (Tier 1)	*Application Services Provider*	*Content Services Provider*
Licence Issue, Revocation, and Renewal	– is dissolved or enters into liquidation, bankruptcy, or an arrangement with its creditors; and – fails to notify CCK of a change in its shareholding, ownership, or control or of a joint venture arrangement.	– fails to notify CCK of a change in its shareholding, ownership, or control or of a joint venture arrangement.	– fails to notify CCK of a change in its shareholding, ownership, or control or of a joint venture arrangement.
Dispute Settlement	The dispute settlement mechanism set out in the Act to apply to any dispute arising from the provisions of the Licence.	The dispute settlement mechanism set out in the Act to apply to any dispute arising from the provisions of the Licence	The dispute settlement mechanism set out in the Act to apply to any dispute arising from the provisions of the Licence

III. Telecommunications Services

170. Part III of the KIC Act makes provisions on telecommunications systems and services. A telecommunication system under the Act means a system for the conveyance, through the agency of electric, magnetic, electromagnetic, electrochemical, or electromechanical energy, of:

- speech, music, and other sounds;
- visual images;
- data;
- signals serving for the impartation (whether as between persons and persons, things and things, or persons and things) of any matter otherwise than in the form of sound, visual images, or data; or
- signals serving for the activation or control of machinery or apparatus including any cable for the distribution of anything falling within the above categories.[122]

171. A telecommunication service, on the other hand, means any of the following:

- a service consisting of the conveyance by means of a telecommunication system of any or all of the categories of the content included in the definition of a telecommunication system above;
- a service consisting of the installation, maintenance, repair, or adjustment of apparatus which is or is to be connected to a telecommunication system; or
- a directory information service, being a service consisting of the provision by means of a telecommunication system of directory information.[123]

172. Part III obliges CA to ensure that there are provided throughout Kenya such telecommunication services and in particular, emergency, public payphone, and directory information services, as are reasonably necessary to satisfy the public demand thereof.[124] In fulfilling this mandate, the Act further obliges CA to:

- protect the interests of all users of telecommunication services in Kenya with respect to the prices charged for and the quality and variety of such services;
- maintain and promote effective competition between persons engaged in commercial activities connected with telecommunication services in order to ensure efficiency and economy in the provision of such services and to promote research and development;
- encourage private investment in the telecommunications sector;
- promote the provision of international transit services by persons providing telecommunication services in Kenya; and

---

122. Section 2.
123. *Ibid.*
124. Section 23(1).

- enable persons providing telecommunication services or producing telecommunication apparatus in Kenya to compete effectively in the provision of such services or apparatus outside Kenya.[125]

173. The Act requires that all persons who operate a telecommunication system or provide any telecommunication services shall do so in accordance with a licence granted under the Act. Contravening this provision is an offence for which a person who is convicted is liable to a fine of up to USD 13,700 or to imprisonment for up to five years, or to both the fine and the term of imprisonment.[126] The licence is to be issued by CA on an application by the prospective licensee and 'subject to such conditions as [CA] may deem necessary'.[127] Some of the conditions under which CA may grant such a licence include, without limitation:

- to provide the telecommunication services specified in the licence or of a description so specified;
- to interconnect to the telecommunication system to which the licence relates, or to permit the connection to such system of such other telecommunication systems and apparatus as are specified in the licence or are of a description so specified, either without charge or subject to a reasonable charge to be determined in accordance with the method specified in the licence;
- to permit the provision by means of the telecommunication system or telecommunication apparatus connected thereto of such services as are specified or of a description so specified;
- to pay such fees as the Commission may prescribe; and
- to fulfil such other conditions as the Commission may prescribe.[128]

174. Once a licence has been granted, CA may renew, vary, modify, or revoke it. The procedure for the application, issue, modification, revocation, and renewal of all licences has been discussed later in the chapter.

175. The Act empowers the Minister for Information and Communications to make regulations generally with respect to telecommunication services, including regulations with respect to:

- the running of telecommunication systems;
- the privacy of telecommunication;
- the provision of telecommunication services and in particular, the manner in which such services shall be offered and performed, the issue of licences and the payment of fees in respect thereof, and such other matters as it deems fit;
- the period during which and conditions subject to which messages and papers relating to telecommunication services belonging to, or in the custody of telecommunication operators shall be preserved;

---

125. Section 23(2).
126. Section 24.
127. Section 25(1).
128. Section 25(3).

- the issue, variation, and withdrawal of approvals in respect of contractors for relevant operations in connection with any telecommunication system and the maintenance of registers of such contractors;
- fees and other charges for any matter permitted or matters required to be done under the Act; and
- the form of any licence, notice, approval, certificate, authority, or other written document required to be issued by or submitted to CA.[129]

176. The contravention of any regulations made by the Minister under this part is an offence punishable by a fine not exceeding USD 4,110 or imprisonment for a term not exceeding three years, or both.[130]

177. The Act creates the nine offences set out in Table 25 with relation to telecommunications services and networks and prescribes the punishments shown against them in the fourth column. As discussed elsewhere in this text, however, one of these offences (section 29) has recently been repealed by the High Court.

129. Section 27(1).
130. Section 27(4).

Table 25 Offences Relating to Telecommunications Networks and Services under the KIC Act

Section of the KIC Act	*Title of Section or Offence*	*Nature of Offence*	*Punishment*
24	*Requirement of a licence*	Operating a telecommunication system or providing a telecommunication service without a licence.	A fine of up to USD 13,700 or imprisonment for up to five years or both the fine and imprisonment.
28	*Dishonestly obtaining a telecommunications service*	Dishonestly facilitating or obtaining a service provided by a person authorized under the Act to provide a telecommunication service with intent to avoid the payment of any charge applicable to the service.	A fine of up to USD 13,700 or imprisonment for up to five years or both the fine and imprisonment.
27(4)	*General regulations for telecommunications services*	Contravention of any regulations made by the Minister under with relation to telecommunications services.	A fine not exceeding USD 4,110 or imprisonment for a term not exceeding three years or both.
34	*Prohibition of unlicensed telecommunication system*	A licensed telecommunications service provider providing a telecommunication service not specified in the licence or connecting the licensed system to any telecommunication system or apparatus not of a description specified in the licence.	A fine not exceeding USD 13,700 or imprisonment for upto three years or both.

Section of the KIC Act	*Title of Section or Offence*	*Nature of Offence*	*Punishment*
29 (Repealed by High Court decision *Geoffrey Andare v. DPP*)	*Improper use of a telecommunications system*	Sending, by means of a licensed telecommunication system: a. A message or other matter that is grossly offensive or of an indecent, obscene or menacing character; or b. a message that the sender knows to be false 'for the purpose of causing annoyance, inconvenience or needless anxiety to another person'.	A fine not exceeding USD 685 or imprisonment for a term not exceeding three months, or both.
30	*Modification of messages*	A person engaged in the running of a licensed telecommunication system, otherwise than in the course of duty, intentionally modifying or interfering with the contents of a message sent by that system.	A fine not exceeding USD 4,110 or imprisonment for a term not exceeding three years or both.
31	*Interception and disclosure*	A licensed telecommunication operator otherwise than in the course of his business – intercepting a message sent through a licensed telecommunication system; or – disclosing to any person the contents of an intercepted message; or – disclosing to any person the contents of any statement or account specifying the telecommunication services provided by means of that statement or account.	A fine not exceeding USD 4,110 or imprisonment for a term not exceeding three years or both.

Section of the KIC Act	*Title of Section or Offence*	*Nature of Offence*	*Punishment*
32	*Tampering with telecommunication plant*	Damaging, removing, tampering with or in any way interfering with any telecommunication apparatus or telecommunication line, post, or other thing whatsoever, being part of or used in or about any licensed telecommunication system or in the use thereof, with intention to: – preventing or obstructing the transmission or to delay any message; or – with the contents of any message; or – committing mischief.	A fine not exceeding USD 1,370 or imprisonment for a term not exceeding three years or both.
33	*Trespass or wilful obstruction of a telecommunications officer*	– Without permission, entering the equipment room of a telecommunications operator; or – entering any enclosure around the telecommunication office in contravention of any rule or notice to the contrary; or – refusing to leave such equipment room or enclosure on being requested to do so by any telecommunication officer; or – wilfully obstructing any such telecommunication officer or a telecommunication operator in the performance of his duty.	A fine not exceeding USD 4,110 or imprisonment for a term not exceeding one year or both.

Source: Kenya Information and Communications Act 2001.

IV. Radio Communications

A. *Meaning of Radio Communications*

178. Under the KIC Act, radio communication means:

> *the emitting or receiving over paths which are not provided by any material substance constructed or arranged for that purpose, of electro-magnetic energy of a frequency not exceeding three million megahertz*[131] *being energy which either: is capable of being transmitted through a telecommunication system; or is used in connection with the determination of position, bearing or distance, or for the gaining of information as to the presence, absence or, motion of any object or objects of any class.*[132]

B. *Scope of Application*

179. The provisions of the Act relating to radio communications apply:

- to all radio communication stations and radio communication apparatus in or over, or for the time being in or over Kenya or the territorial waters adjacent thereto; and
- subject to any limitations which CA may determine through regulations, to all radio communication stations and radio communication apparatus which is released from within Kenya or its territorial waters or from any vessel or aircraft which is registered in Kenya.[133]

C. *Radio Communications Licensing*

180. The Act makes it an offence for a person to establish or use any radio communication station or apparatus except in accordance with the terms of a licence granted under the Act.[134] A radio communication licence is usually a licence authorizing the use of any radio communication station or apparatus or the installation or use of any apparatus for radio communication. Such a licence is granted by CA at its discretion and subject to such terms and conditions as it may deem fit, including, without limitation:

- in the case of a licence to establish a station, limitations as to the position and nature of the station, the purposes for which, the circumstances in which, and the

131. The definition of radio communications as those with a frequency not exceeding 'three million megahertz', although not technically inaccurate, is most likely a typo and should have read 'three hundred thousand megahertz'.
132. Section 2.
133. Section 46.
134. Section 35.

persons by whom the station may be used, and the apparatus which may be imported, installed, or used therein; and
- in the case of any other licence, limitations as to the apparatus which may be installed or used, and the places where, the purposes for which, the circumstances in which and the persons by whom the apparatus may be used.[135]

181. CA's discretion in granting and renewing radio communication licences is taken away with respect to licences for which the applicant seeks for the purpose of conducting experiments in radio communications for scientific research. Once CA is satisfied that the applicant intends to use the licence for that purpose and the applicant has not previously committed any offence under the Act, it is bound by law not to refuse to grant or to renew such a licence and not to revoke it once it has been issued.[136] However, the discretion of CA to impose conditions on the grant or renewal of a licence and to vary such conditions remains unlimited.

D. Regulations on Radio Communications

182. The Act empowers the Minister, acting in consultation with CA, to make regulations generally with respect to radio communication and, without limitation, with respect to:

- the conditions upon which a licence may be granted, renewed, or revoked;
- the licensing fees;
- acts which may or may not be done in connection with the use of a radio communication;
- the conditions under which radio communication apparatus may be kept and maintained;
- imposing on a licensee obligations for the facilitation of the inspection of radio communication apparatus;
- obligations requiring a licensee to keep and produce accounts and records;
- the exhibition at radio communication stations of such notices as may be prescribed;
- the use of radio communication apparatus on board any vessel or aircraft not licensed or registered in Kenya within the limits of Kenya and the territorial waters adjacent to the limits of Kenya;
- controlling the importation, acquisition, manufacture and sale, letting on hire or other disposition of radio communication apparatus;
- the licensing of dealers in radio communication apparatus and the sale, transfer or use of such apparatus;
- the conduct of examinations for radio communication operators, the content of such examination and the issue of certificates of competence in respect thereof; and

135. Section 36.
136. Section 37.

- the issue, variation, and withdrawal of approvals in respect of radio communication stations and radio communication apparatus and apparatus for connection to any telecommunication system licensed under the Act.[137]

E. Use of Interfering Equipment

183. Where CA is of the opinion that any radio communications apparatus does not comply with technical requirements prescribed by it or that either:

- the use of the apparatus is likely to cause undue interference with any radio communication used for any purpose on which the safety of any person or any vessel, aircraft, or vehicle may depend; or
- the use of the apparatus has caused or is causing undue interference with any other radio communication apparatus in circumstances where all reasonable steps to minimize interference have been taken in relation to the situation or apparatus receiving such radio communication.

184. CA may serve on the person who has the possession or control of the apparatus a notice in writing requiring that the apparatus shall not be used or prescribing the terms under which it shall be used.[138]

185. Where such a notice has been issued, the licensee may, whether before or after the expiration of the notice, give notice in writing to CA indicating the reasons why the apparatus in question complies with the requirements applicable to it. Where CA is satisfied with the notice issued by the licence, it may revoke its notice or vary the restrictions imposed on the use of the apparatus. Any question as to whether the apparatus has been made to comply with the requirements of the CA notice shall be settled by the Communications Appeal Tribunal upon the application of the Director General of CA or the person in possession of the apparatus. Any dispute shall, on the application of the Director General or of any person having possession of or any interest in the apparatus, be determined by the Tribunal.[139]

186. The Act makes it an offence to contravene the terms of a notice issued by CA under this part. The particulars of this offence and the other offences created by the Act with relation to radio communications are shown in Table 26.

137. Section 38.
138. Section 41(1).
139. Section 41(2) (3) (4).

Table 26 Offences Relating to Radio Communications under the KIC Act

Section of the KIC Act	*Title of Section or Offence*	*Nature of Offence*	*Punishment*
35	*Licensing requirements*	Using radio communication station or apparatus except in accordance with the terms of a licence granted under section 36 of the Act.	A fine not exceeding USD 68,500 or imprisonment for a term not exceeding three years or both.
41(5)	*Regulations with respect to resistance to interference*	Contravening a notice issued by CCK imposing restrictions on the use of non-compliant communications apparatus or apparatus which interferes with other radio communication used for a safety-of-life service or apparatus which causes undue interference with other radio communication apparatus.	A fine not exceeding USD 6,850 or imprisonment for a term not exceeding three years or both.
44	*Enforcement of regulations as to sales, etc. by manufacturers and others*	Sending or attempting to send, by means of a radio communication, any message the sender knows to be false or misleading and likely to prejudice the efficiency of any safety-of-life service or endanger the safety of any person, or of any vessel, aircraft or vehicle, and, in particular, any message which falsely suggests that a vessel or aircraft is in distress or in need of	A fine not exceeding USD 13,700 or imprisonment for a term not exceeding five years or both.

Section of the KIC Act	*Title of Section or Offence*	*Nature of Offence*	*Punishment*
		assistance or is not in distress or not in need of assistance; or otherwise than under the authority for the Minister in charge of internal security: – using radio communication apparatus with intent to unlawfully obtain information as to the contents, sender, or addressee of a message; – except in the course of legal proceedings or for the purposes of any report thereon, disclosing any information as to the contents, sender, or addressee of any such message, being information which would not have come to his knowledge but for the use of the radio communication.	
45	*Deliberate interference with radio communication*	Using any station or apparatus for interfering with any radio communication.	A fine not exceeding USD 13,700 or imprisonment for a term not exceeding five years or both.

V. Broadcasting Services

A. *Broadcasting Prior to 2009*

187. The licensing and regulation of broadcasting in Kenya has recently become a highly controversial issue. It has resulted in demonstrations by the media and the public, sometimes involving violent confrontations with the police, and a climate of mutual mistrust and suspicion between media operators and the government.

188. Until 2 January 2009 when certain amendments to the KCA of 1998 came into force, Kenya did not have a transparent legal regime for the issuing of broadcasting licences. The Ministry in charge of communications would consider applications for broadcasting permits, and successful applicants would then be referred to CA for the allocation of frequencies. CA's mandate was at that time limited to the regulation of telecommunications, radio communications, and postal services.

1. *Ahmed Rashid Jibril v. East African Television Network Ltd*

189. One case that most aptly demonstrates the inadequacy of this arrangement was *Ahmed Rashid Jibril v. East African Television Network Ltd & 6 others.*[140] The substantive issue of law in this case, namely, the legality of a transfer of shares in a company, belied the fact that the litigation illustrated the political intrigues that were characteristic of a time in Kenya's history when media licences were tightly controlled by the government. The actions that gave rise to the dispute can be traced back to 1998 when the Nation Media Group, one of Kenya's leading daily newspaper publishers, having been unsuccessful in its application for a television broadcasting licence, had indirectly secured for itself a licence by acquiring majority shareholding in a company that had been issued with a licence.

190. To put the dispute into context, the 1990s was a period of great political ferment in Kenya's political history. The call for multi-partyism and public disaffection against the excesses of over three decades of single-party rule climaxed into violent confrontations between civilians and State forces. At the same time, local and international pressure mounted on the Kenyan government to improve its human rights record, particularly, the individual's rights to life, freedom from torture, and the right to assembly and expression. In 1992, the government ceded a constitutional amendment making Kenya a de jure multiparty State, and reluctantly, the government began to relinquish its stranglehold on the basic rights and freedoms of the citizen. It was at this time that Kenya's media began to take some bold steps towards asserting its freedom. In fact, the first cartoon depictions of the then President, Daniel Arap Moi, appeared at this time. However, the regime for the grant of media licences, which was administered by the then Ministry of Transport and

---

140. Civil Case No. 651 of 1998, High Court at Nairobi (Milimani Commercial Courts) – Presided over by Lady Justice Mary Kasango and concluded on 10 Mar. 2006.

Communications through the government's telecoms monopoly, the KPTC, remained tightly controlled and non-transparent.

191. In 1997, the *East African Television Network Ltd (EATN),* a company in which the plaintiff, *Ahmed Rashid Jibril,* and the second and third defendants, Mr and Mrs Sam Shollei, were directors and shareholders, obtained broadcasting licences from the KPTC.

192. In the meantime, Africa Broadcasting Ltd (ABL), which fully owned Nation Printing and Publishing Company, had been unsuccessful in obtaining broadcasting licences ostensibly because it was not regarded with favour by the government.

193. The watershed moment for the dispute was the transfer to ABL of certain shares held in EATN by one of its directors, the second defendant. In the scheme of things, EATN was to be the vehicle through which ABL (and later the Nation Media Group) would enter the electronic media. According to the plaintiff, EATN had been incorporated at the instance of Transnational Bank Ltd, which was the employer of both himself and the second defendant. The Bank had allegedly requested them to subscribe to and become directors of EATN as its trustees and nominees. In that capacity, therefore, the first defendant had no power to sell the shares to his wife (the third defendant), and subsequently to the directors of ABL.

194. For his part, the second defendant gave evidence that EATN was his brainchild and that he had only invited the plaintiff to hold shares in it as his nominee. He further testified that the plaintiff later resigned from EATN and transferred his shares. In 1998, a sale agreement was concluded for the purchase of EATN's 90% shareholding by Africa Broadcasting Network. As part of the agreement, the second defendant was to be the Chairman of the Board of the company. As it turned out, after the sale of shares was announced, the government cancelled EATN's broadcasting licences allegedly because there was a dispute between its directors.

195. The plaintiff, who denied the allegation that he had resigned from EATN, asked the court to declare the sale of EATN's shares null and void and to issue certain orders restraining the defendants from proceeding with the affairs of EATN. The main issues that the High Court was required to determine were whether the plaintiff and the second defendant held their shares in EATN as trustees and nominees of Transnational Bank and whether the transfer of shares had been in conformity with the company's articles of Association.

196. In dismissing the suit, the court (Mary Kasango, J.) held that the plaintiff's share had been lawfully transferred to the third defendant and the third defendant had been duly appointed a director of the EATN. ABL and its directors were purchasers for value without notice of any defect in the second defendant's title to the shares. Having transferred his shares and resigned from the directorship of EATN, the plaintiff had no interest in the company at the time that ABL and its director acquired their shares. The plaintiff was therefore estopped from denying ABL's ownership of shares in EATN.

197. As the Judge remarkably observed:

> *This case, perhaps more than any other, will stand in the annals of history as an example of how Kenya was once ruled by a clique of [a] political elite, and where that elite did not tolerate divergent views and as a consequence, the media was effectively muffled by denial of airways for broadcasting, both in radio and television. This was a case that ought not to have been filed.*

B. Broadcast Licensing after the Kenya Communications (Amendment) Act, 2008

198. The amendments introduced by the Kenya Communications (Amendment) Act, 2008 established CA as a fully fledged regulator for all postal, information, and communication services, including broadcasting. A new Part IVA was inserted in the Act introducing various provisions on broadcasting; including the issuing of broadcasting licences by CA and the terms on which such licences may be issued.

199. Most of the controversy over broadcasting laws centred on section 88 of the KCA, 1998, which gave the government the power to take temporary possession of communication equipment and to restrict the transmission of communication signals under certain circumstances during a national emergency. Even though this provision was part of the Act when it was first passed in 1998, it had not generated as much public debate and near-violent confrontation as it did after the 2008 amendments were published, perhaps because the amendments did not propose to repeal or amend the section. It is also notable that section 88 gave the Minister of Internal Security the power to ban media coverage and reporting of news events, and this power was exercised during the post-election violence in early 2008. Later in 2009, several months after the amendments had been passed by Parliament with section 88 still being part of the law, the government conceded and repealed the section through a supplementary amendment.[141]

200. In its transitional provisions, the amendment provided that CA would respect and uphold the rights of parties previously issued with broadcasting permits by the Minister. However, the holders of the old permits would have a period of one year (expiring on 2 January 2010) to operate under the terms of the old permits. Before the expiry of that period, the transitional provisions required such parties to apply to CA to be licensed under the new provisions of the Act.[142]

---

141. Statute Law (Miscellaneous Amendments) Act, 2009.
142. Section 46R.

1. *Wezan Radio Group Ltd v. CA*

201. In August 2009, these transitional provisions of the Act were tested in a court action filed against CA by a broadcasting investor, Wezan Radio Group Ltd. The action in *Wezan Radio Group Ltd v. Communications Commission of Kenya*[143] was prompted by what Wezan Radio perceived to be a decision by CA to deem the existing permit holders as having complied with the new licensing requirements of the amended law (section 46) even without subjecting them to an evaluation process. The company stated that it had expected that all the old broadcasting permits issued by the Minister prior to the amendment would expire in January 2010 and that in the meantime, CA would put in place an administrative mechanism for evaluating the permit holders afresh along with first-time applicants under the new licensing regime.

202. But had CA made any decision to migrate the existing permit holders without evaluating them? There may not have been any formal decision as such. Wezan Radio instead referred to a newspaper report carried on 21 July 2009 in which the Chairman of CA's Board of Directors, Eng. Phillip Okundi, had reportedly stated at a public event that CA was preparing a mechanism for the regulation of broadcast services in line with the new law and that it expected 'to start migrating existing broadcasters to the new regime starting September this year'.

203. Wezan Radio told the High Court that if CA proceeded to migrate existing broadcasters to the new regime in contravention of the law, all the available frequencies might be taken up before other interested parties such as itself were afforded an opportunity to enter the market. Because the application had been filed under a certificate of urgency, it was heard without the knowledge or the presence of CA. All that Wezan Radio had to demonstrate was that it had an arguable case against CA, who would later be served with the application and accorded an opportunity to defend itself.

204. In her decision, Lady Justice Sitati observed that from the statement attributed to the Chairman of CA, it was not clear whether CA had complied with the KIC Act with regard to the licensing of broadcasters. It was not clear, for instance, if CA had taken account of public interest obligations 'in deciding to migrate the current licence permits to the new regime'. The Judge reiterated that section 46 of the Act placed a heavy burden on CA to apply the due process of the law in considering applications for licences. If CA was to do a wholesale migration of all pre-existing permits to the new regime, the Judge noted, it could not be said that there had been a consideration of the licence application in the manner required under the new law. Therefore, an issue had arisen as to whether CA had properly exercised the powers conferred upon it by the KCA. Wezan Radio had established that it had an arguable case against CA.

143. High Court of Kenya at Nairobi, Miscellaneous Civil Application No. 490 of 2009; R.N. Sitati, J; 27 Aug. 2009.

205. Accordingly, the High Court allowed Wezan Radio to institute Judicial Review proceedings against CA and in the meantime, issued the following interim orders to stand for sixty days:

- the decision of CA purporting to migrate existing television and radio broadcasters from the current provisional legal regime to the new licensing regime without regard to the provisions of the KIC Act and the law governing public procurement was nullified;
- CA was prohibited from 'migrating existing broadcasters to the new regime starting September (2009)' without first complying with the provisions of the law relating to public procurement and the licensing requirements of the KIC Act and from licensing continued broadcasts by any person beyond the 2 January 2010 deadline without the full compliance with those provisions.

206. Wezan Radio was to subsequently file the substantive claim and serve it on CA who would be at liberty to both oppose the claim and to apply for the discharge or non-renewal of the interim orders.

207. This case was an early case in what would become a highly public and controversial process of migrating broadcasting to digital format.

VI. Broadcasting Regulation Provisions of the KIC Act

208. The provisions of the KIC Act relating to broadcasting are contained in Part IVA and in the Kenya Communications (Broadcasting) Regulations, 2009 dated 31 December 2009 and published in Kenya's official Gazette.[144] The regulations were promulgated by Hon. Samuel Poghisio, the Minister for Information and Communications in exercise of his powers under section 46K of the KIC Act. Along with a set of thirteen other pieces of pending subsidiary legislation, the broadcasting regulations were the culmination of a round of legislative drafting and public debate initiatives brought about by the need to update and align subsidiary legislation or ministerial regulations with the new-look KIC Act.

209. The Act provides the following pertinent definitions with relation to broadcasting:

- broadcasting – the unidirectional conveyance of sounds or television programmes, whether encrypted or not, by radio or other means of telecommunications, for reception by the public;
- broadcaster – any legal or natural person who composes or packages or distributes television or radio programme services for reception by the public or sections of the public or subscribers to such a service, irrespective of the technology used;

144. Legal Notice No. 187 of 2009.

- broadcasting service – any service which consists of the broadcasting of television or sound broadcasting programmes to the public, sections of the public, or subscribers to such a service; and
- programme – sound, vision, or a combination of both, intended to inform, educate, or entertain but does not include text or data.[145]

A. Functions of CA

210. The Act provides that the functions of CA in relation to broadcasting services shall be to:

- promote and facilitate the development, in keeping with the public interest, of a diverse range of broadcasting services in Kenya;
- facilitate and encourage the development of Kenyan programmes;
- promote the observance at all times, of public interest obligations in all broadcasting categories;
- promote diversity and plurality of views for a competitive marketplace of ideas;
- ensure the provision by broadcasters of appropriate internal mechanisms for disposing of complaints in relation to broadcasting services;
- protect the right to privacy of all persons; and
- carry out such other functions as are necessary or expedient for the discharge of all or any of the functions conferred upon it under this Act.[146]

B. Classification of Broadcasting Services

211. The Act classifies broadcasting services into three broad service categories:

(1) public broadcasting;
(2) private broadcasting; and
(3) community broadcasting.[147]

212. A further classification is provided for broadcasting service licences into the following classes:

- free-to-air radio;
- free-to-air television;
- subscription radio;
- subscription television;
- subscription management; and
- any other class of licence as may be determined in accordance with the regulations.[148]

145. Section 2.
146. Section 46A.
147. Section 46B(1).
148. Section 46B(2).

213. A free-to-air service is defined as a service that is broadcast without encryption and capable of being received by conventional broadcasting receiving apparatus.[149]

214. On 31 December 2009, the Ministry of Information and Communications published the Kenya Communications (Broadcasting) Regulations, 2009.[150] The bringing into effect of the regulations, which had been strongly opposed by the media, was harshly criticized by both the print and electronic media. The following are the key provisions of the regulations.

C. Licensing Authority

215. The CA is tasked with receiving, publishing, evaluating, and acting on applications by persons wishing to provide broadcasting services in Kenya. The CA is further required to monitor the activities of licensed broadcasters to ensure compliance with all relevant laws and regulations.

D. Fees

216. The CA is tasked with prescribing fees for broadcasting licences, including renewal and transfer of licences. The CA may (although is not required to) exempt public broadcasting services or any other category of broadcaster from payment of fees.

E. Restriction Against Cross-Media Ownership or Concentrations of Media Control

217. The regulations provide that no broadcaster, other than the public broadcaster, shall be directly or indirectly entitled to more than one broadcast frequency or channel for radio and television broadcasting in the same coverage area.[151] However, the proviso to this regulation obliges CA to prescribe a time frame for existing licensed broadcasters to comply with the requirement. A number of licensed broadcasters have multiple licences for national coverage of radio or television broadcasts.

---

149. Section 2.
150. Legal Notice No. 187 of 2009 published vide Kenya Gazette Supplement No. 86 (Legislative Supplement No. 54).
151. The Kenya Communications (Broadcasting) Regulations, 2009, para. 10.

F. Equity Ownership and Control of a Broadcasting Entities

218. A broadcast licensee is required to notify CA 'of any proposed change in ownership, control, or proportion of shares held in it' and any change in shareholding exceeding 15% of the issued share capital or the acquisition by an existing shareholder of at least 5% of additional shares shall require the express consent of CA.[152]

G. Projection of Kenya's Culture and Identity

219. All commercial broadcasters having national coverage are required 'to provide programming that reflects the identity and needs of the people of Kenya'.[153]

H. Licences for Foreign and Subscription Service Broadcasters

220. CA shall, in consultation with the Minister, license foreign commercial broadcasters subject to the availability of frequencies.[154] CA has the discretion to grant licences for subscription broadcasting for satellite, cable, and subscription management services. Such licensee may be required to provide a minimum number of Kenyan channels and diversity in programming. A satellite broadcasting service provider whose signal originates from outside Kenya shall obtain landing rights authorization by the CA to provide its subscription service in Kenya either by directly or through a subscription management service provider.[155]

I. Broadcasting Content Standards

221. A licensee shall ensure that its broadcasts:

- do not contain offensive language, including profanity or blasphemy;
- do not present sexual matters in an explicit and offensive manner;
- do not incite, perpetuate hatred, vilify a person or community on account of race, ethnicity, nationality, gender, sexual preference, age, disability, religion, or culture; and
- are rated in advance by the Kenya Films and Censorship Board.[156]

222. Furthermore, a licensee shall protect children: due care is to be exercised to avoid content that 'may disturb or be harmful to children', that such content is

152. *Ibid.*, para. 10(3).
153. *Ibid.*, para. 12(d).
154. *Ibid.*, para. 12(2).
155. *Ibid.*, para. 14(2).
156. Paragraph 19.

not broadcast outside of the watershed period (between 5.00 a.m. and 10.00 p.m.) and that an interview with a minor shall not be conducted without the consent of the minor's parent's or guardian.[157]

223. Furthermore, a licensee shall provide news coverage: news and information are to be broadcast and presented in an accurate, factual, fair, and balanced manner; that a report is based on fact and where it is not, the report indicates the matter on which it is based; that corrections of errors in reports are broadcast within a reasonable time and 'within a similar time-slot as the original error' and such corrections to include an apology where this is appropriate.[158] A licensee is not to accept sponsorships of news, weather, financial, or traffic reports broadcasts.[159]

224. When broadcasting 'controversial issues of public interest' during live broadcasts, licensees are to ensure that a wide range of opinions are represented and that persons who wish to reply to criticism on such matters are afforded a fair opportunity to do so.[160]

225. Regarding broadcasts during elections or polling periods, a licensee is to give equitable coverage to all political parties and candidates and clearly identify and attribute for the audience the opinion of a political party as such.[161]

226. Regarding advertisements and sponsorships, advertisement broadcasts are to be accurate, lawful, honest, decent, and conforming with the principles of fair competition.[162]

227. The CA may require a licensee to prescribe a minimum amount of time for the broadcasting of local content. However, a broadcaster may have the option of exempting itself from such a requirement by paying a prescribed fee to CA.[163]

228. The CA may prescribe for a broadcaster certain steps for the promotion of access to its programming by persons with hearing and visual disabilities.[164]

229. Finally, the CA shall prescribe a programme code that sets the standards for the time and manner of programming or allow a broadcaster to submit to a programming code prescribed by any registered body of broadcasters.[165]

157. Paragraph 20.
158. Paragraphs 21–23.
159. Paragraph 30.
160. Paragraph 24.
161. Paragraph 25.
162. Paragraph 33.
163. Paragraph 35.
164. Paragraph 36.
165. Paragraph 38.

J. Complaints Procedure

230. Every broadcaster shall develop a procedure for handling complaints by persons who may be aggrieved by its broadcasts. A person who is not satisfied with such procedures may refer a dispute to the CA.[166]

K. Public Emergencies

231. All broadcasters will be obliged to provide notices of public emergencies upon the request of a person authorized by the government and in accordance with guidelines prescribed by CA.[167]

L. Offences and Penalty

232. Any person who contravenes any of the provisions of the regulations commits an offence and upon conviction shall be liable to a fine not exceeding USD 13,700 or to imprisonment for up to three years or to both the fine and imprisonment.[168]

M. Transitional Provisions

233. All persons previously issued with broadcasting permits prior to the commencement of the Kenya Communications (Amendment) Act, 2009 are:

- to apply for broadcast licences to the CA subject to such fees and conditions as the CA may prescribe;
- to retain the radio frequency resources previously assigned to them 'under the same terms and conditions of issuance' provided that the person shall comply with such new terms and conditions as the CA may prescribe;
- to cease to be broadcasters if they fail to apply or to qualify for the new licences;
- if they hold a broadcasting permit and have been assigned more than one frequency for either radio or television broadcasting services in the same broadcast coverage area, to surrender all additional broadcasting frequencies to the CA within a period not exceeding the licence term.[169]

234. The actual implementation of the transition period and Digital Migration are described elsewhere in this chapter.

166. Paragraphs 39 and 42.
167. Paragraph 43.
168. Paragraph 44.
169. Paragraph 46.

VII. General Provisions of Licensing under the KIC Act

235. The Act prescribes the eligibility for licensing and the considerations that go into the granting of a licence. It makes it an offence for any person to provide broadcasting services except in accordance with the terms of a licence issued by CA for that purpose.[170] The following classes of persons are ineligible for the grant of a broadcasting licence:

- political parties;
- persons who have been adjudged bankrupt or who have entered into a composition or scheme of arrangement with their creditors;
- persons of unsound mind; and
- persons who do not fulfil such other conditions as may be prescribed.[171]

236. In considering applications for the grant of a broadcasting licence, CA is obliged to have regard to:

- the observance at all times of public interest obligations in all broadcasting categories;
- diversity and plurality of views for a competitive marketplace of ideas;
- the availability of radio frequency spectrum including the availability of such spectrum for future use;
- efficiency and economy in the provision of broadcasting services;
- demand for the proposed broadcasting service within the proposed broadcast area;
- expected technical quality of the proposed service, having regard to developments in broadcasting technology;
- the suitability, capability, experience, and expertise of the applicant in carrying out the broadcast service;
- financial means and business records, if any, of the applicant; and
- any other relevant matter that CA may consider necessary.[172]

237. Under the broadcasting regulations an applicant for a free-to-air commercial broadcasting services licence is required to furnish to CA 'a business plan' showing the applicant's technical capacity particularly the capacity to provide broadcasting services for at least eight continuous hours in a day, relevant experience and expertise, a programme schedule, and any other information that CA may require.[173]

238. The Act permits CA to include in broadcasting service licences conditions requiring the licensee to:

---

170. Section 46C.
171. Section 46D(1).
172. Section 46D(2).
173. Kenya Communications (Broadcasting) Regulations, 2009 para. 4.

- broadcast in such areas and within such geographical limits as CA may prescribe;
- commit a minimum amount of time as may be prescribed, in its programme schedule to locally produced programmes or, in the alternative, pay such amount of money as may be prescribed, into a Fund to assist the development of the Kenyan production industry;
- pay such fees as CA may prescribe; and
- fulfil such other conditions as CA may require.[174]

A. Public Broadcasting

239. The Act designates the KBC established under section 3 of the KBC Act as the public broadcaster and with the mandate of providing public broadcasting services.[175]

B. Community Broadcasting

240. Under the Act, a community broadcasting service is any broadcasting service which meets all the following requirements:

- is fully controlled by a non-profit entity and carried on for non-profitable purposes;
- serves a particular community;
- encourages members of the community served by it or persons associated with or promoting the interests of such community to participate in the selection and provision of programmes to be broadcast in the course of such broadcasting service; and
- may be funded by donations, grants, sponsorships, or membership fees, or by any combination of these sources.[176]

241. A community broadcasting licence is granted by CA at its discretion and subject to such conditions as it may deem necessary.[177] In considering applications for such licences, CA is to have regard to:

- the community of interests of the persons applying for or on whose behalf the application is made;
- whether the persons, or a significant proportion of them constituting the community, have consented to the application;
- the source of funding for the broadcasting service;
- whether the broadcasting service to be established is not-for-profit; and

174. Section 46C(3).
175. Section 46E.
176. Section 2.
177. Section 46F(1).

– the manner in which members of the community will participate in the selection and provision of programmes to be broadcast.[178]

242. Some of the conditions upon which a broadcasting licence may be granted include obligations for the licensee to:

– ensure that a cross-section of the community is represented in the management of the broadcasting service;
– ensure that each member of the community has a reasonable chance to serve in the management of the broadcasting service;
– ensure that members of the community have a way of making their preferences known in the selection and provision of programmes; and
– conform to any conditions or guidelines as CA may require or issue with regard to such broadcasting service.

243. A list of community broadcasters in Kenya is provided in Table 27.[179]

Table 27 Kenyan Broadcaster Licensees and Their Locations

Licence Holder	*Station*	*Location(s)*
Abeingo FM Networking Self Help Group	West FM	Kakamega
Ata Nayeche FM Radio	Ata Nayeche FM	Kakuma
Koch FM	Koch FM	Nairobi
SIDAREC (Pumwani)	Ghetto FM	Nairobi
Pamoja Development (Kibera)	Pamoja 99.9 FM	Nairobi
St Paul's University (Limuru)	Light FM	Nairobi
Kenyatta University (KU)	KU 99.9 FM	Nairobi
Multimedia University	MMUK	Nairobi
Maseno University	Equator FM	Nairobi
Rware Community Multimedia Centre	Rware CMC	Nyeri
Reto Women Association	Serian 88.9 FM	Maralal
Community Broadcasting Services	Radio Mambo 91.7 FM	Webuye
SDA Baraton University	Baraton University	Kapsabet
Masinde Muliro University	MMUST FM	Kakamega
Daystar University	103.1 Shine FM	Machakos

178. Section 46F(2).
179. Obtained from the Media Council of Kenya, available at http://www.mediacouncil.or.ke/en/mck/index.php/programs/mck-accreditation/kenya-broacasters-2013.

Licence Holder	*Station*	*Location(s)*
Wajir Community Radio Association	Wajir Radio	Wajir
Mang'elete	Radio Mang'elete	Kibwezi
Mau West Development Initiative	Mururi FM	Mt Kenya
Pamoja Development Centre (PADEC)	Pamoja FM	Nairobi
Unjiru TV	UTV	Machakos
Sabaot International Development (SIDO)	BK Radio 98.2 FM	Mt. Elgon
Southern Hills Development Agency	Radio Kaya	Kwale
Bondo CMC	Maendeleo/Sauti FM	Rarieda
Shinyalu Multimedia Centre	Shinyalu FM	Kakamega
Mugambo Telecentre	Mugambo Yetu	Tigania
Konoinia Community	Mtaani Radio	Nairobi
Koinonia Community	Radio Domus	Kajiado
Dominion CMC	Mwenedu FM	Taita

Sources: Othieno Nyanjom 'Factually True, Legally Untrue: Political Media Ownership in Kenya,' Internews, November 2012. Also Peter Oriare, Rosemary Okello Orlale & Wilson Ugangu '*The Media We Want: The Kenya Media Vulnerabilities Study*,' Friedrich Ebert Stiftung, Nairobi, 2010.

C. Private Broadcasting Services

244. A private broadcasting licensee may be required, as part of the conditions for the grant of the licence, to, among other things, provide coverage in geographic areas specified by CA and in the case of television, including drama, documentaries, and children's programmes that reflect a Kenyan theme.[180]

D. Programme Code

245. CA has the power to set standards concerning the time and the manner of programmes to be broadcast by licensees and more particularly, to prescribe and enforce a programming code and a watershed period programming when large numbers of children are likely to be watching programmes.[181] However, where a licensee is a member of a body which has proved to the satisfaction of CA that its

180. Section 46G.
181. Section 46H(1).

members subscribe and adhere to a programming code enforced by that body and provided also that the programming code has been filed with and accepted by CA,[182] that licensee is to be exempted from the provisions of CA's programming code.

246. The CAK has created a Programme Code[183] that entered into force on 1 July 2016[184] and sets the standards for time and manner of programmes to be broadcast in compliance with section 36 of The KIC (Broadcasting) Regulations 2009.

E. Responsibilities of Broadcasters

247. All licensed broadcasters are required to:

- provide responsible and responsive programming that caters for the varied needs and susceptibilities of different sections of the Kenyan community;
- ensure that Kenyan identity is developed and maintained in programmes;
- observe standards of good taste and decency;
- gather and present news and information accurately and impartially;
- when controversial or contentious issues of public interest are discussed, make reasonable efforts to present alternative points of view, either in the same programme or in other programmes within the period of current interest;
- respect the rights of individuals to their privacy;
- respect copyright and neighbouring rights in respect of any work or material;
- keep a programme log or machine-readable record of its programming for a period of one year after the date of broadcasting;
- ensure that advertisements, either in terms of content, tone, or treatment, are not deceptive or are not repugnant to good taste;
- ensure that derogatory remarks based on ethnicity, race, creed, colour, and sex are not broadcast;[185] and
- where a cinematograph film has been submitted for classification or censorship, not broadcast such a film contrary to the conditions given by the Kenya Film and Censorship Board[186]for the broadcasting of such a film.

F. Revocation of Licenses

248. CA may revoke a broadcasting licence where the licensee:

- is in breach of the provisions of the Act or any regulations made under it;

182. Section 46H(2).
183. *See* https://www.article19.org/data/files/medialibrary/38333/Kenya-Programme-Code-analysis-April-2016-Final.pdf.
184. *See* https://www.kts.co.ke/new-programing-code-for-broadcasters-to-be-on-force/.
185. Section 46I(1)(2).
186. Established under the Films and Stage Plays Act (Ch. 222 of the Laws of Kenya).

- is in breach of the conditions of a broadcasting licence; or
- fails to use the broadcasting frequencies assigned to it by CA within one year after their assignment.[187]

G. Regulations on Broadcasting

249. The Minister may, in consultation with the CA, make regulations generally with respect to all broadcasting services and, without limitation, with respect to:

- the facilitation, promotion, and maintenance of diversity and plurality of views for a competitive marketplace of ideas;
- the financing and broadcast of local content;
- mandating the carriage of content, in keeping with public interest obligations, across licensed broadcasting services; and
- prescribing anything that may be prescribed under the Act.[188]

H. Complaints Procedure

250. All broadcasters are required to establish and maintain a procedure by which persons aggrieved by any broadcast or who allege that a broadcaster is not complying with this Act may file complaints.[189] The procedure is to be submitted to CA for prior approval. The complaints should be filed in writing within thirty days of the breach complained against and should set out the grounds upon which they are based, the nature of damage or injury suffered as a result of the broadcast or the violation complained of and the remedy sought.[190]

251. A complainant who is not satisfied with the remedy offered or action taken under the licensee's complaint procedure may appeal to CA.[191] A person who is aggrieved by a decision of CA may appeal to the Communications Appeal Tribunal within thirty days after the decision.[192]

I. Signal Distribution Services

252. CA may also upon application grant a licence authorizing a person to provide signal distribution services upon such terms and conditions as it may deem necessary.[193] It is an offence to provide a signal distribution service without a licence

187. Section 46J.
188. Section 46K.
189. Section 46L.
190. Section 46L(4).
191. Section 46L(2)(3).
192. Section 46L(2)(3)(5).
193. Section 46O(1).

or where a licence has been granted, to provide such a service contrary to the terms of the licence.[194] A signal distribution licence granted may require the licensee to:

- provide signal distribution services as a common carrier to broadcasting licensees;
- provide services promptly upon request, in an equitable, reasonable, non-preferential, and non-discriminatory manner;
- provide capability for a diversity of broadcast services and content;
- provide an open network that is interoperable with other signal distribution networks;
- comply with any other conditions that the Commission may determine; and
- where the licensee is utilizing a frequency resource, to comply with conditions as to the nature and location of transmitters and their transmission characteristics.[195]

253. CA may revoke a signal distribution licence if the licensee:

- is in breach of this Act or regulations made under it;
- is in breach of the conditions of a licence; and
- fails to commence operations within the period prescribed by CA.[196]

J. Broadcasting Content Advisory Council

254. The Act establishes a Broadcasting Content Advisory Council (BCAC) and mandates it with the responsibility of making decisions on:

- the administration of the broadcasting content aspects and provisions of the Act;
- the mechanisms for handling complaints relating to broadcasting services;
- monitoring compliance with broadcasting codes and ethics for broadcasters; and
- such other functions and powers as the Board of the Council may determine.[197]

255. The BCAC was disbanded in January 2014 following the enactment of The KIC (Amendment) Act 2013.[198] The KIC 2009 was amended to align the Act to provisions set out in Article 34 of the Constitution of Kenya. The KIC (Amendment) Act 2013 establishes the Broadcast Standards Committee (BSC) with a mandate to set broadcasting standards.[199]

256. Table 28 outlines broadcasting offences defined in the KIC Act and the punishments prescribed for them.

---

194. Section 46N.
195. Section 46O(2)(3).
196. Section 46P.
197. Section 46S(1)(2).
198. Regulation of Media: Comparative Analysis of Regulation of Broadcasting Services in Kenya, Jackline A. Okore.
199. Section 7.

Table 28 Offences Relating to Broadcasting Services under the KIC Act and Regulations

Section of the KIC Act/ Regulations	*Title of Section or Offence*	*Nature of Offence*	*Punishment*
46C	*Requirement of a licence*	Providing a broadcasting service without a licence or contrary to the terms of a licence.	A fine not exceeding USD 13,700 or imprisonment for a up to five years or both.
46(4)	*Interfering with signal distribution equipment*	A signal distribution licensee changing the location or transmission characteristics of equipment prescribed by CCK.	A fine not exceeding USD 13,700 or imprisonment for a term not exceeding three years or both.
46N(1)	*Signal distribution*	Providing signal distribution services within Kenya or from Kenya to other countries contrary to the terms of a signal distribution licence.	A fine not exceeding USD 13,700 or imprisonment for a term not exceeding three years or both
46Q	*Unlicensed broadcasting service*	Providing a broadcasting service without a broadcasting licence. Where a person has obtained a broadcasting licence: – provides a broadcasting service which is not of a description specified in the licence; – provides a broadcasting service in an area for which he is not licensed to broadcast; or – broadcasts in contravention of the Act or the licence conditions.	A fine not exceeding USD 13,700 or imprisonment for a term not exceeding three years or both.

Section of the KIC Act/ Regulations	*Title of Section or Offence*	*Nature of Offence*	*Punishment*
Kenya Communications (Broadcasting) Regulations, regulation 44	*Offences and penalty*	Contravening any provision of the regulations	A fine not exceeding USD 13,700 or to imprisonment for a term not exceeding three years or both.

Source: Kenya Information and Communications Act 2001.

K. Uptake and Monitoring of ULF Licensees

257. Uptake of the ULF licensing regime has been brisk. The CA maintains and periodically publishes a register of ULF licensees. Table 29 provides the categories of licensees as well as the number of licensees in each category as provided in the March 2017 register.

Table 29 Categories of Licensees[1]

Category of Licensee	*Number of Licensees Listed*
International gateway operators	13
Submarine cable landing rights operators	3
Network facilities provider Tier 1	3
Network facilities provider Tier 2	24
Network facilities provider Tier 3	24
Application service providers	192
Content service providers	304
Business process outsourcing service providers	24
Telecommunications contractors	463
Telecommunications technical personnel	433
Telecommunication equipment vendors	440
Public communication centres	14
Dot ke subdomain name registrar services provider	52

1. Register of ULF Licensees, March 2017.

258. CA continues under the current legal and regulatory framework to monitor the use of spectrum and the activities of broadcasters. For example, the CA issued various notices to a local broadcaster, Royal Media Services Ltd (RMS), in 2012. One of the notices read, in part: '[various] frequencies are being operated without a licence and therefore, in contravention of the law. The current users of these resources are hereby served with a 30 day notice to surrender the frequencies, failing which CCK shall take the necessary action at its disposal.'[200] A second notice read, in part: 'despite being asked to correct the frequency assignment condition anomalies, Royal Media has not taken any action. In this regard, you are required to take corrective measures … to ensure that you install the band pass filters, obtain Type Approval for your transmitters, shut down unauthorised stations and relocate to the designated broadcast sites.'[201]

259. In response to the notices, RMS sued the government, claiming (among other things) that the letters contained false accusations, and further claiming that the CA had acted improperly in allocating frequencies to broadcasters. Specifically, RMS cited two instances of 'mischievous purported allocations': (1) that CCK allocated the frequency 94.3 MHz, thereby interfering with Royal Media's frequency 94.2 MHz; and (2) that CCK allocated another broadcaster frequency No. 100.5 MHz thereby interfering with Royal Media's broadcasts in Kisumu at 104.4 MHz.[202]

260. The court held that the CA (formerly CCK) was properly constituted and empowered to carry out its statutory responsibilities including regulation over broadcasting and other electronic media pursuant to the KIC Act (until such time as parliament establishes the body contemplated under Article 34(5) of the constitution), and that it was not in bad faith that the CA continued to carry out its regulatory function despite the fact that the institution contemplated was not yet established.[203]

261. The court also held that the various letters and notices sent to RMS were not in contravention of the Royal Media's rights protected by Articles 34, 40, and 47 of the Constitution as they were in the nature of notices that afford RMS to show cause why regulatory action should not be taken against it.[204]

262. Hence the court held that regulatory action, which entitles RMS to due process, was not a violation of the Constitution nor did such action interfere with its fundamental rights and freedoms of the petitioner. The petition was thus dismissed.[205] This case, known as *Royal Media Services Ltd & 2 others v. Attorney General & 8 others*, addressed a variety of issues in the ICT sector and is described in more detail later in this chapter.

---

200. *Royal Media Services Ltd v. Attorney General*, Minister of Information & Broadcasting & Communication Commission of Kenya [2013] eKLR.
201. *Id.*
202. *Id.*
203. *Id.*
204. *Id.*
205. *Id.*

VIII. Digital Broadcasting and Digital Migration

263. Digital broadcasting has emerged as a globally accepted standard for next-generation mass media. It presents a method of relaying radio and television signals with various advantages over analogue broadcasting. It enables a more efficient use of bandwidth and the bundling of multiple channels in one frequency. Moreover, digitally broadcast images, video, and audio have a higher quality than their analogue counterparts. The transition from signal to digital broadcasting is arguably the most significant technological cross-over for television and is only closely rivalled, if not slightly surpassed, by the invention of colour television.[206]

264. In the Regional Radio Conference organized by the ITU in Geneva in 2006, a digital broadcasting plan was established for Africa, Middle East, the republics comprising the former Soviet Union, and Europe. Various countries, including Kenya, committed themselves to a series of time-bound events culminating in a complete switchover from analogue to digital broadcasting. The original deadline for analogue switch-off (ASO) according to the ITU timetable was 17 June 2015.

265. In the National ICT Policy released in 2006, the government of Kenya expressed its commitment 'to promote the introduction and uptake of digital broadcasting in the country by managing the transition from analogue to digital broadcasts'.[207] To plan the digital migration process, the government established, in March 2007, a committee of experts and stakeholders in the broadcasting industry known as the Taskforce on the Migration of Terrestrial Television from Analogue to Digital Broadcasting. The Taskforce conducted a study on the appropriate approach that Kenya should take in transiting from analogue to digital broadcasting and presented its report to the Ministry in July 2007.

266. The key recommendations of the report were as follows.

A. *Digital Broadcasting Standards*

267.
- The Digital Video Broadcasting (DVB) family of standards should be adopted in Kenya for digital television broadcasting in accordance with the decisions taken at the 2006 Regional Radio Conference.
- The Terrestrial-Digital Audio Broadcasting (T-DAB) standard should be adopted as the standard for digital sound broadcasting in Kenya.
- The introduction of DVB and DAB services in Kenya should be made through licensed signal distributors.

---

206. R. Tadayoni & T Kristensen, 'Solving the Information Problems of the Digital Age?', paper presented at the Internet Society (ISOC) INET '99 Conference (San Jose, California, USA, June 1999).
207. Paragraphs 4.7, 21.

B. Signal Distribution

268.
- Based on the government's decision to license the national broadcaster, KBC, as a signal distributor, KBC is to form an independent company to run the signal distribution services in order to avoid conflict of interests or cross-subsidies.
- Licensed broadcasters to be allowed to form an independent company to run the signal distribution services in order to utilize their existing infrastructure.
- Existing broadcasters who own infrastructure to negotiate commercial terms with the licensed signal distribution provider for transfer of ownership of the infrastructure.

C. Broadcasting Content

269. The government is to:

- promulgate an appropriate policy on the access, use, and distribution of content in the diverse digital service environment;
- establish a body entrusted with the responsibility of promoting diverse content development by providing financial and other support to the local content development industry;[208] and
- streamline the development and supervision of curriculum used in the media training institutions.

270. For regulating the content and behaviours of the media in Kenya, the Media Council of Kenya (MCK) was established by the Media Council Act 2013. Specifically, the objectives of the MCK include:

- promote the freedom and independence of the media and protect the rights and privileges of journalists in performing their duties;
- prescribe standards of journalists and journalism, including ethical and professional standards, professional education, and training;
- set and regulate ethical and disciplinary standards for journalists; and
- establish and monitor media standards.[209]

271. In addition to the MCK, broadcast content in Kenya is monitored and regulated by the Kenya Film Classification Board (KFCB), which was created by amendment in 2009 of the Films and Stage Plays Act 1962. The KFCB has the following specific objectives:

- regulate the creation, broadcasting, possession, distribution, and exhibition of films by examining films and posters submitted under the act for the purpose of

208. As discussed previously, the Broadcasting Content Advisory has been created under the KIC Act.
209. Media Council Act 2013, s. 6.

classification, imposing age restrictions, and giving consumer advice on the appropriateness of content for various groups; and
- license and issue certificates to distributors and exhibitors of films.[210]

D. Policy and Regulatory Issues in the Transition to Digital Broadcasting

272.
- existing analogue terrestrial broadcasting service to migrate to digital transmission networks based on their own commercial strategy and economic considerations;
- the government to establish a multi-stakeholder working group to coordinate the migration process and set aside funds to cater for the migration;
- Kenya to adopt either a policy-driven approach on the transition to digital broadcasting with a firm nationwide switch-off date or a phased switch-off of analogue services within a period of three years;
- the government to ensure the availability of affordable digital receivers and set-top boxes through fiscal measures;
- the Kenya Bureau of Standards (KEBS) and CA to define the minimum standards for set-top boxes to be used in Kenya;
- importation of analogue-only TV receivers should not be allowed after 2012 in preparation for the ASO deadline of 2015;
- upon switch off of television broadcasting transmitters, the frequency assignments to broadcasters to be revoked by CA and frequencies to no longer be assigned to broadcasters once signal distributors are in place; and
- the regulator to ensure that signal distributors provide services to broadcasters promptly on request.

E. Consumer Issues

273. The government is to institute measures that protect the consumers of broadcasting services in ensuring that their access to quality broadcasting equipment and services is not adversely affected by the migration to digital broadcasting. Some of these measures are to include:

- conduct a public information campaign on digital broadcasting;
- a phased switchover strategy including a voluntary switching phase;
- a working group to receive, process, and respond to consumer concerns;
- providing consumer welfare-oriented incentives to broadcasters; and
- offer tax incentives and other regulatory controls to ensure the affordability of digitally compliant equipment and to prevent the dumping of obsolete equipment in Kenya.

210. Films and Stage Plays Act, s. 15.

274. To facilitate the deployment of the digital infrastructure and generate greater content, the CA (then CCK) developed a new broadcasting licensing framework that unbundled content from distribution and created two categories of licences – content licences and Broadcasting signal distribution (BSD) licences. The government viewed this new 'unbundled' licensing framework as a means to reduce market entry barriers and operating costs for broadcasters, as certain licensors would no longer need to deploy and operate expensive networks, such as television transmitters and associated infrastructure, or acquire spectrum.[211]

275. Initially, Kenya set a target of 2012 as the year when the migration was to be completed – i.e., the transmission of all analogue digital signals was to cease. This date was well ahead of the 2015 deadline set by the International Telecommunications Union (ITU).

276. Then, on 9 December 2009, Kenya became the second African country (after the Republic of South Africa) to start the official transmission of digital broadcasting signals as a step towards the complete migration of all analogue broadcasts to digital broadcasting. The launch of digital broadcasting was presided over by President Mwai Kibaki at the Digital Terrestrial Video Broadcasting Centre at KBC and marked the beginning of a period of simultaneous transmission of digital and analogue broadcasts in the country.

277. Despite the multi-year period of advance notice, the cross-over to digital broadcasting would prove to be contentious. Legal challenges began to surface as the 2012 deadline for ASO approached. Ultimately these challenges were decided in the Supreme Court of Kenya, and the path to that decision is provided in the following case description.

Royal Media Services Limited & 2 others v. Attorney General & 8 others

Parties (in the original case before the High Court):

278.

- Petitioners: 1. Royal Media Services Ltd, 2. Nation Media Services Ltd, and 3. Standard Media Group Ltd.
- Respondents: 1. The Attorney General, 2. Ministry of Information, Communications, and Technology, 3. Communications Commission of Kenya, 4. Signet Kenya Ltd, 5. Star Times Media Ltd, 6. Pan African Network Group Kenya Ltd, and 7. GO TV Kenya Ltd.
- Interested Parties: 1. Consumer Federation of Kenya (COFEK) and 2. West Media Ltd.

211. Telecommunications Management Group Inc., Digital Migration Process in Kenya, January 2017, p. 6.

279. The initial case in the High Court of Kenya[212] related to the nature and extent of the freedom of the media protected under Article 34 of the Constitution of Kenya 2010 and whether it had been violated by the respondents in the context of the migration of terrestrial television broadcasting from the analogue to the digital platform.

280. The petitioners were Kenyan broadcasting companies that collectively controlled 85% of television coverage in the country and that had not been issued BSD licences. The first three respondents are bodies of the state, while the 4th and 6th respondents were companies that had been granted BSD licences by the CA. Other respondents included the holder of a temporary licence for a broadcast subscription management service, a television broadcaster in Kenya, and a media company licensed to broadcast by the CA.[213]

281. At first, the CA awarded only one BSD licence to Signet, a newly created subsidiary of the public broadcaster, KBC. After roll-out was delayed and funding was insufficient, the government opened a competitive tender process and awarded a second licence to Pan African Network Group (PANG), a private Chinese owned entity.

282. From the petition, the court identified three issues:

(i) whether and to what extent the petitioners were entitled to be issued with BSD licences by the CA, and whether issuance of the licences to the other licensees to the exclusion of the petitioners was a violation of Articles 33 and 34 of the Constitution;
(ii) whether implementation of the digital migration constituted a violation of the petitioners' fundamental rights and freedoms and, if so, whether the process should be stopped, delayed, or varied in order to vindicate or ameliorate the petitioners' fundamental rights; and
(iii) whether, as regards the 4th, 5th, 6th, and 7th respondents, they have breached and/or violated the petitioners' IPR.[214]

283. The court determined that the issues had to be resolved bearing in mind that digital migration occurs within a global context, and the process is implemented through a framework established by the International Telecommunication Union Convention, which Kenya ratified in 1964.[215]

---

212. *Royal Media Services Ltd & 2 others v. Attorney General & 8 others* [2013] eKLR, Petition No. 557 of 2013.
213. Justine Limpitlaw, Media Law Handbook for Eastern Africa-volume 2 (Konrad-Adenauer-Stiftung Regional Media Programme: Sub-Saharan Africa, 2016, 437).
214. *Communications Commission of Kenya & 5 others v. Royal Media Services Limited & 5 others* [2014] eKLR.
215. *Royal Media Services Ltd and Others v. Attorney and Others* [2013] eKLR.

284. The High Court held that Petitioners were not entitled to be issued with BSD licences merely on the basis of their established status, or on the basis of legitimate expectation on their part and further, that the implementation of the digital migration was not a violation of the petitioners' fundamental rights and freedoms. Finally, the Court held that the petitioners had not established that their IPR had been infringed.[216] The petition was dismissed.

285. The Petitioners in the High Court appealed the ruling to the Court of Appeals. A panel of three judges of the Court of Appeal delivered separate but largely concurring judgments setting aside the judgment of the High Court and issuing a number of orders:

(i) That the CA's direction to the 4th, 5th, 6th, and 7th respondents to air the appellant's free-to-air programmes without their consent was a violation of the appellant's IPR and was declared null and void.
(ii) In its composition at the material time, the CA (then CCK) was not the independent body envisaged by Article 34(3)(b) of the Constitution, and consequently its public procurement process of determining applications for BSD licences was null and void, and that an independent body constituted strictly in accordance with the above constitutional article should conduct the tendering process afresh.
(iii) That a BSD licence was to be issued to the appellants upon their meeting the terms and conditions set out in the appropriate law and applicable to other licensees, in view of their massive investment in the broadcasting industry.
(iv) That the BSD licence issued to the 6th respondent was null and void and that the CA should refund whatever fees it was paid for the licence.
(v) That the 2nd and 3rd respondents were restrained from switching off the appellants' analogue frequencies, broadcast spectrums, and broadcasting services and that the new switch-off date should be no later than 30 September 2014.[217]

286. Parties from both sides filed appeals in the Supreme Court of Kenya. In a landmark ruling, the Supreme Court reversed the Court of Appeals and held the following:

(i) The annulment of the issuance of a BSD licence to PANG Kenya Ltd by the CA was set aside.
(ii) The order by the Court of Appeal directing the independent regulator to issue a BSD licence to the 1st, 2nd, and 3rd respondents was set aside.
(iii) The CA was required to consider the merits of applications for a BSD licence by the 1st, 2nd, and 3rd respondents, and any other local private sector actors in the broadcast sector, whether singularly or jointly, within ninety days of the judgment.

---

216. *Communications Commission of Kenya & 5 others v. Royal Media Services Limited & 5 others* [2014] eKLR.
217. *Ibid.*

(iv) The CA was to ensure that the BSD licence issued to the 5th appellant be duly aligned to constitutional and statutory imperatives.

(v) The CA, in consultation with all the parties to this suit, had to set timelines for the digital migration, pending the international ASO date of 17 June 2015.[218]

287. The Supreme Court of Kenya further upheld the constitutionality of the CA as the appropriate authority for issuing broadcasting licences under Article 34(3). This, it was held, follows from the Constitution's supremacy clause, which provides a formula by which old legislation would transit into the new constitutional dispensation without creating a vacuum.[219]

288. In its conclusion, proposal and orders, the court signalled certain directions that will have bearing on constitutional initiatives by other agencies of governance, including the following:

(i) The CA was urged to ensure that the sale of set -top boxes was open to competition to avoid creating a monopoly or duopoly. Towards this end, the CA could consider incorporating subsidizing the cost of set -top boxes as part of the requirement for signal distribution licensees.

(ii) The CA must realign operations and licensing procedures to be in tune with Articles 10, 34, and 227 of the Constitution.

289. In the aftermath of the legal actions surrounding digital migration, the final phase of ASO was completed in 2015, just ahead of the deadline of 17 June 2015. The migration ultimately resulted in an increase in population coverage as well as an increase in the number of channels offered to viewers.[220]

290. Kenya's experience in digital broadcasting migration can be examined in the context of the experiences of other East African countries. Whereas Rwanda and Tanzania missed their targeted ASO dates by a mere three months, both Kenya and Uganda experienced a delay of three years. Furthermore, whereas no major court cases were observed in Rwanda and Tanzania, major challenges to the legality of the ASO process were lodged in Uganda and Kenya.[221] These differences are not surprising when viewed through the lens of the different systems of governance. Rwanda and Tanzania have a far greater degree of centralized planning compared with Uganda and Kenya, where the actions of the government are routinely challenged by the private sector.

218. *Ibid.*

219. Justine Limpitlaw, *Media Law Handbook for Eastern Africa-volume 2* (Konrad-Adenauer-Stiftung Regional Media Programme: Sub-Saharan Africa), 2016, 440.

220. 'Digital Migration Process in Kenya,' GSMA Spectrum Report, January 2017.

221. *Ibid.*

§4. Conclusion

291. Kenya has an open-market regulatory framework for its ICT industry that is policed by the CA, the converged multi-sector regulator for telecommunications, broadcasting, ICT, and postal services. The Ministry of Information and Communications, under which the CA operates, has promulgated the ULF, a new technology-neutral licensing regime that brings ICT regulation abreast with changing technology and is helping Kenya to leverage on ICT as a key driver of economic gain. The Ministry especially has been very active in passing or championing legislation, regulations, and policies that allow ICT to remain a driving force in social, economic, and political development.

292. Reform of the legal regime is still a work in progress, with a new ICT Policy and further legislation (especially in cybersecurity but also potentially in data protection and privacy) expected within the next year. Compared with a majority of other African countries, Kenya's regulatory regime is highly advanced and arguably provides a favourable environment for the growth of ICT, particularly e-commerce and e-government.

Chapter 2. Regulation of Competition in the ICT Market

§1. Introduction

293. Kenya has both an all-encompassing general regulation on fair competition contained in the Competition Act (Chapter 504 of the Laws of Kenya) (hereinafter referred to as 'The Competition Act'), which was enacted in 2010, as well as sector-specific statutory and subsidiary legislation on fair competition for the ICT industry contained in the KIC Act, 1998 and its regulations and subsidiary legislations. It may, therefore, be said that Kenya's ICT industry is subject to two regimes of fair competition law. The CAK, created under the Competition Act, appears to be taking a more active role as compared with its predecessor, the office of the Prices and Monopolies Commissioner, in regulating competition across all sectors.

294. There is currently no publicly available framework for guiding the duality of roles of the CA and the CAK, and stakeholders in the ICT sector must account for potential action by either or both regulators. Is regulation and promotion of competition in the ICT sector ultimately the responsibility of the CA or the CAK, or both? If both, what are the limitations of each, and how are conflicts to be resolved? The ICT sector joins a growing list of sectors, including banking and gambling, where the presence of dual regulatory authorities gives rise to such questions.

295. Kenya's situation is not unique or necessarily anomalous, and the answers to these questions lay in the unique nature of the ICT market and the complexities of economics and regulation. Traditionally, in many parts of the world, telecommunications was the monopoly of State-owned entities, such as the KPTC in Kenya and British Telecom in the UK. The 1980s–1990s ushered in the era of privatization. The newly privatized entities were forced to become more efficient by their exposure to market competition. However, concerns arose about residual monopolistic power – the incumbent State monopolies often controlled 100% of the market and have the benefit of economies of scale as well as privileged rights of way in public and private places. It was, therefore, feared that the entities would abuse these advantages and take undue advantage of consumers while making it difficult for new operators to enter the market. The need for their regulation, therefore, arose in part to prevent monopolistic abuses and anticompetitive behaviour.

296. Walden and J. Angel[222] identify two main factors justifying a separate regulatory regime for the telecommunications industry. First, from the standpoint of new operators, the market has very steep barriers to entry. It is expensive for a new operator to enter and set up its own network, even if certain portions of existing infrastructure are shared among operators. Second, all the operators are dependent on each other for the completion of each other's calls.

222. I. Walden & J. Angel, *Telecommunications Law & Regulation* (London: Blackstone Press, 2001).

297. Two additional factors may be relevant to the Kenyan situation. The first is the fact that a newly liberalized ICT market is particularly predisposed to market failure; in Kenya, oligopolistic tendencies by new market entrants mean that the normal market forces of supply and demand do not necessarily secure the benefits of competition for the consumer. Second, a sector-specific regulator is able to accumulate and apply sector-specific knowledge and expertise better than a general competition regulator. These factors, coupled with the existence of a dominant incumbent fixed telephone operator, greatly influence the manner in which competition law is applied in telecommunications. This has given rise to special obligations in the nature of competition rules which may be imposed exclusively on operators in the telecommunications market.

298. The powers of a telecommunications regulator are primarily as follows: licensing, that is, giving of authority to construct, operate, and supply telecoms equipment, networks, and services; management of electromagnetic spectrum; the resolution of disputes between operators (or in certain instances between operators and consumers); and consumer protection.

299. Walden and Angel give the different kinds of models that countries have applied in creating their telecommunications regulator. The US' Federal Communications Commission (FCC) is an autonomous quasi-judicial commission. Kenya and the UK, however, have preferred the model of an independent official or office outside a government ministry – CA and the office of the Director General of Telecommunications, respectively. Post-och Telestyrelsen (PTS) of Sweden is an independent office or official inside a government ministry, and in Romania, the regulator is a government ministry. Incidentally, New Zealand is the only example of a jurisdiction that achieved the liberalization of its telecommunications market solely through the application of traditional competition law.

300. Ultimately, the mandate of a sector-specific industry regulator is likely to be, at least in part, complementary to that of a general competition regulator. Perhaps the mutual powers of the two regulators may be optimized by a framework of cooperation that leaves the sector-specific regulator to handle competition issues unique to the industry, for instance, such as interconnection, co-location, and number portability, while the general competition regulator concerns itself with overarching competition issues such as anticompetitive agreements and practices, joint ventures and mergers, and the concentrations of economic power in one or a few operators manifested in incidents of abuse of dominance.[223] Arguably, once a newly liberalized ICT industry matures into a fully competitive market, the forms of regulatory intervention required will shift, again at least in part, from the sector-specific regulator to the general competition regulator.

223. For instance in July 2008, the Minster for Finance, acting under the Restrictive Trade Practices, Monopolies and Price Control Act, authorized two takeovers involving companies operating in the ICT industry: Lion Cable Television Network Ltd by Wananchi Online Ltd and Trunking Systems Ltd by Wilife Network Ltd and Richard William Bell – *See* Notice No. 5969 Kenya Gazette Vol. CX No. 53 and Notice No. 6848 Vol. CX No. 61.

§2. HISTORICAL BACKGROUND

301. Prior to Kenya's attainment of self-rule in June 1963 and full independence on 12 December 1963, the degree of industrialization and liberalization of the economy was rudimentary.[224] Most consumer items such as sugar, fats, razor blades, *pangas* (farm machetes), and *jembes* (digging hoes), which were needed by the settler community were imported from the UK. In Kenya itself, the interests of the consuming settlers were protected through a regime of price control under the Price Control Act of 16 October 1956.[225]

302. Thereafter, Kenya embarked on a process of rapid industrialization and indigenization of the economy on the attainment of independence on 12 December 1963 through the setting up of import substitution industries to meet Kenyan and EAC requirements and the transfer of non-citizen firms to Kenyans. To this end, the independent administration of Kenya enacted the Trade Licensing Act[226] which legalized the takeover of non-citizen firms by Kenyans through a restrictive system of issuing Trading Licences to certain Trades and Businesses. Through Legal Notice No. 303 of 1964 under the Imports, Exports and Essential Supplies Act,[227] the administration also legalized the control of the importation and exportation of goods of any description and the control of supplies essential to the life or well-being of the community.[228]

303. Briefly, therefore, the commercial activities of Kenya were regulated mainly through instruments provided under the Price Control Act, the Trade Licensing Act, and Imports, Exports and Essential Supplies Act. These instruments included:

– fixing prices of certain goods and services;
– transfer of certain businesses from non-citizens to citizens of Kenya;
– establishment of imports substitution industries;
– imports and exports licensing;
– establishment of import quotas for certain goods;
– complete banning of imports of certain goods;
– letters of 'No Objection' to trading in certain goods;
– allocation of foreign exchange; and

224. For a thorough background of competition law in Kenya, *see*, e.g., Mudida, Robert; Ndiritu, S. Wagura & W. Ross, Thomas. 'Kenya's New Competition Policy Regime'. *World Competition* 38(3) (2015): 437–462, and the referenced cited therein.
225. Peter Muchoki Njoroge, 'Enforcement of Competition Policy and Law in Kenya Including Case Studies in the Areas of Mergers and Takeovers, Prevention of Possible Future Abuse of Dominance and Collusion/Price Fixing' (2004), 3, available at www.ifc.org/ifcext/fias.nsf/AttachmentsByTitle/Conferences_CompetitionPolicyTanz_Peter%2BNjoroge.prn.pdf/$FILE/Conferences_Competition PolicyTanz_Peter%2BNjoroge.prn.pdf.
226. Chapter 497 of the Laws of Kenya.
227. Chapter 502 of the Laws of Kenya.
228. Peter Njoroge (2004).

– fixed exchange rate.[229]

304. Later, the inadequacies of the country's industrialization programme were thrown into relief in the 1970s when the EAC collapsed and the splinter economies of Tanzania and Uganda opened their markets to India, China, and the Asian Tigers. The market for Kenya's domestic market shrunk significantly and struggled to compete with the cheaper, higher quality, and better-packaged imports. This both contributed to and was affected by the general disillusionment among the Kenyan populace with the so-called 'fruits of independence', declining employment opportunities and standards of living.

305. In order to reverse the economic decline, it became an imperative for the government to empower its industries to take advantage of export markets. Therefore, in the mid-1970s, local industries were exposed to a level of competition from the international market when the government relaxed its protectionist stand and allowed some previously banned imports. The aim was to improve 'the marketability … of Kenyan products in the export market, increase job opportunities, lower the cost of living and raise the standard of living for Kenyans … .'[230]

306. In 1982, the Working Party on Government Expenditures prepared a proposal for the development of a competition policy for Kenya. Kenya's momentum for change from a controlled economy to a free economy was amplified by Sessional Paper No. 1 of 1986 on 'Economic Management for Renewed Growth', which noted that:

> *Government will establish the market-based incentives and regulatory structures that will channel private activity into areas of greatest benefit for all Kenyans. In doing so, Government will rely less on instruments of direct control and increasingly on competitive elements in the economy.*[231]

307. Ultimately, in 1988, the Restrictive Trade Practices, Monopolies, and Price Control (RTPMP) Act was passed and given presidential assent. It was later brought into operation on 1 February 1989.

308. The provisions of the Act engendered the regulation of mergers, unwarranted concentrations of economic power, and restrictive trade practices by the office of the Prices and Monopolies Commissioner. However, quite curiously, it retained virtually all the price control provisions contained in the replaced Price Control Act.

309. In a foreword to Sessional Paper No. 2 of 1996 on 'Industrial Transformation to the Year 2020', Kenya's government reiterated the need to promote competition among local traders 'through strict enforcement of anti-monopoly and

229. *Supra* n. 226.
230. *Supra*, 4.
231. Government of Kenya, 'Sessional Paper No. 1 of 1964', 24 para. 2.53.

antitrust laws'. The Sessional Paper also definitively stated Kenya's commitment to follow through on the international trade obligations it had incurred as a signatory to the agreement establishing the World Trade Organization (WTO):

> *The multilateral trade negotiations of the Uruguay round culminated in the establishment of the World Trade Organization (WTO). It set out an ambitious agenda which included reducing trade barriers further. Kenya is a signatory to this Agreement and must work within its trade regulations and recognize that international trade will become more competitive. However, new trade opportunities will emerge as a result of the new multilateral arrangements that will encourage international trade provided Kenya can establish export oriented industries.*

310. Therefore, while Sessional Paper No. 1 of 1986 committed Kenya to the promotion of competition internally, Sessional Paper No. 2 of 1996 committed it to the promotion of competition through the path of comparative advantage and opened the economy to a new vista of both opportunities and challenges for international trade. The paper also committed Kenya to the WTO agreement that arose from the Uruguay Round and underlined Kenya's commitment to abide by WTO's trade agreements that promoted international trade.

311. While the RTPMP Act remained the overarching legal framework for competition regulation in Kenya, in 1998, the KCA was enacted in 1998, creating CA and designating it as the competition regulator for the telecommunications, radio telecommunications, and postal services (and later broadcasting).

312. Then, partially to fulfil constitutional requirements in the area of consumer protection, Parliament enacted the Competition Act 2010 (cap. 504). The Competition Act 2010 expressly repeals the RTPMP. The Competition Act was amended once in 2016 as described below.

§3. The Legal Framework for Fair Competition

I. The Constitution

313. In the emerging digital economy where technology is rapidly taking the place of personal interactions in the supply of goods and services, the consumer has become both more empowered and more vulnerable. Strong consumer protection regimes are an imperative for an Internet-driven market.

314. The Constitution of Kenya 2010 provides specific provisions declaring the rights of consumers. Primarily, such rights are provided in Article 46, which provides that consumers havc the right:

(a) *to goods and services of reasonable quality;*

(b) *to the information necessary for them to gain full benefit from goods and services;*
(c) *to the protection of their health, safety, and economic interests; and*
(d) *to compensation for loss or injury arising from defects in goods or services.*[232]

315. The Constitution also directs Parliament to enact legislation to provide for consumer protection and for fair, honest, and decent advertising.[233] These provisions are to apply to goods and services offered by public entities or private persons.[234] The Constitution contains one additional mention of competition, requiring of the Kenyan government to operate with a fair and inclusive tendering process, particularly protective of historically marginalized persons.[235]

316. In addition to the Competition Act 2010, the KIC Act and its regulations make various provisions for the protection of consumers of ICT services. These pieces of legislation are dealt with in turn.

II. The KIC Act, 1998: Competition in Telecommunications

317. The KIC Act is the framework legislation for the ICT industry. It establishes the CA as the ICT sector regulator and invests it with both specific and general powers to regulate competition in the industry. The Kenya Communications Regulations, 2001 make more particular provisions on fair competition and equality of treatment and provide a redress mechanism.

A. *General Provisions*

318. With regard to telecommunications, the KIC Act obliges CA to:

- ensure, so far as is reasonably practicable, that there are provided throughout Kenya such telecommunication services and in particular, emergency, public payphone, and directory information services, as are reasonably necessary to satisfy the public demand thereof;
- to protect the interests of all users of telecommunications services in Kenya with respect to the prices charged for and the quality and variety of such services;
- to maintain and promote effective competition between persons engaged in commercial activities connected with telecommunication services in Kenya in order to ensure efficiency and economy in the provision of such services and to promote research and development;
- to encourage private investment in the telecommunication sector; and

232. Article 46(1).
233. Article 46(2).
234. Article 46(3).
235. Article 227(2)(b).

- to enable persons providing telecommunications services or producing telecommunication apparatus in Kenya to compete effectively in the provision of such services or apparatus outside Kenya.[236]

319. The CA is directed to carry out the above mandate while maintaining regard to the values and principles of the Constitution of Kenya 2010.[237]

320. Part VIC of the Act is titled 'Fair Competition and Equal Treatment' and constitutes the Act's substantive law on competition. It was introduced into the Act by the Kenya Communications (Amendment) Act, 2008 and is substantially a reproduction of a similarly titled portion of the Kenya Communications Regulations, 2001 that had been earlier promulgated by the Minister for Information and Communications in consultation with CA.

321. However, the new provisions on fair competition in the Act differed from the 2001 regulations in two material respects. First, the portion of the definition of acts of unfair competition in the regulations, which included the act of entering into an agreement or engaging in a concerted practice with any party that unfairly prevents, restricts, or distorts competition, was expanded to include acts amounting to:

- fixing purchase or selling prices or any other trading conditions;
- limiting or controlling production, markets, technical development, or investment;
- sharing markets or sources of supply;
- applying dissimilar conditions to equivalent transactions with other trading parties, thereby placing them at a competitive disadvantage; and
- making the conclusion of contracts subject to acceptance by the other parties of supplementary obligations which, by their nature or according to commercial usage, have no connection with the subject of such contract.[238]

322. Second, and perhaps most significantly, while the fine which CA could impose on an operator who is adjudged to have engaged in anticompetitive behaviour was stated in the regulations to be an amount not exceeding USD 80 for every month during which the contravention continues, the amendment to the Act provided for a fine not exceeding 'the equivalent of 10% of the annual turnover of the licensee for each financial year that the breach lasted up to a maximum of three years'.[239]

323. Part VIc begins with a general prohibition directed at all licensees while in the course of business not to engage in activities intended to or likely to have the effect of unfairly preventing, restricting, or distorting competition.[240] It goes on to

236. Section 23.
237. *Id.*
238. KIC Act s. 84S(2)(b).
239. KIC Act s. 84T(6)(b).
240. Section 84Q.

mandate CA with the duty to promote, develop, and enforce fair competition and equality of treatment among licensees and in that regard to make determinations directed at the licensed systems and services. This mandate is substantially similar to the general mandate of the Competition Authority created by the Competition Act 2010, though specific to the ICT sector.

324. Licensees are required to provide equal opportunity for access to the same type and quality of service to all customers in a given area at substantially the same tariff subject to available appropriate technologies required to serve specific customers.[241] Denial of access or service to a customer by a licensee is not permitted except for delinquency of payment or any other just cause.[242]

325. Either acting upon a complaint or on its own motion, CA may investigate any licensee alleged to have committed any act in breach of fair competition or equal access.[243] Such an act may include but is not limited to:

(1) abuse of a dominant position which unfairly excludes or limits competition between an operator and any other party;
(2) entering into any agreement or engaging in any concerted practice with any other party, which unfairly prevents, restricts, or distorts competition or which tends to:
    (a) directly or indirectly fix purchase or selling prices or any other trading conditions;
    (b) limit or control production, markets, technical development, or investment;
    (b) share markets or sources of supply;
    (c) apply dissimilar conditions to equivalent transactions with other trading parties, thereby placing them at a competitive disadvantage;
    (d) make the conclusion of contracts subject to acceptance by the other parties of supplementary obligations which, by their nature or according to commercial usage, have no connection with the subject of such contract; and
    (e) the effectuation of anticompetitive changes in the market structure and in particular, anticompetitive mergers and acquisitions in the communications sector.[244]

326. Where it appears to CA that a breach of fair competition has been or is being committed, it is to investigate the act and to give written notice to the licensee under investigation stating the nature of and reasons for the investigation and

241. Section 84V.
242. Section 84U.
243. Section 84S(1), 84T.
244. Section 84S(2).

where necessary, requiring the licensee to provide it with further information. Also, where appropriate, the notice is to state the steps to be taken in order to remedy the suspected breach.[245]

327. The licensee under investigation as well as any other person affected by the suspected breach of fair competition may make representations to CA. After considering the representations, CA is to make a decision on the investigation. Where a licensee is found to be competing unfairly, CA may:

- order the licensee to stop the unfair competition;
- require the licensee to pay a fine not exceeding the equivalent of 10% of its turnover for each financial year that the breach lasted up to a maximum of three years; and
- declare any anticompetitive agreement or contracts null and void.[246]

328. In addition to the remedial actions that may be ordered by CA, the offending licensees will be liable for the violation of the right of any person under the laws of Kenya which is a consequence of the act of unfair competition.[247] Any person aggrieved by the decision of CA under this part may appeal to the Communications Appeals Tribunal established under section 102 of the Act.[248]

329. CA may issue a notice in the Kenya Gazette declaring a person or institution to be a 'dominant telecommunications service provider' after having regard to the following:

- the provider's market share being at least 50% of the total revenue of the entire telecommunications market;
- significant market power enjoyed by the telecommunications provider; and
- any other consideration determined by the CA.[249]

330. A person or institution declared to be a dominant telecommunications service provider is required to file tariffs, rates, terms, and conditions of interconnection with CA.

331. Finally, Part VIc gives the Minister the power to make regulations in consultation with CA for the better carrying out of its provisions. The subject of the regulations may include but is not limited to:

- access, including rules of interconnection, by licensees and their subscribers to each other's network;
- the procedure of handling alleged breaches of fair competition;

---

245. Section 84T(2).
246. Section 84T(3)–(6).
247. Section 84T(7).
248. Section 84T(8).
249. Section 84W.

- investigation of a licensee alleged to have committed acts or omissions in breach of fair competition;
- access to information from any licensee with regard to facilitating investigations on alleged breaches of fair competition;
- steps to be taken in order to remedy the breach;
- definition of market segments; and
- account separation.[250]

332. As noted in the preceding chapter, in 2009, CA, acting in consultation with the Ministry of Information and Communications and out of the need to streamline sector regulations in the aftermath of the substantial amendments introduced by the Kenya (Communications) Amendment Act, drafted a set of fourteen regulations which were subjected to rounds of public consultations and redrafting. The regulations covered various aspects of regulation, including consumer protection, numbering, and fair competition, and have since been supplemented with not less than six additional sets of topical regulations.

B. Telkom Kenya's Legal Monopoly over Certain Services

333. In the wake of the liberalization of the telecommunications sub-sector, the government of Kenya secured a legal monopoly for Telkom Kenya, the incumbent nationalized operator, ostensibly to give it a head start and to consolidate its position as the crown jewel in the family of Kenya's newly nationalized institutions. As can be seen by the recent sector statistics provided towards the end of this chapter, however, Telkom Kenya (now operating as Orange) is clearly not dominant in the Kenyan market for consumer mobile telecommunications services.

C. Tariff Regulation

334. In addition to a general power conferred on the Minister to make regulations on any matter for the better carrying out of the provisions of the KIC Act, the Act gives the Minister the power to make regulations, in consultation with CA, with respect to the 'fees and other charges for any matter permitted or matters required to be done under [the] Act in relation to telecommunication services' and with respect to 'access, including rules of interconnection, by licensees … and their subscribers to each other's network'.[251] The KIC (Tariff) Regulations 2010 were adopted with the purpose of providing a framework for determining tariffs and tariff structures, and to:

- ensure licensees maintain financial integrity and attract capital;
- protect the interests of investors, consumers, and other stakeholders;
- provide market incentives for licensees to operate efficiently; and

250. Section 84R, 84W.
251. Sections 27 & 84W.

- promote efficient and fair competition within the framework for a free market economy; and
- ensure compliance with all competition laws.[252]

335. Licensees (i.e., entities licensed under the KIC Act) are directed to set tariffs that are 'just and reasonable' as well as non-discriminatory. A tariff that is not reasonable on its face may be deemed appropriate if the licensee shows 'legitimate commercial reasons for the tariff'.[253] Tariffs must not, however, be set to a level that prevents market entry or distorts competition. All tariff rates must be filed with the CA on a quarterly basis,[254] and the CA is empowered to investigate whether any tariff is anticompetitive.[255]

336. The important regulatory function of the CA as a promoter of competition in the ICT sector is emphasized in the Tariff Regulations. For example, the CA is empowered to declare any service to be a 'regulated service' and in so doing, is empowered to approve or set tariff schedules for the regulated service. A decision declaring a service as a regulated service is to be based on the demonstration that there is a competition concern, including instances where a licensee has been declared to be in a dominant market position and found to be abusing that position. Where there is a competition concern, the CA is to prepare a report showing that:

- effective competition among existing licensees cannot develop;
- there exists strong and non-transitory barriers to entry in the identified market segment;
- there is no other competition law that is sufficient to deal with the competition concern;
- in the case of a retail service, no wholesale remedies are available to address the competition concern in the identified market segment; and
- such other circumstances that the Commission may consider necessary from time to time.[256]

337. The report by the CA must also demonstrate that declaring the service to be a regulated service will prevent a potential abuse.

D. Interconnection

338. The rules governing interconnection are contained in the KIC (Interconnection and Provision of Fixed Links, Access and Facilities) Regulations 2010. The purpose of interconnection is to provide physical and logical linking of telecommunication networks used by the same or different service licensees in order to allow

252. Regulations, s. 3.
253. Regulations, s. 4.
254. Regulations, s. 5.
255. Regulations, s. 10.
256. Regulations, s. 3A.

the users of one licensee to communicate with users of the same or another licensee or to access services provided by another licensee.[257] All interconnection agreements are required to facilitate end-to-end connectivity by ensuring that calls originated on the telecommunications system of an interconnecting operator can be terminated at any point on the telecommunications system of any other telecommunications service provider on a non-discriminatory basis.[258] In general, therefore, interconnection requirements are provided to enhance competition and provide a level playing field among telecommunications companies.

339. Generally, a licensee has the right to choose its interconnection provider for the purpose of routing calls towards the customers of another operator.[259] An operator is at liberty to negotiate an interconnection agreement with another operator save that when a request is made by one operator to another for an interconnection, the requested operator is legally obliged to negotiate an interconnection agreement.[260]

340. An interconnection agreement shall be in writing and shall make provisions for:

- the scope and specification of the interconnection;
- access to all ancillary or supplementary services or access to and use of premises or land necessary to support the interconnection;
- the maintenance of an end-to-end quality service and other service levels;
- charges for interconnection;
- billing and settlement procedures;
- ordering, forecasting, provisioning, and testing procedures;
- points of interconnection or co-location;
- the amount of, or the forecast procedures to be used to determine, interconnect capacity to be provided;
- transmission of call line identity;
- network information;
- information regarding system modernization or rationalization;
- technical specifications and standards;
- interoperability testing, traffic management, measurement, and system maintenance;
- an information handling process and confidentiality agreement;
- duration for and renegotiation of the agreement;
- formation of appropriate working groups to discuss matters relating to interconnection and to resolve any disputes;
- formal dispute resolution procedures;
- definition and limitation of liability and indemnity;
- adequate capacity, service levels, and reasonable remedies for any failure to meet those service levels;

257. Regulations, s. 2.
258. Regulations, s. 5(6).
259. Regulations, s. 4(1).
260. Regulations, s. 4(3).

– force majeure;
– other contractual terms and conditions; and
– any other matters that the Commission may prescribe.[261]

341. Interconnection agreements and extensions of such agreements must be filed with and approved by the CA. The CA can request any additional information needed in order to evaluate an agreement, and decisions by the CA are appealable to the Tribunal.[262]

342. Interconnections are intended to be seamless to a calling party and the party receiving a call. The Regulations provide extensive details pertaining to the mechanisms and infrastructure by which interconnection is implemented. These details are intended to be made transparent by their inclusion in interconnection agreements.[263]

343. The charges for interconnection services should be 'objective, independently verifiable, and fair' and not designed to facilitate cross-subsidies by an interconnect provider of its network.[264] The charges are to be so structured that they distinguish and separately price the fees for the establishment and implementation of physical network connections, the periodic rental charges for the use of the requested operator's network, and variable charges for telecommunications and supplementary services.[265] Charges must be below the retail charges levied by the interconnect provider for the provision of any retail service that makes similar use of those network elements that are required by both the retail and interconnection service. Charges must also be sufficiently below retail service charges to allow for recovery of the incremental retail costs associated with provision of the retail service supported by the interconnection service that the interconnect service provider would have to incur in order to compete effectively with the interconnect provider at the retail level.[266]

344. Parties to an interconnection agreement are required to comply with all relevant service standards of the ITU and other technical standards that the Commission may publish.[267] Moreover, the customers of an interconnect operator are entitled to receive no less favourable treatment than that afforded to the operator's own customers, those of its subsidiaries and affiliates, or other similarly situated service providers.[268]

345. A dominant telecommunications service licensee may be ordered by the CA to provide a 'reference interconnect offer', which is a document setting out the

261. Regulations, s. 5(7).
262. Regulations, s. 5.
263. *See*, Regulations, e.g., ss 13–15.
264. Regulations, s. 12(1).
265. Regulations, s. 12(2).
266. Regulations, s. 12.
267. Regulations, s. 10.
268. Regulations, s. 9.

terms and conditions under which the dominant licensee undertakes to permit interconnection to its telecommunications network in a non-discriminatory manner.[269]

346. An interconnection provider may only terminate an interconnection agreement as a result of a fundamental breach of the agreement that the interconnection operator has failed to remedy. However, the termination must be preceded by a notice to both the interconnection operator and CA.[270] Disputes are to be settled in accordance with the KIC (Dispute Resolution) Regulations 2010.[271]

347. Further regulations apply to a facilities acquirer ('a licensee who provides network services who has leased or shares facilities or has requested to lease or share facilities from a facilities provider') as well as a facilities provider ('a network facilities licensee who has been requested by a facilities acquirer for lease or to share facilities') as pertains to access, sharing, co-location, and leasing of physical infrastructure used in provision of telecommunications services ('network facilities').[272]

E. Interconnection of Fixed Telephone Networks

348. In the fixed network service segment, Telkom Kenya Ltd, the incumbent fixed telecommunications service provider, was given specific pricing targets to implement in charging for its services for a five-year period beginning 1 July 1999. In the initial licence period, Telkom was required to rebalance its tariffs to ensure that as much as possible, its prices reflected the real cost of service provision and eliminated any cross-subsidies between local, long distance, and international telecommunications services. This entailed a rise in local call charges and a drop in long distance and international call charges, respectively. All these charges had to be filed with CA before Telkom could implement them.[273]

349. In the long run, a price-cap method was used to arrive at charges for fixed services. The price-cap method, often denoted by the formula RPI–X% (where RPI referred to the Retail Price Index or the relative prices of a basket of goods and services indexed to inflation – the RPI is reckoned by the Ministry of Finance – while X referred to a productivity factor). Under this regime, charges were not to be allowed to go beyond the price cap until full competition was introduced and demand and supply forces were sufficient to regulate prices. Additionally, the Long Run Incremental Cost (LRIC) method was used to determine costs and ultimately to determine the appropriate interconnection rates between the interconnecting licensees.[274]

---

269. Regulations, s. 18.
270. Regulations, s. 16.
271. Regulations, s. 22.
272. Regulations, ss 19–21.
273. CA's 'Review of Implementation of Interconnection Determination No. 1 of 2007' (2009), 3.
274. *Ibid.*

F. The Kencell Ltd and Telkom Kenya Interconnection Dispute

350. On 6 August 2001, Kencell Communications Ltd (now Airtel (K) Ltd) informed CA that after protracted discussions between themselves and Telkom, they had failed to reach an agreement on an appropriate local call interconnection rate for fixed public payphones.

351. Earlier in February of the previous year, CA had issued to Kencell a licence for the provision of Mobile Cellular services throughout Kenya for a renewable period of fifteen years. Bundled with the licence was a universal service obligation obliging Kencell to also provide public payphone services pursuant to section 25 of the KCA. Kencell rolled out the public payphone service in November 2000 installing a total of 300 payphones by the end of that year.

352. On 12 March 2001, Kencell informed the Commission that it was unable to activate the service on payphones installed in Nairobi due to Telkom's reluctance to accept a negotiated interconnection rate of USD 0.0118 (KES 0.86) per minute which, as Kencell stated in its reference, had been agreed between the two companies' technical working teams. In its reply, Telkom put forward the argument that the tariff of USD 0.217 (KES 1.67) proposed by Kencell was not agreeable as to accept it would amount to subsidizing the customers of Kencell, an act which would not make any business sense to Telkom. Telkom argued that an interconnection rate ought to be cost-based and commercially feasible.

353. Having examined the claims of either party, CA made five observations:

(1) the provision of payphone services was a Universal Service Obligation, a social need for which the cost must, of necessity, be borne by all licensed telecommunications operators;
(2) any decision to prescribe a tariff structure for any service stream or an interconnection charge should take into account costing data submitted by the disputants. In the absence of such cost structures, interconnection charges would be based on retail prices which would also consider unbundling and apportioning charges according to the part of the network used to transport payphone traffic to the other network;
(3) CA acknowledged the existing retail price of USD 0.068 per unit on Telkom's network was subsidized and that as a matter of fact, Telkom's tariff on local and international long distance did not reflect the cost of the service. However, Telkom's argument that it would be subsidizing another network failed to consider that it would equally be charging rates in the long distance and international service stream on the customers of Kencell that did not reflect the cost of providing that service;
(4) it was provided by law, and particularly paragraph 38(1) of the Kenya Communications Regulations, that the rates charged for interconnection should not vary on the basis of the class of customers to be served and that there should not be no less favourable treatment of customers of an interconnecting provider than those of the requesting party; and

(5) finally, CA noted that the contentious price of USD 0.217 was in respect of an end-to-end call and the element of subsidization would probably not apply with regard to interconnection capacity as the interconnection seeker would only use a portion of Telkom's network to relay its traffic.

354. Ultimately, CA's determination was that in the interest of activating the services from installed payphones and pursuant to section 25(2) b of the KCA and section 47 of the Kenya Communication Regulations, the proposed interconnection rate of USD 0.217 for local payphone calls would be applied for Kencell local payphone calls terminating on Telkom's network as an interim interconnection rate with effect from 1 November 2001. The parties were nevertheless left at liberty to negotiate and to table before CA a mutual interconnection agreement within three months. In the meantime, Kencell was directed to supply Telkom with the payphone numbers on its network and to continually update Telkom's records with newly installed and activated payphone numbers.

355. This determination governed the interconnection relationship between Kencell and Telkom until it was superseded by another determination issued in early 2007.

G. Interconnection Rates and Tariffs for Mobile Cellular Services

356. CA's approach to mobile cellular services was one of the minimal interventions, if any, in the form of tariff controls. Probably, CA considered that the market was fully competitive and that calling costs would fall into alignment with the forces of supply and demand. Nevertheless, mobile cellular operators were required to present their pricing structures to CA before they could put them into effect.

357. Between 2006 and 2007, CA conducted a Network Cost Study on retail and wholesale prices in the telecommunications market. The objective of the study was to determine through review of the available institutional, regulatory, and financial information and through a costing exercise, the appropriate costs, and prices of various telecommunications services. The study covered mobile and fixed telecommunications services as well as existing and projected interconnections. The results of the study were meant to provide the necessary regulatory tools in support of a competitive telecommunications environment that can ensure increased investment, returns, and access to services in the long run. Not surprisingly, therefore, one of the short-term regulatory requirements recommended by the study was for CA to realign call termination by issuing a formal determination on interconnection rates.

358. Consequently, in early 2007, CA issued Determination No. 1 of 2007 on 'Cost-Based Interconnection Rates for Fixed and Mobile Telecommunication Networks'. This Determination, which came into effect on 1 March 2007, ushered in a cost-based pricing structure for fixed and mobile telecommunication services in Kenya and superseded all previous rulings and determinations on the subject.

359. CA carried out a first review of the implementation of Determination No. 1 in January 2008 just before the start of the second phase of the interconnection rates scheduled for 1 March 2008. The review established that during the initial stages of the implementation, operators experienced certain legal and technical difficulties in preparing interconnection agreements. However, on the overall, it was reported that the Interconnection Determination provided a framework that spurred growth and competition in the industry.[275]

360. The implementation of the second phase of the Determination commenced on 1 March 2008. During the period of the implementation of the second phase, two new mobile operators entered the market, namely Telkom Kenya under the Orange brand and Econet Wireless Kenya operating under the 'Yu' brand. The new operators negotiated and signed agreements with the other operators on the basis of the rates in the second phase of the Determination, and CA subsequently approved the agreements. During this phase, a total of five interconnection agreements had been filed involving:

(1) Telkom Kenya and Flashcom.
(2) Telkom Kenya and Safaricom.
(3) Telkom Kenya and EM Communications.
(4) Safaricom and Celtel.
(5) Telkom Kenya and Celtel.

H. Impact of the Determination in the Telecommunications Sector

361. CA subsequently conducted a review of the status of implementation of the second phase based on information from the quarterly returns submitted by the operators. To establish the impact of the Interconnection Determination on the sector, CA looked at projected indicators that tended to show the impact of the Determination in the telecommunications market. These include tariffs for voice services, growth in subscriber numbers, and network coverage.

I. Tariffs for Voice Services

362. In its report, CA observed that the implementation of the Determination had continued to result in tariff reductions with reductions being evident in both post-paid and prepaid tariffs within the review period. The average tariff reduction ranged from 15% for post-paid calls to the same network to 37% for post-paid calls to fixed networks. The average charges to fixed network (post-paid and prepaid) were lower than the charges to another mobile network (post-paid and prepaid, respectively), apparently due to lower charges by Telkom Kenya's Orange to the fixed network compared to other mobile networks.[276]

275. CA's 'Review of Implementation of Interconnection Determination No. 1 of 2007' (2009), 2.
276. *Ibid.*, 3.

363. An analysis in 2008 revealed a wide disparity of the average tariffs charged by the operators. The rolling out of Telkom's Orange brand and Econet's Yu took competition in the mobile cellular services market in Kenya to a new level, and despite various entries into and exits from the market, this remains the case. Competition among the operators has been waged in tariffs as well as services offered. The CA is able to monitor promotions and special offers because these require an application from the offering operator. In the last three months of 2016, for example, the CA received twenty applications from the various operators for the offering of promotions and specials.[277]

J. Subscriber Numbers and Growth

364. Between March and October of 2008, the number of mobile cellular subscribers increased by 35% from 11.9 million to 16.2 million. Prepaid subscribers continued to dominate the market and registered increased growth for all operators. While the growth in subscribers could not be attributed solely to the implementation of the Determination, the reduction in end-user tariffs made possible by reduced interconnection and termination rates may have in turn resulted in the uptake of mobile cellular services by a segment of the population that hitherto could not afford them.[278]

365. The Determination No. 1 was intended to provide a three-year 'glide path' for the implementation of interconnection rates and was supplanted on 1 July 2010 by Determination No. 2 of 2010, entitled 'Determination on interconnections rates for fixed and mobile telecommunications networks, infrastructure sharing and co-location; and broadband interconnection services in Kenya'. Determination No. 2 included a review of the 2006 Network Cost Study and had as its primary objective the development of a new competitive interconnection rate framework that accounts for new developments in the communications market.

366. Determination No. 2 of 2010 directed all mobile and fixed telecommunication operators in Kenya to implement the interconnection rates and time schedule shown in Table 30.

Table 30 Interconnection Rates for Mobile and Fixed Operators

Nominal KES	*1 July 2010*	*1 July 2011*	*1 July 2012*	*1 July 2013*
1. Call Mobile Termination Prices				
Mobile Termination	2.21	1.44	1.15	0.99
2. Fixed Termination and Transit for Existing Regulated Services				

277. Communication Authority of Kenya: Sector Statistics Report Q2 FY 2016-2017, s. 6.
278. *Ibid.*, 6. The most recent available subscriber numbers are provided at the end of this chapter.

Nominal KES	*1 July 2010*	*1 July 2011*	*1 July 2012*	*1 July 2013*
Local Termination	1.67	1.33	1.06	0.99
Single-Tandem Termination from Tandem Exchange				
Double-Tandem Termination from Tandem Exchange	2.93	2.61	2.38	
Single-Tandem Termination from Local Exchange				
Double-Tandem Termination from Local Exchange				
Transit Local Exchange to Tandem (Single Tandem)	1.26	1.28	1.32	Not Regulated
Transit Local Exchange to Tandem (Double Tandem)				
Tandem to Tandem Transit				
Local to Local Transit (Single Tandem)				
Local to Local Transit (Single Tandem)				

Source: Kenya Interconnection determination 2 of 2010.

367. Furthermore, the CA determined that SMS wholesale termination rates were unjustifiably high and directed all operators to renegotiate and file with the Commission lower mobile and fixed SMS termination rates within three months. Finally, Determination No. 2 emphasized that the CA would continue to monitor the development of tariffs and access in the sector, including tariffs for interconnectivity of mobile money transfer services, and tariffs for broadband services.

368. As it happened, interconnection rates fell as expected, ultimately landing as shown in Table 31.

Table 31 Actual Interconnection Rates for Mobile and Fixed Operators

Service	*Call Termination Prices (KES)*
Mobile Termination	0.99
Fixed Termination and Transit for Existing Regulated Services	
Local Termination	0.99
Single-Tandem Termination from Tandem Exchange	0.99
Double-Tandem Termination from Tandem Exchange	0.99
Single-Tandem Termination from Local Exchange	0.99
Double-Tandem Termination from Local Exchange	0.99
Tandem to Tandem Transit	No Tariff Cap

Source: Communications Authority of Kenya: Annual Report for the Financial Year 2015/16.

369. Tariffs are continuously monitored by the CA and are reported at least annually. Average tariffs have essentially stabilized in the market and, as of June 2016, range from KES 2.6 per minute within the network to KES 3.7 per minute across networks.[279] Although these average tariffs have essentially not changed in over two years, it should be noted that the average tariffs do not account for the proliferation of special offers and promotions.

K. Premium Rate Services

370. Premium Rate Services (PRS) are communications services provided usually by a third party over the network infrastructure of a licensed telecommunications services provider through designated telephone numbers and telephone calls or messaging services for which prices higher than normal are charged. PRS were previously known as value-added services, but under the new ULF, they are known as Third-Party Content Services (by non-infrastructure based content providers).

371. CA has licensed a number of CSP who are offering various PRS including mass SMS for corporate communications, business messaging, SMS marketing, SMS voting, etc.

279. Communications Authority of Kenya: Annual Report for the Financial Year 2015–2016.

372. Charges for PRS are not regulated, although premium rate service providers (PRSP) are required to ensure that they clearly and conspicuously inform consumers on the service offering and cost of sending and/or receiving a text/voice message service to the number.[280]

L. Numbering

373. The KIC (Numbering) Regulations, 2010, makes various provisions on the management of numbering systems for telecommunications services. It directs the CA to establish a National Communication Numbering and Address Plan – a plan for electronic communications numbers and addresses, postal codes, and national addressing system.[281]

374. A numbering plan is a method of assigning network numbering exchange (NNX) codes to provide unique telephone addresses or identities to a user-network interface.

375. Prior to the assignment and publication of any numbering plan, CA is obliged by the regulations to ensure that such numbering:

- allows sufficient numbers to be made available to licensees;
- is allocated without undue delay;
- allows for the inclusion of as few digits as practicable;
- does not confer an undue advantage on any licensee; and
- minimizes any inconvenience that may be caused by implementation of the numbering plan to a licensee and persons using the telecommunications systems.[282]

376. The CA released a telecommunications numbering and addressing scheme in 2002, and further released an updated Telecommunications Numbering Plan for Kenya in May 2017. These documents detail the allocation of geographical area codes, emergency and other reserved numbers, mobile network codes, and dialling prefixes.[283]

377. As reported in the Numbering Plan of 2017, the CA has prescribed the following numbering plan for Kenya:[284]

- Country Code: +254.
- International Dialling Access Prefix: 000.

280. Procedures and Guidelines for the Management of Telecommunications Short Codes and Premium Rate Numbers in Kenya, 2012.
281. Regulation 4.
282. Rcgulation 5(4).
283. Telecommunications Numbering Plan for Kenya in May 2017, available at http://www.ca.go.ke/index.php/numbering, accessed 1 Jun. 2017.
284. Source: CA.

- Regional (East Africa) dialling prefixes: (a) Kenya 005; (b) Uganda 006; (c) Tanzania 007.
- National dialling prefix: 0.
- Emergency Number: 999 or 112.
- Child helpline: 116.
- Carrier Selection Codes: 17X/18X.

M. Number Portability

378. Number portability enables a telecommunications network to provide users with the ability to migrate from one service provider to another without changing their telephone number.

379. Number portability is an important component of telecommunications market regulation and the dynamics of competition among TSPs. To the service providers, it reduces barriers to market entry and provides the motivation for them to continuously improve both the quality and the prices of their services in order to retain and attract more customers. To end users, number portability eliminates customer detention by offering the flexibility necessary to migrate from one network to another based on the quality, price, and variety of services offered.

380. In 2004, CA initiated a round of public consultations on the desirability of introducing number portability. Arising from the consultation, 'it was felt that the market was not ready as there were only two licensed mobile operators in the country. It was therefore feared that introduction of number portability would have resulted in unnecessary churn'.[285]

381. They argued that since there was a very big difference on the applicable tariffs between on-net and off-net calls and since callers would not be able to tell on which network the called party is served from, there was danger of callers incurring huge bills without prior knowledge. It was consequently resolved to defer the implementation of number portability until there were at least three mobile operators in the market and the difference between off-net and on-net tariffs has narrowed down.

382. In November 2008, CA announced plans to introduce number portability by 2009, although this deadline was not met. Under the Regulations passed in 2010, number portability appears to be merely optional, which state that the numbering and addressing plan *may* set out rules that include:

- the use of different numbers and addresses for different kinds of services;
- the assignment of numbers and addresses;
- the transfer of assigned numbers and addresses;
- the use of assigned numbers and addresses;
- the portability of assigned numbers and addresses;

285. CA Press Release, available at www.CA.go.ke/html/news.asp?newsid=294&area=new.

- the requirements that licensees maintain a plan for assigning and reassigning numbers and addresses;
- the fees for the assignment and transfer of numbers and addresses which may be determined by the CA; and
- any other matters that the CA may prescribe.[286]

383. Notwithstanding the optional nature of number portability under the Regulations, the CA released extensive Procedures and Guidelines for number portability in October 2010.[287] The Procedures and Guidelines 'specify the different stages of the process from the point when a Subscriber requests a new Account via number portability to the point when the Subscriber has an active Account on the Recipient network, the Account on the Donor network has been closed and all other Operators have been informed of the number porting'.[288]

384. Despite the availability of number porting and the established rules and procedures, the practice remains fairly uncommon. In the six months from June–December 2016, only 557 phone number ports were reported to the CA.[289]

N. Geographic Numbers Assigned for Fixed Line Service

385. The Telecommunications Numbering Plan for Kenya describes geographical area codes for fixed telephony services. The country is divided into geographical regions, with each region assigned a two-digit prefix between 20 and 69 for fixed line service. Nairobi and Mombasa, for example, are assigned the prefixes 20 and 41, respectively. The prefix is followed by a two- or three-digit number assigned to the telecommunications operator of the particular line. Thus a fixed line phone number in Nairobi would be 20-yy-xxxxx, with 'yy' indicating the telecommunications operator and 'xxxxx' providing the unique user.

O. Non-geographic Numbers Assigned for Mobile Service

386. The Telecommunications Numbering Plan for Kenya describes non-geographic assigned numbers for licensed mobile cellular providers operating in Kenya. To distinguish mobile lines from these fixed lines, mobile numbers are assigned prefixes greater than 69. Each operator has been allocated a range of unique prefixes under which it may assign subscriber numbers with a fixed number length of nine digits (including the prefix or code), though, usually the digit '0' is included for all calls originating from within the country.[290]

---

286. The Kenya Information and Communications (Numbering) Regulations 2010, Regulation 5(6).
287. Procedures and Guidelines for the Provision of Mobile Number Portability Services in Kenya.
288. *Id.*
289. Communication Authority of Kenya: Sector Statistics Report Q2 FY 2016-2017, s. 1.3.
290. Telecommunications Numbering Plan for Kenya. Source – CA.

P. Quality of Service Standards (QoS)

387. In November 2008, CA published a notice prescribing the minimum service quality thresholds for mobile telephone service operators.[291] The notice was later revoked and replaced with another notice in February 2009.[292] The notice was in the form of a modification of the terms and conditions of the licences issued to GSM operators by CA to the operators under powers given to it by the KIC Act, 1998.[293]

388. The notice, issued by CA's Director General, Mr C.J.K. Njoroge, prescribed the following Quality of Service (QoS) Requirements:

- the licensees would be liable to pay penalties for failure to meet the quality of service requirements; and
- CA reserved the right, upon reasonable notice to the licensees, to review the QoS requirements periodically.

389. Further, CA prescribed the following procedures with regard to compliance assessment on the QoS:

- besides the submission of returns by the licensee on the QoS parameters, CA would continuously conduct independent QoS evaluation of licensees in all the provinces of the country;
- the results of each QoS parameter would be the average of all the measurements done for all the provinces during the entire reporting period of twelve months commencing from the effective date of this notice;
- a licensee would only be assessed on the geographical areas of coverage where the licensee's coverage obligation applies at the time of measurement;
- a licensee shall achieve the threshold of at least 80% of the prescribed QoS parameters, and this is to be borne out by the licensee's returns and the independent QoS evaluations;
- failure to achieve the threshold of at least 80% of the listed QoS parameters, after notification by CA to the licensee, would constitute non-compliance with the QoS requirements, and the licensee will be liable to a penalty under the KIC Act; and
- CA shall, prior to carrying out tests to verify compliance with these conditions, share with the licensee the QoS measurement framework to be used.

390. The purpose of the notice was to ensure 'the provision of better quality of services, provide for an objective and independently verifiable QoS compliance mechanism, provide for reasonable and achievable QoS targets and to level the playing field'.

---

291. Government Printer, 'The Kenya Gazette', Gazette Notice No. 11382 of 2008, 20 Nov. 2008.
292. Government Printer, 'The Kenya Gazette', Gazette Notice No. 1148 of 2009, 5 Feb. 2009.
293. Section 82(2) and (3).

391. Table 32 shows the QoS metrics prescribed by CA for GSM operators. For any mobile operator to be deemed compliant with the QoS standards, they are required to meet a minimum threshold of at least 80% of the overall QoS KPIs against the targets detailed in the table.

Table 32 Quality of Service (QoS) Requirements for GSM Operators as of 2014

Key Performance Indicator	*Target*
Call Completion Rate	≥95%
Call Set Up Success Rate (CSSR)	≥95%
Call Drop Rate	≤2%
Call Block Rate	≤5%
Speech Quality	95% of samples > 3.1
Call Set Up Time	<13.5 Seconds
Handover Success Rate	≥90%
RX Level	Outdoor = −102 dBm Indoor = −95 dBm In Car = −100 dBm

Source: CA Quality of Service Report 2013/14.

392. In the most recent QoS Report available from the CA, all four of the then-present mobile carriers (Safaricom, Essar (Yu), Airtel, and Orange) were found non-compliant as failing to meet minimum thresholds for at least 80% of the key performance indicators (KPIs). Three of the operators met minimum thresholds in five out of eight KPIs, while the fourth operator (Essar) met minimum thresholds in only half of the eight KPIs.[294]

Q. Spectrum Allocations

393. In 2015, the CA allocated 4G broadband spectrum to the telecommunications company Safaricom Ltd.[295] Other telecommunication companies demanded similar allocations, arguing that it was unfair to allow the dominant telecommunications company to launch improved high-speed Internet service before its competitors. Following these demands, the CA allocated spectrum to Airtel and Telkom Kenya in 2016. The three operators were required to pay USD 25 million for their

294. Quality of Service Monitoring Report for Mobile Telecommunication Network Services 2013–2014.
295. Gazette Notice, 19 Aug. 2015.

4G licences, and they were obliged to share at least 30% of their 4G network capacity with smaller players, including MVNOs and tier-two infrastructure providers.[296] Despite these frequency allocations, Safaricom is currently the only provider of 4G LTE services in Nairobi and Mombasa.

III. The Competition Act

394. As stated earlier in the chapter, while the KIC Act, 1998 and its regulations are the sector-specific legislation for the regulation of competition in the ICT industry, the Competition Act 2010[297] is the overarching framework legislation on competition regulation in all industries and markets in Kenya. The latter Act commenced on 1 August 2011, and its declared objectives are:

- increase efficiency in the production, distribution, and supply of goods and services;
- promote innovation;
- maximize the efficient allocation of resources;
- protect consumers;
- create an environment conducive for investment, both foreign and local;
- capture national obligations in competition matters with respect to regional integration initiatives;
- bring national competition law, policy, and practice in line with best international practices; and
- promote the competitiveness of national undertakings in world markets.[298]

395. The Act is a code of statutory provisions establishing the CAK and the Competition Tribunal. The Act defines, prohibits, and provides a mechanism for the detection, reporting, and redress of certain instances of unfair competition, as well as the regulation of activities of market entities public and private. These instances and activities include:

- restrictive trade practices, including: restrictive agreements, practices, and decisions; and restrictive trade practices applicable to trade associations;
- abuse of dominant position;
- mergers; and
- unwarranted concentrations of economic power.

396. The Act also provides a framework for consumer protection law and in this regard is complementary to the Consumer Protection Act, 2012.[299]

---

296. *See* https://www.telegeography.com/products/commsupdate/articles/2016/06/28/kenyan-trio-to-pay-usd25m-each-for-4g-licences/.
297. Chapter 504 of the Laws of Kenya.
298. Competition Act 2010, s. 3.
299. Laws of Kenya, No. 46 of 2012.

397. The overall responsibility for competition policy in Kenya resides with the CAK. Although several of the members of the CAK are appointed by the Minister for Finance, the CAK is intended to be an independent body.[300] The Act provides a large list of functions of the CAK, essentially mirroring the objectives of the Act itself. In addition to the power to enforce the specific restrictions against anticompetitive behaviour, the Act gives the CAK the power to initiate and hold enquiries 'into any matter affecting competition or consumer welfare', and this includes initiating sectoral studies to determine the competitive health of a specific sector.[301]

A. *Restrictive Trade Practices*

398. Part III of the Act broadly prohibits agreements between undertakings, decisions by associations of undertakings, decisions by undertakings or concerted practices by undertakings which have as their object or effect the prevention, distortion or lessening of competition in trade in any goods or services in Kenya.[302] An 'undertaking' is 'any business intended to be carried on, or carried on for gain or reward by a person, a partnership or a trust in the production, supply or distribution of goods or provision of any service, and includes a trade association'.[303] Specific types of prohibited agreements, decisions, and concerted practices mentioned in the Act are those which:

- directly or indirectly fixes purchase or selling prices or any other trading conditions;
- divides markets by allocating customers, suppliers, areas, or specific types of goods or services;
- involves collusive tendering;
- involves a practice of minimum resale price maintenance;
- limits or controls production, market outlets or access, technical development, or investment;
- applies dissimilar conditions to equivalent transactions with other trading parties, thereby placing them at a competitive disadvantage;
- makes the conclusion of contracts subject to acceptance by other parties of supplementary conditions which by their nature or according to commercial usage have no connection with the subject of the contracts;
- amounts to the use of an intellectual property right in a manner that goes beyond the limits of fair, reasonable, and non-discriminatory use; and
- otherwise prevents, distorts, or restricts competition.[304]

399. These practices are prohibited regardless of whether the accused undertaking(s) is/are dominant in a market. For practices involving multiple parties, these

300. Competition Act 2010, s. 7(2).
301. Section 18.
302. Section 21.
303. Section 2.
304. Section 21.

prohibitions apply whether the parties are in a horizontal relationship (i.e., the parties are in direct competition) or a vertical relationship (i.e., the parties are at different levels in a supply chain).

400. Trade associations are defined as any body or person (whether incorporated or not) which is formed for the purposes of furthering the interests of its members or persons represented by its members. The following practices conducted by or on behalf of a trade association are declared by the Act to be restrictive trade practices:

– the unjustifiable exclusion from a trade association of any person carrying on or intending to carry on, in good faith, the trade in relation to which the association is formed; and
– the making, directly or indirectly, of a recommendation by a trade association to its members or to any class of its members which relates to: (i) the prices charged or to be charged by such members or any such class of members or to the margins included in the prices or to the pricing formula used in the calculation of those prices; or (ii) the terms of sale (including discount, credit, delivery, and product and service guarantee terms) of such members or any such class of members and which directly affects prices, profit margins included in the prices, or the pricing formula used in the calculation of prices.[305]

401. A restrictive trade practice is punishable by a fine of up to USD 100,000 or imprisonment for up to five years or both fine and imprisonment.[306]

402. Exemptions may be made for certain restrictive trade practices. The process for obtaining an exemption is initiated with the filing of an application to the CAK by the undertaking or association of undertakings. The CAK is authorized under the Act to grant an exemption 'if it is satisfied that there are exceptional and compelling reasons of public policy as to why the agreement, decision, concerted practice or category of the same, ought to be excluded from the prohibitions' of the Act.[307] The Act provides factors that are to be considered by the CAK in considering the requested exemption, specifically the extent to which the agreement, decision, or concerted practice, or the category thereof contributes to, or results in, or is likely to contribute to or result in:

– maintaining or promoting exports;
– improving, or preventing decline in the production or distribution of goods or the provision of services;
– promoting technical or economic progress or stability in any industry;

305. Section 22.
306. Sections 21(9) and 22(6).
307. Section 26(2).

- obtaining a benefit for the public which outweighs or would outweigh the lessening in competition that would result, or would be likely to result, from the agreement, decision or concerted practice, or the category of agreements, decisions, or concerted practices.[308]

B. Abuse of a Dominant Position

403. Part III of the Act defines and prohibits abuse of a dominant position in the market. A dominant undertaking according to the Act is any undertaking that controls 50% or more of production, supply, or distribution of any product in Kenya or 50% or more of any service rendered in Kenya. For undertakings controlling less than 50% of a relevant market for goods or services, that undertaking can still be found to be dominant if the undertaking has market power.[309] The Act defines market power as the power of a firm to control prices, to exclude competition, or to behave to an appreciable extent, independently of its competitors, customers, or suppliers.[310] It should be noted that a determination of dominance has as a prerequisite the definition of the relevant market. Several methods are widely known in the field of economics for defining a relevant market,[311] but the Act does not provide guidance as to a preferred or mandatory method for such determination.

404. Where an entity has been determined to be dominant in a relevant market, the Act prohibits the entity from abusing such dominance and provides the following examples of abusive conduct:

- directly or indirectly imposing unfair purchase or selling prices or other unfair trading conditions;
- limiting or restricting production, market outlets or market access, investment, distribution, technical development, or technological progress through predatory or other practices;
- applying dissimilar conditions to equivalent transactions with other trading parties;
- making the conclusion of contracts subject to acceptance by other parties of supplementary conditions which by their nature or according to commercial usage have no connection with the subject matter of the contracts; and
- abuse of an intellectual property right.[312]

405. In a 2016 amendment to the Competition Act, Parliament added the abuse of buyer power as prohibited conduct for any dominant entity. The amendment

308. Section 26(3).
309. Section 23.
310. Section 2.
311. Examples include the small but significant and non-transitory increase in price (SSNIP) test as well as an ad hoc determination of similarities of goods/services.
312. Section 24(2).

defines buyer power as 'the influence exerted by an undertaking or group of undertakings in the position of a purchaser of a product or service to obtain from a supplier more favourable terms, or to impose a long term opportunity cost including harm or withheld benefit which, if carried out, would be significantly disproportionate to any resulting long term cost to the undertaking or group of undertakings'.[313] The CAK is to use the following factors to determine buyer power: the nature and determination of contract terms; the payment requested for access infrastructure; and the price paid to suppliers.[314]

406. An entity found to be dominant and engaging in any of the above activities (or any other activity deemed abusive of the dominant position) may be punished by a fine of up to USD 100,000 or imprisonment for up to five years or both fine and imprisonment.[315]

C. The Investigation into Prohibited Practices

407. The CAK plays the dual roles of regulator and investigator in matters of competition. Thus, the Act authorizes the CAK to carry out, on its own initiative or upon receipt of information or a complaint from any person or government entity, an investigation into conduct by an entity that is alleged to violate prohibitions against restrictive trade practices and/or abuse of dominance.[316] The investigative powers of the CAK are wide-ranging and include the power to: compel an entity to furnish documents or other evidence pertaining to the alleged violations; compel an entity or a representative thereof to appear before the CAK to give oral evidence or to produce documentary evidence; enter and search the premises of an entity believed to have relevant information pertaining to the alleged violations; search a computer system during a search of any premises; and seek the assistance of police officers to carry out these powers.[317]

D. Control of Unwarranted Concentration of Economic Power

408. The Act obliges the CAK to 'keep the structure of production and distribution of goods and services in Kenya under review' in order 'to determine where concentrations of economic power exist whose detrimental impact on the economy outweighs the efficiency advantages, if any, of integration in production and distribution'.[318]

313. Section 24(2A) and 24(2D).
314. Section 24(2B).
315. Section 24(3).
316. Section 31(1).
317. Section 32.
318. Section 50(1).

409. An unwarranted concentration of economic power is deemed to be prejudicial to the public interest if, having regard to the economic conditions prevailing in the country and to all other relevant factors, the effect would be:

- to increase unreasonably the cost relating to the production, supply, or distribution of goods or the provision of any service; or
- to increase unreasonably: (a) the price at which goods are sold; or (b) the profits derived from the production, supply, or distribution of goods or from the performance of any service; or
- to reduce or limit competition in the production, supply, or distribution of any goods (including their sale or purchase) or the provision of any service;
- to result in a deterioration in the quality of any goods or the performance of any service; or
- to result in an inadequacy in the production, supply, or distribution of any goods or services.[319]

410. The CAK may investigate any economic sector that it has reason to believe may feature one or more factors relating to unwarranted concentrations of economic power. After completing the investigation, the CAK may make an order directing any person whom it deems to hold an unwarranted concentration of economic power in any sector to dispose of such portion of his interests in production or distribution or the supply of services as it deems necessary to remove the unwarranted concentration.[320]

411. However, the Act mitigates the effects that any order from the CAK may have on a highly integrated manufacturing enterprise. It provides that no order may be issued that would have the effect of subdividing a manufacturing facility whose degree of physical integration is such that the introduction of independent management units controlling different components reduces its efficiency and substantially raises production costs per unit of output.[321]

412. A person aggrieved by an order of the CAK may appeal to the Competition Tribunal. The decision of the Tribunal is appealable to the High Court whose decision shall be final.[322]

E. Mergers

413. The Act requires CAK approval of all mergers and that any merger approved by the CAK is implemented in accordance with any conditions imposed by the CAK on the merger.[323] This requirement applies whenever one or more

319. Section 50(4).
320. Sections 50(2) and 52(1).
321. Section 52(4).
322. Section 53(1) (2).
323. Section 42.

undertakings directly or indirectly acquire or establish direct or indirect control over the whole or part of the business of another undertaking.[324] The Act provides guiding examples of when such an event occurs, as well as the meaning of 'control' within the context of the Act.[325] The CAK, upon receiving an application for a proposed merger, is required to make a determination as to allowing the merger within sixty days unless the CAK requests further information or a hearing conference with the parties.[326]

414. In making a determination in relation to a proposed merger, the CAK may approve the merger unconditionally, approve the merger with conditions, or decline to give approval of the merger.[327] The CAK is directed to take into account the following non-limiting list of factors when deciding on a proposed merger:

- the extent to which the proposed merger would be likely to prevent or lessen competition or to restrict trade or the provision of any service or to endanger the continuity of supplies or services;
- the extent to which the proposed merger would be likely to result in any undertaking, including an undertaking not involved as a party in the proposed merger, acquiring a dominant position in a market or strengthening a dominant position in a market;
- the extent to which the proposed merger would be likely to result in a benefit to the public which would outweigh any detriment which would be likely to result from any undertaking, including an undertaking not involved as a party in the proposed merger, acquiring a dominant position in a market or strengthening a dominant position in a market;
- the extent to which the proposed merger would be likely to affect a particular industrial sector or region;
- the extent to which the proposed merger would be likely to affect employment;
- the extent to which the proposed merger would be likely to affect the ability of small undertakings to gain access to or to be competitive in any market;
- the extent to which the proposed merger would be likely to affect the ability of national industries to compete in international markets; and
- any benefits likely to be derived from the proposed merger relating to research and development, technical efficiency, increased production, efficient distribution of goods or provision of services, and access to markets.[328]

415. A person aggrieved by an order of the CAK may appeal to the Competition Tribunal, and the decision of the Tribunal is appealable to the High Court. Any decision from the High Court shall be final.[329] Any merger carried out without CAK

324. Section 41(1).
325. Section 41(1)(2).
326. Section 44.
327. Section 46(1).
328. Section 46(2).
329. Section 49.

approval is invalid and has no legal effect.[330] Furthermore, a person who contravenes the requirements of obtaining CAK approval of a merger is guilty of an offence and is liable to imprisonment for a term of up to five years or to a fine of up to USD 100,000 or to both imprisonment and fine.[331]

F. Price Controls

416. The Competition Act 2010 contains none of the price control provisions that were central to the RTPMP Act. This is not to say, however, that the Kenyan economy and the ICT sector are now free of price controls. Regarding the ICT sector in particular, the KIC Act provides that the CA is responsible for protecting the interests of all users of telecommunication services in Kenya with respect to the prices charged for and the quality and variety of such services.[332]

417. Regarding general price controls, the government passed the Price Control (Essential Goods) Act, which commenced in September 2011. The Act provides that the Minister may declare any goods to be essential commodities for the purposes of this Act and determine the maximum prices of the commodities in consultation with the industry.[333] The Act does not specify the ministry responsible for such declarations, and perhaps it was intended that such powers are available to all ministers for the goods that are regulated by their respective ministries. Prices of various goods have been regulated by the government from time to time, including the prices of petrol, maize, sugar, and rice, among others.

G. Sector Enquiries by the Competition Authority

418. The Competition Act 2010 grants to the CAK the authority to conduct sector enquiries in order to determine whether there is a need to further encourage competition. Thus far, the CAK has conducted market enquiries into the following sectors: Banking, Agriculture, Tea, Seed, Cement, and Sugar.[334] In addition, the CAK carried out a market enquiry on competition implications of Unstructured Supplementary Service Data (USSD) pricing in mobile support services.[335] The enquiry was initiated on noting a widespread lack of price disclosure in the Telecommunications sector and concerns over consumer protection.[336] The objectives of

330. Section 42(3).
331. Section 42(5).
332. Section 23(2)(a).
333. Price Control (Essential Goods) Act No. 26 of 2011, s. 2.
334. *See* http://bcckenya.org/assets/documents/20160317-Brief_%20by_Competition_Authority_of_Kenya_Director_General_Mr.%20Kariuki_speech_at_BCCK.pdf.
335. Gazette Notice No. 3829, available at http://kenyalaw.org/kenya_gazette/gazette/volume/MTE3MQ--/Vol.CXVII-No.55.
336. *See* http://cofek.co.ke/index.php/news-and-media/863-competition-authority-of-kenya-is-set-to-investigate-telecommunication-companies-for-anti-competitive-behaviour-in-provision-of-mobile-banking-services-to-financial-institutions?showall=.

the study included: determining whether the provision and pricing of USSD services leads to constrained competition in the financial services market and identify any concerns relating to consumer protection; identify potential consumer protection concerns in the use of USSD to deliver mobile financial services, including the display of USSD costs to customers in a clear manner either before or after the service has been accessed;[337] provide a competitive USSD pricing benchmark that gives some measure of unit economic cost; determine whether larger stakeholders in the provision of the services have undue influence on mobile service providers; and carry out a comprehensive measurement of USSD pricing and terms that providers such as banks and CSP charge to consumers.[338] The results of this market enquiry have not yet been made public.

§4. Current Competition and Statistics in the Sector

419. As of the end of 2016, five TSPs were operating in Kenya, with the market share and other statistics shown in Table 33.

Table 33 Selected Data for Telecommunications Operators in Kenya

	Safaricom	*Airtel*	*Finserve*	*Telkom Kenya*	*Sema Mobile Services*
Market share for mobile subscriptions (%)	71.2	17.6	3.8	7.4	0.0
Number of subscriptions	27,738,727	6,849,493	1,496,153	2,897,545	270
Number of agents for mobile money transfer	124,084	18,354	(Unavailable)	800	–
Number of subscriptions for mobile money transfer	21,574,006	6,711,829	1,240,503	1,772,696	–
Value of mobile money transfer transactions*	KES 892.9 billion	KES 6.6 billion	KES 80.0 million	KES 251.6 billion	–

337. Competition Authority of Kenya Newsletter, Issue No. 1, 2017.

338. *See* http://mobile.nation.co.ke/business/Authority-to-probe-mobile-payments/1950106-2742610-format-xhtml-rvdig0/index.html.

	Safaricom	*Airtel*	*Finserve*	*Telkom Kenya*	*Sema Mobile Services*
Number of SMS messages sent/ received	15.1 billion	693 million	9.6 million	75.1 million	15,754

*Transactions recorded during Q2 only, and include deposits, withdrawals, payments to business accounts, and person-to-person transfers.

Source: CA (Sector Statistics Report Q2 FY 2016/17).

420. From the statistics shown above, it is clear that by any of a number of measures, Safaricom is a 'dominant undertaking' as defined in the Competition Act 2010, controlling at least 50% of the market.[339]

421. The CA also monitors the development of Internet usage, and the sectoral statistics show a single year increase of more than 10% in the number of Internet subscriptions (from 23,929,657 in December 2015 to 26,679,222 in December 2016). Fixed telephone lines, satellite connections, Digital Subscriber Line (DSL) connections, fibre optic connections, and cable modems, as a group, account for less than 1% of all Internet connections in Kenya; more than 99% of Internet access connections are via mobile data subscriptions.[340]

422. Finally the sectoral statistics also clearly show the low importance of fixed-line telephony and that fixed line traffic continues to slowly decline in volume. The number of fixed terrestrial lines in December 2016 stood at 72,427, a decline of 15% from the 85,496 lines in operation in December 2015, and a number that is less than 1% of the 38,596,928 mobile subscribers.[341]

§5. Net Neutrality

423. Net neutrality refers to the extent to which ISPs differentiate their treatment of Internet traffic. In a fully neutral situation, an ISP does not differentiate traffic – i.e., all traffic is charged at the same rate and given the same priority in queues, regardless of any factor such as the type of traffic, the origin or destination of the traffic, and the users/providers involved in the traffic. This situation is typically not favoured by ISPs, which would prefer to be able to charge higher rates or offer premium service for certain kinds of traffic. Proponents of net neutrality often argue

339. Communications Authority of Kenya: Sector Statistics Report Q2 Fiscal Year 2016–2017.
340. *Id.*
341. *Id.*

that it is necessary in order to ensure that the Internet remains accessible to all citizens and technologically neutral. Opponents of net neutrality typically argue that it removes market incentives for innovation and slows the development of new services and technologies.

424. The debate over net neutrality took centre stage in 2014 when then-President Barack Obama directed the industry regulating FCC in the US to issue rules strongly preserving net neutrality.

425. There is currently little in express policies or laws addressing net neutrality in Kenya. The ICT Master Plan cites technology neutrality – i.e., the use of common, interoperable standards, and protocols – as a guiding principle for the ICT sector as a whole.[342] The current Draft National ICT Policy 2016 is noncommittal: 'a net neutrality policy may need to be developed to ensure fair competition between different content and service providers. However, a blanket open Internet policy could inadvertently undermine key policy objectives such as the promotion of innovation local content production and universal service.'

426. An issue in Kenya related to net neutrality is zero rating – i.e., the practice, currently carried out by one of Kenya's telecommunications companies, of offering free data for access to selected mobile applications. Most of the zero-rated content is from foreign-hosted Internet resources such as Facebook and Wikipedia. Zero rating has been controversial as limiting the scope of Internet access available for those without the means or desire to pay for unlimited access, and also placing barriers for the development of local content and services. This content-focused controversy can be contrasted with the ISP-focused controversies observed in developed countries and regions.

427. On a regional level, the African Declaration on Internet Rights and Freedoms affirms Openness as its first key principle, and defines Openness as including net neutrality:

> *The Internet should have an open and distributed architecture, and should continue to be based on open standards and application interfaces and guarantee interoperability so as to enable a common exchange of information and knowledge. Opportunities to share ideas and information on the Internet are integral to promoting freedom of expression, media pluralism and cultural diversity. Open standards support innovation and competition, and a commitment to network neutrality promotes equal and non-discriminatory access to and exchange of information on the Internet.*

342. National ICT Master Plan 2017.

§6. CONCLUSION

428. Kenya's prescription of a hybrid regulatory regime, featuring a sector-specific ICT industry regulator and a traditional general competition regulator for all industries has resulted in a nearly well-defined apportionment of regulatory responsibilities and a mechanism of mutual collaboration between the two regulators. Due to a burgeoning growth in investments in the ICT industry in the last decade, the need for a rigorous regulatory regime has only recently become an imperative for Kenya. Already, with CA's direction, Kenya's ICT industry has been mid-wifed through a liberalization process to achieve market leadership in the greater East African region. Still, fears linger in some segments of the market about the independence of CA from executive control and the likelihood of autocratic State interference with operators, particularly broadcasters. Whatever the fate will be of the market, ICT consumers are enjoying the benefits of highly differentiated products and services brought about by vigorous competition in the industry.

429. A discussion of State actions and criminal laws aimed at protecting ICT consumers has been reserved for elsewhere in this text.

Chapter 3. Regulation of Cryptography

430. The issue of encryption was prominent in the international news in 2016, as the US government fought a high-profile legal battle with Apple Corp., attempting to compel the company to develop a method to 'unlock' the iPhone of a known terrorist. The unlocking was necessary because the iPhone stored data in an encrypted format that would be permanently erased upon logging a certain number of unsuccessful attempts at gaining access. The requested access would provide, for those with the key, 'back-door' access to the iPhone in question as well as potentially any other iPhone in circulation. The government's argument was simply that the requested access was necessary for the sake of national security. Privacy advocates and others in the ICT industry opposed the efforts, and indeed the development of any back-door access to encrypted systems, for a variety of reasons. In addition to a threat against the fundamental right of privacy, they argued that such back-door access makes systems less secure and has a net negative effect on the safety of users.

431. Notable discussions on issues of privacy and encryption occasionally surface within the government and public forums in Kenya. As mentioned elsewhere, the Kenya ICTA developed and promulgated a series of nine ICT standards. Several of these standards include requirements and guidelines for encryption of government data and transmissions. For example, the End-User Computing Devices Standard,[343] which regulates the use of personal computers, phones, and other electronic devices by governmental employees and entities, requires users to encrypt stored data and transmissions of data, among other activities. Other standards with significant requirements pertaining to encryption and data security include the Information Security Standard 2016 and the Electronic Records and Data Management Standard 2016.

432. The ability for private citizens or corporations to use encryption is not guaranteed. Although the right of privacy is provided in the Constitution of Kenya 2010, it has yet to be codified by Parliament. Various laws address national and private security, both generally and in the context of ICT systems (e.g., the KIC Act and the National Intelligence Service (NIS) Act). The KIC Act also mentions encryption in the context of broadcasts and digital signatures.[344] Whereas the National ICT Policy of 2006 contained no mention of encryption, the Draft National ICT Policy 2016 cites the use and support of encryption as a policy objective and furthermore cites the lack of legislation on encryption as a policy challenge. Regional agreements such as the African Union Convention of Cyber Security and Personal Data Protection also oblige Member States to ensure a framework for preventing unauthorized access to data and systems.

433. Notwithstanding the efforts by the Government of Kenya mentioned above, and as is the case in other geographic areas, implementation of encryption in Kenya

343. Kenya ICT Authority, 2016.
344. Kenya ICT Act 1998, s. 2.

is driven by the ICT industry. WhatsApp began offering users end-to-end encryption in 2016. Other similar messaging services and OTT services highlight encryption as a selling point for their respective services. The incompatible reality of the growing presence of encrypted services and the continued efforts by governments to monitor ICT activities in the name of national security suggests that a public dispute, similar to the North American dispute involving Apple, is likely.

Chapter 4. Legal Status of Standardization

§1. Background and Legal Authority

434. In line with their mandate, the Kenya ICTA developed a set of nine standards that were released in 2016 and 2017. These standards cover six domain areas relating to public and private ICT activities and devices, although there is a heavy focus on the operations of government entities and the activities of government employees. The standards were developed by the relevant ICTA committees in collaboration with the KEBS, taking into account international requirements, government requirements, stakeholder requirements, public participation, and industry best practices. The resulting documents were released with the intention that they will be reviewed every three years. The documents are summarized below.

I. End-User Computing Devices Standard, ICTA-2.001:2016

435. This document provides policies and standards for the following aspects of user devices:

- Equipment procurement, including technical specifications and minimum hardware and software specifications for government-procured items.
- Government policies on: bring your own device; travel with laptops; file sharing; and accessibility by disabled persons.
- Inventory standards.
- Maintenance, decommissioning, and disposal.
- Protection of data-in-transit and data-at-rest.
- Authentication standards for government activities.

436. Of particular note are the provisions for data protection.[345] For example, the document states that Ministries, Counties, and Agencies shall protect data as it travels across unprotected networks and shall 'implement strong data at rest protection using encryption algorithms'. Government devices are required to have and use full disk encryption, virtual disk encryption, and file/folder encryption where appropriate in the circumstances.

II. Systems & Applications Standard, ICTA-6.001:2016

437. This document covers the area of Systems and Applications. It establishes guidelines for the successful acquisition, deployment, and utilization of software systems and applications. It aims to evaluate quality and ensure the internal usability of the software product.[346] The document was put into operation on 1 January 2017.

345. End-User Computing Devices Standard, Annex D.1 and Annex D.2.
346. *See* http://icta.go.ke/standards/systems-applications-standard/.

438. Areas covered:

– Architectural model for e-government applications.
– Software acquisition, maintenance, and disposal.
– Messaging and collaboration.
– Website development management.

III. Cloud Computing Standard, ICTA-2.001:2016

439. This standard covers an area of ICT infrastructure. It outlines the various considerations for Ministries, Counties, and Agencies (MCAs) in the selection of services and models for online storage of services, applications, and data, such as Software-as-a-Service (SaaS), Infrastructure-as-a-Service (IaaS), Platform-as-a-Service (PaaS); and public cloud, private cloud, community cloud, and hybrid cloud.[347] The standards contain compliance checklists for cloud service selection, selecting cloud deployment model, and Service Level Agreements (SLA). The document was operationalized on 1 October 2016.

IV. Data Centre Standard, ICTA-2.001:2016

440. This standard covers an area of infrastructure and provides guidelines for setting and maintaining Government data centres. The centres are necessary for supporting the large amounts of data stored and handled by Government, and, under the standards, are required to ensure continued service availability. The document was operationalized on 1 October 2016.

441. The Data Centre Standards contain compliance checklists for site space and layout, tiered reliability, cabling infrastructure, and environmental considerations.[348]

V. IT Governance Standard, ICTA. 5.001: 2016

442. The standards on IT Governance define the processes that ensure the effective and efficient use of IT in enabling government institutions to achieve their goals. The standards span IT management and control in the institution's culture, organization, policy, and practices. The document was operationalized on 1 January 2017.

443. The standards contain compliance information and checklists for the following areas:

347. *See* http://icta.go.ke/standards/cloud-computing-standard/.
348. *See* http://icta.go.ke/standards/data-centre-standard/.

- IT service management.
- IT project management.
- IT legal and regulatory.
- Performance measurement to support IT governance.
- Risk management.
- IT resource management.[349]

VI. ICT Human Capital and Workforce Development Standard, ICTA.7.001:2016

444. The standards on ICT Human Capital and Workforce Development address issues of capacity. They seek to enhance the opportunities for interoperability of public service ICT resources, ensuring uniformity in skills and competencies, and guaranteeing uniform quality of government services everywhere and at all times. These standards take into account the needs and aims of all government's e-service delivery competencies and thus provides standards on: ICT professional (technical) personnel in the public sector, ICT end users, and Kenyan citizens ICT training. The document was operationalized on 1 January 2017.[350]

445. The specific areas addressed by the standards include:

- ICT professionals in the public sector requirement and compliance checklist.
- Capacity development for end-user requirement.
- Capacity development for citizen competency requirement.
- Accreditation of ICT institutions/training providers.
- Accreditation of IT professionals.

VII. Information Security Standard, ICTA-3.001:2016

446. This standard addresses the area of IT Security, providing a consistent approach to managing information security risks across Government bodies. The standards provide that Government must have appropriate controls for the protection of information from a wide range of threats in order to ensure continuity in Government operations, minimize risk, and maximize return on Government IT investments. The document was operationalized on 1 October 2016.

447. The IT security standards deal with the following areas:

- Information security policy.
- Organization of information security.
- Asset management.
- Human resource security.

---

349. *See* http://icta.go.ke/standards/it-governance-standard/.
350. *See* http://icta.go.ke/standards/ict-human-capital-workforce-devpt-std/.

- Communications security.
- Operations security.
- Physical and environmental security.
- Cryptography.
- Access control.
- Systems acquisition, development, and maintenance.
- Supplier relationships.
- Information security incident management.
- Information security aspects of business continuity.
- Compliance.
- Compliance checklist for information security.
- Acceptable use of computing resources (assets) sample policy.[351]

351. *See* http://icta.go.ke/standards/information-security-standard/.

Part II. Protection of Intellectual Property in the ICT Sector

Introduction

448. There are three main domains of intellectual property law that are relevant to the ICT sector in Kenya:

(1) copyright and neighbouring rights;
(2) trademarks; and
(3) patents.

449. Kenya is a signatory to several international treaties and conventions for the protection of intellectual property, including the several international instruments falling under the WTO and the World Intellectual Property Organization (WIPO). These include the agreements and treaties shown in Table 34.

Table 34 Selected IPR Treaties and Agreements to Which Kenya Is a Party[1]

Treaty Name	*Date Signed or Ratified by Kenya*	*Subject Matter*
Agreement on Trade-Related Aspects of Intellectual Property Rights (TRIPS)	1 January 1995	Various forms of IPR
Paris Convention	14 May 1965	Various forms of IPR
Patent Cooperation Treaty (PCT)	8 March 1994	Patents
Harare Protocol[2]	24 October 1984	Patents
Berne Convention	11 March 1993	Copyrights
Marrakesh Treaty	28 June 2013 (signed, not yet ratified)	Copyright
WIPO Copyright Treaty	20 December 1996 (signed, not yet ratified)	Copyright

Treaty Name	*Date Signed or Ratified by Kenya*	*Subject Matter*
Madrid Agreement and Protocol	26 March 1998	Trademarks

1. *Source*: World Intellectual Property Organization (WIPO) website and treaty database.

2. A protocol of the African Regional Intellectual Property Organization (ARIPO).

450. At the municipal level, Kenyan laws on IP that are relevant to ICT include the Copyright Act, 2001, the Trade Marks Act cap. 506, the Industrial Property Act, 2001, and the Anti-Counterfeit Act 2008, and others.

451. The protection of software is an issue that is central to the broader question of protection of IP in the ICT sector. Generally in Kenya, as in other countries, software may simultaneously receive protection under copyright law as well as patent law. It can also be said that copyright law, which lacks formality requirements and is explicitly applicable to the protection of software, is well suited for such protection. In contrast, patent law, which has rigorous formality and substantive requirements and is not explicit in its application to software, is less well suited for such protection. Nevertheless, these and other forms of IP protection are relevant and important to the ICT sector, as described in the following chapters.

Chapter 1. Application of Copyright in the Area of ICT

§1. Basic Principles of Copyright

452. The Copyright Act, 2001 is the primary legislation relating to copyright law in Kenya. It came into force in 2001, and it repealed the old Copyright Act of 1966. The new Act was in large part driven by Kenya's need to fulfil its international legal obligations to harmonize its domestic laws on intellectual property with key provisions of the WTO Agreement on Trade-Related Aspects of Intellectual Property Rights (TRIPS) as well as the 1996 WIPO Treaties.[352] The Copyright Act 2001 was updated with various amendments in 2012 and 2014.

I. Works Eligible for Copyright Protection

453. The purpose of the Act is to make provision for the protection of copyright in literary, musical, and artistic works, audiovisual works, sound recordings, and broadcasts.[353]

454. A literary, musical, or artistic work is only eligible for copyright if:

- sufficient effort has been expended on making the work to give it an original character; and
- the work has been written down, recorded, or otherwise reduced to material form.[354]

455. The degree of effort that would be 'sufficient' to give a work an original character and the medium in which a work should be expressed in order for it to be considered as existing in a 'material form' has been the subject of abundant scholarly analysis. However, it may be said in general that within the Commonwealth, courts have refrained from setting too high a standard for this threshold test for copyright works and second, that the artistic quality of the work is not a material consideration. In *Alternative Media Ltd v. Safaricom Ltd*,[355] the High Court of Kenya held that the law does not require a person to prove that his work was uniquely artistic in order for it to qualify for copyright protection as an artistic work under the Act. The case involved a claim for compensation for alleged infringement of copyright in certain artistic and textual material. The Court asserted that an artistic work may be constituted by a work such as a photograph even if 'the quality thereof was not "uniquely artistic". The quality of the … work is immaterial'.

352. The WIPO Copyright Treaty (WCT) and the WIPO Performances and Phonograms Treaty (WPPT).
353. Preamble to the Act and s. 22(1).
354. Section 22(3).
355. Nairobi High Court Civil Case No. 263 of 2004 (October 2005).

456. That the courts adopt a permissive and liberal approach in determining whether a work has satisfied the copyright threshold is exemplified in this case when the Court's humouredly tried to distinguish, for the purposes of originality, a subtle difference between two pictures, both of which depicted a cheery man haloed inside a bright ring:

> *[I]f the artistic work was to [be] found in the fact that the ring offered protection to the person who was celebrating life, that piece of work would be distinguishable from the picture of a man whose head was outside the ring. The man would not be enjoying the protection of the ring!.*[356]

457. The Court was satisfied that even though some of the conceptual elements of the second picture may have been borrowed from the first one, the creator of the second picture had nevertheless expended sufficient effort and skill in obtaining the photograph and the various design elements that were unique to his picture so as to give it a completely original character.

458. The decision in *Alternative Media* can be contrasted with another case, *Nevin Jiwani v. Going Out Magazine & Another.*[357] In this case, the plaintiff, the publisher of *Go Places* Magazine, claimed that the defendant, the publisher of his own magazine, committed copyright infringement by using photographs and text from *Go Places* Magazine. The Defendant argued that it is possible for different people to take pictures of the same object with each having originality.[358] While comparing the two similar pictures for purposes of originality, the court agreed with the plaintiff's argument that 'it was not possible to produce identical photographs of a scene unless it is taken at the same time or there is a copying'.[359] This holding is not, however, consistent with most international copyright jurisprudence. One need to only think of the thousands of nearly identical photographs taken every year of popular landmarks (e.g., Mount Rushmore and the Eiffel Tower) to understand why.

459. An artistic work is defined by the Act to mean, without reference to artistic quality, any of the following works, or works similar thereto:

- paintings, drawings, etchings, lithographs, woodcuts, engravings, and prints;
- maps, plans, and diagrams;
- works of sculpture;
- photographs not comprised in audiovisual works;
- works of architecture in the form of buildings or models; and
- works of artistic craftsmanship, pictorial woven tissues, and articles of applied handicraft and industrial art.[360]

---

356. *Supra*, 6 of the judgment.
357. *Nevin Jiwani v. Going Out Magazine & Another* [2002] eKLR.
358. *Id.*
359. *Id.*
360. Section 2.

460. An audiovisual work, however, means a fixation in any physical medium of images, either synchronized with or without sound, from which a moving picture may be reproduced and includes videotapes and video games but does not include a broadcast. A broadcast is the transmission, by wire or wireless means, of sounds or images or both or the representations thereof, in such a manner as to cause such images or sounds to be received by the public and includes transmission by satellite.[361] A broadcast shall not be eligible for copyright until it has been broadcast.[362]

461. A literary work means, irrespective of literary quality, any of the following works, or works similar thereto:

- novels, stories, and poetic works;
- plays, stage directions, film sceneries, and broadcasting scripts;
- textbooks, treatises, histories, biographies, essays, and articles;
- encyclopaedias and dictionaries;
- letters, reports, and memoranda;
- lectures, addresses, and sermons;
- charts and tables;
- computer programs; and
- tables and compilations of data including tables and compilations of data stored and embodied in a computer or a medium used in conjunction with a computer.

462. A written law and judicial decision are not to be considered as literary works for the purpose of the Act.[363]

II. Meaning of 'Author'

463. The Act defines the author of a work eligible for copyright protection from two perspectives: the nationality or domicile of the author and from the role of the person in the creation of the work.

III. Nationality

464. Copyright is conferred on an eligible work of which the author, if it is a natural person, is a citizen of Kenya or is domiciled or ordinarily resident in Kenya at the time when the work is made, or, if it is a body corporate, is one which has been incorporated under or in accordance with the laws of Kenya.[364] Where a work is the product of joint authorship, it is sufficient if at least one of the co-authors satisfies this requirement.

361. *Supra.*
362. Section 22(2).
363. *Supra.*
364. Section 23(1).

IV. Role in the Creation of the Work

465. The definition section of the Act makes clear provisions with regard to the nature of the relationship between a person and a work by virtue of which that person may claim copyright in the – a litmus test for identifying who the 'author' of a work is for the purposes of the Act. Table 35 provides various works subject to copyright and the corresponding definitions for authors of such works.

Table 35 Definitions of 'Author' in Respect of Various Works under the Copyright Act, 2001

Work	*Litmus Test for Author*
Literary, Musical, and Artistic Work	The person who first makes or creates the work.
A Photograph	The person who is responsible for the composition of the photograph.
A Sound Recording	The person by whom the arrangements for the making of the sound recording were made.
Audiovisual Works	The person by whom the arrangements for the making of the film were made.
A Broadcast	The first broadcaster.
A Published Edition	The publisher of the edition.
A Literary, Dramatic, Musical, or Artistic Work or Computer Program which is Computer-Generated	The person by whom the arrangements necessary for the creation of the work were undertaken.
A Computer Program	the person who exercised control over the working of the program.

Source: Kenya Copyright Act 2001.

466. The Act confers copyright protection on a literary, musical, or artistic work or any audiovisual work if it is first published in Kenya. If the work is a sound recording, it is protected by the Act if it is made or first published in Kenya. Broadcasts are protected if they are transmitted from transmitters situated in Kenya.[365]

365. Section 24(1).

V. Duration of Copyright Protection

467. The duration of protection provided by the Act for various works is shown in Table 36.

Table 36 Duration of Copyright for Various Works under the Copyright Act, 2001

Type of Work	*Date of Expiration of Copyright*
Literary, Musical, and Artistic Work	Fifty years after the end of the year in which the author dies.
Audiovisual Works and Photographs	Fifty years from the end of the year in which the work was either made, first made available to the public, or first published, whichever date is the latest.
Sound Recordings	Fifty years after the end of the year in which the recording was made.
Broadcasts	Fifty years after the end of the year in which the broadcast took place.
Anonymous or Pseudonymous Literary, Musical, or Artistic Works	Fifty years from the end of the year in which the work was first published.

Source: Kenya Copyright Act 2001.

VI. Moral Rights

468. The Act recognizes two separate types of rights subsisting in every work – economic rights of a copyright owner to benefit from economic exploitation of the work and moral rights of the author. The moral rights are inalienable and are regarded as existing 'independently of the author's economic rights and even after the transfer of [such economic] rights'.[366,367] The moral rights include the right to:

- claim the authorship of the work; and
- object to any distortion, mutilation, or other modification of or other derogatory action in relation to the work which would be prejudicial to the honour or reputation of the author.

469. The moral rights are not transmissible during the life of the author, but the right to exercise any of the rights shall be transmissible by testamentary disposition

366. Section 2(1).
367. Section 32(1).

or by the operation of the law following the demise of the author.[368] The Act gives the author the right to seek relief in connection with any distortion, mutilation or other modification, or derogatory action in relation to his work, where the action is prejudicial to his honour or reputation.[369]

VII. Avoiding the Problem of Copyright in Perpetuity: Non-human Authors

470. The fact that copyright may be conferred on a corporate body[370] and that copyright in a literary, musical, and artistic work expires after a period of time measured from the death of the author raises the question: When is copyright having a corporate entity as author deemed to expire? In the copyright laws of some countries, this question is specifically avoided by setting the expiration of such a copyright as a fixed period of time from the first publication of the work. The Copyright Act in Kenya contains no such provision, but it does provide that a copyright in the case of an anonymous literary, musical, or artistic work shall expire fifty years from the end of the year in which it was first published.[371] Accordingly, one likely and tidy answer to this question is to deem a work owned/authored by a corporate entity as being an anonymous work, and therefore expiring fifty years after first publication. This question has not yet been raised in a case in the Kenyan courts, and so the matter deserves a more thorough analysis.

471. By its very nature, a corporate body such as a company has an existence and an identity that is separate from the human actors who comprise its staff. By the perpetual succession of the human actors, a corporate body is not predestined to 'die' in the same sense as a human person. As a matter of fact, some of the world's leading companies have been in existence for periods far exceeding the average human lifespan. Hypothetically speaking, in addition to treating the work as an anonymous work, there may be several other possible answers to the question of expiry when a copyright has a corporate author:

- The first argument stems from a pure and mechanistic interpretation of the law: A corporation dies when its existence is terminated through the legal process for the dissolution of companies. Therefore, where the copyright in a literary, musical, or artistic work is held by a corporation, the copyright expires fifty years from the date of dissolution. An immediately obvious problem with this approach is that it leaves open the remote possibility that the copyright will never expire.
- The second argument is that a corporation is not capable of creating a work and that for all intents and purposes, the duration of the copyright held in a work by a corporation is to be reckoned from the lifespan of the human creator of the work who is an employee of the company. According to this argument then, copyright

368. Section 32(2).
369. Section 32(3).
370. As observed, the definition of an author of an eligible work provided in s. 23(1) includes a corporate body.
371. Section 23(3).

in a literary, musical or artistic work held by a corporation would expire fifty years after the end of the year when the human creator of the work dies. Naturally, this approach assumes that the author can be identified.

472. The first argument fails the moral philosophy test of intellectual property law. The aim of the law is to encourage creativity and innovation by granting, for a limited time, monopoly rights to inventors, authors, and creators to commercially exploit the application and use of their works. After the limited time, the monopoly rights cease, and the property in the work passes into the public domain so that humankind may freely avail itself of its benefits.

473. The second argument is by far the preferred interpretation in cases where the actual human author can be identified. It avoids the moral absurdity of copyright which is either held for too long or which does not expire where it is held by a corporation which on account of mergers, acquisitions, and the perpetual succession of its human actors exists for an indefinite period of time. This interpretation seems to be the one preferred by the law. The Act make a factual and legal distinction between the human creator of a work and the person in whom the copyright in the work is vested.

474. Where the identity of the human actor who creates a work for his company cannot be established, or where his identity and the date when he created the work are deliberately obscured by a corporation, assuming the work to be an anonymous work prevents the employing company from continuing to enjoy the benefits of copyright protection indefinitely.

475. At least for the purpose of reckoning the duration of copyright held by a corporation, it is important for copyright legislation, whether in its preambular definitions or its substantive text, to recognize two distinct entities:

(1) the author of the work; and
(2) the owner of the work, whether that is the author or an entity to which copyright is assigned by an author.

476. Kenya's copyright law clearly makes the distinction. In relation to a literary, musical, and artistic work, the Act defines the term 'author' as 'the person who first makes or creates the work'.[372] In relation to a literary, dramatic, musical, or artistic work or a computer program which is computer-generated, the Act defines an author as 'the person by whom the arrangements necessary for the creation of the work were undertaken', whereas for a computer program, it is 'the person who exercised control over the working of the program'.

477. Further, where a work is commissioned by a person who is not the author's employer under a contract of service or not having been so commissioned is made

372. Section 2(1).

in the course of the author's employment under a contract of service, the copyright shall be deemed to be transferred to the person who commissioned the work or the author's employer, subject to any agreement between the parties excluding or limiting the transfer.[373]

478. The Act further makes specific provisions on how to reckon the lifespan of copyright held by a government, another entity which by its nature has, at least in theory, an indefinite lifespan. Copyright in a literary, musical, or artistic work created pursuant to a commission from the government, an international governmental body, or a non-governmental body is to exist 'until the end of the expiration of fifty years from the end of the year in which it was first published'.[374] Copyright in such a work vests initially in the government or such other body and not in the author.[375]

VIII. Nature of Copyright in Literary, Musical, or Artistic Work

479. Copyright in a literary, musical or artistic work, or audiovisual work means the exclusive right to control the doing of any of the following works in Kenya:

- the reproduction of the original work or its translation or adaptation in any material form;
- the distribution of the work to the public by way of sale, rental, lease, hire, loan, importation, or similar arrangement;
- the communication to the public and the broadcasting of the whole work or a substantial part of it, either in its original form or in any form recognizably derived from the original.[376]

IX. Fair Use and Fair Dealing

480. In all copyright laws throughout the world, exceptions are imposed that limit the ability of a copyright holder to enforce their copyright. This is done often for the sake of fairness but also for the sake of practicality in enforcement. Copyright regimes are generally implemented with one of two different systems of determining whether an exception is applied: fair use or fair dealing. Under the latter system, the law provides a list of specific exceptions, and an activity must fall within one of those listed exceptions in order to qualify as fair dealing. Thus only specifically enumerated categories of activities can be found as exceptions to copyright infringement in a fair dealing system. In contrast, a fair use system provides guidance as to the nature of activities that should be exempted from copyright infringement and allows judges to examine the context of a specific activity in question against the guidance provided. Thus, at least in theory, nearly any category of

373. Section 31.
374. Section 25(1) (2).
375. Section 31(2).
376. Section 26(1).

activity can be exempted from copyright infringement under the right context in a fair use system. Whereas the US operates under a fair use system, much of the rest of the world, including Kenya, operates under a fair dealing system.

481. Accordingly, under the Copyright Act, copyright in literary, musical or artistic works, or audio-visual works shall not include the right to control:

- the doing of any of those acts by way of fair dealing for the purposes of scientific research, private use, criticism or review, or the reporting of current events subject to acknowledgement of the source;
- the reproduction and distribution of copies or the inclusion in a film or broadcast, of an artistic work situated in a place where it can be viewed by the public;
- the incidental inclusion of an artistic work in a film or broadcast;
- the inclusion in a collection of literary or musical works of not more than two short passages from the work in question if the collection is designed for use in a school registered under the Education Act[377] or a university and includes an acknowledgement of the title and authorship of the work;
- the broadcasting of a work if the broadcast is intended to be used for purposes of systematic instructional activities;
- the reproduction of a broadcast referred to in the preceding paragraph and the use of that reproduction in a school registered under the Education Act or a university for instructional activities;
- the reading or recitation in public or in a broadcast by one person of any reasonable extract from a published literary work if it is accompanied by a sufficient acknowledgement of the author;
- the reproduction of a work by or under the direction or control of the government, or by designated public libraries, non-commercial documentation centres, and scientific institutions, where the reproduction is in the public interest and no revenue is derived from it;
- the reproduction of a work by a broadcasting station where the reproduction or copies thereof are intended exclusively for broadcast by that broadcasting authority authorized by the copyright owner of the work and are destroyed before the end of the period of six calendar months immediately following the making of the reproduction or such longer period as may be agreed between the broadcasting authority and the owner of the relevant part of the copyright in the work. Any reproduction of such a work, if it is of an exceptional documentary nature, may be preserved in the archives of the broadcasting authority, but it is not to be used for broadcasting or for any other purpose without the consent of the owner of the work;
- the broadcasting of a literary, musical, or artistic work or audiovisual works already lawfully made accessible to the public with which no copyright collective society is concerned, provided that the owner of the broadcasting right in the work receives fair compensation; and

377. Chapter 211 of the Laws of Kenya.

- any use made of a work for the purpose of a judicial proceeding or any report of any such proceeding.[378]

482. The above list of situations in which copyright law does not allow the author to exercise control is a closed list, and therefore the Copyright Act firmly places Kenya in the category of countries having a fair dealing (rather than fair use) regime. This firm footing was upset in the case of *Royal Media Services Ltd. & 2 Others v. Attorney General & 8 Others.*[379] In this case, dealing with (among other things) the broadcast of free-to-air channels, the Supreme Court of Kenya held that another category, namely public best interest, can serve as the basis for activities to be considered fair use. By introducing a category of fair dealing that is not explicitly listed in the Copyright Act, however, the Court has arguably transitioned Kenya from a fair dealing jurisdiction to one that recognizes court-created exceptions, i.e., a fair use jurisdiction.

X. Nature of Copyright in a Sound Recording

483. Copyright in sound recordings confers the exclusive right to control the doing in Kenya of any of the following acts in respect of the sound recording:

- the direct or indirect reproduction in any manner or form; or
- the distribution to the public of copies by way of sale, rental, lease, hire, loan, or any similar arrangements; or
- the importation into Kenya; or
- the communication to the public or the broadcasting of the sound recording in whole or in part either in its original form or in any form recognizably derived from the original.[380]

484. However, the following uses of a sound recording amount to fair use under the Act and the copyright holder has no right to control them:

- the doing of any of those acts by way of fair dealing for the purposes of scientific research, private use, criticism or review, or the reporting of current events subject to acknowledgement of the source;
- the reproduction of a broadcast referred to in the preceding paragraph and the use of that reproduction in a school registered under the Education Act or a university for instructional activities;
- the reproduction of a work by or under the direction or control of the government, or by designated public libraries, non-commercial documentation centres, and scientific institutions, where the reproduction is in the public interest and no revenue is derived from it;

378. *Supra.*
379. [2013] eKLR. This case is discussed extensively in Part I of this text.
380. Section 28(1).

- the broadcasting of a work already lawfully made accessible to the public with which no copyright collective society is concerned, provided that the owner of the broadcasting right in the work receives fair compensation;[381]
- the making of a single copy of the recording for the personal and private use of the person making the copy, though in such use, the copyright owner shall be entitled to 'fair compensation consisting of a royalty levied on audio recording equipment or audio blank tape suitable for recording and other media intended for recording, payable at the point of first sale in Kenya by the manufacturer or importer for commercial purposes of such equipment or media'.[382] As of 2017, the so-called 'blank tape levy' had been discussed by Kenya Copyright Board (KECOBO) and industry stakeholders on multiple occasions, but the amount of the levy had not been agreed and so collections are not yet underway.

485. Notwithstanding the lack of an agreed 'blank tape levy', the Act makes it an offence to commercially avail any audio recording equipment for the purposes of enabling another person to make single copies of any sound recording for personal or private use, without the payment of the royalty. The offence is punishable by a fine not exceeding two hundred thousand shillings or imprisonment for a term not exceeding four years or both.

XI. Copyright in Broadcasts and Performances

486. Copyright in a broadcast vests the exclusive right to control the doing in Kenya of any of the following acts, namely, the fixation and the rebroadcasting of the whole or a substantial part of the broadcast and the communication to the public of the whole or a substantial part of a television broadcast either in its original form or in any form recognizably derived from the original.[383] Copyright in a television broadcast includes the right to control the taking of still photographs therefrom.[384]

487. However, it constitutes fair use of a broadcast to:

- do any of those acts by way of fair dealing for the purposes of scientific research, private use, criticism or review, or the reporting of current events subject to acknowledgement of the source;
- broadcast a work for purposes of systematic instructional activities;
- reproduce a broadcast for use in a school registered under the Education Act or a university for instructional activities; and
- any use made of a work for the purpose of a judicial proceeding or any report of any such proceeding.[385]

---

381. Section 28(2).
382. Section 28(3).
383. Section 29.
384. *Ibid.*
385. *Ibid.*

488. Section 30 of the Act makes provisions on the rights of performers. A performance means the representation of a work by such action as dancing, playing, reciting, singing, declaiming, or projecting to listeners by any means and a performer means an actor, singer, declaimer, musician, or other person who performs a literary or musical work and includes the conductor of the performance of any such work.

489. A performer has the right to control the following acts with respect to his performance:

- broadcasting the performance except where the broadcast is made from a fixation of the performance authorized by the performer;
- communicating to the public his performance except where the communication: (a) is made from a fixation of the performance; or (b) is made from a broadcast of the performance authorized by the performer;
- making a fixation of a previously unfixed performance;
- reproducing a fixation of the performance in either of the following cases: (a) where the performance was initially fixed without the authorization of the performer or (b) where the reproduction is made for purposes different from those for which the performer gave his authorization; and
- rent for commercial purposes to the public, the original, and copies of their fixed performances.[386]

490. The protection of the rights of the performer exists for fifty years after the end of the year in which the performance was fixed.[387]

491. The Act confers on the performer certain moral rights with respect to his work. During his lifetime and independently of his economic rights, the performer has the following rights with respect to live performances or performances fixed in phonograms:

- the right to be identified as the performer of his performances and to object to any distortion, mutilation, or other modification of his performances that would be prejudicial to his reputation; and
- the right to seek relief in connection with any distortion, mutilation or other modification of, and any other derogatory action in relation to his work where such work would be or is prejudicial to his honour or reputation.[388]

492. The Copyright Act was amended in 2012 to include section 30A, providing a right to equitable remuneration to the performer for the use of sound recordings and audiovisual works. The section provides that if a sound recording is published for commercial purposes or a reproduction of such recording is used directly for broadcasting or other communication to the public, or is publicly performed, a

386. Section 30(1)(b).
387. Section 30(4).
388. Section 30(5).

single equitable remuneration for the performer and the producer of the sound recording shall be paid by the user, and the remuneration shall be shared equally between the producer of the sound recording and the performer.[389]

493. Section 30A further provides that if a fixation of a performance is published for commercial purposes or a reproduction of a fixation of a performance is used for broadcasting or other communication to the public, or is publicly performed, a single equitable remuneration for the performer shall be paid by the user.

494. Section 30A further requires that the remuneration mentioned in the section is to be paid through the respective collective management organization (CMO). Presumably, the proper CMO is the Performers Rights Society of Kenya (PRiSK). This requirement, however, and section 30A generally, became the subject of several lawsuits, ultimately resulting in the nullification of section 30A as described below.

A. *Xpedia Management Ltd. & 4 Others v. The Attorney General & 5 Others*

495. The petitioners included several artists as well as two companies involved in promoting and distributing music through digital platforms.[390] They argued that the requirements in section 30A (that royalties for performers are to be collected and distributed by the relevant CMO) compels them to become members of the CMO or to forfeit their royalties. This, it was argued, violates their right to freedom of association guaranteed under Article 36 of the Constitution, as well as their right to property under Article 40(5). Judge Mumbi Ngugi held for the respondents. Section 30A, according to Mumbi J., does not require petitioners to become members of the CMO. Non-members may collect their royalties from the CMO, and the additional fees charged by the CMO for fees paid to non-members are not sufficiently punitive or restrictive as to be unconstitutional.

B. *Mercy Munee Kingoo & Another. v. Safaricom Ltd. & Another*

496. The petitioners in this case alleged that the respondent was using section 30A to justify payment of royalties generated by ringtones to CMOs rather than to the so-called PRSP that were preferred by the petitioners.[391] Rather than attacking the constitutionality of section 30A per se, however, the petitioners alleged that the process by which section 30A was added to the Copyright Act was unconstitutional. Specifically, the petitioners argued that the legislative process for adding section 30A did not sufficiently involve stakeholders and open public participation. In holding for the petitioners, S.J. Chitembwe, J. stated that section 30A was 'enacted without public participation and it is being retrospectively applied'. Interestingly, and in

389. Section 30A(1).
390. [2016] eKLR.
391. [2016] eKLR.

direct conflict with Justice Ngugi, the judge also held that section 30A 'also limits artists' freedom not to be compelled to join an association of any kind as provided under Article 36 of the Constitution. The petitioners are being forced to receive their royalties through Collective Management Organization yet they have no dealings with them. This is unconstitutional'.

497. The nullification of section 30A has two significant consequences: (1) it calls into question the legitimacy of all other Parliamentary amendments that have been made with the same or similar level of public participation, including specifically all other amendments to the Copyright Act that were enacted at the same time that section 30A was added and (2) it poses a challenge to the operations and collections of PRiSK, the CMO that represents performers.

§2. Administration of Copyright

I. The Kenya Copyright Board

498. The Act establishes the KECOBO[392] and mandates it with the following powers:

- implement and ensure the observance of all copyright laws and international treaties and conventions to which Kenya is a party;
- license and supervise the activities of collective management societies;
- conduct public training, publicity, and education on copyright and related rights;
- ensure the continuous improvement and effectiveness of copyright legislation;
- maintain an effective data bank on authors and their works; and
- administer all matters of copyright and related rights in Kenya.[393]

499. The Board of Directors for KECOBO is composed of a Chairman appointed by the Minister for the time being in charge copyright matters[394] (also known as the Parent Ministry), and a membership that includes government officials, industry representatives, and experts on copyright law. The government officials on the Board include representatives of the Attorney General, the Commissioner of Police, the Ministry of Information and the Parent Ministry, while the industry is represented by seven nominees from industry associations. These associations include software engineers, musicians, film-makers, artists, authors and writers, producers of sound recordings, broadcasting stations, and the distributors of

392. Section 3.
393. Section 5.
394. Currently the Office of the Attorney General, according to the provisions of the Copyright Act as read with the Interpretation and General Provisions Act and consistent with the amendment made by the Statute Law (Miscellaneous Amendments) Act of 2014.

audiovisual works. The Minister has the discretion to appoint to the Board up to four other members by virtue of their knowledge and expertise in matters relating to copyright and other related rights.[395]

500. In 2016, under Kenya Gazette Notice No. 1724 published on 17 March 2016, the president of Kenya, Uhuru Kenyatta, appointed Millicent Ogutu as the chairperson of KECOBO and revoked the appointment of then-Chairperson Tom Mshindi. In the Notice, the President stated that he was exercising the powers conferred upon him under section 7(3) of the State Corporations Act. There were very many questions as to the legality of this particular appointment since the Copyright Act provides that KECOBO's chairperson is to be appointed by the Attorney General. This particular appointment also came after the High Court had recently nullified the appointment of the chairperson of the Anti-Counterfeit Agency by the president through the process of Judicial Review.[396] In his judgment in that case, Justice G. V. Odunga stated that the President must adhere to the provisions of the relevant legislation in making appointments.[397] Issues over the appointment of the KECOBO board chairperson were resolved in a subsequent Gazette Notice.

501. The Executive Director of the Board is in charge of the management of the affairs of the Board's Secretariat and remains under the general direction and supervision of the Board.

II. Assignment and Licences

502. The Act recognizes the right of a copyright owner to transfer the copyright in his work. Transmission of copyright may be done by:

- assignment;
- licence;
- testamentary disposition (i.e., by a will); or

---

395. Section 6.
396. *Republic v. Attorney General & 3 others Ex-Parte Tom Odoyo Oloo* [2015] eKLR.
397. At para. 49: 'Having considered the issues raised herein, I am not satisfied that that both the Constitutional and relevant statutory provisions relating to the appointment of the interested party to the position the subject of these proceedings were not adhered to. Where there is non-compliance with the provisions of the law the minimum that the executive can do is to give some rational grounds for the action otherwise the Court may well be entitled in concluding that there was no reason for acting in the manner it did in which case the decision may well be found to be grossly unreasonable since that is the only term that can be applied to an action taken in breach of the law. Whereas the President had the power to appoint the Chairman of the Anti-Counterfeit Agency, that appointment had to be in compliance with the Constitution and the relevant Legislation since, as I have stated herein above, the President in undertaking his executive functions does so on behalf of the people of the Republic of Kenya and has to bow to the will of Kenyans as expressed in their document delegating their sovereign powers to inter alia the executive, the Constitution. It is the Constitution which sets out the terms under which the delegated sovereign power is to be exercised and those to whom the power is delegated must adhere to it and where certain powers are not expressly delegated, resort must be had to the people by way of a referendum.'

– by the operation of law.[398]

503. An assignment or testamentary disposition of copyright may be limited so as to apply only to the doing of a limited number of acts in relation to the work, or to only a part of the period of the copyright, or to a specified country or other geographical area.[399] A copyrighted work may be the subject of a licence lawfully granting a licensee permission to do any one or more acts controlled by the copyright. A licence may be exclusive or non-exclusive.

504. However, save where copyright is transmitted by the operation of the law, all assignments, exclusive licences, and testamentary dispositions[400] of copyright are required to be made in writing and signed by or on behalf of the person making it.[401] Where an assignment relates to works from outside Kenya, the instrument of assignment shall be accompanied by a letter of verification from the KECOBO.[402] However, a non-exclusive licence may be written or oral, or it may be inferred from conduct and it may be revoked at any time.[403] Where an agreement for assignment of copyright does not specify the period of assignment, the assignment will be deemed to terminate after three years.[404]

III. Authentication

505. Manufacturers and producers of sound and audiovisual works or recordings are required to apply to the KECOBO for the authentication of copyright works.[405] Once the Board considers the documentation furnished with the request and is satisfied that the work is authentic, it issues an approval certificate authorizing the applicant to purchase an authentication device. In 2010, KECOBO began issuing authentication devices in the form of holographic stickers that were to be affixed to every legitimate copy of a work (e.g., every CD or DVD). Uptake of the stickers has been slow despite efforts by KECOBO to encourage copyright holders, including by assisting in enforcement activities.

506. The Act makes it an offence to sell or exhibit any copyright work to which no authentication device has been affixed where such a work is one to which the device is required to be affixed.[406] The Copyright Regulations, 2004 extend the requirement to affix the authentication device to sound recordings and audiovisual works imported into Kenya for sale, rental, hiring, lending, or distribution to the

398. Section 33(1).
399. Section 32(2).
400. Subject to certain formal requirements, an oral will may be made under the Law of Succession Act (Ch. 160 of the Laws of Kenya).
401. Section 32(3).
402. *Ibid.*
403. Section 32(4).
404. Section 32(7).
405. Section 36(1).
406. Section 36(5).

public for commercial purposes. However, the regulation excludes 'computer programs embodied in sound recording or an audiovisual work' from this provision.

IV. Copyright Inspectors

507. The Act empowers the KECOBO to appoint Copyright Inspectors 'for the purpose of enforcing the provisions of [the] Act'.[407] The Act also empowers any member of the Board or a police officer, in his own capacity, to perform the functions of a Copyright Inspector.

508. An Inspector has the power, subject only to exercising it at a reasonable time and upon the production of his certificate of authority, to enter, search, and inspect any premises, ship, aircraft, or vehicle for the purpose of ascertaining whether there is or has been any contravention of the Act.[408] The Inspector may also seize and detain any substance or article which he has reasonable cause to believe is an infringing copy of a work or in relation to which an offence may have been committed under the Act and arrest any person who is reasonably suspected of committing such an offence.[409] He may also seize any documents which may be required in proceedings under the Act.[410]

V. Works in the Public Domain

509. The Act designates the following works as belonging to the public domain:

- works whose terms of protection have expired;
- works in respect of which authors have renounced their rights; and
- foreign works which do not enjoy protection in Kenya.[411]

510. A work that has fallen into the public domain may be used without any restriction.

VI. Collective Administration of Copyright

511. The Act makes provision for the collective administration of copyright through copyright collecting societies registered by the Copyright Board. Each of these CMOs must be a company limited by guarantee and incorporated under the laws of Kenya. It is to be a non-profit making entity with rules and regulations for the protection of the interests of its members. It is to have as its principal objective

407. Section 39(1).
408. Section 40.
409. Sections 41, 42.
410. *Ibid.*
411. Section 45.

the negotiation for the collection and distribution of royalties and the granting of licences in respect of copyright works or performer's rights.

512. As of 2016, three CMOs were operational in Kenya. The Music Copyright Society of Kenya (MCSK) was the oldest of the CMOs and represented the interests of music authors and publishers. The Kenya Association of Music Producers (KAMP) represents the interests of music producers. The Performers Rights Society of Kenya (PRiSK) collects royalties on behalf of performers. Many commercial consumers of music objected to the need to pay separate royalties to three different CMOs, and in 2016 efforts were made to institute a single joint tariff. The joint tariff is expected to go into effect in 2017.

513. A fourth Kenyan CMO, known as KOPIKEN, represented the interests of authors and publishers of printed works (e.g., books and magazines). This organization collected royalties primarily from copy shops and universities. Although KOPIKEN went defunct in 2014, efforts are underway to revive the organization.

514. Currently, no CMO is operating in Kenya on behalf of any activities in the computer software industry.

515. A collecting society may be deregistered by the Board where it fails to adequately fulfil its functions or fails to comply with the provisions of the Act.[412] This, in fact, occurred in 2017, when KECOBO took the unusual decision to refuse to renew the licence granted to MCSK and to grant that licence to a newly formed CMO known as the Music Publishers Association of Kenya (MPAKE).

516. One challenge encountered by the CMOs in Kenya has been adapting to the shift from physical distribution (e.g., via CDs and other tangible media) to digital distribution of music and other content. Development of online and mobile platforms for content distribution is a burgeoning field within the innovation community in Kenya, with numerous start-up companies and SMEs attempting to capture a share of the growing market. As with other areas of technology, such activities evolve and develop at a rapid pace. Integration of rapidly evolving technologies presents a particular challenge to CMOs in terms of maintaining effective and efficient collection and distribution channels.

VII. Competent Authority (Copyright Tribunal)

517. The Act establishes a quasi-judicial Tribunal (referred to in the Act as 'the competent authority'). The Tribunal is to be comprised of a minimum of three and a maximum of five persons appointed by the Minister for the time being in charge of matters relating to copyright. One of the members is to be a person qualified as

412. Section 47.

an advocate or attorney of not less than 'standing of seven years or a person who holds or has held judicial office in Kenya who shall be the Chairman'.[413]

518. The jurisdiction of the tribunal extends to 'any matter [which is required] to be determined by [it]' including:

- where the Board is unreasonably refusing to grant a certificate of registration in respect of a collecting society or is imposing unreasonable terms or conditions on the granting of such a certificate; or
- a collecting society is unreasonably refusing to grant a licence in respect of a copyright work or is imposing unreasonable terms or conditions on the granting of such a licence.[414]

519. Where a dispute has been referred to the Tribunal, it has the power to conduct hearings, giving each party an opportunity to represent its case either in person or through its representatives either orally or in writing, and to thereafter make a determination of the dispute.[415]

520. Members of the Tribunal were duly nominated in 2015–2016. However, due to a lack of resources and the legal uncertainty as to how the Tribunal should receive operational funding, the Tribunal has yet to sit or to begin hearing disputes.

§3. Infringement, Relief, and Defences

I. Infringement

521. Copyright shall be infringed by a person who, without the licence of the owner of the copyright:

- does, or causes to be done, an act the doing of which is controlled by the copyright; or
- imports, or causes to be imported, otherwise than for his private and domestic use, an article which he knows to be an infringing copy;
- with respect to a performance: (a) does, or causes to be done, any of the acts specified in the preceding part or (b) imports or causes to be imported, otherwise than for his own private or domestic use, an article which he knows would have been made contrary to those provisions had it been made in Kenya by the importer;
- circumvents any effective technical measure designed to protect works; or
- manufactures or distributes devices which are primarily designed or produced for the purpose of circumventing technical measures designed to protect works protected under this Act; or

413. Section 48.
414. Section 48(2).
415. Section 48(3).

- removes or alters any electronic rights management information; or
- distributes, imports, broadcasts, or makes available to the public, protected works, records, or copies from which electronic rights management information has been removed or has been altered without the authority of the right holder.[416]

II. Relief

A. Anton Piller Orders

522. If a person has prima facie evidence that his right has been infringed by another party, and he satisfies the court or competent authority that prima facie:

- he has a cause of action against another person which he intends to pursue;
- the other person has in his possession, documents, infringing copies, or other things which constitute evidence of great importance in substantiation of that cause of action, and there is the real and well-founded apprehension that the documents, infringing copies, or other things may be hidden, destroyed, or rendered inaccessible before discovery can be made in the usual way; the court or competent authority may make such order as it considers necessary or appropriate to secure the preservation of the materials as evidence.[417] Such an order may be granted ex parte (upon the application of one party and without the knowledge or presence of the other party).[418]

523. This remedy derived its name from the English decision of *Anton Piller KG v. Manufacturing Processes Ltd & others*[419] in which the conditions for the grant of the orders were laid down by Ormorod L. J. at page 62 as follows:

> *First, there must be an extremely strong prima facie case. Secondly, the damage, potential or actual, must be very serious for the applicant. Thirdly, there must be clear evidence that the defendants have in their possession incriminating documents or things, and that there is a real possibility that they may destroy such material before any application inter-partes can be heard.*

524. In *Microsoft Corporation v. Mitsumi Computer Garage Ltd & another,*[420] Microsoft Corporation filed a suit against Mitsumi Computer Garage Ltd., a company that specialized in the sale of computer hardware and an authorized distributor of Microsoft's software. In its statement of claim, Microsoft asserted its copyright as the creator of a suite of computer programs, being in the nature of 'computer-generated literary works', namely, operating system software known as Microsoft

416. Section 35.
417. Section 37(1).
418. Section 3(2).
419. [1976] 1 Ch. 55.
420. Nairobi (Milimani Commercial Courts) Civil Suit No. 810 of 2001.

Windows 98 and Microsoft Office Professional 2000, comprising of, among others, Microsoft Word 2000, Microsoft Excel 2000, Microsoft Access 2000, and Microsoft PowerPoint 2000. Microsoft stated that Mitsumi had made 'counterfeit/unlicensed computer software programs, which were unauthorized reproductions of [its] software programs'. Along with the statement of claim, Microsoft filed an interlocutory application under a certificate of urgency asking the High Court to issue an ex parte Anton Piller order allowing it enter and inspect the premises of Mitsumi and seize therefrom computers and material necessary to substantiate the claim. Ringera J., being satisfied that Microsoft had satisfied the requirements set out in the *Anton Piller* case, issued an Anton Piller order. Pursuant to that order, Microsoft raided the premises of Mitsumi and seized seventy-six computer systems.[421] According to Microsoft, four of these computers revealed 'a duplication of product identification, and licensing deficiency, thus indicating a duplication of the licences and the illegitimacy of the software' installed on them. At least two of the computers had versions of the Windows 95 operating system software bearing similar product identification numbers.

525. Microsoft asked the Court to issue an injunction restraining Mitsumi from further infringing its copyright, a delivery up or destruction upon oath of all the infringing copies, an enquiry as to damages, and an account by Mitsumi on the profits made by reason of the infringement and general damages. The litigation was eventually settled out of court on terms that have not been made public by the parties.

526. In *Microsoft Corporation v. Microskills Kenya Ltd*[422] Microsoft Corporation sued a local hardware and software reseller, Microskills Kenya Ltd, for copyright infringement. Microsoft alleged that Microskills illegally bundled Microsoft's business software on hundreds of computer systems that it sold to its customers. The High Court found Microskills liable for copyright infringement and awarded Microsoft over USD 342,365 in damages. Thereafter, Microskills moved the High Court on a bankruptcy and winding-up cause ostensibly because it was not in a financial position to settle the award. It remains unclear how much of the award was settled during the winding-up proceedings.

B. Other Remedies

527. The infringement of any right protected under the Act is to be actionable at the suit of the owner of the right[423] and in any action for infringement the following statutory reliefs are available to the plaintiff:

---

421. Microsoft also seized computer equipment belonging to another company, Mitsuminet (Kenya) Ltd, ostensibly under the mistaken belief that it was the property of Mitsumi Computer Garage Ltd. This seizure was subsequently overruled by the court and Microsoft's attempt to amend the statement of claim to join Mitsuminet as a party to the suit was dismissed.
422. Nairobi High Court Civil Case No. 323 of 1999.
423. Section 35(4).

- the relief by way of damages, injunction,[424] accounts or otherwise that is available in any corresponding proceedings in respect of infringement of other proprietary rights;
- delivery up to the plaintiff of any article in the possession of the defendant which appears to the court to be an infringing copy, or any article used or intended to be used for making infringing copies;
- in lieu of damages and at the option of the plaintiff, the award of an amount calculated on the basis of reasonable royalty which would have been payable by a licensee in respect of the work or type of work concerned, and for the determination of which a court may hold a special enquiry;[425] and
- where an infringement of copyright is proved or admitted, and the court, having regard (in addition to all other material considerations) to: (a) the flagrancy of the infringement and (b) any benefit shown to have accrued to the defendant by reason of the infringement is satisfied that effective relief would not otherwise be available to the plaintiff. In assessing damages for the infringement, the court may award such measure of aggravated damages as it may consider appropriate in the circumstances.[426]

III. Defences

528. Where in an action for infringement of copyright it is proved or admitted that an infringement was committed but it is established that at the time of the infringement the defendant was not aware, and had no reasonable grounds for suspecting, that copyright subsisted in the work to which the action relates, the plaintiff shall not be entitled to any damages against the defendant in respect of the infringement whether or not other relief is granted.[427]

A. General Principles of Criminal Liability

529. The Copyright Act defines various offences of copyright infringement and prescribes the penalties for the offences. However, even where a prima facie act of infringement is established by the prosecution, the offence is not committed if the accused person establishes that he had acted in good faith and had no reasonable grounds for supposing that copyright or the right of a performer would be infringed.[428] Copyright infringement is therefore not an offence of strict liability.

---

424. Section 35(7) precludes the issue of an order of an injunction requiring a completed or partly built building to be demolished or preventing the completion of a partly built building. Such an order might be sought by a plaintiff who seeks relief for the infringement of his copyright in an architectural design.
425. *Ibid.*
426. Section 35(6).
427. Section 35(5).
428. Section 38(1).

530. Where a person has in his possession or control two or more infringing copies of a work in the same form, a statutory presumption arises that his possession or his importation of the copies was otherwise than for private and domestic use.[429] This presumption is rebuttable, and it can be dislodged by the evidence of the accused.

531. The general punishment for copyright infringement is a fine not exceeding USD 5,480 or to imprisonment for a term not exceeding ten years or both.[430]

532. No prosecution for an offence of copyright infringement under section 38 of the Act may be instituted after the expiration of the period of three years immediately following the date of the alleged offence. Such prosecution is to be before the High Court or a subordinate court presided by a magistrate of the rank of Resident Magistrate. Further, one-half of all fines imposed and recovered by a court in respect of the contravention of any of the provisions of the Act or its regulations is to be paid into the revenues of the KECOBO and the other half into the general revenues of the Republic Kenya.[431] In practice, however, at least until 2017, KECOBO was not receiving any portion of the fines levied in the courts.

B. Extension of Application of the Act

533. The Act precludes the application of common law rights in copyright to Kenya by providing that no copyright or right in the nature of copyright shall exist otherwise than by virtue of the Copyright Act or other statutory enactment in that behalf.[432]

C. Litigation

1. *John Boniface Maina v. Safaricom Ltd. & 4 Others*

534. The defendant, Safaricom Ltd., introduced in 2008 a caller ring back tone service named *Skiza*.[433] The service allowed Safaricom users to customize their ringtones with music from a wide selection of artists. The plaintiff was a popular Kenyan musician, and many of his works were made available to users through the Skiza system. The plaintiff sued for breach of copyright in his musical works. The court found that the plaintiff presented a plausible case for copyright infringement and issued an injunction prohibiting the defendants from using the plaintiff's music as Skiza ringtones while the case remained pending. Shortly thereafter, the parties settled the dispute out of court, reportedly for the sum of KES 15.5 million (USD

429. Section 38(3).
430. Section 38(4).
431. Section 38(9).
432. Section 51.
433. [2013] eKLR.

150,000).[434] This case paved the way for many other musicians to receive substantial payments for the use of their copyrighted music as ringtones.

§4. Specific Issues for Digital Copyright

I. Born-Digital Works

535. At least for the purpose of defining the various classes of works which are eligible for copyright protection, the Act makes no distinction between works that are created using computers (i.e., works that are born digital) and those that are created on other media, such as paper for artistic works and parchment or canvas for paintings. Therefore, in terms of eligibility for copyright, there is no qualitative difference between a 'painting' created on a computer using a 'painting' software such as Microsoft Paint and a painting done on a canvas using liquid paint. In *Alternative Media Ltd v. Safaricom,*[435] the High Court considered that the definition of an author of a computer-generated work provided in the Act was wide enough to cover a computer graphics designer who was asserting his copyright in a photograph depicting a smiling lady inside an enchanted halo, and which had been created using a computer. The photograph had been printed on the promotional materials and mobile phone airtime recharge vouchers of Safaricom, a leading mobile phone service provider. 'In order to come up with the design', the Court observed, '[he] had to utilize his knowledge, labour and skill so as to produce something which nobody else had yet [sic] done'.[436]

536. The distinction between computer-generated works and other works only becomes material for the purpose of defining the author of a computer-generated work. This challenge is becoming ever more important with the development of artificial intelligence and of systems that are capable of independently creating works of music, art, literature, and software. As shown previously, the author of a literary, dramatic, musical, or artistic work or computer program which is computer-generated is 'the person by whom the arrangements necessary for the creation of the work were undertaken'.

537. It is a matter of conjecture what the meaning of the term 'the person by whom the arrangements necessary for the creation of the work were undertaken' might mean. The imprecision of this wording appears to leave open several pertinent questions for computer programmers or users and the owners of computer systems, in situations where these two classes of persons are separate and distinct:

(1) There is a latent ambiguity in the way the term 'arrangements' has been used in this provision of the Act. The definitive question is whether the term has

434. *See* http://www.businessdailyafrica.com/corporate/Safaricom-reaches-Sh15-5m-settlement-with-musician/539550-2304920-exj11yz/index.html.
435. *Supra* n. 4.
436. *Supra.*

been used as a term of art to refer to the set of operations that are performed by a computer program or whether it has been used in its common parlance form to mean the administrative facilitation provided by an employer (the owner of a computer system) to members of staff (computer programmers) in the sense of 'arranging' for them to perform their duties. Depending on which usage was intended, the author of a computer-generated work would be the computer programmer or the person who caused the computer to perform the operations that generated the work, according to the first usage, or in the other usage, it would mean the person who owns the computer system.

(2) Is there copyright in a work that is generated exclusively by a computer without the intervention of a human actor? If copyright subsists in such a work, in whom does it vest? Some works may be the products (or by-products) of highly automated and integrated computerized processes involving the interaction between two or more computer systems which are far apart and under the control of different persons or the interactions between two or more computer programs. In such situations, the wording of the Act does not make it easy to evaluate the competing claims of the computer programmer, the owner of the computer system, the user of the computer, and the person having the copyright in the computer program responsible for the generation of the work.[437]

538. A tangentially related body of case law currently emerging outside of Kenya involves works made by non-human authors such as animals.[438] Many copyright laws specifically require that an author is a human, yet with the development of advanced computer software, artificial intelligence, and automation, it is increasingly common for works of art to be developed in part or whole without human involvement. Whether such works should be afforded copyright protection, and who should be the owner of such copyrights if they are deemed to exist are matters receiving much attention in certain jurisdictions.

II. Electronic Rights Management

539. Electronic or digital rights management (often referenced by the acronym, DRM) is a general term referring to technologies applied by hardware manufacturers and copyright proprietors to control and impose limitations on the usage of digital content and devices. These technologies identify to the user content that is protected by copyright or other restriction and set out the terms and conditions for the use of such content.[439]

---

437. However, so far, such applications remain rare and highly complex. One example is a process described by Sohal, S. Vikaas et al., 'Intrinsic and Synaptic Dynamics Interact to Generate Emergent Patterns of Rhythmic Bursting in Thalamocortical Neurons', *The Journal of Neuroscience* 26 (2006), available at www.jneurosci.org/cgi/content/full/26/16/4247.

438. An international furor arose when a certain macaque monkey was denied copyright protection for her 'selfie' (a picture taken of the monkey, by the monkey).

439. P. Sumpter, Intellectual Property Law: Principles and Practice (CCH New Zealand Ltd, 2006), 69.

540. Under the interpretation section of the Copyright Act, 2001, 'Electronic rights management information' means any information by right holders which identifies the work or recording.[440] Under the Act, one of the definitions of copyright infringement is removing or altering 'any electronic rights management information' or distributing, broadcasting, or otherwise availing to the public a protected work 'from which electronic rights management information has been removed or has been altered without the authority of the right holder'.[441] In some jurisdictions, copyright laws or supporting laws explicitly make illegal the development of technologies designed to circumvent DRM technologies.

541. DRM technologies may impose technical barriers against copying digital works as opposed to the legal barriers imposed by copyright laws. As such, DRM is often seen as an alternative, or complementary, to copyright law in the protection of creative works. Examples of DRM technologies include watermarks on digital photos, limited instal patches on software (requiring, for example, a purchaser of a software to obtain an authorization code from the manufacturer's website), and encryption algorithms applied to digital content such as movies.

440. Section 2.
441. Section 35(3)(c) & (d).

Chapter 2. Copyright Protection of Software

542. Under the Copyright Act, a computer program is a literary work. A computer is defined as 'an electronic or similar device having information-processing capabilities' and a computer program as 'a set of instructions expressed in words, codes, schemes or in any other form, which is capable, when incorporated in a medium that the computer can read, of causing a computer to perform or achieve a particular task or result'.[442] By defining the computer program as a literary work, all of the provisions of the Copyright Act relevant to literary works are also relevant to software. For example, source code must be fixed in a tangible form and must be original as evidenced by sufficient effort on the part of the author in order to receive copyright protection. For most substantial computer programs, these requirements are easily met.

§1. Litigation

543. The MPesa mobile money platform and other Safaricom products have attracted a number of lawsuits involving intellectual property. One such suit, described below, shows the inherent limitations of copyright protection in the ICT industry, where software-based ideas and innovations are relatively easily reproduced even where there is no access to the original source code.

I. *Faulu Kenya Deposit Taking Microfinance Ltd. v. Safaricom Ltd.*

544. The claimant alleged that it developed a cash advance system suitable for use with a mobile money platform such as MPesa and that it divulged the specifics of the system to Safaricom in a concept paper. The claimant did this with the intent of partnering with Safaricom to provide the cash advance system to users of the MPesa system. Safaricom rejected the offer, but a short time later debuted M-Shwari, a cash advance product similar to the concept proposed by Faulu Kenya. Faulu Kenya sued Safaricom, claiming violation in the copyright of their concept paper, breach of confidence, and violation of a non-disclosure agreement between the parties. The defendant denied the charges and argued that the alleged product was already in use by Airtel Networks Kenya Ltd (and was, as a concept, therefore in the public domain).

545. The published decision of the court[443] was solely regarding a preliminary injunction sought by the claimant. The court denied the injunction, stating: 'Apart from [Plaintiff's] failure to prove its alleged copyright, I tend to agree with the Defendant that the latter has not breached the Plaintiff's confidence. The fact that its

442. Section 2.
443. [2013] eKLR.

bank product was already in the public domain through its prior agreement with Airtel Networks Kenya Ltd would imply that "*its secret, as a secret, had ceased to exist*".'[444]

546. The concept paper prepared by Faulu Kenya was most likely a copyright-eligible work (e.g., as a literary work or other written work), but that copyright would merely protect the specific expression of the paper rather than the concepts/ideas embodied therein. By reproducing the concept, Safaricom would not be infringing the rights granted through copyright. This case vividly shows the limitations of copyright with respect to protection of software; copyright is always limited to protecting specific expressions rather than ideas or concepts, and it is no infringement of copyright to independently create works that embody a similar concept.

§2. No Fair Use of Computer Programs?

547. Further to the fair use/dealing complication introduced by the Supreme Court of Kenya, mentioned in Chapter 1 above, and with regard to computer programs, the Copyright Act makes a rather perplexing provision: 'Copyright of a computer program shall not constitute fair dealing for the purposes of paragraph (*a*) of subsection (1)'.[445] The paragraph (a) of subsection (1) referred to provides that the conferment of copyright does not include the right to control the doing of the prohibited acts (reproduction, distribution, or communication of the work) by way of fair dealing for the purposes of scientific research, private use, criticism or review, or the reporting of current events subject to acknowledgement of the source.

548. To merge and paraphrase the two provisions: Copyright in a computer program shall not constitute the right to reproduce, distribute, or communicate the work for the purposes of scientific research, private use, criticism, review, or the reporting of current events.

549. Even though it may be the product of poor drafting, the provision appears to unequivocally exclude the application of certain limitations under the doctrine of fair use to computer programs. The provision is only qualified by the subsequent subsection which prescribes the four circumstances in which a user can legally make copies of a computer program without the permission of the copyright holder:

- to the extent necessary to correct errors; or
- to make a backup copy; or
- for the purpose of testing a program to determine its suitability for the person's use; or

444. *Id.*
445. Section 26(3).

– for any purpose that is not prohibited under any licence or agreement permitting the person to use the program.[446]

550. Further, the authorization of the right holder of the program shall not be required to decompile the program or to convert the program into a version expressed in different programming language or code for the purpose of obtaining information needed to enable the program to operate with other programs.[447]

551. However, the Act requires that any copies made pursuant to this section should be used only for the purpose for which they were made and that they should be destroyed when the person's possession of the computer program ceases to be lawful.[448]

446. Section 26(4).
447. Section 26(5).
448. Section 26(6).

Chapter 3. Legal Protection of Databases

552. The question whether intellectual property law, particularly copyright law, affords adequate protection for quasi-creative and quasi-original compilations of data (databases) has been a vexing question of international intellectual property law jurisprudence. The debate is largely informed by two important events of the early 1990s. First, the growth of computer use and the emergence of the Internet and second, the landmark decision of the US Supreme Court in *Feist Publications v. Rural Telephone Service Company.*[449] The case involved the question of the copyright in listings in a telephone directory prepared for an area of Kansas by Rural Telephone Service Company, as part of its legal obligations as a telephony service provider. Feist was a publisher of directory information for larger geographical areas. It would, with the licence of the small-area directory service providers, aggregate the information in the small directories and publish it in its larger directory. When Feist failed to obtain a licence from Rural to use the information in Rural's directory for the Kansas area, it copied the information and published it in its directory. Rural sued for copyright infringement.

553. Prior to this case, the substance of copyright in the US law had followed the 'sweat of the brow' doctrine, which gave copyright to anyone who invested significant amount of time and energy into their work, irrespective of the degree of originality.

554. In *Feist v. Rural,* this line of precedent was reversed when the Supreme Court, while acknowledging that the long-standing principle of the US copyright law that 'information' was not copyrightable but 'collections' of information were, ruled that originality is the sine qua non of copyright. The creativity need not be novel, rather the work only needs to possess a 'spark' or 'minimal degree' of creativity to be protected by copyright. The aim of copyright law was not to reward persons collecting information but to encourage creative expressions. In regard to collections of facts, Justice S. O'Connor, one of the presiding judges in the case, stated that copyright could only apply to the creative aspects of collection: the creative choice of what data to include or exclude, the order and style in which the information is presented, etc., but not on the information itself. This has become known as the 'selection and arrangement' doctrine, and stands in contrast with the 'sweat of the brow' doctrine. If Feist were to take the directory and rearrange them it would have destroyed the copyright owned in the data. The court ruled that Rural's directory was nothing more than an alphabetic list of all subscribers to its service, which it was required to compile under law, and that no creative expression was involved. The Court found that the fact that Rural had spent considerable time and money collecting the data was irrelevant to copyright law, and Rural's copyright claim was dismissed.

---

449. 499 U.S. 340 (1991).

555. The decision appeared to limit the protection desired by the creators of databases – or compilations of information and data – which were increasingly becoming an essential feature of the emerging information economy. At the same time, while the UK provided adequate legal protection for databases, European laws generally had a high threshold requirement for originality that put them virtually in the same situation as the US. Later, in 1996, the European Union adopted the Database Directive creating a new intellectual property right (a sui generis right, separate from copyright) in databases.[450]

556. Kenya does not recognize any special IPR of the compilers of databases. Databases are protected under the general rubric of literary works. The Copyright Act defines a literary work to include, irrespective of literary quality, any 'tables and compilations of data including tables and compilations of data stored and embodied in a computer or a medium used in conjunction with a computer'.[451]

557. The law is not explicit on whether the 'sweat of the brow' or the 'selection and arrangement' doctrine should be applied to compilations of data. The threshold requirements, however, for copyright protection for literary, musical, or artistic works in Kenya are originality and reduction of the work in material form, and the Act expressly provides that such a work shall not be eligible for copyright 'unless sufficient effort has been expended on making the work to give it an original character and [it] has been written down, recorded or otherwise reduced to material form'.[452] This language would seem to support the 'selection and arrangement' test for copyright protection of databases in Kenya. So far, however, the legal protection of databases is virgin territory for Kenyan case law. Save for judicial pronouncements obliquely commenting on the thresholds of originality and degree of effort generally observed for literary works,[453] Kenya's courts have not yet had the opportunity to expressly interpret the foregoing provisions of the Copyright Act with respect to the legal protection of databases.

558. As such, the global picture presents a discordant mix of laws on the protection of databases, with Europe providing for a sui generis law, most commonwealth countries relying on either the sweat of the brow doctrine, the selection, and arrangement doctrine or as an alternative in the US and civil law countries, unfair competition, and anti-circumvention laws.[454] 'This creates trade distortions as well as inadequate protection because in some countries, protection is either inadequate or excessive,'[455] and makes a strong case for the need, albeit an ambitious one, to achieve a general international harmony on legal protection of databases.

---

450. E. Derclaye, *The Legal Protection of Databases: A Comparative Analysis* (Massachusetts: Edward Elgar Publishing, 2008), 3.
451. Section 2(1).
452. Section 22(3).
453. *See Alternative Media Ltd v. Safaricom Ltd, supra* n. 4.
454. *Supra.*
455. *Supra.*

Chapter 4. Legal Protection of Computer Chips

559. In Kenya, there is currently no law specifically providing for the protection of integrated circuit designs and integrated circuit masks. A draft bill was prepared in the early 2000s but was not adopted by Parliament. Drawings of integrated circuit designs could possibly obtain protection under copyright law and/or industrial design law, although the functional nature of such drawings would call into question the suitability of such laws for the purpose. An analogy can be found in architectural works (buildings and models thereof), which are clearly functional and yet are specifically mentioned in the Copyright Act 2001 as receiving copyright protection.[456] There is no such specific mention in the Copyright Act for integrated circuits.

560. Provided that the relevant legal requirements (i.e., novelty, inventive step, usefulness) are met, integrated circuit layouts would find protection under the Kenyan patent and utility model laws. Indeed, the Industrial Property Act 2001 provides a definition of Utility Model as including 'any form, configuration or disposition of element of some … electrical and electronic circuitry … '.[457]

561. Notwithstanding the lack of dedicated legislation, Kenya is a party to the Agreement on -TRIPS as well as the EAC Common Market Protocol, both of which provide for the protection of layout designs of integrated circuits. By the operation of Article 2(6) of the Constitution of Kenya 2010, these international agreements automatically form a part of Kenyan law[458] and are therefore discussed below.

562. Article 35 of TRIPS provides, in relevant part:

> *Members agree to provide protection to the layout-designs (topographies) of integrated circuits (referred to in this Agreement as 'layout-designs') in accordance with Articles 2 through 7 (other than paragraph 3 of Article 6), Article 12 and paragraph 3 of Article 16 of the Treaty on Intellectual Property in Respect of Integrated Circuits … .*

563. The 1989 Treaty on Intellectual Property in Respect of Integrated Circuits (also known as the Washington Treaty or IPIC Treaty) was never officially ratified by enough countries to go into effect but was later given effect by its incorporation into TRIPS. The relevant parts of the IPIC Treaty are as follows:[459]

---

456. Copyright Act, s. 2.
457. Industrial Property Act, s. 2.
458. Although the Constitution of Kenya 2010 states explicitly that any 'treaty or convention ratified by Kenya shall form part of the law of Kenya', it is widely argued that enabling legislation is still a requirement for such international agreements to have effect in Kenya.
459. Treaty on Intellectual Property in Respect of Integrated Circuits, Arts 3–4.

> *Article 3 (1) (a) Each Contracting Party shall have the obligation to secure, throughout its territory, intellectual property protection in respect of layout-designs (topographies) in accordance with this Treaty. It shall, in particular, secure adequate measures to ensure the prevention of acts considered unlawful under Article 6 and appropriate legal remedies where such acts have been committed.*
> *Article 4 Each Contracting Party shall be free to implement its obligations under this Treaty through a special law on layout-designs (topographies) or its law on copyright, patents, utility models, industrial designs, unfair competition or any other law or a combination of any of those laws.*

564. As per Article 4 of the IPIC Treaty, Kenya appears to have fully implemented its obligation under TRIPS with respect to the protection of integrated circuit designs by providing for such protection with (at least) utility model certificates.

565. In the EAC, Article 43 of the Common Market Protocol provides a mandate for Kenya and other member nations to work together in offering protection of integrated circuit designs. The relevant parts of the Protocol are as follows:

1. *The Partner States undertake to co-operate in the field of intellectual property rights to:*
   (a) *promote and protect creativity and innovation for economic, technological, social and cultural development in the Community; and*
   (b) *enhance the protection of intellectual property rights.*
2. *For the purposes of paragraph 1, the Partner States undertake to cooperate in the [area of] layout designs of integrated circuits … .*

Chapter 5. Other IPR in the ICT Sector

§1. Trademarks

566. Kenya's legal regime for the registration and vesting of rights in trademarks is embodied in the Trade Marks Act of 1957.[460] The Act materially domesticated the provisions of the Paris Convention for the Protection of Industrial Property of 1883 and later the agreement establishing the WTO Agreement, signed at Marrakesh, Morocco, on 15 April 1994.

567. Even though the Act bars proceedings for the prevention of or recovery of damages for the infringement of an unregistered trademark, it does not affect the rights of a claimant to bring an action for the commercial wrong of passing off.[461] All trademark registrations are to be in respect of goods and services, and the Registrar of Trademarks adopts International Classification of Goods and Services and the International Classification of the Figurative Elements of Marks.[462]

I. General Principles of Trademark Law in Kenya

568. Kenyan law has long recognized that the registered proprietor of a trademark acquires the exclusive right to use the mark in relation to the goods or services for which it is registered and that any person who uses a mark identical with or so nearly resembling that mark as to be likely to deceive or cause confusion in the course of the trade in those goods or services infringes on rights of the trademark's proprietor. This was more recently restated by the High Court of Kenya in *Unilever Plc. v. Bidco Oil Refineries Ltd.*[463]

569. A plaintiff who establishes his claim for the infringement of a trademark is entitled to both general and special damages, the subject of course to meeting the necessary rules of evidence regarding the burden and standard of proof – *Jivanji v. Sanyo Electrical Company.*[464]

570. In *Aktiebolaget Jonkoping-Vulcan Indstricksfa Briksaktiebolag v. East Africa Match Co. Ltd* [1964] EA 62, it was established that as a general rule, the burden of satisfying the court that there has been an infringement of a trademark is on the plaintiff. It is his duty to prove that there exists a resemblance between his

460. Chapter 506 of the Laws of Kenya.
461. Trade Marks Act s. 5. The action of passing off is used by plaintiffs lacking a registered trademark but having a demonstrable history of trading or doing business under a specific mark.
462. *Supra* s. 6.
463. [2004] 1 KLR 57.
464. [2003] KLR 425.

mark and the mark used by the defendant that is deceptive and likely to cause confusion.[465] The marks forming the subject matter of the litigation need not be absolutely identical. The degree of resemblance necessary is not capable of defining a priori, and all that a court can do is to say that no trader should adopt a trademark so resembling that of a rival so that ordinary purchasers exercising ordinary caution are likely to be misled. This proposition of law was later affirmed in *Unilever Plc.v. Bidco Oil Refineries Ltd.*[466]

571. In *Pharmaceutical Manufacturing Co. v. Novelty Manufacturing Ltd,*[467] Ringera J. held that the infringement of a trademark is a tort of strict liability for which proof of damage is not necessary, and the intention and motive of the infringing party are irrelevant considerations. In the same case, Ringera J. also held that the fact that the plaintiff may have acquiesced in the defendant's use of the trademark for a long time does not constitute a defence to the claim: 'As the right [to the exclusive use of the trademark] is a statutory one, acquiescence cannot constitute an estoppel or any other defence which the statute itself does not recognize.'[468]

572. In many cases where a suit is filed to enforce a right held in a trademark, it is customary for the plaintiff to simultaneously ask the court for an interlocutory order of injunction restraining the defendant from continuing to use the mark pending the hearing and determination of the dispute. As with all applications for any other form of interlocutory injunctions, the principles upon which such an application is determined were settled by the Court of Appeal for Eastern Africa (now defunct) in *Giella v. Cassman Brown* & Co Ltd.[469] The plaintiff ought to make out a prima facie case with a probability of success, and an interlocutory injunction will not normally be granted unless the plaintiff might otherwise suffer damage or injury which cannot be compensated by an award of damages. Where the court is in doubt, it will decide the application on a balance of convenience.

573. In *Cut Tobacco Kenya Ltd v. British American Tobacco (K.) Ltd,*[470] the Court of Appeal of Kenya set aside an order of the High Court restraining the defendant from further using a mark which the plaintiff alleged was so similar to its registered trademark as to be deceptive to the buyers of the goods traded by the parties. The Court was not satisfied that the applicant would suffer a loss or damage that could not be compensated by way of damages if the order of injunction was refused and the intended appeal was successful. The Court more recently applied the same reasoning in *G4S Security Services (K.) Ltd v. Group Four Security Ltd.*[471]

465. Section 8 of the Act disentitles the plaintiff to an injunction where 'the defendant establishes to the satisfaction of the court that the use of [the mark] of which the plaintiff complains is not likely to deceive or cause confusion or to be taken as indicating a connexion in the course of trade between the goods'.
466. [2001] KLR 392.
467. [2001] KLR 392.
468. Page 400, line 17.
469. [1973] E.A. 358.
470. [2001] KLR 36.
471. [2007] eKLR.

574. The Trade Marks Act establishes an administrative structure for the registration of both national and international trademarks in Kenya through the Kenya Industrial Property Institute (KIPI) which in turn has been established under the Industrial Property Act. The Trade Marks (International Registration) Regulations domesticate material provisions on international registration of trademarks contained in the Protocol adopted by the Administrative Council of the African Regional Intellectual Property Organization (ARIPO) held in Banjul, the Gambia, in 1993 (the Banjul Protocol); the Agreement relating to the International Registration of Marks, adopted in Madrid, in April, 1891 (the Madrid Convention); and the Madrid Agreement adopted in Madrid, on 27 June 1989 (the Madrid Protocol).[472]

575. The Act forbids any registration of a trademark that interferes with any bona fide use by a person of his own name or of the name of his place of business.[473] It protects a 'well-known trademark', being a mark which is well known in Kenya as being the mark of a national of a country that recognizes the Paris Convention and who is domiciled in, or has a real and effective industrial or commercial establishment in such a country whether or not that person carries on business or has any goodwill in Kenya.[474]

576. The burden on a plaintiff to prove that a mark is a 'well-known' mark appears to be quite high. In 2016, the Registrar of Trademarks at KIPI issued the surprising decision that 'Sony' was not a well-known mark and that the Sony Corporation of Japan was not entitled to the protections that extend to a well-known mark. The decision was made in the context of an opposition hearing filed by Sony Corporation against trademarks filed by Sony Holdings, a Kenyan company. The decision has been appealed and is pending in the Court of Appeals.

577. The proprietor of a trademark which is entitled to protection under the Paris Convention or the WTO Agreement as a well-known trademark is also entitled to restrain by injunction the use of a trademark in Kenya which is identical or similar to his, in relation to identical or similar goods or services, where the use is likely to cause confusion among the users of the goods or services.[475]

578. The Trade Marks Act allows for the defensive registration of well-known trademarks. Where a trademark consisting of an invented word has become so well known in relation to goods which it has been registered and used that the use of the mark in relation to another class of goods would be likely to be taken as indicating a connection in the course of trade between the two sets of goods, the proprietor of the mark in relation to the first class of goods may register the mark as a defensive trademark even though he does not propose to use it in relation to the other set of goods.[476]

---

472. Section 40B.
473. *Supra* s. 11.
474. Section 15.
475. Section 15A(2).
476. Section 30.

§2. PATENTS AND SOFTWARE

579. The application of copyright protection to computer software is relatively uncontroverted and is supported by substantial case law. In contrast, there is a diversity of expert opinion on whether software patents or patents on computer programs *should* be granted and, if they are, then under what conditions software is eligible for patent protection. The pertinent issues in this discourse are mainly:

- how the distinction may be made between software that should be protected merely by copyright and that which is suitable subject matter for a patent;
- whether software patents meet the inventive step and nonobviousness criteria for patentability; and
- whether such patents are a disincentive rather than a stimulus for innovation.[477]

580. By and large, Kenyan law incorporates a number of internationally recognized principles of patent law. The familiar threshold requirements of patentability, that is, novelty, inventive step, and industrial applicability, are part of the statutory law. The Industrial Property Act, 2001 defines invention as 'a solution to a specific problem in the field of technology'[478] whether embodied in a product or a process. An invention is patentable if it is new, in the sense that it has not been anticipated by prior art, if it involves an inventive step, is industrially applicable or is a new use.[479]

581. An invention is considered as involving an inventive step if, having regard to the prior art relevant to the application claiming the invention, it would not have been obvious to a person skilled in the art to which the invention pertains on the date of the filing of the application or, if priority is claimed, on the priority date validly claimed in respect thereof.[480] An invention is considered industrially applicable if, according to its nature, it can be made or used in any kind of industry, including agriculture, medicine, fishery, and other services.[481]

582. Patents are granted for a period of twenty years from the date of filing the application for the patent.[482]

583. The predecessor law to the Industrial Property Act 2001 specifically stated that the following are not considered 'inventions' and are therefore excluded from patentability:[483]

---

477. *See*, generally, A. Gowers (2006), *Gowers Review of Intellectual Property*, The Stationery Office 75 and Intellectual Property on the Internet: A Survey of Issues (Geneva: Wipo, 2003), 62.
478. Section 21(1).
479. Sections 22, 23.
480. Section 24.
481. Section 25.
482. Section 60.
483. Industrial Property Act cap. 509, s. 6(3).

- discoveries or findings that are products or processes of nature where mankind has not participated in their creation (including animals, plants, and microorganisms) and scientific and mathematical methods and theories;
- schemes, rules, or methods for doing business, performing purely mental acts or playing games, and computer programs;
- methods for treatment of the human or animal body by surgery or therapy, as well as diagnostic methods, except products, in particular substances or compositions, for use in any of those methods; or
- mere presentation of information.

584. In contrast, the Industrial Property Act 2001 provides that the following are not inventions and are therefore excluded from patentability:[484]

- discoveries, scientific theories, and mathematical methods;
- schemes, rules, or methods for doing business, performing purely mental acts or playing games;
- methods for treatment of the human or animal body by surgery or therapy, as well as diagnostic methods practised in relation thereto, except products for use in any such methods; and
- mere presentation of information.

585. These two provisions are noteworthy as differing in one major respect: the absence of computer programs in the updated Act. The deletion of computer programs from the list of excluded subject matter, while leaving all other exclusions essentially untouched, strongly suggests that Parliament intended computer programs to be patentable as of 2001. The recorded legislative history of the 2001 Act does not contain any record of Parliamentary discussions around this matter, so the language of the Act must speak for itself.

586. Perhaps because of the subtlety of the above change in the patent law, many lawyers and other professionals continue to believe that software patents are unavailable in Kenya. Nevertheless, granted patent documents are public records, and a search of the KIPI patent database reveals a number of granted patents with claims directed specifically to software or more generally to methods that are carried out using a computer.[485]

587. Kenyan and foreign inventors have the option, when applying for patent protection under the Industrial Property Act 2001, of filing for a patent or a utility model certificate. There are three major distinctions between these types of IPR:

(1) whereas the patent term is twenty years from the filing date, the term of a utility model certificate is ten years from the date of grant of the certificate;

484. Industrial Property Act 2001, s. 21(3).
485. *See*, for example, Kenyan Patent KE337 (Applicant: Nokia Corp.), claiming computer-based systems and methods.

(2) whereas patents require novelty, inventive step, and industrial utility, the grant of a utility model certificate does not require that the applicant demonstrate inventive step; and
(3) whereas patents are subjected to substantive examination at KIPI, as of 2014 all utility model applications are granted without any substantive examination.

588. Regarding software, whereas the patent law is relatively unambiguous in allowing patents directed to software, the definition of 'utility model' in the Industrial Property Act[486] leaves room for interpretation that such rights cannot be applied to processes and therefore do not apply to computer-implemented processes. This interpretation would effectively bar all software from eligibility under utility model certificates.

§3. Trade Secrets

589. Article 39 of TRIPS provides the following requirement:

(1) *In the course of ensuring effective protection against unfair competition as provided in Article 10bis of the Paris Convention (1967), Members shall protect undisclosed information in accordance with paragraph 2 ...*
(2) *Natural and legal persons shall have the possibility of preventing information lawfully within their control from being disclosed to, acquired by, or used by others without their consent in a manner contrary to honest commercial practices so long as such information:*
   (a) *is secret in the sense that it is not, as a body or in the precise configuration and assembly of its components, generally known among or readily accessible to persons within the circles that normally deal with the kind of information in question;*
   (b) *has commercial value because it is secret; and*
   (c) *has been subject to reasonable steps under the circumstances, by the person lawfully in control of the information, to keep it secret.*

Notwithstanding this requirement, there are, currently, no specific provisions in any law in Kenya for the protection of trade secrets.

486. Section 2 of the Act defines 'utility model' as meaning 'any form, configuration or disposition of element of some appliance, utensil, tool, electrical and electronic circuitry, instrument, handicraft mechanism or other object or any part of the same allowing a better or different functioning, use, or manufacture of the subject matter or that gives some utility, advantage, environmental benefit, saving or technical effect not available in Kenya before ... '.

Chapter 6. Internet Domain Name Registration

§1. Background

590. Domain names are the familiar and easy-to-remember names for Internet computers, such as '<www.ecommerce.go.ke>'. They map to unique Internet Protocol (IP) numbers (e.g., 98.37.241.30) that serve as routing addresses on the Internet. The Domain Name System (DNS) translates Internet names into the IP numbers needed for transmission of information across the network.

591. The domain namespace is constructed as a hierarchy. It is divided into Top-Level Domains (TLDs), with each TLD divided into Second-Level Domains (SLDs), and so on. More than 200 national, or country code TLDs (ccTLDs) are administered by their corresponding governments or by private entities with the appropriate national governments' acquiescence.

§2. Establishment and Functions of Kenya Network Information Centre (KeNIC)

592. Kenya Network Information Centre (KeNIC) is a private non-profit-making organization whose responsibilities include managing the Domain Name registration service for .ke domains under the authority delegated by the Internet Corporation for Assigned Names and Numbers (ICANN).

593. KeNIC is the designated administrator of Kenya's ccTLD, that is, .ke, as well as its second level domains. KeNIC was established in 2002 as a private–public partnership through a consultative process involving the CA and the fledgeling ICT industry. Previously, the pioneering work of Dr Shem Ochuodho of Kenya and Mr Randy Bush of the US had let to the establishment of domain name registry services as early as 1993. Viewing domain names as a strategic national resource that should be managed in the best interests of the public and the industry, the founder members of KeNIC envisioned that a non-profit making body with government and industry oversight would be ideal to administer the country's domain name.[487]

594. KeNIC's Board is comprised of representatives from the CA, Telkom Kenya, GITS, Directorate of E-Government, TESPOK, Kenya Education Network (KENET), and other industry stakeholders. The Kenya ICT Action Network (KICTANet), Domain-Name Registrar Association of Kenya (DRAKE), and Kenya Internet Marketing Association (KIMA) are associate Board members.

---

487. *See* www.kenic.or.ke.

I. The Functions of KeNIC

595. KeNIC organizes the space for .ke names via classifications designed to divide the .ke namespace in such a way that it facilitates the accommodation of different kinds of institutions and sectors of activity.

596. The functions of KeNIC are to:

- act as a trustee for the .ke ccTLD;
- become the .ke domain administrative contact as well as technical contact;
- administer the .ke ccTLD and its Second-Level Domains;
- maintain and promote the operational stability and utility of the .ke ccTLD;
- ensure a cost-effective administration of the .ke ccTLD and its subdomains;
- notify ICANN of any change to the contact information about the .ke ccTLD;
- provide name services for all .ke and ensure that the database is secure and stable;
- allow ICANN to access .ke zone files and registration data and continuously maintain a KeNIC website at all times with all the registration information;
- meet all its financial obligations to ICANN; and
- comply with all global ICANN Internet policies and help in their development.[488]

597. Over and above the management of Kenya's domain namespace, KeNIC has been established with a clear mandate to represent the views of the Kenyan Internet community during both local and international events and conferences. It is further mandated to carry out such other activities as it sees fit that will promote the growth and development of the sector within Kenya. The .ke Domain Namespace has been divided into several third-levels. These are provided, along with the number of registered domains, in Table 37.

Table 37 Registered Domains in Kenya[1]

Subdomain	*Purpose*	*Number of Registered Domains*	*Percentage of Total*
.co.ke	Companies	57,752	92.8
.go.ke	Government entities	372	0.6
.or.ke	Non-profit-making organizations or NGOs	1,859	3.0
.ac.ke	Institutions of higher education	763	1.2

488. *Ibid.*

Subdomain	*Purpose*	*Number of Registered Domains*	*Percentage of Total*
.sc.ke	Lower and middle institutes of learning	770	1.2
.ne.ke	Personal websites and e-mail	181	0.3
.me.ke	Personal websites and e-mail	336	0.5
.mobi.ke	Mobile content	43	0.1
.info.ke	Information	139	0.2
Total		62,215	

1. Source: Kenya Network Information Centre (KeNIC) (www.kenic.or.ke) as of December 2016.

598. The CA announced in 2015 that they were preparing regulations that would require all businesses registered or operating in Kenya to purchase a local domain.[489,490] The stated rationale for this requirement was to encourage a more rapid proliferation of locally hosted domains. After receiving vehement pushback from the business community, the CA seems to have dropped this as a priority.

II. Registering a Domain Name

599. Any person who desires to register a subdomain under the .ke country-code-top-level-domain would have to lodge an application with KeNIC. All applications are processed subject to KeNIC's terms and conditions set out in its domain name registration policy.[491] In submitting to KeNIC's registration process, an applicant will have undertaken to provide full and accurate information to KeNIC. The registration agreement embodies three affirmations on the part of the applicant:

(1) that to the knowledge of the applicant, the registration of the domain name will not infringe upon or otherwise violate the rights of any third party;
(2) that the applicant is not registering the domain name for an unlawful purpose; and
(3) that the applicant will not knowingly use the domain name in violation of any applicable laws or regulations.

489. Source: Kenya Network Information Centre (KeNIC) (www.kenic.or.ke) as of December 2016.
490. *See* http://www.mediamaxnetwork.co.ke/business/153900/ca-rules-to-compel-firms-to-take-local-domains/.
491. *See* www.kenic.or.ke/index.php?option=com_content&task=view&id=43&Itemid=61, 23 Dec. 2009.

600. KeNIC's registration procedures expressly make it the responsibility of the applicant to determine whether the domain name registration infringes or violates someone else's rights, and KeNIC repudiates all liability for any damage or consequential loss resulting from the registration.

601. In practice, the registration of a domain name is administered by any of a growing number of private registrars that are independently licensed by KeNIC to carry out such function.

602. Under the procedure, KeNIC reserves the right to cancel, change, or transfer the domain name registration under any of the following circumstances:

- upon written or appropriate electronic instructions from the registrant or his authorized agent to take such action;
- upon an order from a court or arbitral tribunal of competent jurisdiction;
- upon a decision of an Administrative Panel under KeNIC's or under any other equivalent mechanism for domain name dispute resolution; and
- upon the failure by the registrant to remit domain name registration or renewal fees within the required period.

III. Domain Name Dispute Resolution under the KeNIC Policy

603. KeNIC's activities for the resolution of disputes on registration of domain names is governed by KeNIC's Uniform Domain Name Dispute Resolution Policy and the Uniform Domain Name Dispute Resolution Policy Rules. KeNIC's policy and rules are based on the Uniform Domain Name Dispute Resolution Policy and the Rules for Uniform Domain Name Dispute Resolution Policy adopted by ICANN. Indeed, part of KeNIC's policy statement states that its management of the delegated domain namespace will be 'in the interest of the Kenya Internet Community and being mindful of the global Internet community interest consistent with ICANN policies'.[492]

604. Under ICANN's policy, most types of trademark-based domain name disputes must be resolved by agreement, court action, or arbitration before a registrar will cancel, suspend, or transfer a domain name. Disputes alleged to arise from abusive registrations of domain names (e.g., cybersquatting) may be addressed by expedited administrative proceedings that the holder of trademark rights initiates by filing a complaint with an approved dispute resolution service provider.[493]

605. Evidence that a domain name is an abusive registration may be provided by any or all of the following non-exhaustive factors:

492. *See* www.kenic.or.ke/index.php?option=com_content&task=view&id=13&Itemid=38, accessed on 23 Dec. 2009.
493. *See* www.icann.org/en/udrp/udrp-policy-24oct99.htm, 23 Dec. 2009.

(1) circumstances indicating that the Registrant has registered or otherwise acquired the domain name primarily to:

(i) sell, rent, or otherwise transfer the domain name to a Complainant or to a competitor of the Complainant, or any third Party, for valuable consideration in excess of the Registrant's reasonable out-of-pocket expenses directly associated with acquiring or using domain names;
(ii) block the registration of a name or mark in which the Complainant has rights;
(iii) disrupt unfairly the business of the Complainant; or
(iv) prevent the Complainant from exercising their rights.

(2) circumstances indicating that the Registrant is using, or has registered, the domain name in a way that leads people or businesses to believe that the domain name is registered to, operated, or authorized by, or otherwise connected with the Complainant;
(3) evidence, in combination with other circumstances indicating that the domain name in dispute is an abusive registration and that the Registrant is engaged in a pattern of making abusive registrations;
(4) false or incomplete contact details provided by the Registrant in the WHOIS database;
(5) domain name is identical or confusingly similar to a trademark or service mark in which the Complainant has rights;
(6) evidence that the domain name was registered as a result of a relationship between the Complainant and the Registrant and the Registrant has:

(i) been using the domain name registration exclusively; and
(ii) paid for the registration or renewal of the domain name registration.

(7) any other factor that in the opinion of the Arbitrator may be indicative of abusive registration.

606. Furthermore, a registered domain name may be deemed an offensive registration if the domain name advocates hatred that is based on race, ethnicity, gender, or religion or that constitutes incitement to cause harm.

607. To invoke the policy, a trademark owner should either:

- file a complaint in a court of proper jurisdiction against the domain name holder (or where appropriate an in rem action concerning the domain name); or
- in cases of abusive registration submit a complaint to an approved dispute resolution service provider (*see* below for a list and links).

608. The policy sets out the type of disputes for which a registrant would be required to submit to a mandatory administrative proceeding. The proceedings are conducted before the High Court or an administrative dispute resolution service provider, of which several are known in Kenya.

IV. Dispute Proceedings

609. A registrant is required to submit to a mandatory administrative proceeding in the event that a third party (a 'complainant') asserts that:

- the registrant's domain name is identical or confusingly similar to a trademark or service mark in which the complainant has rights;
- the registrant has no rights or legitimate interests in respect of the domain name; and
- the registrant's domain name has been registered and is being used in bad faith.[494]

610. The policy provides that in the administrative proceeding, it is the duty of the complainant to prove each of these three elements.

V. Evidence of Registration and Use Not in Bad Faith

611. The policy sets out at least three criteria for demonstrating a registrant's rights or legitimate interests to the domain name where a complaint is lodged against its registration. These criteria, which are not stated to be exhaustive, include:

(1) before being aware of the Complainant's complaint, the Registrant has:

  (i) used or made demonstrable preparations to use the domain name in connection with a good faith offering of goods or services;
  (ii) been commonly known by the name or legitimately connected with a mark which is identical or similar to the domain name; or
  (iii) made legitimate non-commercial or fair use of the domain name.

(2) the domain name is used generically or in a descriptive manner, and the Registrant is making fair use of it;
(3) that the Registrant has demonstrated fair use, which use may include websites operated solely in tribute to or fair criticism of a person or business, provided that the burden of proof shifts to the Registrant to show that the domain name is not an abusive registration if the domain name is identical to the mark in which the Complainant asserts rights, without any addition; and
(4) any other factor that in the opinion of the Arbitrator may be indicative that the domain name is not an abusive or offensive registration.[495]

---

494. KeNIC Alternative Domain Name Dispute Resolution Policy.
495. *Id.*

612. In addition, the Policy specifies the following:

(1) Trading in domain names for profit and holding a large portfolio of domain names are of themselves lawful activities. The Arbitrator shall review each case on its merits.
(2) Sale of traffic, that is, connecting domain names to parking pages and earning click-per-view revenue, is not of itself objectionable under this Policy. However, the Arbitrator shall take into account:
  (a) the nature of the Domain Name;
  (b) the nature of the advertising links on any parking page associated with the Domain Name; or
  (c) that the use of the Domain Name is ultimately the Registrant's responsibility.[496]

§3. Domain Name Litigation and Africa

613. There is one published decision of the High Court of Kenya pertaining to domain name disputes. In the case of *James Ngoci Waweru & 2 Others v. James Mutitu Mworia & Another*,[497] one of the plaintiffs, a company by the name of Autoscope Ltd, sought an interlocutory injunction directing one of the defendants, a company by the name of Empire Microsystems Ltd, to release the domain name www.autoscope.co.ke. High Court Judge Mutava, J. found that the evidence presented at the initial hearings was insufficient to support the grant of an interlocutory injunction and allowed the defendant to keep the domain name. No further decisions have been released in the case, but it is notable that the contested domain name is now non-functional.[498]

614. In 2011, ICANN invited bids for new generic TLD names as part of an international expansion programme.[499] For geographically relevant domains, control over new TLDs would be granted by ICANN where an applicant could show endorsement by at least 60% of local governments in the region.[500] Several applications were lodged for control of the .africa domain. A Kenyan company, Dot Connect Africa (DCA) obtained the endorsement of the United Nations Economic Commission for Africa (UNECA) and the African Union Commission (AUC) as early as 2008.[501] However, in 2010 the AUC withdrew its endorsement and asked ICANN to put the domain on the list of reserved TLDs. This would have had the effect of rendering the domain unavailable for individual firms, but ICANN declined the request.[502]

496. *Id.*
497. [2012] eKLR.
498. As of May 2017, the domain name www.autoscope.co.ke is non-functional.
499. *See* https://www.standardmedia.co.ke/business/article/2001233467/inside-kenya-sa-fight-to-control-africa-domain on 17 May 2017.
500. *Ibid.*
501. *Ibid.*
502. *Ibid.*

615. In 2012, DCA submitted its application to ICANN, and in 2014 South Africa's ZA Central Registry (ZACR) also applied for the domain.[503] In 2016 ICANN granted the domain to ZACR, and DCA filed a lawsuit against ICANN in the US to challenge the decision.

616. In April 2016, DCA was granted a preliminary injunction barring ICANN from granting control of .africa to ZACR. This injunction was annulled by Superior Court Judge Howard Halm in February 2017, and the case is still pending. Meanwhile, the launch of the .africa domain has begun and will progress in three phases. The first phase opened in April 2017 and allows trademark holders to apply to register for a .africa domain name matching their registered trademarks.[504] The second phase is for premium applications and highly desirable domain names. The third phase, scheduled to begin July 2017, will allow for any applications from the general public.[505] Registrations are to be carried out by ten accredited registrars.[506]

§4. Conclusion

617. Kenya has an intellectual property legal regime that incorporates contemporary international legal principles on intellectual property law. It is governed by Kenyan statute law, which is applied and interpreted with the aid of the English common law and international legal instruments. While Kenya does not have a sui generis legal regime for the protection of the intellectual property in databases, this species of works is also protected under the general rubric of literary works. The registration of domain names and the resolution of domain name disputes is governed by statutory trademark law as well as by the administrative procedures prescribed by ICANN through KeNIC, Kenya's registrar, and administrator for ccTLD names. Enforcement of IPR in all sectors, including the ICT sector, is seen as a challenge and a burden on rights holders, although progress has been made and will continue, slowly, for the foreseeable future.

503. *Ibid.*
504. *See* http://nic.africa/en/home/ on 17 May 2017.
505. *See* http://www.itweb.co.za/index.php?option=com_content&view=article&id=159468 on 17 May 2017.
506. *See* https://registry.net.za/accredited/dotafrica.php on 17 May 2017.

Part III. ICT Contracts

Chapter 1. Hardware Contracts, Software Contracts, Distribution Agreements, and Maintenance Contracts

§1. Hardware Contracts

618. Computer hardware may refer to a wide range of items from a single peripheral device to a large-scale networked computer system. Consumers of hardware include individual citizens, SMEs, and large corporations, associations, educational institutions, and the government. The design, sale/lease, installation, maintenance, upgrade, replacement, and disposal of computer hardware are activities that may be governed by hardware contracts, and such contracts therefore vary widely in complexity and customization.

619. Although there is no specific legislation in Kenya to govern hardware contracts, general contract law and practice are applicable. Due to the unique nature of certain issues that may arise in the course of hardware and activities involving hardware, hardware contracts may include provisions that are not typically found in common contracts for the sale/lease of goods.

620. In Kenya, a good is defined in the Sale of Goods Act as including all chattels personal other than things in action and money, and all emblements, industrial growing crops, and things attached to or forming part of the land which are agreed to be severed before sale or under the contract of sale. As mentioned above, computer hardware typically refers, at least in part, to one or more physical elements of a computer system. These physical elements, once they are the subject matter of a contract, can be categorized as personal chattels, and the hardware contract would then be a contract for the sale of goods.

621. This concept was discussed in the UK case of *Beta Computers (Europe) Ltd v. Adobe Systems Ltd.* The Court in this case sought to distinguish a contract for the use of a physical manifestation of computer software and a licence to use the software itself. It was ruled that the contract for the sale of the hardware in which the software was embedded was a contract for the sale of goods.[507] The contract, in a

507. *Beta Computers (Europe) Ltd v. Adobe Systems Ltd* (1996), The Court of Session (Outer House) of Scotland.

Kenyan context, would, therefore, be governed by the Sale of Goods Act, the Law of Contract Act, and the general law of contract followed from common law.

622. The Sale of Goods Act gives a number of provisions regarding the formation of a contract for the sale of goods, the effects of such a contract, the performance of the contract, and the rights of an unpaid seller.[508] These provisions would be used in dealing with matters relating to contracts for the sale of computer hardware in Kenya.

§2. SOFTWARE CONTRACTS

623. As with hardware contracts, there is no law in Kenya specifically addressing software contracts or the issues that are unique to software contracts. Furthermore, there is, as yet, little in the way of jurisprudence regarding contractual disputes over software.

624. Whereas the Sale of Goods Act mentioned above is clearly applicable to hardware contracts and the sale of hardware, the situation is less clear for software. In particular, software in Kenya is typically licensed (rather than sold) to an end user, and it is often accompanied by a licensing agreement. The use of licensing is appropriate because software is included in the definition of 'literary work' in the Kenya Copyright Act and therefore receives copyright protection.[509] An important implication of this is that the vendor has the ability to retain substantially more rights in a licensing transaction as opposed to a sale of goods. For example, a software vendor can attach terms of use to a software licence, including limitations on appropriate uses of the software and prohibitions against modifications of the software. Whether software is sold or licensed may also be a determining factor in whether the First Sale Doctrine applies to the software.[510] Finally, end users are often unaware of the terms of a software licence or are ill-equipped to understand the terms of a licence. For this reason, so-called 'shrink wrap' licences that are effective upon purchase of software have been the subject of much interest in other jurisdictions.

625. Although this situation is not unique to Kenya, there is currently a lack of judicial guidance in Kenya as to whether software is sold or merely licensed and a particular lack of guidance as to the implications of this issue.

508. Sale of Goods Act (2012).
509. Copyright Act 2001, s. 2.
510. In intellectual property law, the First Sale Doctrine states that a legitimate (i.e., authorized) sale of a good that is protected by intellectual property rights exhausts those rights, such that the purchaser of the good is allowed to resell the good without further obligation to the original holder of the intellectual property rights. If the First Sale Doctrine does not apply to software (e.g., because the software is licensed rather than sold), an end user cannot legitimately resell the software.

§3. TURNKEY CONTRACTS

626. Turnkey contracts in ICT may involve hardware, software, firmware, or any combination of these. No law in Kenya specifically mentions or addresses turnkey contracts in the context of ICT projects and products. Standard contract law and provisions of the KIC Act relevant to contract law are presumably applicable.

627. A general provision for turnkey contracts can be found in the Procurement Manual for Works produced by the Public Procurement Oversight Authority (PPOA) (*see* Chapter 3 below for a discussion of this Authority). The Manual refers to Turnkey contracts as 'similar to Design and Construct [contracts] in that the Contractor has responsibility for both design and construction. However, turnkey contracts are usually employed in more complex situations where it is usually not feasible to formulate the full project scope and detailed specifications at the onset.'[511] The Manual, which applies to government procurement processes, suggests the following processes:

> *The two stage tendering process is sometimes employed for turnkey contracts. The first stage is to solicit for design concepts that aim to capture the vision of the Employer for the intended works based on initial thoughts and preliminary briefings. The Request for proposals on the design concept may be issued to a pre-qualified list of Contractors. The concept that best meets the Employer's vision is accepted and detailed technical and financial proposals are then sought on the selected concept during the second stage of the tendering process.*[512]

628. A number of media reports describe turnkey contracts for various government (non-ICT) projects, including power generation facilities, airport security systems, and roadway construction projects.

§4. DISTRIBUTION AGREEMENTS

629. Distribution agreements are those where a party – the distributor – is granted the right to sell the goods or services of another – the supplier – to clients or customers. In the context of ICT, two types of distribution agreements are most common: distribution of hardware and software and distribution of content. The distribution of content via broadcasting rights is discussed elsewhere in this text. This section, then, refers to contracts for distribution of hardware/software and the distribution of content via mechanisms other than broadcasting.

630. Distribution contracts for physical and consumer goods such as tyres and beverages have been common in Kenya for many decades. Distribution contracts for

511. Public Procurement Oversight Authority, *Procurement Manual for Works*, April 2009 (First edition), s. 6.7.
512. *Id.*

hardware and software are relatively new, and there is no specialized law in Kenya to deal with such matters. Many elements of distribution contracts in ICT are the same as those in other fields, such as exclusivity and price ceilings or price floors. Whether in ICT or any other field, these elements of a distribution contract are regulated in Kenya by laws such as the Competition Act and the Law of Contract Act. Some elements, however, are very specific to the field of ICT. For example, distribution contracts should address whether software updates or future versions of hardware devices are included in the distribution agreement. Another important and specific example in ICT is technical support and whether and for how long the supplier agrees to provide technical support to the supplied products.

631. The ubiquity of distributors in Kenya of devices from international ICT companies such as Samsung and Huawei Technologies is evidence that distribution contracts are commonplace. In many cases such contracts go beyond the mere sale of devices and allow distributers to offer servicing/repair of damaged devices. The terms of such distribution contracts are typically not publicly available.

§5. Maintenance and Management Contracts

632. Maintenance and management contracts are generally used for large-scale installations of software and/or hardware, such as large corporate computer systems or integrated systems involving numerous entities inputting or processing data. The contracts can take a variety of forms, and the provisions of such contracts vary according to the situation.

633. Facilities management contracts may involve a provider agreeing to keep hardware and/or software in good condition, with periodic updates and upgrades. Such contracts may require the provider to make regular or as-needed site visits, although many modern software packages include remote management options. A further option involves the customer returning equipment to a workshop for repair or upgrade.

634. There are no ICT-specific provisions in contract law in Kenya that relate to maintenance and management contracts.

Chapter 2. Network Services Contracts

635. The Communications Authority (CA) under its Unified Licensing Framework (ULF) uses the term NFP to describe all entities 'who shall own and operate any form of communications infrastructure (based on satellite, terrestrial, mobile or fixed)'.[513] This definition encompasses two service providers the Kenyan market:

(1) ISPs.
(2) TSPs.[514]

636. NFP, therefore, enter into network service contracts with customers such as the general public, businesses, education institutions, and the government.

§1. Governing Law: KIC Act 1998

637. The ULF attempts to reduce the need for multiple-licensing, i.e., the separation of licences obtained on the basis of the services offered and technology used. This way, network service providers (NSPs) can obtain more than one licence for the use of multiple systems of operation. Thus, a NFP may enter into contracts with individuals and groups for various different services.[515] For example, a telecommunications company may enter into contracts with customers for the provision of telecommunication services, mobile Internet, and home-based wireless Internet.[516] This framework has allowed mobile phone operators to emerge as Kenya's largest providers of Internet services.[517]

638. The formation of a contract between a customer and a NSP involves fulfilment by the provider of a number of prerequisites. The most important prerequisite is the acquisition of a licence from the CA, legitimizing the provision of service under the different categories. This is recognized in section 25(1)(b) of the KIC Act, which states that licences shall authorize the provision of telecommunications service.

513. Communications Authority of Kenya, *Telecommunications*, available at http://www.ca.go.ke/index.php/telecommunication.
514. Communications Authority of Kenya, *Telecommunications Market Structure under the Unified Licensing Framework*, available at http://www.ca.go.ke/images/downloads/TELECOMMUNICATION/LicensingProcedures/New%20Market%20Structure%20Under%20The%20Unified%20Licensing%20Framework%20-February%202017.pdf.
515. Research ICT Africa (RIA!) (2012). Regulatory Framework. In T.M. Waema & M.N. Ndung'u, *Understanding What Is Happening in ICT in Kenya* (pp. 5–6). Nairobi, available at https://www.researchictafrica.net/publications/Evidence_for_ICT_Policy_Action/Policy_Paper_9_-_Understanding_what_is_happening_in_ICT_in_Kenya.pdf.
516. *See* https://www.safaricom.co.ke/.
517. *Ibid. See* note 3.

639. Once licensed, a provider can offer services according to their stated terms and conditions provided in user agreements. Such user agreements are subject to regulation under several provisions of the KIC Act, as described below.

§2. E-TRANSACTIONS

640. E-transactions are allowed under the Act according to section 83J, which states that an offer and acceptance may be expressed by means of electronic messages. A wide range of services is available from various Kenyan providers (e.g., mobile money transactions and purchase of airtime and data bundles) that are executed solely via e-transactions.

§3. ANTI-COMPETITION

641. No contract may use anti-competition tactics in order to secure and keep customers. This is provided under section 84S of the KIC Act, which states that contracts shall not contain any clauses that subject customers or other contracting parties to supplementary obligations that have no connection with the subject of the contract. Furthermore, under section 84T, the Act authorizes the CA to render null and void any contracts that are anticompetitive.

642. Furthermore, the Regulations associated with the KIC Act states that anti-competition concerns will arise (and may therefore require intervention by the CA) where there is a likelihood that a service provider may 'make the conclusion of contracts subject to acceptance by the other parties of supplementary obligations which, by their nature or according to commercial usage, have no connection with the subject of the contracts.'[518]

§4. INTERMEDIARIES

643. Intermediary licensees are licensed under the Network Facility Provider (NFP) category within the ULF. These licences are needed by ICT companies in order to increase or spread business to the less populated and rural areas.

644. The most common intermediaries in Kenya are telecommunications agents for mobile money platforms, for example M-Pesa agents. The exchange of money and information on mobile money platforms generally happens through text or USSD messages. This way, telecommunications companies are aware of all transactions carried out on their behalf by their agents. Written proof of the transactions is recorded in books with the customer's signature and unique code of transaction, for the telecommunications companies' records and to avoid theft.

518. Fair Competition and Equality of Treatment Regulations 2010, s. 8A(2)d.

§5. LIABILITY

645. Unlicensed individuals are prohibited from providing network services. Section 34(1) of the KIC Act states that 'A person who, while not holding a valid licence under section 25, runs a telecommunication system or provides a telecommunication service, commits an offence'. A fine of up to one million shillings and/or imprisonment for a term not exceeding five years can be applied to anyone convicted under this section of the Act.

646. Section 28 of the Act states that 'A person who dishonestly facilitates or obtains a service provided by a person authorised under this Act to provide telecommunication services with intent to avoid payment of any charge applicable to the provision of that service commits an offence and shall be liable on conviction to a fine not exceeding one million shillings, or to imprisonment for a term not exceeding five years, or to both'.

647. With regard to the privacy of contracts that NSPs may enter into, section 31 of the Act states that a telecommunications operator who intercepts a message 'in the course of his business: (a) intercepts a message sent through a licensed telecommunication system; or (b) discloses to any person the contents of a message intercepted … commits an offence and shall be liable on conviction to a fine not exceeding three hundred thousand shillings, or to imprisonment for a term not exceeding three years, or to both.'

§6. GEOGRAPHICAL LIMITATIONS

648. NSPs may impose geographical restrictions for the availability of their services, particularly where infrastructure such as fibre optics is available in limited areas.

Chapter 3. Government Contracts

649. The Government Contracts Act[519] of Kenya dates from 1957 (i.e., pre-independence) and has been amended numerous times, with the latest amendment in 2005.[520] Section 2 of the Act defines a government contract as one that is:

- made on behalf of the government;
- reduced in writing;
- made in the name of the government; and
- signed either by the accounting officer or by the receiver of revenue of the Ministry or for the department of the Government concerned, or by any public officer duly authorized in writing by such accounting officer or receiver of revenue.

650. Section 4 of the Act states that only contracts made in the prescribed form will be deemed to be made by the Authority of the government.

651. The Cornell Law School's Legal Information Institute[521] draws three major distinctions between government contracts and private sector contracts. First, government contracts are subject to a number of statutes and regulations to enhance competition and accountability. Second, there exist special clauses for government contracts that are not present in private contracts. Lastly, the government being a sovereign entity is treated differently in litigation.

652. Governments largely depend on public procurement to provide goods and services to the public. Obtaining these goods and services by the government is a crucial step in public service. Indeed, the role of players in public procurement is to provide 'the right thing in the right place at the right time while maintaining public trust'.[522] The dynamic nature of societal needs, therefore, creates a dynamic public procurement landscape, with contracts being formed to supply all manner of goods and services.

653. ICT products and services are increasingly a subject of government contracts. As this happens, governments are creating frameworks designed to enable efficiency in public procurement.[523] This chapter provides an exposition on the Kenyan legal and policy framework governing public procurement of ICT products.

---

519. Chapter 25 of the Laws of Kenya.
520. The Act has not yet been vetted with respect to compliance with the Constitution of Kenya 2010.
521. *See* https://www.law.cornell.edu/wex/government_contracts.
522. Public Procurement Manual for 2016, Gambia, 1.
523. For instance, England has the Queensland Information Technology Contracting (QITC) framework, 2017, available at (https://www.business.qld.gov.au/industries/science-it-creative/ict/tendering-government/contracting-framework).

§1. LEGAL FRAMEWORK

I. The Constitution of Kenya (2010)

654. The constitution lays the foundation for public procurement laws and practices in Kenya, chiefly in Article 227. Here, principles[524] are provided that inform public procurement, together with an order for Parliament to prescribe a framework for the implementation of public procurement policies.

II. Public Procurement and Asset Disposal Act (2015)

655. The Public Procurement and Asset Disposal Act is a consequence of Article 227 of the Constitution of Kenya 2010. The Act replaced the Public Procurement and Disposals Act of 2005, becoming the chief statute governing public procurement and asset disposal by government entities.

656. The Act provides that the National Treasury is responsible for, among other things, designing and prescribing 'an efficient procurement management system for the national and county governments to ensure transparent procurement and asset disposal ... '.[525] The National Treasury is also responsible for developing public procurement and asset disposal policy.

657. The Act also establishes the Public Procurement Regulatory Authority (known and referred to in Kenya as the PPOA). Among the Authority's functions include working with the National Treasury to monitor the operation and performance of the public procurement system.[526]

658. As a relatively new law, the Public Procurement and Asset Disposal Act 2015 is noteworthy for the deference it pays to the devolved system of government mandated by the Constitution of Kenya 2010. Throughout the Act, clear references are made to the role of the national government and the role of the county governments. Considering the importance of government procurement to the national and local economy, the Act is a clear effort on the part of Parliament to delineate the roles of different levels of government under the new constitutional framework.

III. Public Procurement Manual for ICT

659. In performing its many functions, the Public Procurement Regulatory Authority has issued several area-specific manuals. Included among these is the

---

524. The system is to be fair, equitable, transparent, cost–effective, and competitive.
525. Section 7.
526. Section 9.

Public Procurement Manual for ICT, issued in May 2009.[527] The ICT manual was prepared to address issues in public procurement of ICT that may not arise in other sectors and is to be read in the context of the Act and any other general manuals.

660. The Procurement process for ICT products and services in government[528] is provided in the manual as follows:

(i) Identifying procurement needs:[529] This is done by the procurement entity of the concerned government entity. The manual provides for factors for consideration in identifying the procurement needs of various ICT products individually.
(ii) Procurement planning.[530]
(iii) Choice of procurement method: The manual proposes open tendering as the preferred procurement method, guided by section 21 of the Public Procurement and Disposal Act (PPDA).
(iv) Selection of ICT suppliers:[531] Selection is to be based on capability appraisal.
(v) Inspection and acceptance of services.[532]
(vi) Contract administration:[533] It is expected that most ICT contracts will require ongoing support from the supplier. The contracts should therefore include confidential clauses that sufficiently cover the government agency's interests.
(vii) Evaluation.

In practice, all government procurement in Kenya is routed through an online platform known as the Integrated Financial Management System (IFMIS).[534]

§2. POLICY FRAMEWORK

I. The ICTA's Government Enterprise Architecture Framework

661. Another body that plays a key role in government ICT contracts is the ICTA. Established in 2013, the authority is in charge of enforcing ICT standards in government. In performing this mandate, the authority has developed the Government Enterprise Architecture (GEA) Framework to 'ensure coherence and unified approach to acquisition, deployment, management and operation of ICTs across

527. The ICT procurement manual predates the Public Procurement and Asset Disposal Act 2015. Nevertheless, the Public Procurement Regulatory Authority has stated that the ICT procurement manual is still in force insofar as it does not contradict the Act. *(Source: personal communication with the Public Procurement Regulatory Authority).*
528. *Note: this process is provided for in the 2006 manual. It is not clear whether any changes have been introduced post the enactment of the PPADA 2015. I have written to the Public Procurement Oversight Authority and am awaiting confirmation.
529. Section 5.
530. Section 6.
531. Section 9.
532. Section 11.
533. Section 12.
534. *See* http://www.ifmis.go.ke/.

state agencies'.[535] This means that even when contracting, government agencies must adhere not only to the Public Procurement and Disposal of Assets Act but also to the standards set by GEA.

II. ICT Policy 2016

662. The Draft ICT Policy 2016, in paragraph 17.3, includes provisions for ICT trade and export, as well as several considerations that government should make so as to increase the contribution for the ICT industry to national GDP. These include giving preferential treatment to local developers in tendering government projects and requiring that a minimum percentage of a contract sum is reserved for local partnerships for skill transfer purposes.

III. The Kenya ICTA: Standards

663. Several of the nine Standards developed by the ICTA address various aspects of government contracting. For example, the Cloud Computing Standard contains provisions on SLA, thereby requiring Ministries, Counties, and Agencies to implement minimum standards when adopting technologies that are accompanied with such agreements. The Human Capital and Workforce Development Standard also contains provisions on SLA as well as guidance on the appropriate skills required for personnel involved in external and internal contracting activities.

535. From their official page, available at http://icta.go.ke/standards/why-gea-was-developed/.

Part IV. Electronic Transactions

Chapter 1. Legal Status of Electronic Transactions

664. Throughout the 1990s and early 2000s, even with (or perhaps because of) the increased use of information and communications technologies, there was a lingering uncertainty about the legality of electronic transactions. This was largely because the new ways of doing business in the domain of e-commerce presented a paradigm whose defining features were not matched by any existing legal vocabulary. The terms 'e-commerce', 'e-mail', 'digital signatures', etc. did not feature in any piece of legislation – at least not in a sense that left no doubt that the law was giving formal legal recognition to them.

665. As is customary with legal controversies, two schools of thought emerged, each with its own interpretation of the legal position. The first school of thought regarded the legality of electronic communications as being excluded by non-reference. According to this school, until the law was amended to expressly recognize the validity of electronic communications, they would have no legal consequence and would not give rise to any legally binding obligations. According to the other school, because the law did not expressly exclude electronic communications and transactions, they were included by non-exclusion, and no legislative amendment was necessary. This school felt that a purposive interpretation of the existing legislation would serve to include electronic communications and transactions that are equivalent or approximately equivalent to their offline counterparts. For instance, all references to 'writing' and 'signature' were construed to include communications that were electronically written and signed. Even under such a liberal interpretation of the law, however, there is ambiguity – e.g., whether an electronic signature is merely a digital image of a physical signature or may also include other less conventional forms of signature.

666. This ambivalence in the definitive legal position must have provoked at least two kinds of responses by existing and potential e-commerce protagonists: a guarded engagement with the Kenyan market or, in the alternative, no engagement at all. Ultimately, the ambiguity was largely put to rest with the passage of the Kenya Communications (Amendment) Act, 2008. Legislative and other governmental actions since 2008 have consistently added to the legitimacy of e-commerce.

667. With such barriers removed, the digital marketplace and e-services have been enthusiastically embraced within Kenya. Mobile money platforms, described below and pioneered in Kenya from 2006, have become a backbone of the formal and informal economies. Web- and mobile-based start-up companies have proliferated, as have the organizations that support such endeavours.

668. The new frontier in this area, and a source of numerous and significant constitutional questions, is found in the data that are inevitably generated by an increasingly online society and economy. Issues of data protection, access to data, data ownership, appropriate use of data, and liability with respect to data are emerging in virtually every area of the law, the economy, government, and society.

§1. The KIC Act

669. Part (VIA) of the KIC Act makes various provisions on electronic transactions. The part prescribes the following as the functions of the CA in relation to electronic transactions:

- facilitating electronic transactions and cybersecurity by ensuring the use of reliable electronic records;
- facilitating e-commerce and eliminating barriers to e-commerce such as those resulting from uncertainties over writing and signature requirements;
- promoting public confidence in the integrity and reliability of electronic records and electronic transactions;
- fostering the development of e-commerce through the use of electronic signatures to lend authenticity and integrity to correspondence in any electronic medium;
- promoting and facilitating the efficient delivery of public sector services by means of reliable electronic records;
- developing sound frameworks to minimize the incidence of forged electronic records and fraud in e-commerce and other electronic transactions;
- promote and facilitate the efficient management of critical Internet resources; and
- develop a framework for facilitating the investigation and prosecution of cybercrime offences.[536]

I. Electronic Cash

670. The new part contains provisions giving formal legal recognition to electronic transactions. However, the Act provides that its provisions regarding the legal recognition of electronic documents and electronic transactions are not to apply to three classes of documents or transactions:

(1) the creation or execution of a will;
(2) negotiable instruments; and

536. Section 83C.

(3) documents of title.[537]

671. However, the law empowers the Minister for Information and Communications to amend the exclusion, by including or excluding from the provision any class of transactions or matters.

672. The exemption means that the old rules requiring writing or signatures shall continue to apply to these documents so that they may not legally exist except in paper form and that they may not be signed otherwise than by hand – they may not be legally signed using digital signatures. In the Memorandum of Objects and Reasons traditionally annexed to any Bill presented to Parliament by its sponsor, the Ministry of Information and Communications did not give the rationale for the exclusion clause.

673. The exempted documents bear a common legal characteristic – they are documents that, by their nature, have to be retained in their original form in order for them to be valid. The possessor of a vehicle log book or a land title deed (documents of title) will be the owner of the vehicle or land described on it or a person who came to be in possession of the document by virtue of him having acquired a legal interest or right in the property – for instance, a bank or lender to whom the property has been offered as a security for a loan issued to the registered owner. There is no dissociating the value the documents represent and the paper on which they are constituted. Therefore, the mechanism used to transfer the value is the physical transfer and delivery of the paper itself.

674. If the validity of certain documents depended on the retention of their original, how then could such retention be guaranteed with respect to electronic documents which in their nature are non-material, volatile, and susceptible to mass replication and distribution at a speed and quality not previously anticipated by existing technology? Perhaps this dilemma was too much for Kenya's Parliament to contemplate. Like the parliaments of Canada, Singapore, and Hong Kong before it, Kenya excluded wills, negotiable instruments, and documents of title from the law.

675. In considering its Electronic Transactions Bill, Hong Kong had floundered in its attempt to justify the exemption of these classes of documents and transactions from its application: 'the Bill should not go as far as to require acceptance of electronic documents and digital signatures in all types of transactions before the community at large is ready for such a change.'[538] The justification proffered for the exemption of negotiable instruments sounded even less convincing: 'As for bills of exchange (e.g., cheques), it is conventionally exchanged by hand and there is little demand for it to be exchanged by electronic means.'

537. Section 83B.
538. The Report of the Hong Kong Legislative Council, available at at www.legco.gov.hk/yr98-99/english/bc/ bc19/papers/b194111c.pdf, 1.

676. The exclusion of negotiable instruments bears two self-evident contradictions – it stands against one of the declared objectives of the legislation: the promotion of e-commerce and second, it appears to outlaw existing industry practice. By 2009, the year when the legislation was passed, one of Kenya's mobile phone service providers had pioneered the transfer of money by mobile phone, an innovative service that won both local and international acclaim. With Safaricom's M-Pesa® service,[539] subscribers who are registered for the service deposit hard currency with a registered agent. Safaricom has a burgeoning network of registered agents throughout the country as the M-Pesa business model is easily integrated into small-scale retail businesses for fast moving consumer commodities, which are a common feature in both urban and rural Kenya. The agent then updates the subscriber's M-Pesa account with the amount deposited. The subscriber may, thereafter, send money from his M-Pesa account to a payee through a programmed text message or a USSD interface. The payer's account is immediately credited with the amount sent, and the payee's account is debited with the amount. The payee may withdraw the money from a registered Safaricom agent or from automated teller machines operated by banks or providers that have a special arrangement with Safaricom. All the transactions are recorded and managed on Safaricom's network. The idea of cash value stored on a mobile phone spawned creative new ideas for the marketplace, including loan services and savings schemes. Some players in the service industry as well as sellers of commodities soon started to accept M-Pesa payments in their sale transactions; some commercial banks leveraged the service to expand their mobile banking services, and some employers integrated their employee payroll payments with the service. Soon after M-Pesa was introduced, it became clear that the platform would be a runaway success, and other mobile carriers in Kenya introduced similar platforms. Despite such competition, M-Pesa retained and continues to retain a substantial majority share of the market for mobile money transactions. Table 38 provides selected statistics illustrating the widespread and substantial use of M-Pesa services.

Table 38 Statistics on Safaricom's Mobile Phone Money Transfer Service: M-Pesa

Number of agents	124,084
Number of subscriptions	21,574,006
Number of transactions	356,786,745
Value of transactions	KES 892,878,930,121
Number of mobile commerce transactions	222,092,539
Value of mobile commerce	KES 408,641,371,835
Person-to-person transfers	KES 423,693,636,524

Source: Communications Authority of Kenya, Sector Statistics Report Q2 FY 2016/17.

539. The service was launched on 6 Mar. 2010.

677. Considering the vast sums of money flowing through M-Pesa and other mobile money systems in Kenya, it is remarkable the low number of verifiable instances of fraud, money laundering, or other nefarious uses of such systems. This lack of known instances of fraud may, however, result from the lack of disclosure rules in Kenya – private organizations are not required to disclose breaches of security and loss of data. As a result, customers are not necessarily informed when such breaches occur. Nevertheless, although newspaper articles appear on a semi-regular basis, court cases on the topic remain relatively rare.[540]

678. The phenomenal growth of the M-Pesa service was a testament to the market's hunger for a convenient and paperless way of transferring money or money's worth. It offered a glimpse of a market that was taking its first step towards the perfect paperless money economy: where national currency issuers such as central banks and the Federal Reserve issue currency not in paper form but in the form of electronic currency; the use of a technological platform that offers electronic currency bearing the same guarantees as the banknote – unique and serially numbered, capable of transfer without retention, tamper–proof and capable of detecting alteration, replication, or copying; and widely accepted as legal tender.

679. With advances in financial cryptography, humankind has already made a mental shift into a frame of reference that is willing to admit that such a technological platform is possible. Indeed, when the idea of electronic money was first presented, most products were based on the idea of digital coins stored offline on smart cards or on user's hard disks. But as one scholar reported:

> *Despite the technological hype, consumers were apathetic, merchants were unimpressed, and most schemes disappeared as quickly as they had surfaced. Still, a number of risks were identified, and possible legal regulation based on 'digital coin' metaphors and smart card technology was debated.*[541]

680. It would be an embarrassing indictment of the digital age if its repertoire of technological innovations did not include a secure and widely accepted digital equivalent of the banknote and if paper money forever remained the only currency of e-commerce.

681. There remains no doubt, however, that the Government of Kenya does not endorse the use of digital currencies. In a Public Notice from 2015, the Central Bank

540. Two examples of cases involving fraud via M-Pesa are: *Kinya Beatrice v. Republic* [2014] eKLR; and *Peter Kimani Ngure v. Republic* [2015] eKLR.
541. Kohlbach, Manfred, 'Making Sense of Electronic Money', *The Journal of Information, Law and Technology(JILT)* 1 (2004), available at http://elj.warwick.ac.uk/jilt/04-1/kohlbach.html.

of Kenya stated unequivocally that 'Bitcoin and similar products are not legal tender nor are they regulated in Kenya. The public should therefore desist from transacting in Bitcoin and similar products'.[542,543] This warning was accompanied by a list of selected risks associated with buying, holding, or trading virtual currencies.

682. Notwithstanding the firm advisory from the Government of Kenya, a homegrown cryptocurrency was launched from Nairobi in 2013. Known as BitPesa,[544] the blockchain-based currency is currently operating mainly in East Africa and Nigeria.

683. The reluctance by countries such as Kenya to give legal recognition to digital currency may not be entirely attributed to shortness in legislative courage. The subject of electronic money is entangled with two areas of knowledge that do not lend themselves to easy understanding: the fiction of a legal tender as a means of transferring value and financial cryptography. On top of these complex issues is the easy to understand problem of money laundering and the use of digital currencies for criminal activities. Whatever the reason, the exclusion of negotiable instruments from the provisions of electronic transactions forecloses on possible future developments in electronic cash by denying industry the creative space to evolve current ideas of paperless money into fully fledged digital currency.

A. Republic v. National Transport & Safety Authority & 10 Others Ex Parte James Maina Mugo

684. This application for Judicial Review related to a Legal Notice from the National Transport and Safety Authority on the operation of public service vehicles (PSVs).[545] The Notice sought to begin implementation of a 'cash light' PSV fare payment system – a system intended to provide a method for cashless payment of PSV fares. The application was dismissed on non-substantive grounds, thereby removing a barrier to entry of such a cashless system. Nevertheless, for a variety of reasons more practical in nature (e.g., poor user experience, lack of interest, and motivation by PSV operators), the cashless payment system was not successful, and PSVs remain cash-based.

---

542. Bitcoin was developed in 2008 as a decentralized peer-to-peer payment network or Internet protocol that enables value to be transferred over a communications channel. Bitcoin uses the distributed ledger system known as blockchain, was the first practical implementation of a cryptocurrency, and is currently the most prominent triple entry bookkeeping system in existence.
543. Public Notice from the Central Bank of Kenya, 'Caution to the public on virtual currencies such as bitcoin,' December 2015.
544. *See* www.bitpesa.co, accessed 1 Jan. 2018.
545. [2015] eKLR.

II. Cheque Truncation (Paperless Cheque Clearing)

685. It stands out as one of Kenya's legislative contradictions that while the framework legislation for the ICT industry expressly excludes negotiable instruments from the class of documents that can legally exist in paper form, the law governing negotiable instruments was amended in the same year to make provisions on paperless cheque clearing. Kenya's Finance Bill, 2009, the Act of Parliament that was the legislative offshoot of the annual budget speech, introduced the term 'cheque truncation' into Kenya's law. By an amendment to the Bills of Exchange Act[546] cheque truncation is defined as: 'a system of cheque clearing and settlement between banks based on electronic data or images or both electronic data and images, without the conventional physical exchange of instruments.'

686. Paperless cheque clearing has the potential of reducing the floating time by replacing the paper cheque, which has to be hand-delivered at the clearing house to the drawer's bank, with a digital image of the cheque which is sent by electronic means. Even more importantly, an effective paperless cheque clearing system would be a good control experiment for the development of a national electronic cash system.

687. In actual fact, the practice of paperless cheque clearing had previously been recognized by law, albeit with a limitation in scope, in an amendment introduced to section 74 of the same Act back in 2005. The law somewhat limited the application of the practice to dishonoured cheques, permitting the bank to which the cheque had been presented to return an electronic version of the cheque to the holder rather than the paper cheque itself. Perhaps by introducing the definition of the term 'cheque truncation' into the law, Kenya's Parliament intended to not only bring the law up to speed with industry terminology but also lay the basis for the establishment of cheque truncation as a fully fledged industry practice. The Finance Bill also gives the Central Bank the power to make rules giving effect to and regulating the practice.

688. Under the Bills of Exchange Act, where a cheque presented for payment is dishonoured by non-payment, the presenting banker may issue to the holder an 'image return document' (presumably a digital image representation of the dishonoured cheque with the appropriate endorsement).[547] For all intents and purposes, the image return document is deemed in law 'to be the cheque to which it relates and may be presented for payment to the presenting banker by the holder to whom it is issued' subject to the banker's endorsement of its validity and any validity period given by the banker.

689. The KIC Act substantially incorporates into the laws of Kenya key provisions of the United Nations Commission on International Trade Law (UNCITRAL) Model Law on Electronic Commerce, particularly those relating to the recognition

546. Chapter 27 of the Laws of Kenya.
547. Section 74B.

of electronic records, the 'originality' of such records, digital signatures, and the formation of contracts through electronic data interchange.

690. The CA developed and released guidelines in 2015 for the adoption and promotion of best practices in e-commerce.[548] The guidelines cover the following topics:

- remote payment;
- security;
- delivery standards;
- tracking postal items; and
- international and local packages.

691. A persistent barrier to the uptake of e-commerce in Kenya remains the lack of a national physical addressing system. The lack of a standardized and universal addressing system complicates the delivery of goods and, in most cases, precludes the development of fully automated commercial activities. The CA is responsible for the development of a national addressing system and has held several stakeholder meetings on the topic, but the country remains without such a system.

692. On a regional level, the East African Legislative Assembly on 8 October 2015 passed the EAC Electronic Transactions Bill 2014, paving way for the business and corporate world to transact business using digital means.[549] The Act has the following objectives: to allow for seamless electronic transactions among EAC partner states; to encourage electronic-based transactions as a more efficient mode of linking both the private sector and governments in the region; to promote technology neutrality in applying legislation to electronic communications and transactions; and to develop a safe, secure, and effective environment for the consumer, business, and the governments of the partner States to conduct and use electronic transactions.[550] The effects of this regional instrument are yet to be fully realized.

A. Republic v. Commissioner of Domestic Taxes

693. Digital and online commercial activities bring new challenges in a variety of areas including taxation. In *Republic v. Commissioner of Domestic Taxes (Large Taxpayers Office) Ex parte Barclays Bank of Kenya Limited*,[551] the dispute concerned whether the KRA was entitled to demand withholding tax from Barclays

548. Communications Authority of Kenya: Revised Guidelines for the adoption of Postal e-commerce (CA/Guildelines/LCS/001P/2015).
549. *See* https://www.tralac.org/news/article/8248-region-set-to-realize-e-business-as-eala-enacts-eac-electronic-transactions-bill.html, accessed on 27 Apr. 2017.
550. *See* http://www.cskonline.org/about-us/kenya-ict-press/834-eala-to-debate-bill-on-regional-electronic-transactions-next-week, accessed on 27 Apr. 2017.
551. [2015] eKLR.

Bank on payments made: (1) to card companies such as VISA International Services Association, MasterCard Inc., and American Express Ltd; and (2) as an interchange fee to other banks referred to as the issuers. The court held that KRA ought to have clearly identified the category in which the tax was sought and that their decision to broadly state that the payments amounted to professional or management fees did not meet the level of clarity required in taxation.

§2. Liability for Transactions

694. An individual is liable for any electronic transactions he/she initiates, although the courts have yet to decide a case where the identity of an initiator of a transaction is in dispute. The courts have, however, held that negligence by an operator of an electronic transaction system is a factor when apportioning liability for debts, as shown in the following case.

I. *Anthony Kimani Ngige v. Co-Operative Bank of Kenya Ltd.*

695. The plaintiff, an account holder with the defendant, incurred substantial losses through online gambling activities.[552] These losses caused the plaintiff's account to show a large negative balance. The plaintiff argued that this should have been impossible since the account was a savings account and since no applications were made for overdrafts or loans. The defendant argued that a malfunction in their electronic banking system allowed the plaintiff to debit more than the amount stored in the account, and thus for the savings account to show a negative balance. The defendant stated that this malfunction allowed seven people, including the plaintiff, to incur substantial debits over a period of several months. All such debits were related to Internet-based gambling transactions carried out by the seven individuals.

696. The court held that the plaintiff did indeed carry out the online gambling transactions that resulted in the negative balance. The court also held that the defendant bank knew of the malfunctioning system and failed to timely rectify the malfunction. As a result, the plaintiff's debts were partially the result of negligence on the part of the defendant bank. The finding of negligence allowed the court to hold that the plaintiff was not required to pay the incurred debts and that the defendant bank must absorb the negative balance.

552. [2017] eKLR.

Chapter 2. Regulation of Electronic Signatures and Certification Services

§1. Digital Signatures

697. The Act provides that where a law requires the signature of a person, that requirement is met in relation to an electronic message if an advanced electronic signature is used that is as reliable as is appropriate for the purpose for which the electronic message is generated or communicated, in light of all the circumstances, including any relevant agreement.[553]

698. An advanced electronic signature is considered to be reliable for the purpose of satisfying the requirements of the law if it meets the following conditions:

- it is generated through a signature creation device;
- the signature creation data are, within the context in which they are used, linked to the signatory and no other person;
- the signature creation data are, at the time of signing, under the control of the signatory and of no other person;
- any alteration to the electronic signature made after the time of signing is detectable; and
- where the purpose of the legal requirement for a signature is to provide assurance as to the integrity of the information to which it relates, any alteration made to that information after the time of signing is detectable.[554]

699. Where any law provides that information or any other matter shall be authenticated by affixing a signature or that any document shall be signed or bear the signature of any person, such a requirement shall be deemed to have been satisfied if such information is authenticated by means of an advanced electronic signature affixed in such a manner as may be prescribed by the Minister.[555]

700. The Act forbids any person from operating an 'electronic certification system' without a licence.[556] A person who contravenes this provision commits an offence and upon conviction is liable to a fine not exceeding USD 4,200 or to imprisonment for a term not exceeding three years or both.[557]

701. A licence to provide electronic certification services may include conditions requiring the provider to:

- make use of hardware, software, and procedures that are secure from intrusion and misuse;

553. Section 83O(1).
554. Section 83O(3).
555. Section 83P.
556. Section 83D.
557. *Ibid.*

- provide a reasonable level of reliability in its services which are reasonably suited to the performance of intended functions;
- adhere to procedures that ensure that the secrecy and privacy of the electronic signatures are assured; and
- observe such other standards as may be specified by regulations.[558]

§2. Regulations for Electronic Signatures

702. The Minister for information and communications may, in consultation with the CA, prescribe regulations on:

- the type of electronic signature;
- the manner and format in which the electronic signature shall be affixed;
- the manner and procedure which facilitates identification of the person affixing the electronic signature;
- control of the processes and procedures to ensure adequate integrity, security, and confidentiality of electronic records or payments; and
- any other matter which is necessary to give legal effect to electronic signatures.[559]

703. As per the mandate provided in the KIC Act,[560] the CA enacted the KIC (Electronic Transactions) Regulations, 2016, with the following objectives:

- promote legal certainty and confidence in respect of electronic communications, electronic transactions, and e-commerce;
- promote e-government services and electronic communications, electronic transactions, and e-commerce with public and private bodies, institutions, and citizens;
- ensure that electronic communications, electronic transactions, and e-commerce conform to the highest international standards;
- encourage investment and innovation in respect of electronic communications, electronic transactions, and e-commerce in the Republic;
- ensure compliance with accepted International technical standards in the provision and development of electronic communications, electronic transactions, and e-commerce;
- ensure that the national interest of the Republic is not compromised through the use of electronic communications, electronic transactions, and e-commerce.[561]

704. The Regulations apply to all 'service provides', which are defined quite broadly as 'any person in Kenya who offers on a commercial basis, the sale, hire or

558. Section 83E.
559. Section 83R.
560. Section 83C.
561. Regulation 3, Kenya Information and Communications (Electronic Transactions) Regulations, 2016.

exchange of goods or services through an electronic transaction'. The Regulations require all services providers to acquire authorization from the CA[562] and to comply with a number of provisions largely focused on principles of consumer protection. The Regulations prohibit the sending of 'spam' (i.e., unsolicited communications)[563] and also include a safe harbour provision for service providers that 'merely provide access' to third-party materials that infringe the rights of others.[564]

562. Regulation 4, Kenya Information and Communications (Electronic Transactions) Regulations, 2016.
563. Regulation 8, Kenya Information and Communications (Electronic Transactions) Regulations, 2016.
564. Regulation 11, Kenya Information and Communications (Electronic Transactions) Regulations, 2016.

Chapter 3. Legal Aspects of Electronic Banking

705. The Act makes an express legal recognition of electronic records. Any law providing that information or other matter shall be in writing is deemed to have been satisfied if such information or matter is made available in electronic form and is accessible so as to be usable in an electronic form.[565]

§1. Retention of Information in Original Form

706. Under the Act, any law requiring information to be presented or retained in its original form is deemed to be complied with if there exists a reliable assurance as to the integrity of the information from the time when it was first generated in its final form as an electronic message or otherwise and where it is required that information be presented, that information is capable of being displayed to the person to whom it is to be presented.[566] The criteria for assessing the integrity of the information is whether the information remains complete and unaltered, apart from the addition of any endorsement and any change which arises in the normal course of communication, storage, and display. The standard of reliability required is to be assessed in the light of the purpose for which the information was generated and in considering all the relevant circumstances.[567]

I. Judicial Interpretation of Electronic Transactions Law: The KEMSA Case

707. Probably the first definitive judicial test for the newly enacted provisions of the KIC Act regarding the recognition of electronic documents came to the High Court of Kenya in *Republic v. Public Procurement Administrative Review Board Ex-parte Kenya Medical Supply Agency & 3 Others*.[568] In the case, the High Court held that a scanned document may not be regarded as an 'original' for the purposes of the PPDA, 2005 particularly where in its guidelines to potential bidders, a procuring entity requires the submission of 'original' documents. In an application to review the decision of the Procurement Review and Appeals Board in which the Board had applied a recently enacted law recognizing the legality of electronic documents and the originality of documents rendered in electronic form, the High Court reversed the Board's decision and excluded the application of the new electronic documents law from the Procurement Act.

708. The decision highlighted what may be an awkward dilemma for legislative drafting and statutory interpretation: Where one Act of Parliament excludes the application of any other Act in the interpretation of its provisions and a later Act

565. Section 83G.
566. Section 83I(1).
567. Section 83I(2).
568. [2010] eKLR High Court at Nairobi (Nairobi Law Courts), J. Gacheche J, 4 Mar. 2010.

makes provisions of a general nature to be applied in the interpretation of all other Acts, how is the apparent conflict between the two Acts to be resolved. While section 5 of the PPDA, 2005 provides that where there is a conflict between the Act or the regulations made under it and any other Act in matters relating to procurement and disposal, the Procurement Act and its regulations are to prevail, the provisions of the KIC Act, 1998 recognizing the legality of electronic documents and 'electronic originals' is to apply to all Acts of Parliament, particularly to those that contain provisions providing for documents to be in writing.

709. The decision interpreted two important provisions of the KIC Act: first, where any law provides that information or other matter shall be in writing then, notwithstanding anything contained in such law, such requirement shall be deemed to have been satisfied if such information or matter is:

- rendered or made available in an electronic form; and
- is accessible so as to be usable for a subsequent reference.[569]

710. This provision expressly recognizes the legality of electronic documents and extends its application to other Acts of Parliament providing for any matter or document to be done in writing.

711. Second, where any law requires information to be presented or retained in its original form, that requirement is met by an electronic record if:

- there exists a reliable assurance as to the integrity of the information from the time when it was first generated in its final form as an electronic message or otherwise; and
- where it is required that information be presented, that information is capable of being displayed to the person to whom it is to be presented.[570]

712. It is further provided that the criteria for assessing the integrity of the information shall be whether the information has remained complete and unaltered, apart from the addition of any endorsement and any change which arises in the normal course of communication, storage, and display and further, that the standard of reliability required shall be assessed in the light of the purpose for which the information was generated and in light of all the relevant circumstances.

713. This provision expressly recognizes that a document may, subject to the conditions specified, be deemed to be an 'original' even if it does not exist in paper form and where it is merely an electronic abstraction or representation of a paper document.

714. The conflict between these provisions and the PPDA, 2005 was thrown into relief when a dispute over the procedure followed in the procurement of Human

569. Section 83G.
570. Section 83I.

Immunodeficiency Virus – Acquired Immune Deficiency Syndrome (HIV-AIDS) drugs by the government came to the courts.

A. *The Dispute*

715. In March of 2009, a consortium of agencies and firms involved in procurement and supply chain management comprised of the Kenya Medical Supply Agency (KEMSA), Crown Agents, the agency for German Technical Cooperation (GTZ), and John Snow Inc. advertised a tender for the supply of antiretroviral drugs on behalf of Kenya's Ministry of Health. Among other requirements, the Instructions to Tenderers provided that bidders were to submit 'an original and … copies' of their bidding documents, including a price schedule, and that 'in the event of any discrepancy between them, the original shall govern'. It was further provided that the original and all copies of tender documents were to 'be typed or written in indelible ink and … signed by the tenderer'.

716. One of the bidders for the supply of the drugs was Hetero Drugs Ltd. In the evaluation of the tender documents for all the bidders, the consortium declared Hetero's bid non-responsive ostensibly because it had contravened the Instructions to Tenderers by submitting a scanned copy of a price schedule instead of an 'original document'. Hetero's bid was therefore disqualified at the preliminary stage and ultimately, the tender was awarded to three pharmaceutical companies.

717. Hetero moved to the Public Procurement Administrative Review Board, a statutory body established to deal with complaints from parties to a public procurement process. After considering the arguments of both Hetero and the consortium, the Board relied on section 83G of the KIC Act, 1998 to find that Hetero's price schedule 'was acceptable as an original' even though it was a scanned copy. The Board decided in favour of Hetero and ordered the consortium to admit Hetero's bid and also to carry out a fresh evaluation of all the tenders.

718. The consortium then filed judicial review proceedings in the High Court challenging the decision of the Board. The consortium's argument was that whereas section 83G of the KIC Act provided for situations where 'the law' required that information be submitted in writing, the requirement in this case was not contained in a law but in bidding guidelines:

> *The [Board] failed to appreciate that the effect of its decision is to give tenderers the liberty to submit copies of documents where originals are required therefore making it impossible for procuring entities to establish the authenticity of documents. The entire purpose of the Public Procurement and Disposal Act which is to make public procurement a fair, transparent and accountable process will be defeated if tenderers are allowed to submit copies of documents instead of originals.*

719. The Board also relied on section 5 of the PPDA, which provided that if there was a conflict between the Act or the regulations thereunder and any other Act or regulations in matters relating to procurement and disposal, the Act or the regulations 'shall prevail'.

720. The definitive question before the High Court then became: Does a scanned document qualify as an original document for purposes of the tender and generally, for purposes of the PPDA?

B. The Decision of the High Court

721. Lady Justice J. Gacheche, who presided over the judicial review application, made the following holdings:

- Under the Public Procurement and Disposal Regulations 47 and 48 made under the PPDA, it is a mandatory requirement that tenders are to be submitted 'in the required format' and that a 'procuring entity is to reject all tenders which are not responsive'. Under section 64 of the Act, a tender is responsive 'if it conforms to all the mandatory requirements set out in the tender documents'.
- Though the Court noted the proviso to section 64 which provided that 'minor deviations that do not materially depart from the requirements set out in the tender documents' would not render the tender non-responsive, the requirements that the bids should be compliant were mandatory and to be fulfilled to the letter. One of such requirements was that the tender was to be submitted in the required format.
- The PPDA did not cater for matters pertaining to e-procurement yet the copy that the Board attempted to admit was a scanned copy instead of the original.
- The KIC Act section 83G was a direct contradiction of the requirement in the Instructions to Tenderers prepared by the consortium that bidders were to prepare an 'original' and to clearly mark the original bid documents and the copies. The PPDA prevailed over the KIC Act in matters pertaining to public procurement and disposal.
- The Board had no jurisdiction to waive the obvious mandatory statutory requirements. It had exceeded its jurisdiction in dealing with issues that were not pleaded before it and in doing so, it had reached a wrong conclusion. Its decision was ultra vires.

722. Ultimately, the consortium's application was allowed, and an order of certiorari was issued quashing the decision of the Procurement Review and Appeals Board.

§2. Retention of Electronic Records

723. Where any law provides that documents, records, or information shall be retained for any specific period, that requirement is to be deemed to have been satisfied where such documents, records, or information are retained in electronic form. However, this is subject to the conditions that:

- the information contained therein remains accessible so as to be usable for subsequent reference;
- the electronic record is retained in the format in which it was originally generated, sent, or received or in a format which can be demonstrated to represent accurately the information originally generated, sent, or received; and
- the details which will facilitate the identification of the original destination, date and time of dispatch, or receipt of such electronic record are available in the electronic record.[571]

§3. Formation and Validity of Contracts

724. In the context of contract formation, the Act provides that an offer and acceptance of an offer may be expressed by means of electronic messages and that where an electronic message is used in the formation of a contract, the contract shall not be denied validity or enforceability solely on the ground that an electronic message was used for the purpose.[572] However, out of the law's respect for the doctrine of freedom of contract, the law leaves contracting parties at liberty to prescribe the manner in which an offer and an acceptance may or may not be expressed. As between the originator and the addressee of an electronic message, a declaration of intent or other statement is not to be denied legal effect, validity, or enforceability solely on the ground that it is in the form of an electronic message.[573]

725. However, there is an important exclusion. The Act excludes the use of electronic messages to express an offer or an acceptance in instances where another law expressly provides a different method for the formation of a valid contract.[574] For instance, the Auctioneers Act makes special provisions governing the manner in which public auctions are to be conducted.[575] Under the common law, the contract at a public auction is deemed to have been entered into at the fall of the auctioneer's hammer. Under the Law of Contract Act,[576] all contracts for the sale of land or the disposition of any interest in land are required to be 'in writing', signed by

571. Section 83H.
572. Section 83J(1).
573. Section 83K.
574. Section 83J(2).
575. Auctioneers Act s. 21.
576. Chapter 23 of the Laws of Kenya.

all the parties thereto and with the signature of each party being attested by a witness.[577] It has long been a requirement of the law and an established practice that along with insurance and suretyship contracts, contracts for the sale of land or any interest in land are to be 'in writing'.

726. This raises the recursive contradiction that is expressed in the following two opposing propositions:

> *Proposition 1: Because under the KIC Act, any law requiring anything to be in writing is deemed to have been complied with if such thing is in electronic form, then contracts for insurance, sale of land, suretyship, etc. which are required by law to be 'in writing', can legally be created through electronic records.*
> *Proposition 2: Because the KIC Act excludes the formation of a contract through electronic records 'where another law expressly provides a different method for the formation of a valid contract', then the term 'in writing' as used in laws making special provisions for the formation of certain contracts, such as the Law of Contract Act and the Insurance Act, should not be construed as including electronic records.*

This contradiction remains unresolved, with still little or no guidance to be found from the Kenyan courts.

§4. ATTRIBUTION OF ELECTRONIC RECORDS

727. An electronic message is attributed to the originator if it is sent by the originator himself, or by a person who had the authority to act on behalf of the originator in respect of the electronic record or by an information system programmed by or on behalf of the originator to operate automatically.[578] As between an originator and an addressee, an addressee is entitled to regard an electronic message as being that of the originator, and to act on that assumption, if:

- in order to ascertain whether the electronic message was that of the originator, the addressee properly applied a procedure previously agreed to by the originator for the purpose; or
- the electronic message as received by the addressee resulted from actions of a person who had the authority to act on behalf of the originator in respect of the electronic record.[579]

577. *Ibid.*, s. 3.
578. Section 83L(1).
579. Section 83L(1).

Chapter 4. Consumer Protection of Users of Electronic Services

728. Part VI of the Competition Act provides, in part, a framework for the protection of consumer welfare. The framework is supported by the Consumer Protection Act 2012, as well as the provisions of the KIC (Consumer Protection) Regulations, 2010.

729. The consumer protection provisions of the Competition Act 2010 prohibit the following:

(1) False or misleading representations. The supplier of goods or services may not falsely represent that goods are of a particular standard, quality, value, grade, composition, style, or model or have had a particular history or particular previous use. Furthermore, the Act prohibits false representation pertaining to whether goods or services are new, are of a particular quality/standard, have obtained an endorsement or sponsorship, or have uses or benefits that they do not have. The supplier may not make false representations about the price, availability, or origin of goods or services, or the existence of warranties or guarantees.[580]

(2) Unconscionable conduct. The prohibition against unconscionable conduct by a supplier of goods or services is broad-ranging and applies also to unconscionable conduct in business transactions. A specific prohibition is provided against unilateral charges and fees attached to banking, microfinance, and insurance products where the consumer is not made aware of such charges and fees prior to the provision of the service. The Act furthermore provides a number of factors that shall be considered when determining whether conduct is unconscionable:
   (a) the relative strengths of the bargaining positions of the person and the consumer;
   (b) whether, as a result of conduct engaged in by the person, the consumer was required to comply with conditions that were not reasonably necessary for the protection of the legitimate interests of the person;
   (c) whether the consumer was able to understand any documents relating to the supply or possible supply of the goods or services;
   (d) whether any undue influence or pressure was exerted on, or any unfair tactics were used against, the consumer or a person acting on behalf of the consumer by the person acting on behalf of the person in relation to the supply or possible supply of the goods or services; and
   (e) the amount for which, and the circumstances under which, the consumer could have acquired identical or equivalent goods or services from another supplier.[581]

580. Section 55.
581. Section 56 (similar factors are provided, in section 57, as pertains to parties in a business transaction).

(3) Goods failing to meet established safety and information standards. The CAK is empowered to establish consumer product safety standards as well as consumer product information standards that must be met by goods and services offered for sale.[582] The CAK is also empowered to: issue notices to the public declaring goods to be unsafe or failing to meet established information standards and issue product recalls for goods failing to meet safety or information standards.[583]

730. The Act provides a framework for assigning liability on the supplier for losses or damages suffered by a consumer and resulting from the supply of goods that are unsafe, defective, or unfit for their intended purpose. The framework includes exemptions that apply for actions beyond the control of the supplier, as well as acceptable defences that, when established by a supplier, are effective to remove liability.[584]

731. The penalty for violation of any of the provisions of Part VI of the Act are imprisonment for a term not exceeding five years, a fine not exceeding ten million shillings, or both.[585]

732. A more comprehensive framework for consumer protection is provided in the Consumer Protection Act 2012, which also establishes the Kenya Consumers Protection Advisory Committee (KECOPAC). Unlike the CAK, which falls within the Ministry for Finance, KECOPAC falls within the Ministry for Industry, Trade and Cooperatives. The mandate of KECOPAC is broad and includes 'monitoring the working and enforcement of laws that directly or indirectly affect the consumer',[586] presumably including the consumer protection provisions of the Competition Act 2010. It is therefore clear from these laws that the CAK and KECOPAC are meant to have complementary roles in providing protective oversight for the Kenyan consumer.

733. In addition to CAK and KECOPAC, yet another layer of consumer protection is provided by the Communications Authority as per their mandate under the KIC (Consumer Protection) Regulations, 2010. These regulations provide the following rights to consumers:

- receive clear and complete information about rates, terms, and conditions for available and proposed products and services;
- be charged only for the products and services they subscribe to;
- where possible, select a service provider and service of the customer's choice;
- personal privacy and protection against unauthorized use of personal information;

582. Section 62.
583. Sections 59, 60, 61.
584. Sections 63, 64, 66.
585. Section 70.
586. Consumer Protection Act 2012, section 90(j).

- accurate and understandable bills for products and services authorized by the customer, and to fair, prompt redress in the event of a dispute in the provision of the products and services;
- protection from unfair trade practices, including false and misleading advertising and anticompetitive behaviour by licensees; and
- equal opportunity for access to the same type and quality of service as other customers in the same area at substantially the same tariff limiting variations to available or appropriate technologies required to serve specific customers.[587]

734. TSPs are required by the Regulations to take various actions and establish various procedures, including: take appropriate technical and organizational measures to safeguard the security of their services;[588] establish a customer care system for receiving and handling customer enquiries and complaints;[589] establish mechanisms enabling parents to block access of children to harmful content;[590] provide various information to customers regarding services and associated fees;[591] and provide free access to emergency safety and assistance services.[592]

735. Regarding confidentiality of data, the KIC Regulations prohibit a telecommunications licensee from monitoring, disclosing, or allowing any person to monitor or disclose, the content of any information of any subscriber transmitted through the licensed systems by listening, tapping, storage, or other kinds of interception or surveillance of communications and related data. Prior consent may be required before a licensee may sell or offer for free, to a third party, any information collected by the licensee. Without prior consent, the licensee must provide conspicuous notice to a customer that their information could be used, or is intended to be used, without authorization, by the entity collecting the data for reasons unrelated to the original communications, or that such information could be sold (or is intended to be sold) to other companies or entities. The licensee is furthermore required to establish mechanisms by which customers may be able to know that information is being collected about them through their use of various telecommunications services and systems.[593]

CONCLUSION

736. Kenya's legal regime for e-commerce incorporates internationally recognized legislative principles and standards. The market for electronic transactions in Kenya is also fairly well developed, particularly with the use of the mobile phone to transfer money from one subscriber to another. With such development have come new and unanticipated challenges. The new frontier in electronic transactions

587. Regulations, s. 3.
588. Regulations, s. 4.
589. Regulations, ss 5, 7.
590. Regulations, s. 9.
591. Regulations, s. 10.
592. Regulations, s. 19.
593. Regulations, s. 15.

is, increasingly, the trade of personalized data. In e-commerce and other online activities, the value of data generated in an exchange often surpasses the value of the exchange itself. Retailers and other advertisers are willing to pay for customer behaviour data, whether or not such data are anonymized. The lack of key legislation codifying the right to privacy and the protection of data currently leaves a great deal of uncertainty as to the legality of such transfers of data, and the lack of mandatory disclosure requirements means that consumers usually have no knowledge about data losses and security breaches.

Part V. Non-contractual Liability

Chapter 1. Negligence

§1. General Provisions

737. In tort law, a claim for negligence requires showing that the accused had, and breached, a duty of care to the accuser and that the breach of the duty of care caused damages to the accuser. In the context of ICT in Kenya, a wide variety of actions can result in a claim for negligence, and those actions can broadly be categorized into two areas: computer malpractice and the negligent use of a computer.[594]

738. Computer malpractice may occur, for example, where computers are improperly installed and/or programmed by an individual purporting to be an ICT specialist. If such improper installation or programming results in an injury or other loss, and the specialist was partially or wholly responsible for the improper installation or programming, the specialist may be found negligent. For example, an automated high-speed railroad system requires a great degree of computer control based on sensor data and scheduling. Errors in the computer systems that control such a railroad system may be the result of negligence on the part of the installer/programmer. In a county that is rapidly modernizing infrastructure to include substantial amounts of automation and computer control, Kenyan ICT specialists may become particularly vulnerable to claims of negligence. Nevertheless, as mentioned elsewhere in this text, the Kenyan ICT community has resisted repeated efforts by the CA to implement a certification system for ICT specialists.

739. The negligent use of a computer as a tort offence results from the principle that any computer user has a duty to use the computer with an ordinary level of care towards others. The types of economic activity that predominate in Kenya inform the types of offences that are likely to occur. For example, Kenya is a regional hub for the banking sector. Negligent use of a computer in financial activities might involve, for example, a banking employee carelessly and erroneously entering transactional data into a computer system, particularly where such activity results in a financial loss.

594. Longabaugh, M.L., 'Applying Tort Theory to Information Technology' (2006), self-published online.

740. Violations of many of the criminal provisions in Kenya's body of ICT laws could simultaneously give rise to a civil claim for negligence. In particular, two areas in the ICT context are likely to be the subject of claims for negligence: data protection and maintenance and intermediaries. Data protection is discussed immediately below, while intermediary liability is the subject of the next chapter.

741. Although Kenya lacks a dedicated data protection law, there are provisions of the Kenya ICT Act that pertain to data. Particularly, unauthorized access to data,[595] or modification of data,[596] are criminal offences under the Act. It is not difficult to imagine that a court could hold a computer system operator liable for negligently allowing the acts that give rise to such criminal offences. For example, failure by a system operator to take standard measures to protect a system (e.g., with passwords and restricted access) would conceivably result in personal liability for negligence.

742. Although negligence as a cause of action is most frequently associated with the actions of real persons, some jurisdictions including Kenya allow corporates to be held liable for breaching a duty of care. The critical test is whether the harm resulting from the negligent action/activity was foreseeable.[597] Kenyan courts also allow corporations to share liability in cases where negligence is attributed to more than one party.[598]

743. The concept of corporate liability for negligence has become increasingly relevant worldwide as data breaches have become more common and more harmful to the general public. Reports of the theft of personal and sensitive data for thousands or even millions of customers are a regular occurrence in jurisdictions that require such reporting (e.g., the US[599]). In a jurisdiction such as Kenya that lacks a data protection law, one potential option for customers seeking remedies in view of the theft of personal data may be to initiate a cause of action for negligence by the custodian of the data.[600]

§2. Specific Provisions in Kenyan Law and Policy

744. The KIC Act contains only a single reference to negligence. Any person who vandalizes any telecommunication apparatus or other telecommunication infrastructure commits a criminal offence and is liable to a fine or a prison term, or both.

595. Kenya ICT Act, s. 83W.
596. Kenya ICT Act, s. 83X.
597. *East African Oil Refineries Ltd v. Republic* [1981] KLR 109.
598. *Nickson Muthoka Mutavi v. Kenya Agricultural Research Institute* [2016] eKLR.
599. *See*, for example, news reports on hacking activities against numerous United States companies including Equifax and Uber. An incomplete list is found at https://www.identityforce.com/blog/2017-data-breaches (last accessed 5 Dec. 2017).
600. For example, the American company Uber has been sued for negligence in relation to a data breach that occurred in 2017. *See* https://www.bloomberg.com/news/articles/2017-11-22/uber-sued-for-negligence-after-disclosing-massive-data-breach (last accessed 5 Dec. 2017).

In this case, vandalism includes negligent destruction of such infrastructure.[601] The KIC Act Regulations contain a provision for liability of certification service providers: 'A certification service provider shall, by issuing or guaranteeing a certificate to the public, accept liability for damage caused to any person who reasonably relies on the certificate unless the certification service provider can prove that it was not negligent.'[602] Apart from these very specific references, the law in Kenya is silent on issues of negligence as specifically applied to ICT. Furthermore, there appear to be no published judicial decisions specifically on this issue.

745. The National ICT Policy from 2006 includes provisions protecting against negligence in terms of communications through broadcasting. Under Part 4.3.5 on Professional Standards the Policy states that, as a matter of public interest and right to information, there is 'need to report news truthfully, accurately and fairly, without intentional or negligent departure from the facts'.[603] This same provision appears in the draft National ICT Policy 2016.

746. As mentioned previously, the Kenya ICTA has developed a set of nine Standards that apply primarily to government ICT systems, administrators, and users. Although these standards do not mention negligence specifically, there are several provisions pertaining to liability. For example, the Systems and Application Standard contains a provision that System Administrators of e-mail systems in the Ministries, Counties, and Agencies shall be held liable in case of breach of any licensing requirements and obligations.[604] Also, for example, the Cloud Computing Standard requires that Ministries, Counties, and Agencies should incorporate into any SLAs a liability clause covering issues such as data loss/misuse and interoperability.[605]

747. Finally, the Kenya ICT Act Regulations briefly address the issue of the liability of users (i.e., subscribers to a telecommunications service). Specifically, the user 'shall be liable for activities carried out using a subscription medium registered in that person's name'.[606] The liability of the user can be removed 'if that subscriber can prove that when the activities were being carried out, the subscriber was not in control of the subscription medium'.[607]

---

601. Kenya Information and Communications Act, ss 2 and 32.
602. Section 11, Kenya Information and Communications (Electronic Certification and Domain Name Administration) Regulations 2010.
603. Ministry of Information and Communications. (2006, January). *National Information and Communications Technology (ICT) Policy.*
604. Kenya ICT Authority, Systems and Application Standard, 2016, p. 59.
605. Kenya ICT Authority, Cloud Computing Standard, 2016, p. 12.
606. Kenya Information and Communications (Registration of Subscribers of Telecommunications Services) Regulations 2014, s. 12(1).
607. *Id.*, s. 12(2).

Chapter 2. Liability of Intermediaries: Network Operators and Service Providers

748. The modern Internet ecosystem involves a wide range of intermediary entities providing various services directly or indirectly linking users with content and services. The various entities are often classified into at least the following (sometimes overlapping) categories: network operators; MNOs; MVNOs; NSP; ISPs; online service providers (OSPs); ASP; and CSP, among others. Legislation and case law addressing the liability of intermediaries often have a heavy focus on ISPs and OSPs, even though the defining characteristics of these and other categories are often the subject of debate and confusion. For the purpose of this text, intermediaries are those entities that provide services and/or content to users of networks, whether via fixed-line or mobile infrastructure.

§1. POLICY

749. The National ICT Policy 2006 makes no references to intermediary liability of any sort. The draft National ICT Policy would require the government to develop 'rules on the formal recognition of intermediaries [in e-commerce], their role as well as their exemption from liability in e-transactions'.[608]

§2. LAW AND REGULATIONS

750. With regard to regulation, intermediaries in Kenya are entities licensed by the CA.[609] The activities of Kenyan intermediaries are assessed and regulated as per the general provisions of criminal law and civil liability (e.g., negligence and tort law), as well as some specific legal provisions described in the following paragraphs.

I. Consumer Protection Act of 2012

751. Section 11(1) states that 'no person shall advertise an Internet gaming site that is operated contrary to any written law' and section 11(2) states that 'no person, *other than an Internet service provider*, shall arrange for or otherwise facilitate advertising prohibited under subsection (1) on behalf of another person.'[610] (italics added)

752. Read together, these sections seem to introduce a 'safe harbour' exception so that an ISP can continue operating even if it is hosting adverts that are otherwise

608. Section 17.2, Draft National ICT Policy 2016.
609. Alice Munyua, Grace Githaiga & Victor Kapiyo, Intermediary Liability in Kenya, available at http://www.apc.org/sites/default/files/Intermediary_Liability_in_Kenya.pdf.
610. Consumer Protection Act 2012, s. 11.

illegal. The provisions do not require that the ISP must be unaware of the content of the advertisement, nor do the provisions mention or impose any requirement for monitoring by the ISP.

II. The National Cohesion and Integration Act of 2008

753. Section 62 of the National Cohesion and Integration Act 2008 imposes liability on any newspaper, radio station, or media enterprise for publishing any utterance that amounts to the offence of ethnic or racial contempt.[611] This provision was likely intended to target traditional media enterprises, which are characterized by a high level of control over published content. Such a model is substantially different from social media and other Internet-based platforms that allow users to post content without mediation by the platform owner, but there is no mention in the Act of a requirement for monitoring content. As a result, the Act could be applied against intermediaries, and intermediaries could be held liable if they are found to be publishing such utterances. To date, however, the Act has yet to be applied in this manner against intermediaries in Kenya.

754. The Act further makes it a crime for any person to publish or distribute written material 'which is threatening, abusive or insulting or involves the use of threatening, abusive or insulting words or behavior … if such person intends thereby to stir up ethnic hatred, or having regard to all the circumstances, ethnic hatred is likely to be stirred up'.[612] This provision is also silent as to the nature of a publication, and whether the provision applies to intermediaries.

III. The Sexual Offences Act

755. This Act makes any person liable for the promotion of sexual offences with children through the manufacture, distribution, supply, or display of articles or content;[613] the promotion of child sex tourism;[614] and for the distribution of child pornography.[615]

IV. The Kenya Information and Communication Act

756. As discussed elsewhere, section 29 of the KIC Act has been revoked by judicial decision but stated that it was an offence for any person to send messages that are grossly offensive, indecent, obscene, or those that are false and are intended to cause annoyance, inconvenience, or needless anxiety on others.

---

611. National Cohesion and Integration Act 2008, s. 62.
612. *Ibid.*, s. 13.
613. Sexual Offences Act, s. 12.
614. *Id.*, s. 14.
615. *Id.*, s. 16.

757. Section 30 of the KIC Act makes persons operating telecommunications systems liable should they, outside of the normal course of duty, intentionally modify or interfere with the contents of messages sent through their systems.[616] Similarly, section 31 makes a licensed telecommunication operator liable should they, outside the normal course of business, intercept or disclose the contents of messages sent through their telecommunication systems.[617] Finally, section 84(d) makes any person liable for the publication or transmission of obscene information (i.e., material that is 'lascivious or appeals to the prurient interest and its effect is such as to tend to deprave and corrupt persons').[618]

V. The Penal Code

758. Sections 194–200 of the Penal Code provide the legal boundaries of criminal defamation and libel. In particular, a person is guilty of libel if they publish or convey defamatory material about a person with the intent to defame that person. A definition for 'publication' is provided[619] but does not address the situation of intermediaries having no actual knowledge of the content of material published on their systems and platforms.

VI. Copyright

759. Intermediary liability with respect to publication of content that infringes third party copyrights has been the subject of intense scrutiny for well over two decades. The Digital Millenium Copyright Act (DMCA) in the US established, in 1998, a framework for determining ISP liability and other forms of intermediary liability in the context of copyright infringement, among other aspects of liability. The European Union adopted similar legislation[620] shortly after the DMCA came into effect.

760. The Kenya Copyright Act creates liability on any person for the violation of any copyrights, and this includes among others, the distribution, broadcast, and the availing to the public of protected works without the licence or consent of the copyright owner.[621] There is currently no safe harbour provision that exempts an ISP from liability (e.g., for ISPs that do not screen content uploaded by users); where infringing material is found on a platform hosted by an ISP, it is possible that the ISP would be guilty of copyright infringement under the current copyright law. There is in Parliament, at present, a proposed amendment to the Copyright Act that would provide such a safe harbour for ISPs. The proposed amendment is modelled

616. Kenya Information and Communications Act 1998, s. 30.
617. *Id.*, s. 31.
618. *Id.*, s. 84D. This language appears to be a reference to the Miller Test for obscenity, which was first described in the United States Supreme Court case of *Miller v. California*, 413 U.S. 15 (1973).
619. Penal Code, s. 196.
620. Electronic Commerce Directive 2000/31/EC.
621. Section 35, Kenya Copyright Act 2001.

after the DMCA and includes notice and takedown requirements for allegedly infringing materials. The proposed amendment does not, however, address certain emerging issues in copyright law, such as whether news aggregation websites violate copyright laws, and whether the provision of hyperlinks to copyrighted materials are an infringement (either by the ISP or by the individual responsible for providing the hyperlink).

VII. Trademarks

761. Under the Trade Marks Act in Kenya, a variety of commercial activities are illegal when such activities use a mark that is identical to or resembling a registered mark.[622] There are a variety of ways in which intermediaries may become implicated in activities that involve trademark infringement. Perhaps the most common activity involves a user attempting to sell infringing goods on a platform hosted by the intermediary. The Kenyan courts are yet to rule on a case of this nature, but given the proliferation of online marketplaces based in Kenya, the following case is provided as indicative of a likely outcome.

762. In *L'Oreal SA v. eBay* (C-324/09), the English High Court referred to the Court of Justice for the European Union (ECJ) for clarity on certain issues, particularly focusing on Article 14 of the E-Commerce Directive.[623] The ECJ held that online marketplace providers may be liable under Article 14 of the E-Commerce Directive for activities of their users if the providers play an active role in the promotion or sale of the trademarked goods, or if they have gained knowledge of facts or circumstances which should have put them on notice that the offers for sale were unlawful and they failed to act expeditiously.[624]

VIII. Common Law

763. In common law, intermediaries can be liable for the actions of others under various theories, including contract law, tortious actions, economic torts, and vicarious liability. For example, contract violations such as breach of contract, conditions, or warranties, and economic torts such as fraud and tortious interference will result in intermediary liability for economic loss. Economic and non-economic losses result in specific causes of action against intermediaries that include defamation, copyright infringement, negligence, nuisance, invasion of privacy, breach of confidence, infliction of emotional distress, pain and suffering, and so on. Finally,

---

622. Trade Marks Act 1957, ss 7 et al.
623. *L'Oréal SA v. eBay International AG,* Court of Justice of the European Union, Case C-324/09, 12 Jul. 2011.
624. Joel Smith & Joanna Silver 'L'Oréal v eBay: A Warning to Online Marketplace Operators' *Journal of Intellectual Property Law & Practice* (2011), doi: 10.1093/jiplp/jpr144, first published online: 25 Aug. 2011.

'claims based on vicarious liability can also be made leading to liability of intermediaries for the acts or omissions of their employees.'[625]

764. Finally, intermediaries make frequent use of contractual disclaimers in an attempt to limit liability. Terms and conditions that are required of users often include disclaimers, waivers of liability, and warnings against illegal activities conducted through the various platforms. Social media platforms are especially prone to abuse, and there are many reported instances of such platforms revoking user privileges in response to illegal or prohibited behaviour.

625. *See* http://www.apc.org/sites/default/files/Intermediary_Liability_in_Kenya.pdf.

Chapter 3. Product Liability

765. Product liability refers to the law applicable to the liability of manufacturers and other persons for damage caused by a product, including damage in consequence of a misdescription of the product or of a failure to give adequate notice of its qualities, its characteristics, or its method of use.[626] Product liability does not generally require a written contract between the manufacturer and the buyer or end user but instead stems directly from a sale of goods.

766. The law in Kenya on product liability is rooted in the following constitutional provision:[627]

(1) *Consumers have the right:*
  (a) *to goods and services of reasonable quality;*
  (b) *to information necessary for them to gain full benefit from goods and services;*
  (c) *to the protection of their health, safety, and economic interests; and*
  (d) *to compensation to loss or injury arising from defects in goods or services.*

(2) *Parliament shall enact legislation to provide for consumer protection and for fair, honest and decent advertising.*

(3) *This Article applies to goods and services offered by public entities or private persons.*

767. Shortly after the adoption of the Constitution of Kenya 2010, Parliament passed consumer protection legislation in the form of the Consumer Protection Act 2012. The Act contains the only specific reference within the laws of Kenya to ISPs. Specifically, the Act provides:[628]

(1) No person shall advertise an Internet gaming site that is operated contrary to any written law.

(2) No person, other than an ISP, shall arrange for or otherwise facilitate advertising prohibited under subsection (1) on behalf of another person.

(3) For the purpose of subsection (1), a person advertises an Internet gaming site only if the advertising originates in Kenya or is primarily intended for Kenya residents.

(4) For the purpose of subsection (1), 'advertise' includes:
  (a) providing, by print, publication, broadcast, telecommunication, or distribution by any means, information for the purpose of promoting the use of an Internet gaming site;
  (b) providing a link in a website for the purpose of promoting the use of an Internet gaming site but does not include a link generated as the result of a search carried out by means of an Internet search engine; and

---

626. Convention of 2 Oct. 1973 on the Law Applicable to Products Liability, Article 1.
627. Article 46, Constitution of Kenya (2010).
628. Section 11, Consumer Protection Act 2012.

(c) entering into a sponsorship relationship for the purpose of promoting the use of an Internet gaming site.

768. The Act further contains provisions regulating Internet agreements – i.e., 'consumer agreements formed by text-based Internet communications'.[629] Such agreements are allowable but place an enhanced burden on the supplier of the agreement in the form of three specific requirements:

(1) Before a consumer enters into an Internet agreement, the supplier shall disclose the prescribed information to the consumer.[630]
(2) A supplier shall deliver to a consumer who enters into an Internet agreement a copy of the agreement in writing within the prescribed period after the consumer enters into the agreement.[631]
(3) A consumer may cancel an Internet agreement at any time from the date the agreement is entered into until [a prescribed number of days after].[632]

769. In addition to the above-mentioned provisions specific to ICT, the provisions of the Act are generally applicable to the ICT industry and provide a number of protections for consumers of ICT products. Most significant of these is section 5, as follows:

(1) The supplier is deemed to warrant that the goods or services supplied under a consumer agreement are of a reasonably merchantable quality.
(2) The implied conditions and warranties applying to the sale of goods under the Sale of Goods Act shall apply with necessary modifications to goods that are leased, traded, or otherwise supplied under a consumer agreement.
(3) Any provision, whether part of the consumer agreement or not, that purports to negate or vary any implied condition or warranty under the Sale of Goods Act (cap. 31) or any condition or warranty under this Act is void.
(4) If a term or acknowledgement referenced in subsection (3) is a term of the agreement, it is severable from the agreement and shall not be evidence of circumstances showing intent that the deemed or implied warranty or condition does not apply.[633]

770. In addition to the Consumer Protection Act 2012, the Competition Act 2012 contains a part on consumer welfare, including provisions on product safety standards and liability for defective or unsuitable goods.[634] Again, these are not specific to the ICT sector but are general enough to be applied to that sector. Finally, the Regulations attached to the Kenya ICT Act include the KIC (Consumer Protection)

629. Section 2, Consumer Protection Act 2012.
630. Section 31, Consumer Protection Act 2012.
631. Section 32, Consumer Protection Act 2012.
632. Section 33, Consumer Protection Act 2012.
633. Section 5, Consumer Protection Act 2012.
634. *See* Part VI (Consume Welfare) of the Competition Act 2012.

Regulations 2010. These regulations do not mention product liability but do require protection of the rights of customers with regard to data privacy, false advertising, and billing transparency, among other items.

Part VI. Privacy Protection

Chapter 1. Regulation of Personal Data Processing and Data Protection

§1. The Constitution of Kenya

771. Prior to 2010, there was no constitutional guarantee protecting the privacy of individual citizens, and Kenyan practice on the right to privacy and confidentiality was guided largely by English common law – a system of law that developed from the judicial opinions of the English judiciary. The right to privacy is now expressly provided in the Constitution of Kenya, 2010 as part of Chapter 4, the Bill of Rights:

> *Every person has the right to privacy, which includes the right not to have:*
>
> (a) *their person, home or property searched;*
> (b) *their possessions seized;*
> (c) *information relating to their family or private affairs unnecessarily required or revealed; or*
> (d) *the privacy of their communications infringed.*[635]

772. A schedule for the enactment of laws by Parliament satisfying the various provisions, rights, and structures is contained within the Constitution.[636] Certain Articles in the Bill of Rights are singled out for more rapid codification, but the right to privacy receives the 'default' treatment that Parliament is required to enact suitable legislation within five years of passage of the Constitution. As of 2017, however, there exists no such legislation and, indeed, no draft bills that progressed passed the early drafting stages. Accordingly, the right to privacy in Kenya remains a constitutional guarantee, although Parliament has yet to define the metes and bounds of the right.

635. Article 31, Constitution of Kenya, 2010.
636. Schedule V, Constitution of Kenya, 2010.

§2. The KIC Act

I. Directory Information Services

773. Section 23(1) of the Act obligates the CA to ensure that there are provided throughout Kenya, such telecommunication services, including directory information services, as are reasonably necessary to satisfy the public demand. The CA was taken to court in 2013 over this requirement, with the petitioner alleging that the CA is required, yet failed, to provide an efficient and effective toll-free emergency response number.[637] The court holding 'directed the [Communications Authority of Kenya] to initiate dialogue with stakeholders particularly the phone companies and the police for the provision of a toll-free telephone facility'. Although emergency service was restored in 2013, it was limited to the metropolitan area of Nairobi and was often unreliable due to disruptions from prank callers.

774. The KIC Act contains minimal provisions for data protection. Specifically, telecommunication operators are required to ensure that registration details of subscribers are maintained in a 'secure and confidential manner' and are not disclosed without written consent of the subscriber.[638] Exceptions to this requirement are made under three situations:

(1) for the purpose of facilitating the performance of any statutory functions of the Authority;
(2) in connection with the investigation of any criminal offence or for the purpose of any criminal proceedings; or
(3) for the purpose of any civil proceedings under the Act.[639]

II. Ministerial Regulations on Privacy of Telecommunication

775. The KIC Act empowers the Minister for Information and Communications to make regulations with respect to *the privacy of telecommunication.*[640] The contravention of the Minister's regulation would attract a fine of USD 4,375 or imprisonment for a term of up to three years or to both imprisonment and fine. This resulted in development and adoption of the following regulations:

- The KIC (Consumer Protection) Regulations, 2010, for protecting and safeguarding the interests of consumers in relation to the provision of ICT services and equipment.

637. *Okiya Omtatah Okoiti v. Attorney General & 8 Others* [2014] eKLR.
638. Section 27A(2).
639. Section 27A(3).
640. Section 27.

- The KIC (Dispute Resolution) Regulations, 2010, which outlines the powers of the CA and the process and procedures governing dispute resolution. The Dispute Resolution Regulations apply to disputes between: (a) a consumer and a service provider; (b) a service provider and another service provider; or (c) any other persons as may be prescribed under the KIC Act, 1998.
- The KIC (Registration of subscribers of Telecommunication services) Regulations, 2012.

776. Section 15(1) of the KIC Act (Consumer Protection) Regulations, 2010, provides 'Subject to the provisions of the Act or any other written law, a licensee shall not monitor, disclose or allow any person to monitor or disclose, the content of any information of any subscriber transmitted through the licensed systems by listening, tapping, storage, or other kinds of interception or surveillance of communications and related data.' This regulation appears to have been violated in 2017, when reports were made of mobile carriers placing 'middle boxes' (i.e., surveillance and/or optimization devices) on their data networks.[641]

III. Prohibition Against Unlawful Interception and Disclosure of a Message

777. The Act also makes it an offence for a telecommunications operator to intercept or disclose a message sent through the operator's system or to disclose the statement or account of its subscriber. The prescribed punishment for the offence is a fine not exceeding USD 4,375 or imprisonment for a term of up to three years or both imprisonment and fine.[642]

IV. Prohibition Against Disclosure of Personal Information Through Radio Communication Apparatus

778. Except where the authority of the Minister for Internal Security has been given, the Act forbids any person from using radio communication apparatus with the intention of obtaining information on the contents, the sender, or addressee of any message.[643] It also forbids, except in the course of legal proceedings, the disclosure by any person of any information as to the contents, sender or addressee of any message coming to him or her through a radio communication.[644] A conviction for contravening any of these provisions will lead to a fine of up to USD 12,500 or imprisonment for up to five years or both fine and imprisonment.

641. 'Safaricom and Internet Traffic Tampering,' CIPIT Research Brief March 2017. Downloadable at http://www.cipit.org/index.php/accordion-a/level-2 last accessed May 2017.
642. Section 31.
643. Section 44(b)(i).
644. Section 44(b)(ii).

V. General Restrictions on Disclosure of Information

779. The Act also places a restriction on CA or any other person from disclosing without consent any 'information with respect to any particular business' which:

- has been obtained under or by virtue of the Act; and
- relates to the private affairs of any individual or to any particular business during the lifetime of the individual or business.[645]

780. However, the Act provides for three instances in which disclosure may be lawfully made:

(1) in the course of the performance of the duties of the CA;
(2) in the investigation of a criminal offence or for the purpose of any criminal proceedings; and
(3) for the purpose of any civil proceedings brought under or by virtue of the Act.[646]

Any disclosure of information that contravenes this section is punishable by a fine of up to USD 1,370.

§3. The Banking Act[647]

781. Section 31 subsection (1) of the Banking Act forbids the Central Bank of Kenya (the equivalent of the USA's Federal Reserve Bank) from disclosing 'the financial affairs of a person unless the consent in writing of that person has first been given'. While this subsection applies to the Central Bank, subsection (2) is wider in scope and covers all persons who come to be in possession of personal information in the course of conducting their affairs under the Banking Act. Such information is not to be published or disclosed except in the circumstances and in the manner provided by the Act.

782. The persons to whom personal financial information may be disclosed under the Banking Act:

- a monetary authority or financial regulation authority;[648]
- the Deposit Protection Fund Board;[649]
- credit reference bureau;[650] and

645. Section 93.
646. *Ibid.*
647. Chapter 488 of the Laws of Kenya.
648. Section 31(3)(a).
649. Section 31(3)(b).
650. Section 31(5).

– any other institution to which a disclosure is made in 'good faith'.[651]

I. *Barbra Georgina Khaemba v. Cabinet Secretary, National Treasury & Another*

783. The Petitioner, a businesswoman, sued the national government over the constitutionality of the Banking (Credit Reference Bureau) Regulations, 2013.[652] In particular, the Petitioner claimed that such Regulations violate several articles of the Constitution of Kenya 2010, including Article 31 (the Right to Privacy). Regarding the violation of the right to privacy, the Petitioner observed that Rule 26(1) of the Regulations provides that any credit reference bureau shall protect the confidentiality of customer information which is negative or positive and shall only release such customer information to the customer, the Central Bank or a requesting subscriber, a third party as authorized by the customer concerned or as required by law. This rule, according to the Petitioner, should be interpreted as allowing anyone to access her personal and confidential credit information. The court held that, to the contrary, the Regulations limit disclosure of information to the individuals and institutions that have a legitimate interest in such information. Furthermore, in the event that an individual feels his/her right to privacy has been violated, the Regulations provide a means for redress:

> *Nothing contained in sub-regulation (1) shall affect the right of any person to make a claim against a Bureau, an institution or chairperson, director, member, auditor, adviser, officer or other employee or agent of such Bureau or institution, as the case may be, in respect of loss or damage caused to him on account of any such disclosure made by anyone of them and which is unauthorized or fraudulent or contrary to provisions of these Regulations, guidelines or any other law to which these Regulations relate.*[653]

The petition was therefore dismissed.

§4. Other Acts Affecting the Right to Privacy

784. The Police Service Act in section 47 sets out that the right to privacy (as well as the freedom of expression, association, assembly, demonstration, and picketing) may be limited only for the purposes of ensuring:

(a) the protection of classified information;
(b) the maintenance and preservation of national security;
(c) the security and safety of officers of the Service;
(d) the independence and integrity of the Service; and

651. Section 31(5).
652. [2016] eKLR.
653. Banking (Credit Reference Bureau) Regulations, 2013, Regulation 19(2).

(e) the enjoyment of the rights and fundamental freedoms by any individual does not prejudice the rights and fundamental freedoms of others.[654]

785. Furthermore, police officers are allowed, under a variety of specific conditions, to enter premises, search premises, make arrests, and seize property without a warrant.[655]

786. The National Police Service Act is only one piece of legislation that imposes limits on the right to privacy (and other fundamental freedoms) in the name of state security. The Prevention of Terrorism Act provides that an official agent of a national security organ is taking actions to investigate, detect, or prevent a terrorist act, such an agent is authorized to: search persons, homes, or property; seize possessions; or investigate, intercept, or interfere with a person's communications.[656] Furthermore, the NIS Act provides relatively broad authority to official agents of the NIS to impose on the right of privacy: 'The right to privacy set out in Article 31 of the Constitution, may be limited in respect of a person suspected to have committed an offence to the extent that … the privacy of a person's communications may be investigated, monitored, or otherwise interfered with.'[657] The only limitation placed on this power is that the NIS must first obtain a warrant.

§5. Licensing Requirements in Data Protection

787. The CA has issued various classes of licences for the provision of telecommunications services. These include GSM licences for mobile telephony operators. Under the KIC Act, the CA may impose such terms and conditions on a licensee as it may deem appropriate for the purpose of carrying out the purposes of the Act. Some of those terms may relate to an aspect of personal information.

788. The CA implemented a new licence regime (the Uniform Licence Framework, ULF) beginning in 2009. The old-generation licences were not made public, and the terms under which they were issued remain known only to the CA and the licensee. However, the new licences issued under the ULF are available to the public. The ULF is discussed in detail in Chapter 2.

789. The ULF unites all species of licences under a scheme of classification that broadly recognizes three types of licences:

(1) NFP Licence.
(2) ASP Licence.

---

654. Section 47(1), 47(2), and 47(3), National Police Service Act No. 11A of 2011.
655. The specific conditions, limitations, and procedural requirements for warrantless entry, arrest, search, and seizure are given in ss 57, 58, and 60, National Police Service Act No. 11A of 2011.
656. Section 35(2) and 35(3), Prevention of Terrorism Act No. 30 of 2012. *See also* the discussion of this Act as it relates to cybersecurity in Chapter 7.
657. Section 36, National Intelligence Service Act No. 28 of 2012.

(3) CSP Licence.[658]

790. Two of these licences have provisions on the use of personal information. The Applications Provider Licence, Condition 4, obliges the operator to participate in the provision of directory services as and when required by the CA to do so. The condition further provides that any information which the licensee holds in relation to a person for the purpose of providing directory enquiry services shall be used for that purpose only and may not be provided to any third party without the consent of the person to whom the information relates. CSP Licence Condition 1.1.6 requires the licensee shall ensure that the licensed services are desirable to the public and in particular ensure that the content does not result in unreasonable invasion of privacy. Furthermore, the KIC Act (Consumer Protection) Regulations 2010 provides that customers have the right to 'personal privacy and protection against unauthorized use of personal information'.[659]

791. On 20 July 2009, during an event to mark the tenth anniversary of the CA, President Mwai Kibaki, through a speech read on his behalf by Vice President S. Kalonzo Musyoka, directed 'the Ministry of Information and Communication to put in place within six months an elaborate databank that will ensure all mobile telephone subscribers are registered'.[660] The directive was preceded by a report of the President's concern over a reported increase in phone-related crime.

792. The President's directive, albeit well-meaning, needed to be more clearly expressed in order for it to be properly applied. The clearest form of expression that it could have been given is legislation, and the second clearest form of expression is in regulations. As it happened, both have been satisfied. As earlier noted, the KIC Act empowers the Minister for Information and Communications to make regulations with respect to 'the privacy of telecommunication'.[661] Furthermore, the Act now states that the Minister may make regulations with respect to 'the registration

---

658. 'Network Facilities Provider (NFP)' means a licensee authorized by the Commission to build and commercially operate Telecommunication/electronic communications systems, for example fixed network operators, mobile cellular operators, and data carriers.

'Application Services' means electronic communications services which are normally provided for remuneration and consists wholly or mainly in the conveyance of signals on electronic communications networks including telecommunications and transmission services over electronic communications networks including those used for broadcasting, but exclude services providing or exercising editorial control over, content transmitted using electronic communications networks and services, for example, ISPs, IxPs, and GMPCS service providers.

'Content Services' means information of any kind normally provided at a fee and is delivered over electronic communications networks and services. They include broadcasting content, financial information services, and other information society services, for example premium rate service providers, audio text service providers, credit card validation services, and web-based public commercial information providers.

659. Section 3(1)(d).
660. *The Daily Nation*, 21 Jul. 2009.
661. Section 27(1) and 27(2)(b).

of telecommunications subscribers.'[662] In addition, the Act explicitly states that telecommunications providers cannot issue a SIM or otherwise provide telecommunications services to a person without first obtaining the person's name, identification number, date of birth, gender, and address.[663] Similar basic identification and registration information is required of corporate persons and statutory bodies.

793. These powers were finally realized in 2014, with adoption of the KIC (Registration of Subscribers of Telecommunications Services) Regulations 2014 and, subsequently, adoption of the KIC (Registration of SIM Cards) Regulations 2015. The Regulations make it a requirement for all subscribers of telecommunication services to be registered with the following information provided to the operator at the time of registration:

- subscriber number;
- official name;
- date of birth;
- gender;
- physical address;
- postal address, where available;
- any other subscriber number associated with the subscriber;
- an original and true copy of the national identity card, military card, passport, or alien card;
- an original and true copy of the birth certificate, in respect of the registration of minors;
- an original and true copy of the certificate of incorporation and a true copy of the national identity card or passport of at least one director, where relevant; and
- an original and true copy of the certificate of registration, where relevant.[664]

794. The operator is required by the Regulations to verify certain of the official state-issued documents presented by the subscriber. It is incumbent on the subscriber to notify the operator when any of the registered information is changed.[665]

795. For existing subscribers not registered when the Regulations became effective, a period of thirty days was given within which the subscriber was required to present their subscription medium for registration.[666] Similarly, the regulations pertaining to SIM card registration allowed a period of six months for registration of existing subscribers.[667] Failure to so register was to result in deactivation of the unregistered subscription medium or SIM card. The periods provided in the Regulations were relatively brief given that the directive required the registration of tens

662. Section 27(1) and 27(2)(gg).
663. Section 27A(1)(a).
664. Kenya Information and Communication (Registration of Subscribers of Telecommunications Services) Regulations 2014, Regulation 5(1).
665. *Ibid.*, Regulation 6.
666. *Ibid.*, Regulation 4(1).
667. Kenya Information and Communication (Registration of SIM Cards) Regulations 2015, Regulation 13.

of millions of devices and SIM cards. For comparison, Spain had over 20 million prepaid mobile phone users and gave operators a period of one year to complete the registration process.

796. The operator is required to maintain a physical and/or digital record of the subscriber information that is collected. Such information is required to remain confidential unless the subscriber provides written consent for disclosure by the operator. This confidentiality may be broken for the following purposes:

- for the purpose of facilitating the performance of any statutory functions of the Commission;
- in connection with the investigation of any criminal offence;
- for the purpose of any criminal proceedings; or
- for the purpose of any civil proceedings under the Act.[668]

797. While civil libertarians may argue that the registration of subscriptions amounts to an infringement on the privacy of individuals, the State argues that the move is necessary as a matter of national security and is in the interests of safeguarding the welfare of the consumers of mobile phone services. The two arguments are equally compelling, though the State's argument may have more weight at least until the constitutional guarantee of an individual's right to privacy is codified. Even then, constitutional rights may be abrogated in the interests of public welfare and national security. It is notable that there has been virtually no sustained or organized opposition to collection of subscriber information in Kenya.

668. Kenya Information and Communication (Registration of Subscribers of Telecommunications Services) Regulations 2014, Regulation 10.

Chapter 2. Protection of Telecommunications Privacy

§1. ACCESS TO INFORMATION

I. The Constitution of Kenya

798. In addition to the right to privacy, the Bill of Rights also provides for access to information:

(1) *Every citizen has the right of access to:*
  (a) *information held by the State; and*
  (b) *information held by another person and required for the exercise or protection of any right or fundamental freedom.*
(2) *Every person has the right to the correction or deletion of untrue or misleading information that affects the person.*
(3) *The State shall publish and publicise any important information affecting the nation.*[669]

799. The government took several steps in view of this constitutional provision. Most prominently, at least early on was the development of the Kenya Open Data Initiative. Launched in 2011 by President Mwai Kibaki, the online Kenya Open Data Portal provided key government data through a free-to-access online portal and was the first of its kind in sub-Saharan Africa. The portal was designed to be user-friendly by providing various online visualization and download tools, and by providing application programming interface (API) access for software developers.

800. In addition to being able to access government data on the Open Data Portal, beginning in 2010 private citizens and organizations made numerous applications for release of information from various government entities. Such applications were largely successful, although may have been hampered by a lack of standardized procedures. For example, the constitutional provision does not specify the format of the data to be released, thereby allowing government entities to comply with the requirement even without supplying user-friendly (e.g., machine-readable) formats.

II. Access to Information Act 2016 and Other Acts

801. To satisfy Article 35 of the Constitution of Kenya 2010, Parliament passed the access to Information Act, 2016. The Act restates the principles that: (1) data held by the government shall be accessible to the citizens of Kenya; and (2) data held by private bodies shall be accessible to citizens of Kenya where that information is required for the exercise or protection of any right or fundamental freedom.[670] The Act delineates the limitations on these rights, which limitations are

---

669. Article 35, Constitution of Kenya, 2010.
670. Section 4, Access to Information Act 2016.

largely to prevent violations of the freedoms of other citizens, to prevent violations of the law, or to undermine the security of Kenya.[671] Importantly, the Act provides standardized procedures for, among other things: applications for the release of data, processing of such applications, appeals against denial of access, fees for access, and the format of data to be released.[672] Having passed in the late 2016, this act has yet to be the subject of any cases brought in the High Court.

802. The National Police Service Act also provides, albeit vaguely, the right of access to information that shall be limited only for the purposes of ensuring:

- the protection of classified information;
- the maintenance and preservation of national security;
- the security and safety of officers in the Service;
- the independence and integrity of the Service; and
- the enjoyment of the rights and fundamental freedoms by any individual does not prejudice the rights and fundamental freedoms of others.[673]

III. Privacy and Technology

803. The Thin SIM technology was described previously in this text and was the basis of a lawsuit in 2015. The petitioner based their claims, in part, on the constitutional right to privacy[674] and constitutional consumer rights,[675] arguing that there was a serious risk of 'contamination' of user data resulting from ongoing Thin SIM trials and pending commercial use. The petitioner further argued that the Thin SIM technology should not be approved in the absence of a data protection law, as there is a risk of uncontrolled transmission of personal data to third parties when using the technology. The court found the petitioner's arguments unconvincing and dismissed the case, thereby removing a legal barrier to development and deployment of the Thin SIM.[676]

§2. A Case for Law Reform

804. As a country that seeks to leverage the BPO business model as a key driver towards the attainment of Vision 2030, Kenya needs to legislate the right to privacy and to provide for the circumstances and manner in which personal information may be collected and used. Already, the newly established EAC has put together a task force on the harmonization of cyber laws within the member countries. In its report, the task force has underlined the need for member countries to deal with the issue of privacy and data protection:

---

671. Section 6, Access to Information Act 2016.
672. Part III, Access to Information Act 2016.
673. Section 48, National Police Services Act 2011.
674. Article 31, Constitution of Kenya 2010.
675. Article 46, Constitution of Kenya 2010.
676. *Bernard Murage v. Finserve Africa Ltd & 3 Others* [2015] eKLR.

> *The Task Force recognises the critical importance be of data protection and privacy and recommends that further work needs to carried out on this issue, to ensure that (a) the privacy of citizens is not eroded through the Internet; (b) that legislation providing for access to official information is appropriately taken into account; (c) the institutional implications of such reforms and (d) to take into account fully international best practice in the area.*[677] *[Underlining supplied].*

805. Although the new constitution includes the right to privacy, Parliament has yet to codify that right, and so the scope and limitations of the right remain unclear. This is also true with respect to data protection, even as the volume of data collected by public and private institutions grows at an unprecedented rate.

677. The East African Community Cyberlaw Framework – September 2008 Recommendation No. 19.

Part VII. Computer-Related Crime

Chapter 1. Introduction and General Legal Development of Criminal Law

806. Because of increasing use of computers in various spheres of human activity, the Internet or cyberspace continues to impact both positively and negatively on social, economic, cultural, and political aspects of Kenyan society. Nevertheless, while cyberspace has provided secure tools and spaces where people can enjoy their freedom of expression, information, and privacy of communication, the same benefits of anonymity and privacy that are hardwired into the architecture of the Internet also extend to those who employ ICTs for criminal activities and use the Internet to commit offences. As the Internet and digital activities become ubiquitous to our daily lives, the risk posed by such criminal and offensive activities grows ever more substantial. The latest Internet usage report from the CA showed that there were about 35.5 million Internet users in Kenya as of December 2015, amounting to around 82.6% of the country's total population. It is also estimated that by 2020, the number of networked devices will outnumber people by six to one.[678] Such proliferation of devices and access translates, for the cybercriminal, to a proliferation of targets and opportunities.

807. With increased access to mobile phones and the Internet, incidents of the use of ICTs to commit traditional crimes – such as hate speech, surveillance in support of robberies, or kidnapping and the use of mobile phones to make ransom demands – as well as the use of ICTs to commit new forms of crime – such as SMS fraud, hacking, phishing, denial of service, and network security attacks – are increasingly being reported in Kenya. The increased uptake of mobile and online banking by commercial banks in Kenya and the phenomenal success of mobile phone money transfer services have raised the stakes for phone-assisted fraud and information theft. The use of mobile phones and the Internet to commit offences, particularly SMS fraud, raised the concern of Kenya's government. With increased access to broadband, which translates to increased access to and use of ICTs, it became an imperative for the State to ensure that policy and regulation is developed to address cybercrime.

678. *See* http://www.ca.go.ke/images/downloads/STATISTICS/Sector%20Statistics%20Report%20Q2%20FY%202015-2016.pdf.

808. For a long time, the lack of specific cybercrime/cybersecurity legislation, as well as a lack of skills and tools needed for forensic investigations, made it difficult to punish those who use ICT tools to commit crime. With the passing of the Kenya Communications (Amendment) Act in January 2009, twenty-three new offences or cybercrimes were introduced to the law of Kenya. On 20 July 2009, during an event to mark the tenth anniversary of the CCK and following concern over reported increase in phone-related crime, President Mwai Kibaki directed the Ministry of Information and Communication to put in place an administrative mechanism for the registration of all subscribers of mobile phone services.

809. In a study conducted by the KICTANet,[679] a multi-stakeholder ICT lobby comprised of a network of members from civil society groups, private and public sectors, development partners, and media, and it was observed that though the Kenya Communications (Amendment) Act of 2009 created new cybercrimes and prescribed punishments for them, the provisions dwell primarily on offences committed against information technology infrastructure, like data interference and misuse of the technical aspects of devices. No provisions have been made for cybercrimes against the person, such as cyberstalking, chat room abuse, impersonation, and identity theft. This, the report observed, may be attributed to legislative challenges which Kenya was not able to surmount as observed by Goodman and Brener (2000):[680] there is an inherent technical difficulty of conception and scope in defining the laws that need to be put in place for the apprehension and prosecution of cybercrime. There is a difficulty in defining the extent to which these laws should be cybercrime specific as legislation drafters question whether cybercrimes are novel offences or merely old offences committed using the aid of ICTs and therefore not requiring a substantial legislative intervention.

810. More recent reports from the region leave little doubt that cybersecurity issues are growing in frequency and in magnitude, and that cybersecurity is a major concern to all levels of government and the private sector, as well as special interests such as human rights activists. One report indicates that there has been a major shift between 2012 and 2016: cybercriminals during this time have become more targeted and sophisticated and less opportunistic. Throughout this time, however, employees and other insiders have remained as the top cybercrime threat to Kenyan organizations.[681] Any effective approach towards reducing the impact of cybercrime must, therefore, address the obvious lack of awareness, policies, and enforcement of procedures that are internal to such organizations.

811. This chapter looks first at the offences provided by the Kenya Communications (Amendment) Act, 2009, and second at the broader issues of cybercrime in Kenya.

---

679. KICTANET (2010), Women and Cybercrime in Kenya – The Dark Side of ICTs.
680. M.D. Goodman & S. Brenner, The Emerging Consensus on Criminal Conduct in Cyberspace 10, No. 2 (Oxford: International Journal of Law and Information Technology, 2000), 3.
681. Kenya Cyber Security Report 2016, Serianu Ltd.

Chapter 2. Cybercrime in Kenya: The KCA and the Penal Code

812. Prior to the enactment of the Kenya Communications (Amendment) Act of 2009, Kenyan law did not contain any express references to any forms of cybercrimes. Up to that time, perhaps the earliest attempt to legislate against cybercrime was with the prohibition against the improper use of a telecommunication system contained in section 29 of the then KCA of 1998. However, the scope of this provision was very limited, as it applied only to the use of a telecommunications system to send a message that is offensive, indecent, obscene, or menacing.

813. Among the policy objectives declared in the Memorandum of Objects and Reasons to the Kenya Communications (Amendment) Bill was the need to 'provide for electronic transactions-related offences including cybercrime and re-programming of mobile telephones'. The law made sweeping changes to the KCA of 1998, including the introduction of twenty-three cyber crimes. The discussion and table below outlines the offences, the nature of the acts constituting the offence, and the punishment prescribed for each one of them.

§1. The Penal Code

I. Information as a Thing Capable of Being Stolen

814. The Kenya Communications (Amendment) Act amended section 267 of the Penal Code[682] to include information in the class of things that are capable of being stolen. Previously, the list of things capable of being stolen included generally 'every inanimate thing whatever which is the property of any person, and which is movable'.[683] A person commits the offence of theft or stealing under the Act if he 'fraudulently and without claim of right takes anything capable of being stolen, or fraudulently converts to the use of any person, other than the general or special owner thereof, any property'.[684] A person who takes anything capable of being stolen or who converts any property is deemed to do so fraudulently if he does so with any of the following intents:

- an intent permanently to deprive the general or special owner of the thing of it;
- an intent to use the thing as a pledge or security;
- an intent to part with it on a condition as to its return which the person taking or converting it may be unable to perform;
- an intent to deal with it in such a manner that it cannot be returned in the condition in which it was at the time of the taking or conversion;

682. Chapter 63 of the Laws of Kenya. The amendment introduced a new subs. (9) to the section.
683. *Ibid.*, s. 267(1).
684. *Ibid.*, s. 268(1).

– in the case of money, an intent to use it at the will of the person who takes or converts it, although he may intend afterwards to repay the amount to the owner.[685]

815. Under the Penal Code, any person who steals anything capable of being stolen (i.e., now including information) is guilty of the felony termed theft and is liable, unless owing to the circumstances of the theft or the nature of the thing stolen some other punishment is provided, to imprisonment for three years.[686] The Code defines an electronic record as a 'record generated in digital form by an information system which can be transmitted within an information system or from one information system to another, and stored in an information system or other medium'.[687] In the chapter of the Code that deals with offences relating to documents, the term 'document' is defined not to include a trademark or any other sign used in connexion with articles of commerce 'though they may be written or printed or in electronic form'.[688]

II. Forgery

816. The Penal Code defines forgery as the making of a false document with intent to defraud or to deceive.[689] It further provides that any person who forges any document or electronic record is guilty of an offence which, unless otherwise stated, is a felony and he is liable, unless owing to the circumstances of the forgery or the nature of the thing forged some other punishment is provided, to imprisonment for three years.[690]

817. A person makes a false document who:

(1) makes a document purporting to be what, in fact, it is not; or
(2) alters a document without authority in such a manner that if the alteration had been authorized it would have altered the effect of the document; or
(3) introduces into a document without authority while it is being drawn up a matter which if it had been authorized would have altered the effect of the document; or
(4) signs a document:
   (a) in the name of any person without his authority, whether such name is or is not the same as that of the person signing; or
   (b) in the name of any fictitious person alleged to exist, whether the fictitious person is or is not alleged to be of the same name as the person signing: or

685. *Ibid.*, s. 268(2).
686. *Ibid.*, s. 275.
687. Section 4.
688. Section 346.
689. Section 345.
690. Section 349.

(c) in the name represented as being the name of a different person from that of the person signing it and intended to be mistaken for the name of that person; or
(d) in the name of a person personated by the person signing the document, provided that the effect of the instrument depends upon the identity between the person signing the document and the person whom he professes to be.

(5) or fraudulently:
(a) makes or transmits any electronic record or part of an electronic record;
(b) affixes any digital signature on any electronic record; or
(c) makes any mark denoting the authenticity of a digital signature, with the intention of causing it to be believed that such record, or part of document, electronic record, or digital signature was made, signed, executed, transmitted, or affixed by or by the authority of a person by whom or whose authority he knows that it was not made, signed, executed, or affixed.

(6) without lawful authority or fraudulently, by cancellation or otherwise, alters a document or an electronic record in any material part thereof, after it has been made, executed or affixed with a digital signature either by himself or by any other person, whether such person is living or dead at the time of such alteration; or

(7) fraudulently causes any person to sign, seal, execute, or alter a document or an electronic record or to affix his digital signature on any electronic record knowing that such person by reason of deception practised upon him does not know the contents of the document or electronic record or the nature of the alteration.[691]

III. Making Documents or Electronic Records Without Authority

818. The Penal Code further makes it an offence for any person who, with intent to defraud or to deceive, without lawful authority or excuse makes, signs, or executes for or in the name or on account of another person, whether by procuration or otherwise, any document or electronic record or writing, or knowingly utters such document or record or writing so made, signed, or executed by another person. The offence is a felony punishable by imprisonment for seven years.[692]

IV. Uttering Cancelled or Exhausted Document or Electronic Record

819. The Code makes it an offence for a person to knowingly utter any document or electronic record which has by any lawful authority been ordered to be revoked, cancelled, or suspended, or the operation of which has ceased by effluxion of time, or by death, or by the happening of any other event. A person who does

691. Section 347.
692. Section 357.

such an act is guilty of an offence of the same kind, and is liable to the same punishment, as if he had forged the document or electronic record.[693]

§2. Cybercrimes under the KIC Act

820. The KIC Act, including its various amendments, specifically address cybercrimes. Section 83C places authority for addressing cybercrimes clearly within the purview of the CA (variously referred to in the Act as the 'Commission' or as the 'Authority'):

> *83C. Functions of the Commission in relation to electronic transactions and cyber security*
>
> (1) *The functions of the Commission in relation to electronic transactions shall be to:*
> - (a) *facilitate electronic transactions and cyber security by ensuring the use of reliable electronic records;*
> - (b) *facilitate electronic commerce and eliminate barriers to electronic commerce such as those resulting from uncertainties over writing and signature requirements;*
> - (c) *promote public confidence in the integrity and reliability of electronic records and electronic transactions and cyber security;*
> - (d) *foster the development of electronic commerce through the use of electronic signatures to lend authenticity and integrity to correspondence in any electronic medium;*
> - (e) *promote and facilitate efficient delivery of public sector services by means of reliable electronic records;*
> - (f) *develop sound frameworks to minimize the incidence of forged electronic records and fraud in electronic commerce and other electronic transactions and cyber security;*
> - (g) *promote and facilitate the efficient management of critical Internet resources; and*
> - (h) *develop a framework for facilitating the investigation and prosecution of cybercrime offences.*
>
> (2) *The Cabinet Secretary, in consultation with the Authority may make regulations with respect to cyber security.*

821. The KIC Act also provides positive duties on telecommunication services subscribers. In addition to providing the registration details required in the Act, and to notifying the service provider of any change to those details, a subscriber is also required to promptly report to the service provider or the police when a SIM card is lost or stolen. A subscriber is prima facie liable for all activities carried out using

693. Section 354.

their registered SIM, and this liability is removed for any activities carried out after the subscriber has reported the SIM lost or stolen.[694]

822. Table 39 outlines various cybercrimes contained in the KIC Act and the punishments prescribed for them, as provided by the KIC Act and various amendments to the act. After introducing various cybercrimes into the Act by amendment in 2009, further substantial amendments to the Act were made in 2013 and in 2015.

694. Section 27C.

Table 39 Cybercrimes under the KIC Act

Description of Offence	*Section of the KIC Act*	*Nature of Act Constituting the Offence and Other Provisions*	*Minimum Punishment Prescribed*
(1) Improper use of telecommunicationsystem	29 (now repealed)	By means of a licensed telecommunication system, sending a message or other matter that is grossly offensive, indecent, and obscene or menacing or sending a message that one knows to be false for the purpose of causing annoyance, inconvenience, or anxiety to another.	A fine not exceeding USD 685 or imprisonment for a term not exceeding three months or both.
(2) Damaging or denying access to a computer system	83Y	Without lawful authority or excuse doing an act which causes directly or indirectly: – a degradation, failure, interruption, or obstruction of the operation of a computer system; or – a denial of access to, or impairment of any program or data stored in, the computer system.	A fine not exceeding USD 2,740 and or imprisonment for a term not exceeding two years or both.
(3) Tampering with computer source documents	84C	Knowingly or intentionally conceals, destroys, or alters, or intentionally or knowingly causes another person to conceal, destroy, or alter any computer source code, computer program, computer system, or computer network, where the computer source code is required to be kept or maintained by law for the time being in force.	A fine not exceeding KES 300,000 or imprisonment for a term not exceeding three years or both.

Description of Offence	*Section of the KIC Act*	*Nature of Act Constituting the Offence and Other Provisions*	*Minimum Punishment Prescribed*
(4) Publishing of obscene information in electronic form	84D	Publishes or transmits or causes to be published in electronic form, any material which is lascivious or appeals to the prurient interest and its effect is such as to tend to deprave and corrupt persons who are likely, having regard to all relevant circumstances, to read, see, or hear the matter contained or embodied therein.	A fine not exceeding KES 200,000 or imprisonment for a term not exceeding two years or both.
(5) Publication for fraudulent purpose	84E	Any person who knowingly creates, publishes, or otherwise makes available an electronic signature certificate for any fraudulent or unlawful purpose	A fine not exceeding KES 1,000,000 or imprisonment for a term not exceeding five years or both.

Description of Offence	*Section of the KIC Act*	*Nature of Act Constituting the Offence and Other Provisions*	*Minimum Punishment Prescribed*
(6) Reprogramming mobile telephones	84G, H, I	Knowingly or intentionally, not being a manufacturer of mobile telephone devices or authorized agent of such manufacturer, changes mobile telephone equipment identity or interferes with the operation of the mobile telephone equipment identity. Has in his custody or under his control anything which may be usedfor the purpose of changing or interfering with the operation of a mobile telephone equipment identifier and intends to use the thing unlawfully for that purpose or to allow it to be used unlawfully for that purpose. Supplies anything which may be usedfor the purpose of changing or interfering with the operation of a mobile telephone equipment and knows or believes that the person to whom the thing is supplied intends to use it unlawfully for that purpose or to allow it to be used unlawfully for that purpose.	A fine not exceeding KES 1,000,000 or imprisonment for a term not exceeding five years or both.

Description of Offence	*Section of the KIC Act*	*Nature of Act Constituting the Offence and Other Provisions*	*Minimum Punishment Prescribed*
		Offers to supply anything which may be used for the purpose of changing or interfering with the operation of a mobile telephone equipment identifier and knows or believes that the person to whom the thing is offered intends if it is supplied to him to use it unlawfully for that purpose or to allow it to be used unlawfully for that purpose. Although there is no offence if— the reprogrammingis done, or the possession of anything that can change the mobile telephone equipment identity is had, for bonafidespersonal technological pursuits or other technological review endeavours.	

Source: Kenya Information and Communications Act 2001.

823. Section 29 of the KIC Act is of particular interest. This section was used in at least two criminal prosecutions;[695] in both cases the defendant was accused of sending offensive messages via a telecommunications system. In 2015, however, the High Court of Kenya declared that section 29 of the KIC Act was incompatible with the Constitution of Kenya 2010 and declared the section to be 'null and void'.[696]

§3. Further Development of Law and Policy

824. Apart from the legislation mentioned above, a number of attempts have been made at passage of legislation specifically for cybersecurity and cybercrimes. In part these attempts are independently guided by national policy, and in part they are a response to the passage of the African Union Convention on Cyber Security and Personal Data Protection.

I. African Union

825. At the 23rd Ordinary Session of the Assembly of Ministers, in June 2014, the AU adopted the Convention on Cyber Security and Personal Data Protection (AUCCSPDP). The AUCCSPDP will enter into force up ratification by fifteen Member States.[697] The AUCCSPDP covers the areas of: electronic transactions; personal data protection; and cybersecurity and cybercrime.

826. In the area of electronic transactions, the AUCCSPDP requires that entities engaged in online e-commerce activities provide to 'those for whom the goods and services are meant' a variety of identity information about the entity. This includes the entity's name, contact information, tax identification numbers, and applicable regulatory/licensing information. The AUCCSPDP is also notable for prohibiting direct marketing where the recipient has not given consent to receive the marketing, a provision that appears to specifically target unwanted ('spam') e-mail.

827. In the area of personal data protection, the AUCCSPDP requires that Member States establish a national protection authority – 'an independent administrative authority with the task of ensuring that the processing of personal data is conducted in accordance with the provisions of this Convention.'[698] Any entities engaged in collecting, processing, transmitting, storing, or using personal data are subject to the Convention and must report their activities to the national protection authority. To

695. *C V v. Republic* [2015] eKLR; also *Milan Mirembo Nyota v. Republic* [2014] eKLR.
696. *Geoffrey Andare v. The Hon. Attorney General and others*, Petition 149 of 2015.
697. As of early 2017, the AUCCSPDP has been signed by eight AU Member States and has not yet been ratified by any Member States. Kenya was represented at the time of adoption of the convention and voted in support of adoption but has not yet signed or ratified the convention. *See* https://www.au.int/en/treaties/african-union-convention-cyber-security-and-personal-data-protection.
698. AUCCSPDP, Art. 11(1).

guide such activities, and particularly the processing of personal data, the Convention provides six basic principles: consent and legitimacy of personal data processing; lawfulness and fairness of personal data processing; purpose, relevance, and storage of processed personal data; accuracy of personal data; transparency of personal data processing; and confidentiality and security of personal data processing.[699]

828. In the area of cybersecurity and cybercrime, a primary goal of the AUCCSPDP is to harmonize legislation among Member States, and a major requirement is that Member States shall develop all of the following:[700] a national policy covering cybersecurity and protecting critical information infrastructure; a national strategy for implementing the national policy and building necessary capacity and partnerships; national legislation against cybercrime; and national regulatory authorities capable of acting in all aspects of cybersecurity application.

829. Certain provisions of the convention are clearly inspired by the Convention on Cybercrime of the Council of Europe (i.e., the Budapest Convention). Nevertheless, the AUCCSPDP is at once broader and narrower: broader for including substantial provisions pertaining to e-commerce; and narrower for lacking provisions pertaining (e.g.,) to intellectual property and jurisdiction.

II. Cybersecurity Law and Policy

A. Cybersecurity

830. The Kenyan Ministry of Information and Communication passed, in 2014, a National Cybersecurity Strategy.[701] The policy provides four strategic goals towards promotion of cybersecurity by the government: enhancing the nation's cybersecurity posture (e.g., protecting critical infrastructure); building national capacity (e.g., increase overall awareness within the country of cyber threats); fostering information sharing and collaboration (e.g., develop laws and regulations along with stakeholders, and balance security with privacy and economic development); and providing national leadership (e.g., continue to develop relevant national strategies).

831. Several attempts have been made at the passage of national legislation pertaining specifically to cybersecurity and cybercrime. Two attempts were made in 2016. The Ministry of Information and Communication, via the Kenya ICTA, sponsored and prepared the Computer and Cyber Crimes Bill, 2016, with the assistance of an inter-agency task force. Concurrently, the Kenyan Senate (i.e., one branch of the bicameral Parliament) independently authored and debated the Cyber Security

699. AUCCSPDP, Art. 13.
700. AUCCSPDP, Art. 24.
701. *See* http://icta.go.ke/national-cyber-security-strategy/.

and Protection Bill, 2016. The two bills have many similarities indicating a common understanding of the most pressing issues. These include provisions against unauthorized access, unauthorized interception, forgery, fraud, and cyberbullying, among others. The Senate version of the bill was abandoned shortly after introduction. The Kenyan Parliament continued to debate the ICTA cybercrime bill throughout 2017.

B. Policing

832. The Prevention of Terrorism Act of 2012 was amended in 2014 with provisions pertaining to the interception and admissibility of electronic communications. The amendments are clearly drafted so as to skirt the fine line between state surveillance and constitutional guarantees. First, the amendments allow high-ranking police officers (rank of Chief Inspector of Police or above) to apply for a court order that authorizes the interception of communications.[702] Such interception can be accomplished in one of two ways: a communications service provider can be required to intercept and retain relevant communications or the police officer can enter a physical premise to instal a device for interception and retention of relevant communications.[703] Communications intercepted according to the provisions of the act are automatically admissible as evidence in a court proceeding.[704]

833. The amendments to the Prevention of Terrorism Act were more lenient for National Security Organs, which may intercept communications 'for the purpose of detecting, deterring and disrupting terrorism in accordance with procedures to be prescribed by the Cabinet Secretary'.[705] In a direct effort at minimizing constitutional-based challenges of this provision, the amendment specifically adds '[t]he right to privacy under Article 31 of the Constitution shall be limited under this section for the purpose of intercepting communication directly relevant in the detecting, deterring and disrupting terrorism'.[706] Nevertheless, the constitutionality of this provision was soon challenged, and in a landmark case, the High Court held that the amended act does not violate the right to privacy afforded by the Constitution of Kenya 2010. The court used a test for limiting a fundamental freedom that is based on Article 24 of the constitution: consider the nature of the right sought to be limited, the importance of the purpose of the limitation, and the relation between the limitation and its purpose, and whether there are less restrictive means of achieving the intended purpose. In view of this test, the court held that the interests of national security, as well as the safeguards attached to the provision (i.e., judicial

702. Prevention of Terrorism Act, 2012, s. 36(1). The application to the court must be preceded by the police officer requesting and obtaining written consent from the Inspector General or the Director of Public Prosecutions – s. 36(2).
703. Prevention of Terrorism Act, 2012, s. 36(3).
704. Prevention of Terrorism Act, 2012, s. 36(5).
705. Prevention of Terrorism Act, 2012, s. 36A.
706. Prevention of Terrorism Act, 2012, s. 36A(3).

involvement and penal consequences for violations), were sufficient to justify the incursion on the fundamental right of privacy.[707]

C. Cybersecurity Response Capacity

834. Government efforts to establish capacity in combatting cybercrime began in 2000, although initial efforts were later abandoned. By early 2009, Kenya's police force began working on the re-establishment of the cybercrime unit, and as of 2016, the unit was fully functioning with a substantial staff and good forensics capabilities. Cybercrime investigators within the police unit include those with training received in the US, and the unit follows international best practices, including the use of universally recognized forensics tools such as EnCase and Cellebrite tools.

835. Kenya has been working with the International Criminal Police Organization (Interpol) to combat cybercrime and for a while held the vice-chairmanship of an Interpol technical working group on cybercrime. Kenya is, therefore, able to leverage on Interpol's technical guidance for combating cybercrime, including detection, forensic evidence collection, and investigation and the Information Technology Crime Investigation Manual, which provides a technological law enforcement model to improve the efficiency of combating cybercrime.

836. Kenya has at least three operational national-level emergency response teams for cybersecurity incidents (known variously as Computer Emergency Response Teams, (CERTs) or Computer Incident Response Teams, CIRTs). The first is based at the Kenya Educational Network Trust (KENET), a not-for-profit entity designated by the Government of Kenya as the National Research and Education Network (NREN) and providing Internet access to universities in Kenya. The KENET-CERT focuses on assisting member institutions (i.e., universities belonging to KENET) in combatting cybercrime, maintaining data security, and sharing resources.

837. A second operational response team is the Industry Computer Security and Incident Response Team (iCSIRT). This is a private sector initiative, operated by the Technology Service Providers of Kenya (TESPOK), a professional, non-profit organization representing the interests of Technology service providers in Kenya. The TESPOK–iCSIRT offers traditional security training and services primarily to Kenyan ISPs, and secondarily to other organizations and agencies in the region.

838. The third operational CERT fulfils the requirement that the CA establish a national cybersecurity management framework. Known as the National KE-CIRT/CC, it is a collaboration with the ITU and maintains a working relationship with

707. *Coalition for Reform and Democracy (CORD) & 2 Others v. Republic of Kenya & 10 Others,* [2015] eKLR.

national CIRTs in the US and elsewhere. The National KE-CIRT/CC provides information to assist constituents to reduce vulnerabilities, and emergency response when an incident has occurred, and has the following specific goals:

- Offering advisories on Cybersecurity matters and coordinating the cyber incident response in collaboration with relevant actors locally, regionally, and internationally.
- Acting as the national trusted point of contact for information security matters.
- Gathering and disseminating technical information on computer security incidents.
- Carrying out research and analysis on computer security.
- Capacity building in information security and creating and maintaining awareness on cybersecurity-related activities.
- Facilitating the development of a NPKI, among others.

839. In 2014, the KE-CIRT/CC received and responded to thirty-one cyber incidents as shown in Table 40.

Table 40 Types of Cybercrime Incidents Reported and Responded to by KE-CIRT/CC, 2014/15

Type of Incident	*Percentage of All Incidents*
Impersonation	36%
Fraud	19%
Denial of Service	14%
Phishing and Spamming	14%
Online Abuse	12%
SQL injection	5%

Source: Communications Authority of Kenya; Annual Report for Financial Year 2014/15.

Note: Structured Query Language (SQL).

840. During the year under review, the National KE-CIRT/CC continued to collaborate with relevant stakeholders in the management of cybercrime. In addition, the Authority identified two sponsors for its application to join the Forum for Incident Response and Security Teams (FIRST), an international confederation of trusted CIRTs who cooperatively handle computer security incidents and promote incident prevention programs.

841. In addition to the above national-level CERTs, in a survey, 10% of Kenyan organizations reported having an in-house CERT.[708]

708. Kenya Cyber Security Report 2016, Serianu Ltd.

842. Kenya continues to increase capacity in the area of response to cyber threats and security breaches. Kenya remains a part of the ITU Global Resource Centre (GRC)/ International Multilateral Partnership Against Cyber Threats (IMPACT). The objective of IMPACT is to support ITU Member States in dealing with Cybercrime through the establishment of national CERTs, capacity building, and information sharing.

D. The Case for Law Reform

843. A review of these provisions of criminal law against international best practices in legislative drafting, penology, and ICT legislation raises several issues, described below.

844. Section 84D of the KIC Act is titled *Publishing of obscene information in electronic form* and it provides that:

> *Any person who publishes or transmits or causes to be published in electronic form, any material which is lascivious or appeals to the prurient interest and its effect is such as to tend to deprave and corrupt persons who are likely, having regard to all relevant circumstances, to read, see or hear the matter contained or embodied therein, shall on conviction be liable to a fine not exceeding two hundred thousand shillings or imprisonment for a term not exceeding two years or both. [Underlining supplied].*

845. TSPs such as ISPs are important players in the ICT industry and the social and economic development. In return for their investment in the architecture for ICT penetration and their role in facilitating the communication necessary for social and economic advancement, they need to be protected from an operational risk that faces the TSP business model: criminal and civil liability for third-party content transmitted through their networks. In addition to the ISPs providing Internet access, another category of TSPs, namely OSPs are important to the ICT industry. These are various providers of software, storage, and platforms, and now include a variety of 'as a service' providers, e.g., Software-as-a-Service (SaaS), Data-as-a-Service (DaaS), and Network-as-a-Service (NaaS). Quintessential OSPs include the proliferating selection of social media platforms such as Twitter and Facebook, which are now frequently used in commerce as well as for social interactions.

846. Three important forms of such liability include:

(1) liability for copyright infringement;
(2) liability for defamation; and
(3) liability for crude, vulgar, and offensive matter.

847. Generally, TSPs such as ISPs, OSPs, and mobile operators do not generate most of the information and content streamed through their networks, software, and platforms. In many cases, particularly social media platforms, massive amounts of data are generated and processed by millions of individual users. It is widely considered to be important to specifically legislate their immunity from these forms of liability. A misunderstanding of the nature of TSPs and their manner of operation is likely to find them bound up with traditional legal definitions of 'publishers' under the laws of defamation, copyright, and vulgarity and to hold them liable for the harm or damage caused by content generated by and exchanged between the users of their networks. In fact, this risk has already materialized for TSPs in some jurisdictions.[709] In jurisdictions such as the US and the European Union, such risks are addressed via provision of so-called 'safe harbours' – i.e., waivers of liability applied to ISPs and OSPs so long as they satisfy certain criteria and arms-length interactions with the content creators.[710] The safe harbour against liability for offensive or illegal content generally applies until the ISP or OSP becomes aware of the content, at which point is triggered a duty on the part of the ISP or OSP to investigate and/or remove the content. This process is known as the 'notice and take down' requirement.

848. Nearly twenty years after the introduction in the US of the first safe harbour provisions for ISPs and OSPs, it is now widely accepted that the law should not leave it to implication that TSPs are not to be deemed to be under any general obligation to monitor information traffic on their networks unless they are notified or otherwise become aware of illegal content. However, under the doctrine of freedom of contract, TSPs who wish to waive the protection given to them by the law will remain free to contractually assume an obligation to monitor and intercept harmful traffic for their clients.

849. In Recommendation No. 11, the EAC Cyber law Framework prepared in September 2008 recommends that Partner States give consideration to the adoption of rules to 'protect communication intermediaries from liability for third-party content'.

850. Recent efforts in Kenya to provide legislative clarity on liability of TSP and other intermediaries have been made in the form of draft amendments to the Copyright Act 2001, as well as inclusion of such provisions in draft Cybersecurity bills, which is described in the next section and chapter.

E. Computer Misuse and Cybercrimes Act, 2018

851. The ICTA of Kenya, under the Ministry of Information, began the multi-stakeholder process of drafting cybercrime legislation in 2015. The resulting bill was bought to Parliament in 2016 and was adopted by Parliament in 2018. Shortly

709. *See*, for instance, *Stratton Oakmont, Inc. v. Prodigy Services Co.*, 1995 WL 323710 (N.Y. Sup. Ct. 1995).

710. *See*, e.g., the Digital Millennium Copyright Act of 1998 in the United States and the E-Commerce Directive (Dir. 2000/31/EC of the European Parliament and of the Council of 8 Jun. 2000, OJ L 178, 17 Jul. 2000) in the European Union.

after the President of Kenya signed the bill into law, a local NGO filed a petition in the High Court urgently seeking conservatory orders to suspend the coming into force of certain sections of the Act.[711] The day after receiving the petition, the High Court suspended twenty-six sections of the Act until further court proceedings scheduled for later in 2018.

852. The Computer Misuse and Cybercrimes Act 2018, as passed into law, criminalizes a variety of acts, including the following (sections suspended by the High Court are indicated):

- Unauthorised access (§14).
- Access with intent to commit further offence (§15).
- Unauthorised interference (§16, suspended).
- Unauthorised interception (§17, suspended).
- Illegal devices and access codes (§18).
- Unauthorised disclosure of password or access code (§19).
- Cyber espionage (§21).
- False publications (§22, suspended).
- Publication of false information (§23, suspended).
- Child pornography (§24, suspended).
- Computer forgery (§25).
- Computer fraud (§26).
- Cyber harassment (§27, suspended).
- Cybersquatting (§28, suspended).
- Identity theft and impersonation (§29, suspended).
- Phishing (§30).
- Interception of electronic messages or money transfers (§31, suspended).
- Wilful misdirection of electronic messages (§32, suspended).
- Cyber terrorism (§33, suspended).
- Inducement to deliver electronic message (§34, suspended).
- Intentionally withholding message delivered erroneously (§35, suspended).
- Unlawful destruction of electronic messages (§36, suspended).
- Wrongful distribution of obscene or intimate images (§37, suspended).
- Fraudulent use of electronic data (§38, suspended).
- Issuance of false e-instructions (§39, suspended).
- Reporting of cyber threat (§40, suspended).
- Employee responsibility to relinquish access codes (§41, suspended).
- Aiding or abetting in the commission of an offence (§42).

853. The High Court also suspended, pending a full hearing, a provision providing the composition of a newly created National Computer and Cybercrimes Coordination Committee, as well as the following sections:

- Search and seizure of stored computer data (§48).
- Record of and access to seized data (§49).

---

711. *Bloggers Association of Kenya (BAKE) v. Attorney General & 5 others* [2018] eKLR.

- Production order (§50).
- Expedited preservation and partial disclosure of traffic data (§51).
- Real-time collection of traffic data (§52).
- Interception of content data (§53).

854. Most offences committed by individuals attract a penalty of KSE 10 million or KSE 20 million, but penalties rise to KSE 50 million if committed by a body corporate. A person acting in the capacity of a principal officer shall be enjoined to the body corporate if she/he commits the offences under the act in exercise of managerial functions.[712] Courts are also granted authority under the act to confiscate property or assets acquired from offences committed under the act, even though the confiscation occurs after the conviction of the offender.[713] The court can also grant compensation for the any loss or damage sustained from the commission of an offence under the act.[714]

855. The act shall be applied having regard to the Mutual Legal Assistance Act, 2011, which serves to improve international cooperation between states in a bid to fight cybercrime. The act makes provision for a Central Authority tasked with receiving and responding to requests for legal assistance.[715] The requests involve assistance in investigation into criminal activity.[716]

856. Given the cross-border nature of cybercrimes, the act also grants courts in Kenya jurisdiction to try offences committed in Kenya by a Kenyan citizen or a person resident in Kenya. The courts are similarly granted jurisdiction to try offences that are committed outside Kenya if they are committed against a Kenyan citizen or against property belonging to the Government of Kenya outside Kenya.[717]

857. The Act repeals[718] provisions from the KIC Act, 1998, specifically:

- Alteration, deletion, suppression etc. of telecommunication system (§83U).
- Regulations (§83V).
- Unauthorized access to and interception of computer service (§83W).
- Unauthorized modification of computer material (§83X).
- Unauthorized disclosure of password (§83Z).
- Unlawful possession of devices and data (§84A).
- Electronic fraud (§84B).
- Unauthorized access to protected systems (§84F).

712. Section 43, Computer Misuse and Cybercrimes Act 2018.
713. Section 44, Computer Misuse and Cybercrimes Act 2018.
714. Section 45, Computer Misuse and Cybercrimes Act 2018.
715. Section 57, Computer Misuse and Cybercrimes Act 2018.
716. Section 57(2), Computer Misuse and Cybercrimes Act 2018.
717. Section 66, Computer Misuse and Cybercrimes Act 2018.
718. Schedule, Computer Misuse and Cybercrimes Act 2018.

§4. Application of Criminal Law: Prosecutions for Cybercrimes

858. Criminal provisions intended for prosecuting cybercrime have been used in various cases freedom of expression 'offences'. Up to twenty-seven bloggers were arrested between January and April 2015 and charged under the now nullified section 29 of KIC Act, which provided for the improper use of a telecommunication system. In January and February 2016, the policy summoned ten social media users over their online communications.[719] The majority of complainants of freedom of expression offences online have been politicians.

§5. Criminal Procedure as Applied in the Area of ICT in Kenya

859. As mentioned above, a draft Computer and Cybercrimes Bill 2016 is before Parliament and provides for criminalization of a variety of acts. In addition to substantive criminal provisions, the draft bill contains procedural provisions that are meant to augment the ordinary criminal procedure regime.

860. In particular, the Bill provides certain investigative procedures that would aid in tackling criminal activity. For instance, it grants police officers or other authorized persons the authority to apply for a warrant to access, search, and immediately seize a specific computer system or part of it, a computer data storage medium, or computer program and data, provided it can be proved that they are required for conducting investigations or could have been used in order to commit an offence.[720] The officer is granted the warrant subject to the condition that she/he can establish reasonable grounds for applying for the search warrant.[721] The officer is not, however, authorized to acquire physical custody of the computer program, computer system, data, or computer data storage medium, unless it is necessary under certain circumstances such as the fact that it is not practicable to seize or secure the computer data, or it is necessary to ensure that data shall not be destroyed, altered, or otherwise interfered with.[722]

861. Once a warrant is issued the police officer can:

- Access, seize, or secure the specified computer system, program, data, or computer data storage medium.
- Access, inspect, and check the operation of any computer system to which the warrant issued under this section applies.
- Access any information, code, or technology which is capable of unscrambling encrypted data contained or available to such computer system into an intelligible format for the purpose of the warrant issued under this section.

---

719. State of Internet Freedom in Africa, 2016, CIPESA (September, 2016).
720. Section 21(1), The Computer and Cybercrimes Bill (2016).
721. *Ibid.*
722. *See* s. 21(2)(d) read with s. 21(7)(a), *The Computer and Cybercrimes Bill* (2016).

- Require any person possessing knowledge concerning the functioning of the computer system or measures applied to protect the computer data therein to provide, as is reasonable, the necessary computer data or information, to enable the police officer or any authorized person in conducting such activities as authorized under this section.
- Require any person in possession of decryption information to grant them access to such decryption information necessary to decrypt data required for the purpose of the warrant issued under this section, except where such decryption may contravene the protection of such person against self-incrimination under the laws of Kenya.[723]
- Require any person possessing the appropriate technical knowledge to provide such reasonable technical and other assistance as they may require for the purposes of executing the warrant issued under this section.[724]

862. A police officer is also authorized to enter any premises without a warrant but under special circumstances where she/he suspects that an offence has been committed, and she/he then can take possession of a computer system.[725]

863. Police officers are also authorized to apply for production orders. These are orders requiring a person to submit specified computer data in his or her possession and data stored in his or her computer system or computer data storage medium. Production orders may also be an order requiring a service provider offering services in Kenya to provide subscriber information.[726] The police officer must establish that the data or the subscriber information is necessary for conducting investigations.[727]

864. The Computer and Cybercrimes Bill also provides for expedited preservation of traffic data.[728] This means that police officers can, by serving a notice to a specific person in control of a service provider, require him or her to undertake expeditious preservation of available traffic data regardless of whether one or more service providers were involved in the transmission of that communication; or disclose sufficient traffic data concerning any communication in order to identify the

723. Under s. 9 of the Bill 'decrypted information' refers to information or technology that enables a person to readily unscramble encrypted data into an intelligible format.
'Encrypted information' refers to data which has been transformed from its plain text version to an unintelligible format, regardless of the technique utilized for such transformation and irrespective of the medium in which such data occurs or can be found for the purposes of protecting the content of such data.
724. The powers listed in this part are obtained from s. 21(3) of the Computer and Cybercrimes Bill (2016).
725. Section 22, Computer and Cybercrimes Bill (2016).
726. Section 24(1), Computer and Cybercrimes Bill (2016).
727. Section 24(1), Computer and Cybercrimes Bill (2016).
728. Under s. 2 of the Bill, traffic data is defined as computer data relating to a communication by means of a computer system, generated by a computer system that formed a part in the chain of communication, indicating the communication's origin, destination, route, time, date, size, duration, or the type of underlying service.

service providers and the path through which communication was transmitted.[729] The officer must first establish that the data is required for purposes of criminal investigation and that there is a risk of vulnerability that the data may be lost, modified, destroyed, or rendered inaccessible.[730]

865. Furthermore, the bill provides for real-time collection of traffic data. It states that a police officer, on noting that certain data is necessary for investigation into an offence, can apply to the court for an order to permit the officer to record or collect traffic data through the application of technical means in real time; or require a service provider to collect or record traffic data through the application of technical means; or cooperate with the police in the collection or recording of traffic data in real time.[731]

866. The Bill also allows for interception of content data. This takes the form of an order obtained from a court to permit a police officer to collect or record content data through the application of technical means or cooperate and assist the competent authorities in the collection or recording of content data, in real time, of certain communications. The police officer must establish that the traffic data is required for the purpose of conducting investigations to a serious offence.[732]

867. Persons are not authorized to obstruct the police from lawfully exercising their powers under the Bill and would be liable to a fine not exceeding KSE 5 million or a term not exceeding three-year imprisonment or to both.[733] Police officers as well are not authorized to misuse the exercise of powers granted under the Bill, and they would be subject to a fine not exceeding KSE 5 million or a term not exceeding three-year imprisonment or both.[734]

868. Finally, the Bill provides that service providers are only liable for offences committed by users if they had actual knowledge, actual notice, or wilful and malicious intent; or had thereby aided, abetted or facilitated, by action or omission, the use of by any person of any computer system controlled by the service provider in connection with offences denoted under the Bill.[735]

§6. Conclusion

869. Until the enactment of the Kenya Communications (Amendment) Act, 2008, Kenya's penal laws did not, at least in the style of their wording, define any of the general species of offences collectively referred to as cybercrimes, for instance, hacking (unauthorized access to a computer system) and phishing (theft of

729. Section 25(1), Computer and Cybercrimes Bill (2016).
730. Section 25(1), Computer and Cybercrimes Bill (2016).
731. Section 26(1), Computer and Cybercrimes Bill (2016).
732. Section 27(1), Computer and Cybercrimes Bill (2016).
733. Section 28(1), Computer and Cybercrimes Bill (2016).
734. Section 28(2), Computer and Cybercrimes Bill (2016).
735. Section 30(1), Computer and Cybercrimes Bill (2016).

information). At best, such offences would at the time have been tried using the traditional definitions of existing offences, such as theft and forgery. The challenge for cyber law reform has therefore been more semantic than substantive: whether to update the definitions of traditional offences with current notions and definitions of cybercrime or to define cybercrimes and prescribe punishments for them under a new piece of legislation. Kenya's reform of penal legislation has been three-pronged, creating a balance between the two approaches: first, the Penal Code, which is the definitive criminal law statute for Kenya, was amended to include electronic records in its penal provisions relating to documents. Second, the KIC Act, the framework legislation for the ICT industry, was amended to introduce a set of twenty-three types of cybercrimes. Third, Kenyan Government is currently engaged in efforts to create new legislation that is specific to cybercrime.

870. The Kenyan government has made significant efforts to increase its capacity to detect, investigate, and prosecute cybercrime with sophisticated tools, resources, and knowledge. The private sector has been slower to show (publicly, at least) an appreciation for the seriousness of cybercrime issues. As is the case elsewhere, the increasing use of ICTs for business and social interactions, and the global challenge of cross-border cybercrime, remain a challenge for the private sector, government, law enforcement, and the judiciary.

Part VIII. Electronic Evidence

§1. Introduction

I. General Principles of the Law of Evidence

871. There are two principal sources of the law of evidence in Kenya. The first and primary source is Kenya's codified law of evidence, the Evidence Act.[736] The second source is judge-made law, particularly those principles of evidence that are applied by the superior courts of record in the UK and the Commonwealth in general, and increasingly now by the High Court of Kenya. The Evidence Act, like many other Acts of Parliament in force in Kenya, is descended from British law and therefore codifies some of the common law doctrines and principles of the law of evidence. These include:

- the general rule that all evidence must be relevant to the fact in issue;[737]
- how presumptions of fact may be regarded as proved by the operation of the law;[738]
- the admissibility of statements forming part of the res gestae;[739]
- the rule against the admissibility of hearsay evidence and the exceptions thereto;[740]
- the preference for primary evidence over secondary evidence and the exceptions thereto including the rules governing the production of documents in evidence;[741]
- the burden of proof;[742]
- estoppels;[743]
- the admission of the evidence of a child of tender years;[744]
- the compellability and privileges of witnesses;[745] and

736. Chapter 80 of the Laws of Kenya.
737. Section 5.
738. Section 4.
739. Sections 6–24.
740. Sections 33, 34.
741. Sections 35–106.
742. Sections 107–119.
743. Sections 120–123.
744. Section 124.
745. Sections 128–143.

– the procedure in calling evidence.[746]

872. In *Republic v. Stojanovic Milan & another,*[747] Kenya's High Court echoed the general rule that any matter which is relevant and of a probative value is admissible in evidence and that the two exceptions to this rule are that:

(1) an accused person is entitled not to be compelled to give evidence incriminating himself. Incriminating statements by accused persons must have been made voluntarily in order for them to be admissible; and
(2) a court has the discretion to exclude a matter for which the prejudicial effect would exceed its probative value. A judge has the discretion to disallow evidence if the strict rules of admissibility would operate unfairly against an accused person.

873. Subject to a few exceptions prescribed by law, the burden of proving the existence of any fact relating to any legal right or liability in both criminal and civil proceedings in the courts of law in Kenya rests on the person asserting that right or alleging the existence of such fact or the person who wishes the court to rely on the existence of that fact.[748] The burden of evidence also rests on 'the person who would fail if no evidence were given at all on either side'.[749] The standard of proof in civil cases is usually proof on a balance of probabilities, while in criminal cases,[750] it is proof beyond reasonable doubt.[751]

874. In its original form, the Evidence Act became law on 10 December 1963, although the act has been amended on numerous occasions over the course of fifty years. Regarding electronic evidence, two issues are of primary importance: admissibility of the evidence and the form and formalities of submission of such evidence.

II. Electronic Evidence

875. Three distinct periods may be traced in the development of Kenya's statutory law on the admissibility of electronic evidence and judicial interpretations of such law:

– Period I: 1963–1999 – Admission of electronic evidence not expressly legislated but governed by general principles of the English common law on the admissibility of evidence.

746. Sections 144–175.
747. [2008] eKLR.
748. Sections 107, 109.
749. Section 108.
750. *See*, for instance, *Richard Nderitu Kariuki v. Republic* [2009] eKLR.
751. *Gudhka v. Dodhia* [1982] KLR.

- Period II: 2000–2008 – Admission of 'computer-generated printouts' in evidence expressly legislated by amendments introduced to the law on the production of documents in evidence.
- Period III: 2009 and beyond – Admission of 'electronic records' as a special category of evidence expressly legislated by statute.

These periods are addressed in the sections below.

§2. Period I: 1963–1999 – Common Law Principles and the Admission of Electronic Evidence

876. In Kenya's jurisprudence, the earliest judicial interpretations on the admission of electronic evidence may be found in cases dealing with tape recordings.

I. *Nguku v. Republic*

Court asserts the general rule of the admissibility of all relevant evidence as it applies a general rule of evidence to evidence in a tape recording.[752]

877. In this case, the Court of Appeal of Kenya cited with approval the English case of *Republic v. Maqsud Ali,*[753] in which a tape record of a conversation was admitted in evidence even though the only witness who had overheard it was not conversant with the language and could not make out what was said. The English Court of Criminal Appeal had held that a tape recording is admissible in evidence provided the accuracy of the recording can be proved, the voices recorded properly identified, and that the evidence is relevant and otherwise admissible. The Court nevertheless stated that such evidence 'should always be regarded with some caution', and each case would depend on its own circumstances such that no exhaustive set of rules may be laid down by which the admissibility of such evidence may be judged.

878. Agreeing with the decision, Kenya's Court of Appeal observed that:

> The courts are having to adopt constantly to modern techniques and new aids and it would be wrong to deny to the law of evidence the advantages to be gained thereby. Provided a proper foundation is laid, that is to say the accuracy of the tape recording can be proved and the voices recording properly identified, there is no reason why a tape recording cannot be admitted, if relevant, as well as any other evidence.[754]

752. [1985] KLR 412.
753. [1965] 2 All ER 464.
754. *Nguku v. Repulic, infra.*

879. In the same decision, the Court observed that where a party fails to produce certain evidence, a presumption arises that the evidence, if produced, would be unfavourable to that party; this presumption is not confined to oral testimony but can apply also to evidence of tape recording which is withheld.[755] The prosecution had declined to produce in evidence a tape recording of a conversation during which the appellant was alleged to have solicited a bribe ostensibly because the recording was inaudible due to excessive interference from ambient noise. The Court was of the opinion that if the tape contained evidence supporting the prosecution's case, it was advisable that the tape should have been played in court 'if only to show that it was not intelligible'.

II. *Achieng v. Republic*

Tape recording may be admitted in evidence but actual oral testimony required to identify the voices.[756]

880. This was an appeal to the Court of Appeal against the decision of the High Court declining to reverse the conviction of the appellant by a subordinate court for the offence of corruption. The charge and evidence against the appellant were that while employed as a civil servant, he had solicited and received a bribe as an inducement to provide a public service that he was under a legal duty to provide. On the day on which the offence was said to have been committed, police officers had laid a trap for the appellant using an agent provocateur. During the entrapment, the agent provocateur issued to the appellant a banknote laced with forensic powder and by the use of a concealed voice recorder captured an apparently incriminating conversation between him and the appellant.

881. For reasons not disclosed in the record of the case, the tape recording of the conversation was either not produced in evidence or was found unreliable. However, in the appellant's second appeal against his conviction, the Court of Appeal had occasion to comment on the evidential value of the recording. It observed that the tape recording could only have been produced in evidence as an *aide-memoire* to a police officer who had overheard the conversation between the appellant and the agent provocateur. That police officer had to be called to identify the voices in the recording. Ultimately, due to gaps in the evidence of the prosecution, not the least of which was the failure to produce in evidence an audible and admissible recording of the incriminating conversation, the Court of Appeal allowed an appeal and quashed the appellant's conviction.

---

755. This passage has been cited with approval in the more recent decision of the Court of Appeal in *Lazarus Wanjala Musubili & another v. Republic* [2005] eKLR.

756. [1988] KLR 436.

III. *Jane Betty Mwaiseje & 2 Others v. Republic*

Video recording admitted in evidence as judicial interpretations of evidence law keep up with the use of recordings in police investigations.[757]

882. The three appellants in this case had been tried before the High Court on a charge of murder. Part of the material produced in evidence by the prosecution had been video recordings of the statements made by two of the accused persons during the course of investigations, including footage of the appellants leading the police to various scenes relating to the killing of the victim and the place where he had been buried. After the appellants alleged that the video recordings and the transcripts of the recordings were not admissible in evidence because they had been obtained through torture and duress, the High Court held separate proceedings (known in Kenyan criminal procedure as a trial within a trial) to enquire into the admissibility of the statements contained in the recordings. After the enquiry, the Court was satisfied that the statements were voluntarily made and properly recorded and it allowed the prosecution to adduce them in evidence.

883. Ultimately, on the basis of the video recordings and other evidence, the appellants were found guilty, and each one of them was sentenced to death.

884. One of the grounds argued by the appellants in their appeal against their conviction in the Court of Appeal was that the High Court had wrongfully admitted the video evidence. The appellants argued that the police had not complied with due process in obtaining the statements from the appellants, and there had been no evidence to show that the video recording equipment used by the police was serviceable and reliable. Second, they argued that because there was no provision in law that allowed for the inclusion of video recordings in committal documents (a statutory term denoting the sum total of the prosecution's material which meets the evidence threshold for proceeding with a murder charge), the recordings should not have been allowed in evidence.

885. In dismissing the appeal, the Court of Appeal observed that the law on committal procedure had been introduced in 1982, a time when the use of videotapes was not an established practice in police investigations. For that reason, the Court declined the invitation to regard evidence recorded on a videotape, or in any other form not in use hitherto, as having been excluded by the law on the committal procedure. The intention of that law, the Court noted, was to give the defence adequate notice of the evidence that an accused person was expected to face. As in the *Nguku* case, the judges in this case reiterated that the courts of law would not be blind to new technologies being developed to assist in police investigations.

---

757. Criminal Appeal No. 17 of 1991, Court of Appeal at Nairobi, J.R.O. Masime, A.M. Cockar & R.S.C. Omolo, JJ.A. 28 Oct. 1992.

IV. *Republic v. Parvin Simon Dhalay & Another*

Computer-generated transcripts of phone call records admitted in evidence.

886. This was a criminal case in which a father and his son were arraigned before the High Court on a murder charge.[758] Part of the prosecution's evidence was a computer-generated printout of the record of certain international telephone calls made from the deceased person's house in the period preceding her apparent assault and subsequent death. The defence had objected to the admission of the computer printout on the ground that it could have been fabricated. The Court nevertheless admitted the printout in evidence and relied on it, along with other evidence, in convicting the first accused person and sentencing him to death.

887. Even though the question of the admissibility of the printout was not elaborately addressed in the arguments of counsel or in the decision of the Court, this case marks the climax of an early inclination by Kenyan courts to regard computer-generated evidence as being subject to the ordinary rules of evidence, rather than a special category of evidence which was not to be admitted in the absence of special legislation.

§3. Period II: 2000–2008: – Admission of 'Computer PrintOuts', Microfilms, and Facsimile Copies

888. By the turn of the twenty-first century, computers had become a regular feature of social and business affairs in Kenya. However, legal uncertainties lingered over how material contained in a computer could be produced in evidence. At the centre of this controversy was the question whether printouts of evidence contained in a computer were primary or secondary evidence. Classifying such evidence as primary evidence appeared to conveniently dispose of one dilemma for the justice system: it would not be feasible to require a litigant to bring a computer system in court and to conduct the court through a live session of the evidence by displaying the 'primary evidence' on the computer screen. In 2000, Kenya's Parliament passed the Finance Act,[759] which introduced an amendment to the provisions of the Evidence Act regarding the production of documents in evidence. The amendment included the definition of a computer as:

> *any device that receives, stores and processes data, or information applying stipulated processes to the data and supplying results of that data or information; and any reference to information being derived from other information shall be construed to include a reference to its being derived therefrom by calculation, comparison or any process.*[760]

758. High Court at Nairobi, Criminal Case No. 33 of 1996, 30 Jan. 1997.
759. Act No. 9 of 2000.
760. Evidence Act s. 3.

889. By the substantive amendment, all microfilms and reproductions of matter embodied in a microfilm, facsimile copies and 'a statement contained in a document and included in printed material produced by a computer' were to be deemed to be 'documents' for the purposes of the Act and 'admissible in evidence without further proof or production of the original'.[761] Effectively then, computer-generated documents were not to be regarded as copies but as primary evidence of the contents of the computer to the extent printed thereon.

890. However, there were certain conditions that such evidence was required to meet in order for it to pass the test of admissibility:

- the computer printout must have been produced by the computer during the period in which the computer was regularly used to store or process information for the purposes of any activities regularly carried on over that period by a person having lawful control over the use of the computer;
- the computer was, during the period to which the proceedings related, used in the ordinary course of business regularly and was supplied with information of the kind contained in the document or of the kind from which the information so contained was derived;
- the computer was operating properly or, if not, any respect in which it was not operating properly was not such as to affect the production of the document or the accuracy of its content; and
- the information contained in the statement was derived from information supplied to the computer in the ordinary course of business.[762]

891. Probably to mitigate the apparent difficulties that may be encountered in satisfying these conditions, the amendment further provided for the admission in evidence of a certificate by 'a person holding a responsible position in relation to the operation' of the computer system certifying that the printout or the computer system meets any one or more of those conditions.[763]

A. *Flugence Otieno Kessa v. Republic*

892. Finally, the definition of bankers' books was expanded to include computer printouts and electronic versions of such books.[764] However, by this time, the courts did not have any particular difficulty in justifying the admission of electronic versions of bankers' books into evidence. In *Flugence Otieno Kessa v. Republic,*[765] the Court of Appeal presided over an appeal by a computer systems administrator in a commercial bank who had been convicted of fraud and theft. Once the systems administrator's responsibilities at the bank had been to erase the records of all

761. Evidence Act s. 65(5).
762. Section 5(6).
763. Section 5(7).
764. Section 3.
765. Court of Appeal at Mombasa; Criminal Appeal 80 of 2000; J.E. Gicheru, R.S.C. Omolo & A. Lakha JJ.A; 18 Aug. 2000.

accounts closed by the bank's clients from the computer records. The charges against him arose from an allegation by the bank that as the person in charge of the bank's computer records, he had manipulated the records of the accounts of certain clients of the bank by falsely purporting to show that those accounts had accrued interest and then proceeding to trade in those accounts himself by issuing payments and cheques out of them in the guise of the actual account holders. Some of these account holders were called by the prosecution, and copies of bank statements and other records of certain transactions done using their accounts were produced in evidence.

893. The appellant had been tried and convicted by a magistrate's court and sentenced to imprisonment for six years. His first appeal was dismissed by the High Court. In dismissing his second appeal, the Court of Appeal concurred with the findings of fact made by the other courts and confirmed the conviction and sentence.

B. *Barclays Bank Plc. v. Arts 680 Ltd*

894. It would not be long after the coming into force of the amendments that the admission of computer-generated evidence began to pass before the Kenyan courts almost without objection. In *Barclays Bank Plc. v. Arts 680 Ltd*[766] the plaintiff bank had sued a hotel owner in the High Court for the recovery of USD 21,000 which the bank alleged was due to it from the hotel in connection with the use by the hotel of an electronic point of sale terminal for credit card transactions. Under the terms of a merchant agreement, the hotel would provide its goods and services to credit card holders in return for the bank's agreement to honour the claim for payment. However, the hotel was to obtain the authority of the bank for all transactions with cardholders that exceeded USD 100. The bank claimed that the hotel had breached the merchant agreement by not only making a sale for the sum of USD 21,000 without the bank's authorization but also fraudulently issuing to itself a false authorization code for the transaction. The hotel denied the claim and asserted that it had complied with all the terms of the merchant agreement in completing the transaction. Among the evidence produced by the bank were computer-generated printouts of the bank's authorization log report which showed that no authorization had been issued on the day on which the transaction in question was made; and a log of the Visanet Systems, 'an international computerized payment system for card issuers and acquirers of Visa international cards' which showed that the bank's account had been debited with the sum of USD 21,000. Based on the pleadings, the documentary and oral evidence given by the parties, the High Court was satisfied that the hotel had conducted the transaction in question without the bank's authority and in breach of the merchant agreement. Indeed, the Court observed that the transaction may have been fictitious. Therefore, in accordance with the terms of the merchant agreement, the Court found that the bank was entitled to recover the sum of USD 21,000 from the defendant.

766. High Court at Nairobi (Milimani Commercial Courts), Civil Case No. 435 of 1996. T. Mbaluto J., 16 Feb. 2001.

C. *Kay Construction Company Ltd v. Malezi Muthama*

895. In *Kay Construction Company Ltd v. Malezi Muthama,*[767] a magistrate's court had entered judgment against a Nairobi based company in a suit filed by a claimant for compensation for injuries suffered, while he was allegedly employed by the company. The company filed an appeal against the decision in the High Court, which reviewed the evidence, including a computer-generated printout identifying the employees of the company which was adduced in evidence by the company for the purpose of showing that the claimant had not been its employee at the material time. The Court considered the computer printout along with other evidence and noted that there was no evidence to support the findings made by the Magistrate's Court. The appeal was allowed, and the Magistrate's Court decision was reversed.

896. However, a little earlier in *Johnson Joshua Kinyanjui v. Republic,*[768] the High Court, while presiding over a criminal appeal, had rejected the record of the evidence contained in computer printouts because the prosecution had not called an 'expert' to 'verify their authenticity'. The appellant had been tried in a Magistrate's Court and convicted on a charge of making a document without authority and forgery. He had subsequently been sentenced to concurrent terms of imprisonment of eighteen months for each of the offences. Along with other evidence tendered by the prosecution and admitted during the trial were certain computer printouts.

897. In deciding the appellant's appeal against his conviction and sentence, the High Court observed that 'several documents including computer prints were produced. However, no expert evidence was adduced to verify their authenticity'. On that basis and due to certain inadequacies found in the other evidence against the appellant, the appeal was allowed. This case illustrates that, at least for forgery cases, there is a potential conflict between section 70 of the Evidence Act (which requires proof, presumably by an expert witness, that a signature belongs to the person to which it is allegedly attributed) and section 65 of the Evidence Act (which allows for admissibility of computer printouts but does not require expert opinion for authentication). This potential conflict was neither addressed nor resolved in the case.

D. *Cynthia Kuvochi Luyegu & 6 others v. Tourism Promotion Services Ltd & Another*

898. Finally in 2006, in *Cynthia Kuvochi Luyegu & 6 others v. Tourism Promotion Services Ltd & another*[769] and *Titus B. Murugu v. Republic,*[770] the High Court admitted into evidence computer-generated transaction logs in cases of alleged

767. High Court at Nairobi, Civil Appeal No. 361 of 2001, D.K.S. Aganyanya J., 24 Sep. 2002.
768. High Court at Nairobi, Criminal Appeal No. 580 of 2001, A.M. Msagha J., 30 May 2002.
769. [2006] eKLR.
770. High Court at Mombasa, Criminal Appeal No. 145 of 2004, D.K. Maraga J.

fraud and theft by employees who were said to have manipulated computer records of monies received by them to defraud their employers.

§4. PERIOD III: 2009 AND BEYOND – ELECTRONIC RECORDS AS A SPECIAL CATEGORY OF EVIDENCE

I. Amendments to the Evidence Act Made in 2008

899. By 2009, computers had not only permeated many aspects of Kenyan business and social life, but individuals as well as corporations were frequently transacting exclusively by electronic means. The records of such transactions were being preserved only in electronic form, and the term 'paper trail' began to acquire a certain ambiguity. With online banking, customers of commercial banks could not only remotely access their account information but also could transact with third parties; some government institutions were using their websites and mobile phones to deploy public information[771] and even more significantly, mobile phone service providers, with the pioneering success of Safaricom, enabled their customers to transfer money electronically using their phones.[772] The old distinctions between paper and electronic records were giving way to the demands of commerce and more efficient means of communications. However, uncertainties lingered over the legal implications of this trend: virtually every piece of legislation contained one or more references to the filing of prescribed forms and documents 'in writing'[773] and 'signed'. Were these references in the law to be construed as incorporating documents 'written' on electronic media and signed using electronic or digital signatures?

900. It would later become a quasi-philosophical debate whether the law excluded the use of electronic documents and electronic signatures by not expressly making a reference to them or whether it recognized their legality by not expressly providing that they were illegal.

901. In December 2002, when the curtain came down on President Daniel Arap Moi's twenty-four year rule and Kenya ushered in a new government comprising of erstwhile and progressive reformers, it was both one of Africa's most peaceful transitions of power from a long-serving incumbent to a victorious opposition and a time of great promise for the country. It was during the first term of the new regime headed by President Mwai Kibaki that the government conceived what would be the boldest policy, institutional and legislative intervention in Kenya's ICT industry

---

771. For instance, by this time, the results of hundreds of thousands of final year secondary and primary school candidates could be accessed through a short messaging service (SMS) provided by the Kenya National Examinations Council (KNEC); the millions of electricity consumers served by the Kenya Power and Lighting Company could check the status of their bills through a similar service.
772. Through an international award-winning service known as 'M-Pesa', 'M' for mobile and 'pesa' being the Swahili word for money.
773. For instance, the Law of Contract Act (cap. 23) s. 3 required all contracts for the sale or disposition of any interest in land to be in writing.

since 1998. The new regime's blueprint for national development, the ERS-WEC, boldly declared the need to 'review the legal framework to remove impediments that have discouraged adoption and use of e-commerce'.[774] However, even though the momentum for reform would be set back by the hard priority choices of rebuilding a ruined economy amid scarce resources, simmering political intrigues and infighting among the country's leadership and in the violent aftermath of the close of the new regime's first term after the elections of 2007, the most serious threat to national peace and stability since the country's independence,[775] a legislative breakthrough was eventually achieved in 2008.

902. The Kenya Communications (Amendment) Act, 2008, which received presidential assent to become law on 2 January 2009, brought about broad changes to the legal environment in which Kenya's ICT industry operated by introducing sweeping amendments to the KCA, 1998, and to the Evidence Act. In the latter, new provisions asserted the legal recognition of electronic records and provided for the admission of such records in evidence.

A. *Admission of Electronic Records and Reproductions of Such Records*

903. The amendments introduced new Part VII, specifically sections 106(A) through 106(I), to the Evidence Act. These sections provide for the manner in which the contents of electronic records may be proved in a court of law. In most part, the provisions sounded similar to the provisions on the admission of computer printouts introduced to section 65(5) of the same Act in 2000:[776]

> *[A]ny information contained in an electronic record which is printed on a paper, stored, recorded or copied on optical or electro-magnetic media produced by a computer (herein referred to as computer output) shall be deemed to be also a document, if the conditions mentioned in this section are satisfied in relation to the information and the computer in question and shall be admissible in any proceedings, without further proof or production of the original, as evidence of any contents of the original or of any fact stated therein where direct evidence would be admissible.*[777]

904. However, there was a subtle yet very important difference between this amendment and the 2000 amendment. While the 2000 amendment gave legal recognition to material that is printed or otherwise derived from a computer record by the use of a peripheral output device, such as a printer and microfilm, the 2009 amendment did not restrict the legal recognition to a derivation or reproduction of the electronic record but it extended it to the electronic record itself 'stored,

774. Economic Recovery Strategy for Wealth and Employment Creation (2003), para. 9.6.
775. *See*, The Report of the Commission of Inquiry Into Post-election Violence (CIPEV), 2008.
776. *See* n. 26 *supra*.
777. Evidence Act s. 106B(1).

recorded or copied on optical or electromagnetic media'. Effectively, for evidentiary purposes, an electronic record such as a computer file was a 'document' even if it was not reproduced in some material form such as a printout.

905. Nonetheless, the similarity between the two amendments is closer in respect of the conditions that are to be satisfied in order for an electronic record to meet the admission threshold. In the later amendment, it had to be established that:

- the computer output containing the information was produced by the computer during the period over which the computer was used to store or process information for any activities regularly carried out over that period by a person having lawful control over the use of the computer;
- during the said period, information of the kind contained in the electronic record or of the kind from which the information so contained is derived was regularly fed into the computer in the ordinary course of the said activities;
- throughout the material part of the said period, the computer was operating properly or, if not, then in respect of any period in which it was not operating properly or was out of operation during that part of the period, was not such as to affect the electronic record or the accuracy of its content; and
- the information contained in the electronic record reproduces or is derived from such information fed into the computer in the ordinary course of the said activities.[778]

906. Where over any period, the function of storing or processing the electronic record involves the operation of one or more computers and one or more combinations of computers, then for the purposes of the law, all the computers used for that purpose during that period are to be deemed to constitute a single computer.[779]

907. The amendment also made provision for the identification of an electronic record and for establishing that the electronic record satisfied the above threshold conditions to be done through a certificate signed by a person occupying a responsible position in relation to the operation of the computer in question or in the management of the activities relating to the creation of the electronic record (such as a systems administrator).[780] Such a certificate 'shall be evidence of any matter stated [therein] and ... it shall be sufficient for a matter to be stated to the best of the knowledge of the person stating it'.[781]

908. Except in the case of a secure signature, if the electronic signature of any subscriber is alleged to have been affixed to an electronic record, the Evidence Act requires that the fact that such an electronic signature is the electronic signature of the subscriber must be proved.[782]

778. Section 106B(2).
779. Section 106B(3).
780. Section 106B(4).
781. *Ibid.*
782. Section 106C.

909. Further, in order to ascertain whether an electronic signature is that of the person by whom it purports to have been affixed, the court may direct the production of the electronic signature certificate by that person or the certification service provider or require any other person to apply the procedure listed in the electronic signature certificate and verify the electronic signature purported to have been affixed by that person.[783]

B. Presumptions of Evidence

910. The 2008 amendments also introduced several presumptions relating to the evidential value of electronic records:

- presumption as to the electronic record of the official Gazette: A court is to take cognizance of every electronic record purporting to be the official Gazette, or purporting to be an electronic record directed by any law to be kept by any person, if such electronic record is kept substantially in the form required by law and is produced from its proper custody;
- presumption as to electronic agreements: A court is to presume that every electronic record purporting to be an agreement containing the electronic signatures of the parties was concluded by affixing the digital signature of the parties;
- presumption as to electronic records and electronic signatures: In proceedings involving a secure electronic record, the court is to presume, unless the contrary is proved, that the secure electronic record has not been altered since the specific point of time the secure electronic signature was affixed and that the secure signature is affixed by the subscriber with the intention of signing or approving the electronic record. No presumption of authenticity and integrity arises in respect of any record other than a secure electronic record or a secure digital signature.
- presumption as to electronic signature certificates: A court is to presume that the information listed in an electronic signature certificate is correct, except for information which has not been verified if the certificate was accepted by the subscriber; and
- presumption as to electronic messages: A court is to presume that an electronic message forwarded by the originator through an electronic mail server to the addressee to whom the message purports to be addressed corresponds with the message as fed into his computer for transmission, but a court is not to make any presumption as to the person by whom such a message was sent.[784]

II. Amendments to the Evidence Act Made in 2014

911. Three additional amendments to the Evidence Act were made via passage of the Security Laws Amendment Act No. 19, 2014. The first amendment is to section 33 ('Statements by deceased person') and provides for admissibility, in certain

783. Section 106D.
784. Sections 106E–106I.

delineated situations of: 'Statements, written or oral or electronically recorded, of admissible facts made by a person who is dead, or who cannot be found, or who has become incapable of giving evidence or whose attendance cannot be procured, or whose attendance cannot be procured' (amendment underlined).

912. The second amendment to the Evidence Act adds new section 63(A), providing that: *A court may receive oral evidence through teleconferencing and video conferencing.* This new provision removes any doubt as to the permissibility of teleconferencing and video conferencing.[785] Nevertheless, the infrastructure and equipment required to make such practices feasible may not necessarily be available in all courts throughout the country.[786] Furthermore, in at least one instance the court has denied the use of video conferencing evidence, reasoning that video conferencing evidence is appropriate only where it is of essential character.[787]

913. The third, and potentially most influential, amendment to the Evidence Act is the addition of new section 78(A), entitled *Admissibility of electronic and digital evidence*, and which provides in full:

(1) *In any legal proceedings, electronic messages and digital material shall be admissible as evidence.*
(2) *The court shall not deny admissibility of evidence under subsection (1) only on the ground that it is not in its original form.*
(3) *In estimating the weight, if any, to be attached to electronic and digital evidence, under subsection (1), regard shall be had to:*
   (a) *the reliability of the manner in which the electronic and digital evidence was generated, stored or communicated;*
   (b) *the reliability of the manner in which the integrity of the electronic and digital evidence was maintained;*
   (c) *the manner in which the originator of the electronic and digital evidence was identified; and*
   (d) *any other relevant factor.*

785. In *Livingstone Maina Ngare v. Republic* [2011] eKLR, the High Court reviewed, and ultimately overruled, the decision made by the Magistrate's court to reject the admission of video evidence of witnesses who refused to return to Kenya out of fear for their lives.

786. The case of *Abdiaziz Ali Abdulahi & 23 others v. Republic* [2014] eKLR is a High Court review of a case originally before the Chief Magistrate's Court at Mombasa, involving a charge of Piracy for the hijacking of a vessel upon the high seas. Certain video conference testimony was to be given by witnesses located in Tehran, Iran, but this proved impossible 'owing to disruptions caused by the appellants themselves.' Furthermore, later, 'the video went missing and the victims disappeared.'

787. *Republic v. Titus Ngamau Musila Katitu* [2016] eKLR. In this case, the members of the family of the deceased wished to deliver a testimony from Norway, as they feared for their lives if they were to come to Kenya. The evidence sought was not an eyewitness report of the murder, but rather to identify the body of the deceased. The court, however, believed evidence that is to be transferred via video link has to be of an essential character, i.e., *'fundamental to the end of justice'*. Therefore, finding that the video link was not an eyewitness report that sought to identify the perpetrator of the crime, the request by the prosecution was rejected.

(4) *Electronic and digital evidence generated by a person in the ordinary course of business, or a copy or printout of or an extract from the electronic and digital evidence certified to be correct by a person in the service of such person, is on its mere production in any civil, criminal, administrative or disciplinary proceedings under any law, the rules of a self-regulatory organization or any other law or the common law, admissible in evidence against any person and rebuttable proof of the facts contained in such record, copy, printout or extract.*

914. Section 78A of the Evidence Act therefore unconditionally provides for the admissibility of electronic messages and digital material. In effectively removing the issue of admissibility, however, section 78A assigns significant responsibility to the courts. First, the Evidence Act does not provide further definition of 'electronic messages' and 'digital material'. Interpretation of such categories of evidence is left to the courts. Second, although all electronic messages and digital material are now ostensibly admissible, the weight of such evidence remains a subjective determination. Third, the 2014 amendment did not change section 106 of the Evidence Act, although many of the conditions as to the admissibility of electronic evidence provided in that section would seem to be effectively nullified by section 78A. It is possible that such conditions were left intact in order to guide the courts in determining the weight of such evidence.

915. Since 2009, numerous court cases have addressed issues of electronic evidence, although few have addressed the apparent incongruity of section 78A with section 106.

1. Stegma Enterprises Limited v. Viktar Maina Ngunjiri

916. In Stegma Enterprises Limited v. Viktar Maina Ngunjiri,[788] the defendant opposed the admission of CDs and photographs as documentary evidence by the plaintiff. The court found that, on the basis of section 106(B)(4) of the Evidence Act, the CD would be inadmissible due to the lack of a certificate that serves the purpose of verifying its authenticity. This holding seems to be inconsistent with the unconditional admissibility of electronic evidence provided by section 78A of the Evidence Act.

2. Republic v. Mark Lloyd Steveson

917. In *Republic v. Mark Lloyd Steveson,*[789] the court was faced with determining whether an e-mail and a document attached to an e-mail need to be properly authenticated in order for them to be admitted into evidence. According to the court, the purpose of authentication was to demonstrate a reasonable probability that the

788. [2016] eKLR.
789. *Ibid.*

proposed evidence was what the proponent claimed it was. Introduction of electronic evidence under section 78A of the Evidence Act does not remove this requirement.[790] For example, the court should seek a level of certainty that there was no material alteration of the evidence after it came into the custody of the proponent. The court then provided several example ways for authenticating an e-mail message, and it indicated that parties should refer to section 106 for further guidance.

3. *Republic v. Barisa Wayu Mataguda*

918. In *Republic v. Barisa Wayu Mataguda,*[791] the State attempted to enter into evidence a DVD containing CCTV footage relevant to the alleged crime. The evidence was submitted without any certificate of authenticity. The court recognized the DVD as electronic evidence governed by section 106 of the Evidence Act but denied the State's request. The court held that it was abundantly clear from the Evidence Act that 'for electronic evidence to be deemed admissible it must be accompanied by a certificate in terms of S. 106B(4)'. Interestingly, the court further stated: 'If this CCTV footage was available then it amounted to primary evidence and could very easily and simply have been produced as evidence ... It would have been far more logical to produce the CCTV footage in its raw form.'

919. This case is cited, and a similar outcome results, in the 2016 case of *Stegma Enterprises Limited v. Viktar Maina Ngunjiri*, discussed above.[792,793]

§5. Conclusion

920. Kenya has a well-developed evidence law jurisprudence that is both codified in statute and guided by the English common law and case law. Thus, the rules of evidence, particularly the circumstances and the restrictions under which various species of evidence may be admitted, are fairly well developed by statute. Moreover, Kenya has recently codified into statute a substantial portion of the guidelines provided by the UNCITRAL Model Law on Electronic Commerce on the admission of electronic evidence.

921. However, a study of Kenyan case law reveals that particularly with the rules relating to electronic evidence, a few judges may be too restrictive in their approach. Even in the light of a general common law rule of evidence (which has

---

790. Specifically, the case states: 'section8A of the Evidence Act made it explicit that electronic messages were admissible as evidence in Kenya provided that they satisfied the other requirements for such admission. That section did not obviate the need for establishing the relevance of the proposed evidence in the same way it did not excuse the need for authentication of the proposed evidence.'

791. [2011] eKLR.

792. [2016] eKLR.

793. The same issues are also addressed, with the same outcome, in the case of *Nonny Gathoni Njenga & Another v. Catherine Masitsa & Another* [2014] eKLR.

been codified into statutory law) that all evidence relevant to prove a fact in issue is generally admissible, electronic evidence does not seem to enjoy the same overwhelming presumption of authenticity as other species of evidence, such as testimony or exhibit evidence. Though a number of judicial opinions have applied the purposive approach and held electronic evidence up to the same threshold of admissibility as other species of evidence, there is a lingering minority holding onto the unspoken rule that electronic evidence has to dislodge a presumption of 'unauthenticity'. In at least one of the judicial opinions reviewed, the High Court apparently rejected evidence contained in a computer printout *suo motu* even without any objection being raised to its admissibility by the party against whom it was to be adduced. In this regard, there appears to be a chasm between statute law – which has been recently amended to incorporate electronic evidence – and case law.

Part IX. Emerging Issues

922. The ICT sector is among the most rapidly changing sectors, and advances in the ICT sector tend to noticeably and rapidly influence other aspects of the economy, government, and society. In practical terms, the Computer Age and the Internet Age in Kenya are barely three decades and one decade old, respectively, yet no other sector has had such wide-ranging and meaningful influence.

923. It is axiomatic to say that law and policy have difficulty keeping pace and adapting to the developments in the ICT sector. Nevertheless, the Ministry of Information and Communications and other government entities make commendable efforts to address issues as they arise and to make use of technologies as they become mainstream. For example, as described in this chapter, many government entities make extensive use of social media for engaging with the general public and specific stakeholders.

924. In a similar spirit, this chapter will highlight several developments and topics that are emerging as important from a legal, regulatory, and/or policy outlook. The developments and topics are presented from the perspective of their potential for fundamentally changing some aspect of society, rather than a discussion of the most current news for each development or topic, as such news will surely and quickly be out of date. It is notable that most of these topics are well established in developed countries and regions, and yet even in such places the legal, regulatory, and/or policy implications of these topics remain largely undetermined.

§1. Social Media

925. Few phenomena have changed the nature of society as completely and rapidly as social media, and this is as true in Nairobi as it is in Silicon Valley. Most jurisdictions, including Kenya, have yet to pass laws that specifically deal with social media, choosing instead to apply non-specific laws to activities carried out on social media.

926. Generally, anything that is illegal in the offline world is also illegal in the online world. Thus, the laws that are commonly applied to social media activities include tort law (defamation, breach of confidence, fraud, etc.), criminal law (stalking, bullying, harassment, etc.), employment law (rights of an employee to speak, privacy, etc.), and intellectual property law (copyright and trademark law, etc.).

More recently emerging issues in social media law include liability for re-posting content of a third party, the metes and bounds of the 'right to be forgotten' in Europe and elsewhere, and the privacy of search data.

927. Only a small number of reported lawsuits in Kenya have involved the social media actions of a litigant as fundamental to a cause of action in the lawsuit. Most of these have involved a cause of action for defamation and are based on the social media posts of a defendant.[794] An equally small number of reported lawsuits have involved evidence taken from social media activities to support a cause of action that is not directly related to social media. As discussed in Chapter 5, electronic evidence is admissible in court, and there are no reports of difficulty for litigants seeking to admit evidence from social media activities. Considering that few social media data are stored locally within Kenya, it seems only a matter of time before the courts will be asked to decide on issues of jurisdiction, production of records, and authenticity of such data. Lawsuits addressing other activities on social media are also to be expected in Kenyan courts.

§2. Internet of Things

928. The proliferation of Internet-connected devices (other than mobile phones) seen in other jurisdictions has been relatively slow to reach a significant scale in Kenya. Nevertheless, the government is aware of this trend, commonly known as the Internet of Things (IoT). The Draft National ICT Policy 2016 contains the following statement of needs in order to support the IoT environment: 'increase IP addresses, number of smart nodes and the amount of upstream data the nodes generate which is expected to raise new concerns about data privacy, data sovereignty, and security.' Both the private sector and the public sector are attempting to apply the IoT to addressing the relatively unique challenges of life in Kenya. For example, the Red Cross of Kenya has plans to instal Internet-connected fire sensors and GPS devices in Kenyan slums to help speed up the process of locating fires and sending help.[795,796] Also, for example, the Kenya Wildlife Service, beginning in 2014, has made use of the satellite radio collars to help monitor the movement and location of lions. Such monitoring assists the Service in preventing human attacks on the lions, as well as safeguarding human inhabitants near the Nairobi National Park.[797]

794. *See*, e.g., *Republic v. Geoffrey Andari*, [2015] eKLR involving posts on Facebook in alleged violation of the Penal Code. *See also CFC Stanbic Bank v. Consumer Federation of Kenya & 2 Others*, [2014] eKLR, involving defamation for posts on Facebook and Twitter. *See also Safaricom Ltd. v. Porting Access Kenya Ltd. & Another*, [2011] eKLR, involving defamation for a retweet.
795. *See* http://muva.co.ke/blog/5-ways-Internet-things-improving-lives-kenya/accessed 1 Jun. 2017.
796. *See* https://redcrosschat.org/2015/02/24/home-fires-preparedness-campaign-expandingto-kenya/ accessed 1 Jun. 2017.
797. *See* http://www.kws.go.ke/content/one-lion-collared-nairobi-national-park-0 accessed 1 Jun. 2017.

§3. DATA

929. Big Data refers to various methods for capturing, storing, and analysing extremely large sets of data. Analysis of such large data sets may result in the ability to forecast behaviours or events and may provide useful insights into complex phenomenon such as human behaviour, weather, traffic, and biological systems.

930. The Draft National ICT Policy 2016 recognizes that Big Data is associated with challenges and potential benefits, and calls on the government to develop a Big Data Strategy, promote local expertise in Big Data, and develop infrastructure for supporting Big Data ventures. At the same time, the draft policy recognizes that successfully promoting Big Data includes the need to promote two supporting factors: adequate machine-to-machine (M2M) communications infrastructure and standardized M2M protocols and adequate data centres for storage and processing of data.

931. A variety of applications of Big Data have already been observed in Kenya, particularly in the areas of soil quality,[798] agro-weather forecasting,[799] and crop insurance systems.[800] The financial transaction data gathered from mobile money platforms is also an ideal data set for various analyses, provided that issues of privacy and ownership are adequately addressed.

§4. NETWORK REDUNDANCY AND INTERNET DISRUPTIONS

932. A challenge that accompanies the adoption of technology is that many aspects of society become somewhat or completely dependent on the proper functioning of that technology. For example, a transition to an e-government platform results in a certain amount of dependency on the platform, and some government services may become partially or entirely unavailable when the platform malfunctions, requires maintenance, or is the target of a breach of cybersecurity.

933. Since the connection of the first fibre optic undersea cable in 2010, undersea cables have been severed or otherwise severely disrupted on numerous occasions.[801] Each time a cable connection is interrupted, bandwidth is noticeably reduced, and Internet activities are affected for a period of time that may last up to several weeks.

---

798. *See* Africa Soil Information Service (AfSIS), available at http://africasoils.net/ accessed 1 Jun. 2017.
799. *See* http://www.worldbank.org/en/news/loans-credits/2017/02/09/kenya-climate-smart-agriculture-project accessed 1 Jun. 2017.
800. *See* https://www.uap-group.com/sites/kenya/pages/Corporate-Crop-Insurance-Kenya.aspx accessed 1 Jun. 2017.
801. *See*, for example, the reported outage for the SEACOM cable, available at http://seacom.mu/2017/04/08/seacom-subsea-cable-experiencing-service-affecting-outage-8-april-1900-gmt/ accessed 1 Jun. 2017.

934. In addition to unintentional disruptions caused by accidental damage to the physical infrastructure providing network services, a recurring pattern of intentional Internet disruptions has been observed across Africa. These disruptions may take the form of targeted blocking of selected websites and/or complete disconnection of the country from the Internet. Most often, complete Internet shutdowns are observed during or near the time of political elections. This phenomenon has been observed in Cameroon, Democratic Republic of Congo, Egypt, Ethiopia, Gabon, the Gambia, and Zambia.[802]

935. Whereas the solution to intentional Internet shutdowns will likely always remain in the hands of politicians, intelligent network design can provide a solution for unintentional network disruptions. As such, the CA recently released guidelines for network redundancy, resilience, and diversity (NRRD).[803] The guidelines 'are intended to collect information on the status of NRRD by Authority licensees and provide the empirical basis of potentially necessary regulatory interventions and appropriate procedures for use by network operators in support of sustained reliable and available Information and Communications Technology (ICT) networks in Kenya'.[804]

936. The Guidelines are provided to monitor: (1) network redundancy to improve the availability and fault tolerance of a system or service by duplicating one or more components of the system; (2) network resilience to enable a network to provide and maintain an acceptable level of service in the face of various faults and challenges to normal operation; and (3) network diversity to ensure that alternatives are available when challenges impact particular elements or processes.

937. The Guidelines apply to all operators in Kenya of the following networks: MNOs; ISPs; Fixed Wireless Access (FWA) Networks; International Gateway (IGW) Networks; SCN; Internet Exchange Points (IXPs); and Fixed Network Operators (FNOs). Targets for uptime/availability are provided for each of the various types of operators and their applicable metrics. Non-compliant operators are given an initial three-year grace period (expiring in 2020) during which no penalties will be levied.

Conclusions

938. The single most influential event in the fifty-four years since Kenya's independence has been, arguably, the adoption of the new constitution in 2010. Many laws have been passed to implement the guarantees provided by, and the functions

802. *See*, for example, available at https://www.nytimes.com/2017/02/10/world/africa/african-nations-increasingly-silence-Internet-to-stem-protests.html?_r=0 accessed 1 Jun. 2017. *See also State of Internet Freedom in Africa 2016*, CIPESA, September 2016.
803. Communications Authority of Kenya: Guidelines for Network Redundancy, Resilience, and Diversity on Information and Communication Networks in Kenya, 1 Jul. 2017.
804. *Id.*

described in, the Constitution. The process of ensuring that all laws predating 2010 are compliant with the Constitution is not yet complete. Devolution of powers from the central government to the counties is also an ongoing process. The effects of these events will be the subject of books, lawsuits, Parliamentary debates, and academic scholarship for many years.

939. All of these events are occurring in the context of a period of time characterized by dramatic and sweeping technological advancements. Many manual processes within government and industry have been automated and digitized. Communications, access to information and services, the fight against corruption and crime, and economic productivity are just a few of the areas that have seen dramatic changes due to developments in technology – indeed nearly every aspect of society, government, and law is affected.

940. A major difference between the influence of the new Constitution and the influence of technological advancement is that the former is self-imposed and (mostly) controllable, whereas the latter is almost entirely beyond the control of the Kenyan government or any other single entity. This means that the changes brought by the new Constitution are (mostly) predictable, whereas it is impossible to predict the future of technology and how society will adapt to such changes.

941. In many ways Kenya is part of the cohort of African nations leading the continent out of its colonial past and into an unknown and unpredictable future. A new generation of Kenyans is coming of age without any first-hand knowledge of life without the Internet or mobile phones. One thing is certain – the ICT sector will continue to play a vital role as this generation enters the workforce and collectively sets a course for the country.

Selected Bibliography

Books

Derclaye, E. *The Legal Protection of Databases: A Comparative Analysis.* Massachusetts: Edward Elgar Publishing, 2008.

Gowers, A. *Gowers' Review of Intellectual Property.* HM Treasury, London, 2006.

Limpitlaw, J. *Media Law Handbook for Eastern Africa-volume 2.* Konrad-Adenauer-Stiftung Regional Media Programme: Sub-Saharan Africa, 2016.

Sumpter, P. *Intellectual Property Law: Principles and Practice.* CCH New Zealand Ltd, 2006.

Walden, I. & Angel, J. *Telecommunications Law & Regulation.* London: Blackstone Press, 2001.

Articles and Reports

Article 19. 'Statement on Kenya's Freedom of Information Policy'. February, 2007.

Brenner, S. & Goodman, M.D. 'The Emerging Consensus on Criminal Conduct in Cyberspace'. *Oxford, International Journal of Law and Information Technology* 10, no. 2 (2000): 3.

CIPESA. *State of Internet Freedom in Africa 2016*, September 2016.

CIPIT. *Safaricom and Internet Traffic Tampering,* CIPIT Research Brief, March 2017.

Communications Commission of Kenya: Sector Statistics Report, April 2008–June 2009.

Communications Authority of Kenya: Annual Report for the Financial Year 2015–2016.

Economic Survey, 2003 – Kenya Bureau of Statistics.

Government Printer. *Sessional Paper No. 1 of 1964.*

Government Printer. 'The Kenya Gazette'. Gazette Notice No. 11382 of 2008, 20 November 2008.

Government Printer. 'The Kenya Gazette'. Gazette Notice No. 1148 of 2009, 5 February 2009.

Selected Bibliography

Government Printer. Gazette Notice No. 10335 of 2008, 2829. 'Information and Communications Technology Sector Policy Guidelines'. No. 10335 of 2008, 2829.

Government Printer. Legal Notice No. 187 of 2009 published vide Kenya Gazette Supplement No. 86 (Legislative Supplement No. 54).

Government Printer. Gazette Notice No. 7481 of 2007. 'Information and Communications Technology Sector Policy Guidelines'. Vol. CIX-No. 55, 10 August 2007, 2542.

GSMA. *Digital Migration Process in Kenya,* GSMA Spectrum Report, January 2017.

Hong Kong Legislative Council: Report of the Hong Kong Legislative Council, 2000.

Smith, J. & Silver, J. 'L'Oréal v eBay: A Warning to Online Marketplace Operators', *Journal of Intellectual Property Law & Practice* (2011).

Kenya Bureau of Statistics. Gross Domestic Product, 2009 Third Quarter Report.

Kenya Bureau of Statistics. Kenya Economic Survey, Nairobi: Government Printer, 2003.

Kenya Bureau of Statistics. Kenya Economic Survey, 2017.

Kenya Ministry of Planning and National Development: Economic Recovery Strategy for Wealth and Employment Creation, 2003–2007.

KICTANET. *Women and Cybercrime in Kenya – The Dark Side of ICTs'*. Nairobi, 2009.

Kohlbach, M. 'Making Sense of Electronic Money', *The Journal of Information, Law and Technology (JILT)* 1 (2004).

Goodman, M.D. & Brenner, S. 'The Emerging Consensus on Criminal Conduct in Cyberspace', *International Journal of Law and Information Technology* 10, no. 2 (2000): 3.

Ministry of Information & Communications. *National Information & Communications Technology (ICT) Policy* (2006): 1.

National Economic and Social Council: Kenya Vision 2030 (Abridged/Summary Edition), 1.

Office of the President: Presidential Circular No. 1 of 2005 'Structure and Organization of the Government'. 2005.

Research ICT Africa. Waema, T.M. & Ndung'u, M.N. *Understanding What Is Happening in ICT in Kenya* (2012).

Serianu Ltd., Kenya Cyber Security Report, 2016.

Tadayoni, R. & Kristensen T. 'Solving the Information Problems of the Digital Age?'. Paper presented at the Internet Society (ISOC) INET '99 Conference. San Jose, California, USA, June 1999.

WIPO. Intellectual Property on the Internet: A Survey of Issues. Geneva, 2003.

On-line Publications and Databases

Communications Authority of Kenya: www.ca.go.ke.

International Telecommunications Union: www.itu.int/ituweblogs.

Kenya Industrial Property Institute: www.kipi.go.ke.

Kenya Law Reports (KLR): www.kenyalaw.org.
Kenya Network Information Centre: www.kenic.or.ke.
Manfred, K. 'Making Sense of Electronic Money'. *The Journal of Information, Law and Technology(JILT)* 1 (2004) http://elj.warwick.ac.uk/jilt/04-1/ kohlbach.html.
Njoroge P.N. *Enforcement of Competition Policy and Law in Kenya Including Case Studies in the Areas of Mergers and Takeovers, Prevention of Possible Future Abuse of Dominance and Collusion/Price Fixing,* www.ifc.org/ifcext/fias.nsf/ AttachmentsByTitle/ Conferences_CompetitionPolicyTanz_Peter%2BNjoroge.pr n.pdf/$FILE/ Conferences_CompetitionPolicyTanz_Peter%2BNjoroge.prn.pdf, 2 0 February 2010.
Vikaas, S.S., et al. 'Intrinsic and Synaptic Dynamics Interact to Generate Emergent Patterns of Rhythmic Bursting in Thalamocortical Neurons'. *The Journal of Neuroscience* 26 (2006) www.jneurosci.org/cgi/content/full/26/16/4247.

Selected Bibliography

Index

The numbers here refer to the paragraph numbers.

Index

Index

Index